# ATONEMENT

# ATONEMENT

*Jewish and Christian Origins*

EDITED BY

*Max Botner, Justin Harrison Duff & Simon Dürr*

WILLIAM B. EERDMANS PUBLISHING COMPANY
GRAND RAPIDS, MICHIGAN

Wm. B. Eerdmans Publishing Co.
4035 Park East Court SE, Grand Rapids, Michigan 49546
www.eerdmans.com

Published 2020
Printed in the United States of America

26  25  24  23  22  21  20      1  2  3  4  5  6  7

ISBN 978-0-8028-7668-3

**Library of Congress Cataloging-in-Publication Data**

A catalog record for this book is available from the Library of Congress.

# CONTENTS

Acknowledgments ix

Abbreviations x

Introduction xiii

## PART 1
### CRITICAL ISSUES AND THE DEVELOPMENT
### OF ATONEMENT LEGISLATION IN THE HEBREW BIBLE

1. **Atonement** 3
   *Christian A. Eberhart*

   Introductory Comments 3
   General Remarks on Sacrificial Rituals in the Hebrew Bible 7
   The Hand-Leaning Gesture in the Context of Sacrificial Rituals 11
   The Reception of Isaiah 52:13–53:12 13
   The Death and Resurrection of Jesus (Romans 4:25) 17

2. **Sin, Sacrifice, but No Salvation** 21
   *Deborah W. Rooke*

   The *Karet* Penalty 22
   Cut Off–But from What? 26
   Conclusion 39

3. **Atonement beyond Israel** 40
   *David P. Wright*

   P's *ḥaṭṭā't* System 42
   H's *ḥaṭṭā't* in Numbers 15:22–31 45
   Introduction (Numbers 15:22–23) 47

Specific Cases (vv. 24–26, 27–29)                                    49
Intentional Sin (vv. 30–31)                                          58
Conclusion                                                           62


**PART 2**
**ANTHROPOLOGY, COSMOLOGY, AND MEDIATORS IN**
**EARLY JEWISH AND CHRISTIAN ATONEMENT THEOLOGIES**


4.  **When the Problem Is Not What You Have Done**
    **but Who You Are**                                              67
    *Carol A. Newsom*

        The Origins of the Shift                                    71
        Later Second Temple Developments                            77
        Conclusion                                                  88

5.  **The High Priest in Ben Sira 50**                              89
    *Crispin Fletcher-Louis*

        Ben Sira 50                                                 90
        Hebrew Ben Sira 49:16–50:21                                 92
        Priestly and Temple Service Makes All Present to God        94
        Priesthood as a Representative Office Summing Up All Reality 98
        Conclusion                                                  111

6.  **Get the Story Right and the Models Will Fit**                 112
    *N. T. Wright*

        Introduction: The Distorted Story                           113
        Contours of the Biblical Narrative                          115
        Contours of Jesus's Saving Death                            121
        The Cross in Its Narrative Framework                        127
        Conclusion                                                  129

7.  **"Seeing," Salvation, and the Use of Scripture**
    **in the Gospel of John**                                       131
    *Catrin H. Williams*

        Composite Citations                                         131
        Composite Allusions                                         134
        "Lamb of God" (John 1:29, 36) as a Composite Allusion       135
        John's "Lifting Up" Sayings—Seeing the Exalted One          143

Seeing the Pierced One     149
Conclusion     153

8. **Sealed for Redemption**     155
   *T. J. Lang*

   Sealed by the Spirit in Ephesians 1:13     157
   Sealing Terminology in the Realm of Commerce     159
   Promise and Pledge of Inheritance     162
   The Spirit as "Ἀρραβών of Our Inheritance"     164
   The Redemption of the Acquisition     165
   Conclusion     168

9. **What Goes On in the Heavenly Temple?**     171
   *Martha Himmelfarb*

   The Book of the Watchers and the Heavenly Temple     172
   2 Enoch     176
   The Songs of the Sabbath Sacrifice     178
   The Book of Revelation     183
   Epistle to the Hebrews and Testament of Levi     188
   Conclusions     191

*Bibliography*     193

*Contributors*     217

*Index of Modern Authors*     219

*Index of Subjects*     224

*Index of Scripture and Ancient Sources*     230

# ACKNOWLEDGMENTS

This book originated in the symposium "Atonement: Sin, Sacrifice, and Salvation in Jewish and Christian Antiquity," held at the University of Saint Andrews in June 2018. We wish to thank everyone who took the time to make the pilgrimage to our little seaside town on the east coast of Scotland. We are especially grateful to our plenary speakers and presenters for their willingness to contribute to this volume, which we hope will advance the rich tradition of the Saint Andrews Symposium for Biblical and Early Christian Studies.

Our symposium would not have been possible without generous funding from St. Mary's College (School of Divinity) and from the Centre for Academic, Professional and Organisational Development (CAPOD) at the University of Saint Andrews. I (Max) would also like to thank my LOEWE colleagues at Goethe-Universität, especially Christian Wiese and Nina Fischer, for their support in organizing the conference. It is my pleasure to publish this book within the framework of the Hessian Ministry for Science and Art funded by the LOEWE research hub "Religiöse Positionierung: Modalitäten und Konstellationen in jüdischen, christlichen und islamischen Kontexten" at Goethe-Universität Frankfurt am Main/Justus-Liebig-Universität Gießen.

We would also like to thank the faculty and postgraduate community at St. Mary's College for their support in hosting the conference. A huge thanks to Madhavi Nevader, T. J. Lang, and Elizabeth Shively, who were kind enough to chair our parallel sessions and to ensure that things ran smoothly. A special thanks is also owed to Marian Kelsey, who patiently bounced ideas over the course of planning the symposium, and to the administrative secretaries at St. Mary's College, especially Deborah Smith, who helped keep all the details in place. Our gratitude is also due to Tavis Bohlinger for covering the symposium on the Logos Academic Blog (https://academic.logos.com).

Finally, we are indebted to Trevor Thompson of Eerdmans Press for his support in helping this book come to fruition. Eerdmans has proven to be a welcoming home for our volume, and we are deeply grateful to Trevor and the entire Eerdmans team for making each stage of the publication process seamless and enjoyable.

# Abbreviations

| | |
|---|---|
| AJEC | Ancient Judaism and Early Christianity |
| AnBib | Analecta Biblica |
| *AOT* | *The Apocryphal Old Testament* |
| AOTC | Abingdon Old Testament Commentaries |
| ATANT | Abhandlungen zur Theologie des Alten und Neuen Testaments |
| ATD | Das Alte Testament Deutsch |
| AYB | Anchor Yale Bible |
| AYBRL | Anchor Yale Bible Reference Library |
| BBB | Bonner biblische Beiträge |
| BDB | Brown, Francis, S. R. Driver, and Charles A. Briggs. *A Hebrew and English Lexicon of the Old Testament* |
| BETL | Bibliotheca Ephemeridum Theologicarum Lovaniensium |
| BGU | *Aegyptische Urkunden aus den Königlichen Staatlichen Museen zu Berlin, Griechische Urkunden* |
| *Bib* | *Biblica* |
| *BR* | Biblical Research |
| BTS | Biblical Tools and Studies |
| BWA(N)T | Beiträge zur Wissenschaft vom Alten (und Neuen) Testament |
| BZABR | Beihefte zur Zeitschrift für altorientalische und biblische Rechtsgeschichte |
| BZAW | Beihefte zur Zeitschrift für die alttestamentliche Wissenschaft |
| BZNW | Beihefte zur Zeitschrift für die neutestamentliche Wissenschaft |
| CAT | Commentaire de l'Ancien Testament |
| CBET | Contributions to Biblical Exegesis and Theology |

| | |
|---|---|
| *CBQ* | *Catholic Biblical Quarterly* |
| *EBR* | *Encyclopedia of the Bible and Its Reception* |
| EKKNT | Evangelisch-katholischer Kommentar zum Neuen Testament |
| FAT | Forschungen zum Alten Testament |
| HAT | Handbuch zum Alten Testament |
| HCOT | Historical Commentary on the Old Testament |
| HdO | Handbuch der Orientalistik |
| HSM | Harvard Semitic Monographs |
| *HTR* | *Harvard Theological Review* |
| *HUCA* | *Hebrew Union College Annual* |
| ICC | International Critical Commentary |
| *IDBSup* | *Interpreter's Dictionary of the Bible: Supplementary Volume* |
| JAJSup | Journal of Ancient Judaism Supplements |
| *JBL* | *Journal of Biblical Literature* |
| *JECS* | *Journal of Early Christian Studies* |
| *JJS* | *Journal of Jewish Studies* |
| JPS | Jewish Publication Society |
| *JQR* | *Jewish Quarterly Review* |
| *JRS* | *Journal of Roman Studies* |
| JSJSup | Supplements to the Journal for the Study of Judaism |
| *JSNT* | *Journal for the Study of the New Testament* |
| JSOTSup | Journal for the Study of the Old Testament Supplement Series |
| *JTI* | *Journal of Theological Interpretation* |
| *JTS* | *Journal of Theological Studies* |
| LCL | Loeb Classical Library |
| LHBOTS | The Library of Hebrew Bible/Old Testament Studies |
| LNTS | The Library of New Testament Studies |
| LSJ | Liddell, Henry George, Robert Scott, Henry Stuart Jones. *A Greek-English Lexicon*, 9th ed. with revised supplement |
| LSTS | The Library of Second Temple Studies |
| NCB | New Century Bible |
| NICOT | New International Commentary on the Old Testament |
| NIGCT | New International Greek Testament Commentary |
| NovTSup | Supplements to Novum Testamentum |
| *NTS* | *New Testament Studies* |

| | |
|---|---|
| OBO | Orbis Biblicus et Orientalis |
| OTP | *Old Testament Pseudepigrapha* |
| OtSt | *Oudtestamentische Studiën* |
| PSB | *Princeton Seminary Bulletin* |
| RB | *Revue biblique* |
| RBS | Resources for Biblical Study |
| RevQ | *Revue du Qumran* |
| SBLDS | Society of Biblical Literature Dissertation Series |
| SJ | Studia Judaica |
| SSEJC | Studies in Scripture in Early Judaism and Christianity |
| STDJ | Studies on the Texts of the Desert of Judah |
| SUNT | Studien zur Umwelt des Neuen Testaments |
| SVTP | Studia in Veteris Testamenti Pseudepigraphica |
| TBN | Themes in Biblical Narrative |
| TSAJ | Texte und Studien zum antiken Judentum |
| VT | *Vetus Testamentum* |
| VTSup | Supplements to Vetus Testamentum |
| WBC | Word Biblical Commentary |
| WMANT | Wissenschaftliche Monographien zum Alten und Neuen Testament |
| WUNT | Wissenschaftliche Untersuchungen zum Neuen Testament |
| ZABR | *Zeitschrift für altorientalische und biblische Rechtsgeschichte* |
| ZAC | *Zeitschrift für Antikes Christentum/Journal of Ancient Christianity* |
| ZAW | *Zeitschrift für die alttestamentliche Wissenschaft* |
| ZNW | *Zeitschrift für die neutestamentliche Wissenschaft und die Kunde der älteren Kirche* |

# Introduction

Despite a dizzying array of questions and concerns, the concept of atonement remains vital to religious life in the twenty-first century. The holy day Yom Kippur (Day of Atonement), for instance, marks the annual moment at which millions of Jewish worshippers around the globe seek to restore intimacy with God. The Rabbi Jonathan Sacks remarks,

> We fast, we pray and we muster the courage to face the worst about ourselves. We are empowered to do so by our unshakeable belief that God loves, forgives, and has more faith in us than we do in ourselves. We can be better than we are, better than we were. And though we may have stumbled and fallen, God is holding out his hand to lift us, giving us the strength to recover, endure and grow to become the person He is calling on us to be: a blessing to others, a vehicle through which His light flows into the world, an agent of hope, His partner in the work of redemption.[1]

Atonement is not relegated, however, to religious discourse. For example, Ian McEwan's acclaimed novel *Atonement*, on which the 2007 film of the same name is based, tells the story of Briony Tallis, an elderly British woman who attempts to atone for a childhood miscalculation through the process of writing. As an author with sole control over her characters' outcomes, Briony likens herself to God and recasts the history of her loved ones with the happy outcomes she believes they deserve. At one point, she describes her correction of the past and her fresh testimony of their love as "a stand against oblivion and despair."[2] McEwan's protagonist thus stands as a powerful symbol of humanity's fraught and complicated desire to rectify guilt, shame, and destructive acts, particularly offenses against persons long dead.

---

1. Jonathan Sacks, "The Most Personal of Festivals," http://rabbisacks.org/the-most-personal-of-festivals/.

2. Ian McEwan, *Atonement: A Novel* (New York: Doubleday, 2002), 351.

Since popular notions of atonement draw inspiration from ancient Judaism and Christianity, sacrificial rituals often become central to their logic and process. While the destruction of the Second Temple in 70 CE may have spelled "an end to the bloody sacrifices of the Jews and the Christians and thus eventually to paganism itself,"[3] Jewish and Christian communities continued to preserve and interpret sacrificial rituals through the production of texts, art, and architecture.[4] Their mental maintenance of sacrificial *imaginaires* has profoundly affected the theological imaginations of their successors, for better or for worse.

Consider the language used by the congregational minister Horace Bushnell, in his speech "Our Obligation to the Dead," which he delivered at the end of the Civil War:

> As the mild benignity and peaceful reign of Christ begins at the principle: "without the shedding of blood, there is no remission," so, without the shedding of blood, there is almost nothing great in the world, or to be expected for it. For the life is in the blood, – all life; and it is put flowing within, partly for the serving of the nobler use

3. So Elias J. Bickerman, *Jews in the Greek Age* (Cambridge: Harvard University Press, 1988), 139. Bickerman's statement, of course, is a retrospective judgment. As David Biale notes, "The 'end of sacrifice' in Western religion was . . . a complex and dialectical process rather than an abrupt caesura" (45). Many Jews continued to hope for the restoration of the Jerusalem Temple (see, e.g., Jonathan Klawans, *Purity, Sacrifice, and the Temple: Symbolism and Supersessionsim in the Study of Ancient Judaism* [New York: Oxford University Press, 2006], 203–11), and there is ample evidence that some Jews and Christians participated in animal sacrifice well beyond the first century CE. On this see Daniel Stökl Ben-Ezra, *The Impact of Yom Kippur on Early Christianity*, WUNT 163 (Tübingen: Mohr Siebeck, 2003).

4. For an overview of Jewish and Christian attempts to preserve the legacy of the Second Temple and its sacrificial system, see Hugh W. Nibley, "Christian Envy of the Temple," *JQR* 50 (1959/60): 97–123, 229–40; Steven Fine, *This Holy Place: On the Sanctity of the Synagogue during the Greco-Roman Period*, Christianity and Judaism in Antiquity 11 (Notre Dame, IN: University of Notre Dame Press, 1997); Stökl Ben-Ezra, *The Impact of Yom Kippur*; Herbert L. Kessler, "The Codex Barbarus Scaligeri, the *Christian Topography*, and the Question of Jewish Models of Early Christian Art," in *Between Judaism and Christianity: Art Historical Essays in Honor of Elisheva (Elisabeth) Revel-Nehere*, ed. Katrin Kogman-Appel and Mati Meyer, The Medieval Mediterranean 81 (Leiden: Brill, 2009), 139–54; Rachel Hachlili, *Ancient Synagogue—Archaeology and Art: New Discoveries and Current Research*, HdO 105 (Leiden: Brill, 2013), esp. 46–50, 163–220, 292–338; Rina Talgam, "The Representation of the Temple and Jerusalem in Jewish and Christian Houses of Prayer in the Holy Land in Late Antiquity," in *Jews, Christians, and the Roman Empire*, ed. Natalie B. Bohrmann and Annette Yoshiko Reed (Philadelphia: University of Pennsylvania Press, 2013), 222–49.

in flowing out on fit occasion, to quicken and consecrate whatever it touches.[5]

Bushnell's appeal to the lifeforce of blood trades on language in the Pentateuch (cf. Lev 17:11), and his insistence that "without the shedding of blood, there is no remission [i.e., 'forgiveness']" resonates with early Jewish and Christian traditions (cf. Heb 9:22; b. Yoma 5a).[6] While one might dispute his interpretation of the biblical material,[7] Bushnell's conviction that blood spilled in battle has the power to expiate the land of the United States is a remarkable, if not disturbing, indication that talk of the "end of bloody sacrifices" requires qualification.[8] "The matter wanted here," Bushnell declared at the end of his speech, "is blood, not logic, and this now we have on a scale large enough to meet our necessity."[9] Blood provides the material currency of progress, a red-streaked path of suffering and death oriented toward a better future. Such, at least, thought Bushnell, is the logic of the cross.

While Bushnell's unsavory vision of national atonement is eccentric, one claim often rings true for students of ancient Judaism and Christianity: "the matter wanted here is blood, not logic."[10] Indeed, more than two millennia

---

5. Horace Bushnell, "Our Obligation to the Dead," in *Building Eras in Religion* (New York: Charles Scribner's Sons, 1881), 325–328, here 325.

6. On blood manipulation in the Hebrew Bible, see William Gilders, *Blood Ritual in the Hebrew Bible: Meaning and Power* (Baltimore: Johns Hopkins Press, 2004). On blood manipulation in Tannaitic and Aramaic literature, see Mira Balberg, *Blood for Thought: The Reinvention of Sacrifice in Early Rabbinic Literature* (Oakland, CA: University of California Press, 2017). For a discussion of the blood of Jesus and its sacrificial operations in early Christian literature, see Christian A. Eberhart, *Kultmetaphorik und Christologie: Opfer-und Sühneterminologie im Neuen Testament*, WUNT 306 (Tübingen: Mohr Siebeck, 2013), 78–129.

7. For instance, Bushnell interprets the *hapax legomenon* αἱματεκχυσία in Heb 9:22 as an indisputable reference to the "shedding of blood" or blood-spilling that occurs through an act of slaughter. This interpretation is possible, but concurrences of the noun αἷμα and the verb ἐκχέω in Septuagint ritual contexts suggests the writer has in mind the manipulation or "pouring out" of blood from a bowl or vessel at the altar for burnt offerings in the process of the Levitical sin offering. See David M. Moffitt, *Atonement and the Logic of the Resurrection in the Epistle to the Hebrews*, NovTSup 141 (Leiden: Brill, 2011), 291n157.

8. Unwittingly, Bushnell is reviving ancient discourse about the intersection of war and human sacrifice, on which see Laura Nasrallah, "The Embarrassment of Blood: Early Christians and Others on Sacrifice, War, and Rational Worship," in *Ancient Mediterranean Sacrifice*, ed. Jennifer Wright Knust and Zsuzsanna Várhelyi (New York: Oxford University Press, 2011), 142–66.

9. Bushnell, "Our Obligation," 328.

10. To be sure, blood and the moment of slaughtering sacrificial gifts is not the sine qua

of Jewish and Christian theorizing on the logic of atonement suggests that its "logic" is, in fact, highly flexible. Different strata of the Hebrew Bible bear witness to developments in sacrificial rituals[11] and their tradents continue to interpret their traditions in light of an ever-changing world: of temples, real and imagined; of mediators, human and angelic; of promises, realized or deferred. Any account of atonement, then, is but one offering in a vast marketplace of atonement theologies.[12]

The chapters in this volume provide points of entry into the marketplace of atonement. Rather than restrict our study to key terms, such as the *piel* of כפר (cf. the Greek simplex ἱλάσκομαι),[13] we have asked our contributors to

non of ancient sacrifice; see, e.g., Jonathan Z. Smith, "The Domestication of Sacrifice," in *Violent Origins: Walter Burkert, René Girard and Jonathan Z. Smith on Ritual Killing and Cultural Formation*, ed. R. G. Hamerton-Kelly (Stanford: Stanford University Press, 1987), 191–205; Marcel Detienne and Jean-Pierre Vernant, eds., *The Cuisine of Sacrifice among the Greeks*, trans. Paula Wissing (Chicago: University of Chicago Press, 1989); Kathryn McClymond, *Beyond Sacred Violence: A Comparative Study of Sacrifice* (Baltimore: Johns Hopkins University Press, 2008). Christian Eberhart (*Studien zur Bedeutung der Opfer im Alten Testament: Die Signifikanz von Blut- und Verbrennungsriten im kultischen Rahmen*, WMANT 94 [Neukirchen: Neukirchener, 2002]), argues that ritual burning is the constitutive element of sacrifice in Lev 1–7, a central feature of Greek sacrifice as well (see F. S. Naiden, *Smoke Signals for the Gods: Ancient Greek Sacrifice from the Archaic through the Roman Periods* [New York: Oxford University Press, 2013]).

11. On the development of sacrifice in the Hebrew Bible, see Gary A. Anderson, *Sacrifices and Offerings in Ancient Israel: Studies in Their Social and Political Importance*, HSM 41 (Atlanta: Scholars Press, 1988).

12. For example, Robert Jensen points out that there has never been a formal doctrine of atonement to which Christians must adhere: "If you deny that Christ is 'of one being with the Father' or that the Son and Jesus are but one hypostasis, you are formally a heretic. But you can deny any explanation of how the atonement works, or all of them, or even deny that any explanation is possible, and be a perfectly orthodox believer" ("On the Doctrine of Atonement," *PSB* 27 [2006]: 100–8, here 100).

13. For discussion of כפר in the ritual contexts of the Hebrew Bible, cf. David P. Wright, *Disposal of Impurity*, SBLDS 101 (Atlanta: SBL, 1987), 291–99; Jacob Milgrom, *Leviticus 1–16: A New Translation with Introduction and Commentary*, AYB 3 (New York: Doubleday, 2000), 1079–84; Jay Sklar, *Sin, Impurity, Sacrifice, Atonement: The Priestly Conceptions*, Hebrew Bible Monographs 2 (Sheffield: Sheffield Phoenix Press, 2005). For discussion of the translation ἱλάσκομαι and its cognates in Septuagint traditions, see C. H. Dodd, "Ἱλάσκεσθαι: Its Cognates, Derivates and Synonyms in the Septuagint," *JTS* 32 (1930), 352–60; Takamitsu Muraoka, *A Greek-English Lexicon of the Septuagint* (Leuven: Peeters, 2009), 151–52; Dirk Büchner, "Ἐξιλάσασθαι: Appeasing God in the Septuagint Pentateuch," *JBL* 129 (2010): 237–60. The terms כפר and ἐξιλάσκομαι appear in a diverse range of contexts in the biblical tradition (e.g., the burnt offering, cf. Lev 1:4) and invite a diverse range of reflections on the active subjects, objects, and means of *atonement*. For instance, in both ritual and nonritual

examine atonement as a broader phenomenon that negotiates a constellation of features: sin, sacrifice, and salvation. Recognizing that each feature has its own complicated history,[14] we offer them as heuristic categories in order to interrogate the ways in which ancient Jewish and Christian writers envisaged the concept of atonement, broadly conceived.

## Plan of the Book

The essays gathered in Part 1 of the volume outline critical issues in the study of atonement and trace the development of atonement legislation in the Hebrew Bible. Christian Eberhart's chapter aims to introduce pivotal issues surrounding the concept of atonement in biblical studies. He focuses on four, in particular: 1) sacrifice and atonement in Leviticus, 2) the function of hand-leaning gestures in Levitical sacrifice, 3) early Christian reception of Isaiah's fourth servant poem (Isa 52:13–53:12), and 4) early Christian reflection on the life, death, and resurrection of Jesus. To this end, Eberhart argues, it is incumbent upon exegetes and theologians today to find "avatars"—or suitable representatives—to communicate the redemptive framework of the Christ-event.

---

contexts, Israel's deity is rarely the active subject of atonement in the biblical tradition (exceptions in the MT include 2 Chr 30:15–20 and Ezek 16:63). Normally, the active subject is an intermediary figure, such as Moses or a priest. In ritual contexts, Israel's sanctuary typically features as the direct accusative object of atonement (כפר), though it can, along with other nonhuman objects, function as the indirect object, taking the pattern כפר + על (cf. Lev 16:16). When atonement concerns persons, the Priestly writers consistently use the verbal pattern כפר + על / בעד (cf. also 11QT 16:14–17:2, 26:9). In LXX traditions, this pattern is paralleled by ἐξιλάσκομαι + direct accusative object or ἐξιλάσκομαι + περί, respectively.

14. On the concept of sin in early Judaism and Christianity, see Jonathan Klawans, *Impurity and Sin in Ancient Judaism* (New York: Oxford University Press, 2000); Gary A. Anderson, *Sin: A History* (New Haven: Yale University Press, 2009); Joseph Lam, *Patterns of Sin in the Hebrew Bible: Metaphor, Culture, and the Making of a Religious Concept* (Oxford: Oxford University Press, 2016). For the situation of Jewish sacrifice in the broader context of ancient Mediterranean religions, see Stanley K. Stowers, "On the Comparison of Blood in Greek and Israelite Ritual," in *Hesed Ve-emet: Studies in Honor of Ernest S. Frerichs*, ed. Jodi Magness and Seymour Gitin (Atlanta: Scholars Press, 1998), 179–96; Jennifer Wright Knust and Zsuzsanna Várhelyi, eds., *Ancient Mediterranean Sacrifice* (New York: Oxford University Press, 2011); Christopher A. Foraone and F. S. Naiden, eds., *Greek and Roman Animal Sacrifice: Ancient Victims, Modern Observers* (Cambridge: Cambridge University Press, 2012); Naiden, *Smoke Signals*; Daniel C. Ullucci, *The Christian Rejection of Animal Sacrifice* (New York: Oxford University Press, 2012); Daniel C. Ullucci, "Sacrifice in the Ancient Mediterranean: Recent and Current Research," *CBR* 13 (2015): 388–439.

The next two chapters examine topics related to atonement in the Pentateuch. Deborah Rooke interrogates instances in the Priestly source where atonement becomes impossible, resulting in the offender being "cut off" from the community. While there has been much debate about the nature of the *karet* penalty, Rooke argues that its rhetorical function was equally significant to the tradents of P: "to inculcate the values of the Priestly legislators into the minds of the community for whom they were writing." Subtle distinctions in the ways the *karet* penalty is articulated in P may evince a concern to order hierarchically even the most heinous offenses.

David Wright concludes Part 1 by tracing the Holiness school's expansion of the Priestly source's regulations on the "sin" or "purification" offering (*ḥaṭṭāʾt*). Through careful textual analysis, Wright shows that H amends regulations on the *ḥaṭṭāʾt* to include the immigrant (*gēr*) living in the land of Israel. In contrast to the ethical concerns of Deuteronomy and the Covenant Code, however, H is strictly concerned with the *gēr* as a legal category. If the sins of the *gēr* can pollute the land, as H maintains, then it is vital that the principal source of atonement, the *ḥaṭṭāʾt* sacrifice, is made available to them.

The seven essays gathered in Part 2 explore the intersection of anthropology, cosmology, and mediatorial figures in ancient Jewish and Christian atonement theologies. Carol Newsom leads off by delineating the early Jewish construction of a debased anthropology. According to this framework, human persons lack the requisite moral agency assumed in the classic model of atonement. In fact, humans are so corrupted that the only possibility for atonement and reconciliation is radical divine intervention. Such anthropological pessimism, however, is not an end in itself. Rather, it underscores "the religious paradox that it is only by immersing oneself in deep abjection that one is prepared for exaltation."

In contrast to the pessimistic anthropology outlined by Newsom, Crispin Fletcher-Louis traces an exalted view of idealized humanity in Sirach. A close reading of the Hebrew version of Sira 49:16–50:21 suggests that the high priest Simeon, as depicted in his priestly service, is the locus of *at-one-ment*, the place where the divine glory, the people of Israel, and the cosmos are held together. The sage's encomium to Simeon, according to Fletcher-Louis, supports the thesis that some Jews conceived of the office of the high priest as the place where the rift between humanity and divinity is overcome.

N. T. Wright takes up and advances Eberhart's suggestion that early Christian atonement theology holds the various elements of the Christ-event together in a narrative framework. While Wright concedes that atonement "models" have a necessary place in Christian theology, he suggests that they often become "imprecise ways of saying the same thing," particularly when decoupled from the biblical story. The interpretive key to Jesus's saving death, Wright proposes, is the Passover narrative, understood by early Christians as God's victory over sin and death (*Christus Victor*) through the cross of his Messiah (substitution). It is within this narrative that vicarious substitution, participation in Christ, and eschatological joy in the new creation have their raison d'être.

Wright's thesis about the significance of Passover in early Christian atonement theology is tested in Catrin Williams's careful analysis of the ways John the evangelist uses composite citations and allusions to recast soteriological images. The designation of Jesus as the "Lamb of God," for example, creatively weaves together traditional language from the Exodus Passover narrative with motifs from Isaiah's fourth servant poem—thus, John's "Lamb" does what no other Passover lamb ever did or was intended to do: he "bears" the sin of the world. Isaiah's servant poems are so pervasive, in fact, that they provide the evangelist with linguistic resources to articulate both the saving effects of Jesus's death and the sensory and noetic operations through which these are grasped by his disciples.

T. J. Lang's chapter on atonement in Ephesians marks a transition from the canonical Gospels to the Pauline corpus. Lang attends, in particular, to the collocation of "sealing" and "redemption" language, which he argues Paul (or one of his followers) draws from the realm of commerce. Seals on ancient tablets, testaments, and manumission documents validated their ownership and integrity, while the motif of redemption/ransom entailed the acquisition of persons. Thus, in Ephesians, God's Spirit is both the seal of God's "possession"—i.e., human persons who have been ransomed by the "currency" of Christ's blood—and the "down payment" of their inheritance.

Martha Himmelfarb concludes the book by asking the question, What goes on in the heavenly temple? Developing and conflicting ideas emerge in early Jewish and Christian texts. While a number of early apocalypses, such as the Book of the Watchers, conceive of heaven as the locus of an angelic liturgy of praise, the liturgies do not appear particularly interested in the imagery of the sacrificial cult or the concept of atonement. Conversely, the Songs of the Sabbath Sacrifice, Revelation, and the Testament of Levi, each in its own way, imagines a number of cultic gifts mediated in celestial space, with a particular focus on the aroma of the gift. Material blood manipulation in the heavenly realms, however, is absent or suppressed. Hebrews alone, notes Himmelfarb, "dares to imagine blood in heaven in a one-time ritual of atonement."

## PART ONE

*Critical Issues and the Development
of Atonement Legislation
in the Hebrew Bible*

# CHAPTER ONE

# Atonement

## *Amid Alexandria, Alamo, and Avatar*

CHRISTIAN A. EBERHART

At many times and in many ways, religious communities and the academy have employed, defined, developed, explored, and criticized the topics of atonement, sin, sacrifice, and salvation. This essay will try to provide some introductory remarks on the subject matter as well as a recapitulation of previous discussions and results. It will start with reflections on what the term *atonement* means, proceed to study sacrificial rituals in the Hebrew Bible with specific interest in their interpretation, and conclude by looking at how these rituals and the topic of atonement have been adopted in early Christian literature, with a focus on references to the famous Suffering Servant Song in Isa 52:13–53:12 LXX. Along the way, I will advocate closer readings of biblical texts in order to highlight plausible models of reception within early Jewish and Christian contexts. I will participate in the corporate endeavor of better understanding these texts in their historical framework, and I will point out stumbling blocks as we try to explore an ever-changing and important— but certainly not the only—paradigm for reconciliation and salvation in the socioreligious continuum we call early Judaism and Christianity.

## Introductory Comments

What is atonement? It is difficult to define and determine the meaning of this term as it refers to a concept that has been used in a variety of religious traditions over a long period of time. We convened for a symposium at the University of St. Andrews to study this topic, and our investigation led us into the historical depth of Israelite and early Jewish traditions as well as to dogmatic core areas of Christianity. On the one hand, this event dealt with the actual and remembered worship space of the religious, cultural, and sociopolitical epitome of Judaism: the Jerusalem Temple. On the other hand, it also dealt with key referents within the history of Christianity. Not all Christians, however, universally agree on the central place of atonement. To paint the image with broad strokes, Eastern Orthodoxy (and in a similar way, Eastern Catholicism) emphasizes the concepts of incarnation and *theosis*—i.e., the deification of humanity.[1] In Western Christianity, however, atonement occupies a more central place in the teachings of the church. As a result, a diverse spectrum of atonement theories has been developed throughout history.[2]

To approach our topic of inquiry, it is helpful to start in the year 1526 CE. At that time, William Tyndale (1494–1536), a leading personality in the English Reformation movement, coined the term atonement. For Tyndale, the term literally meant *at-one-ment*. It conceptually presupposes that humans and God are separated and that humans cannot directly or immediately communicate or interact with God. Religious ideas and theories that envision methods of overcoming this separation are often said to belong to the category of atonement. Conceptual equivalents are *expiation* and *propitiation*. All three terms tend to address the removal or elimination of wrath, sin, guilt, or impurities. They do not, however, cover the same spectrum of meaning. Linguistically, propitiation and atonement evoke interpersonal relations: propitiation conveys the appeasement of a person or deity, while atonement is a spatial category conveying the encounter with a person or deity. The latter spatial category is what Tyndale had in mind when he created the term. By contrast, expiation connotes cleansing, purgation, or purification; the term can refer to impersonal or personal objects. With this specific meaning, expiation can be construed as a subcategory, or the modus operandi, of atonement and propitiation. The elimination of defilement may thus lead to the restoration of relationships.

---

1. Cf. Clark Carlton, *The Faith: Understanding Orthodox Christianity—An Orthodox Catechism* (Regina: Orthodox Press, 1997), 139–46; Stephen Finlan, *Problems with Atonement: The Origins of, and Controversy about, the Atonement Doctrine* (Collegeville, MN: Liturgical Press, 2005), 3–5, 117–24.

2. For an overview of the history of research on atonement, see Christian A. Eberhart, "Introduction: Constituents and Critique of Sacrifice, Cult, and Atonement in Early Judaism and Christianity," in *Sacrifice, Cult, and Atonement in Early Judaism and Christianity: Constituents and Critique*, ed. Henrietta L. Wiley and Christian A. Eberhart, RBS 85 (Atlanta: Society of Biblical Literature Press, 2017), 12–24. (Not all allusions or references to my previous publications can be provided in this contribution.)

But for many scholars today, the concept of atonement is fraught with problems. For one, Hebrew Bible scholars tend to use the term in ways different from New Testament scholars, whose use, in turn, differs from that of systematic theologians. This has, at times, led to misunderstandings and confusion in academic debates.[3] More serious than this inconsistent use of the term is a widespread dissatisfaction with the concept of atonement itself, which has led to what I would call an "identity crisis," at least in Western Christianity.[4] While atonement is located at the core of theories about salvation, it does not always seem to evoke positive connotations. In light of this, the organizing committee of this conference should be commended for its decision not only to commence this event *at one* o'clock p.m., but also to leave the term atonement in the conference title. (I wonder whether there was a discussion among the members of the organizing committee regarding the marketability of the event if it featured this term.) Elsewhere, however, a certain uneasiness about this term frequently results in strategies to avoid it altogether. This applies also to the German word *Sühne*, a frequent equivalent of atonement.[5] The problem is that, for many, atonement is inevitably associated with blood, violence, gore, slaughter, and death. Books have therefore been written about *Problems with Atonement*.[6]

Since this book also addresses "sin" and "sacrifice," I might add that, mutatis mutandis, similar concerns have been registered regarding these terms. And since, in Christianity, most of these terms belong to the interpretive layer that deals with the death of Jesus of Nazareth on the cross, atonement becomes all the more gloomy.[7] Not surprisingly, an outsider to the Christian religion

---

3. I further discuss this point in subsequent paragraphs.

4. See Christian A. Eberhart, *The Sacrifice of Jesus: Understanding Atonement Biblically*, 2nd ed. (Eugene, OR: Wipf & Stock, 2018), 8.

5. A popular alternative to *Sühne* is the German word *Entstörung*, but it is difficult to translate into English. Dictionaries provide equivalents such as "disturbance suppression," "fault clearance," "interference elimination," "suppression shielding," or "anti-jamming." None of these terms can easily be applied in a religious context. One could perhaps add that *Entstörung* might also be rendered as "reconciliation," which is at least familiar from traditional discourse in academia and the church.

6. Finlan, *Problems with Atonement*. As for the German equivalent, an article published in 2000 conveys its main argument in its title, stating that atonement, guilt, and failure are not central to Christianity and that a loving God does not want sacrifice (Adolf Holl, "Ein liebender Gott will keine Opfer! Sühne, Schuld und Scheitern sind nicht das Zentrum des Christentums, und Gott ist kein Sadist: Warum Jesus mit einem Opferlamm rein gar nichts zu tun hat," *Publik-Forum* 8 [2000]: 24–26).

7. It barely needs to be mentioned that, over the past two millennia, the cross has become a key symbol representing Christianity; hence its ubiquity in Christian architecture and liturgical practice—for example, on top of steeples of church buildings of all Christian

recently "criticized the ugliness of the crucifixion scene."[8] The frequent habit of wearing golden crosses on necklaces does not mitigate the historical truth that crucifixion was a cruel and shameful method of capital punishment in antiquity reserved for non-citizens and slaves in the Roman Empire.[9] It is true, therefore, to say that "the Christian savior had died the worst of deaths, that of a slave and criminal."[10] What was Christianity to do with the particular dilemma that its charismatic leader had died in this fashion? Since it was impossible to deny the historical factuality of Jesus's crucifixion, early Christianity soon developed atonement concepts to articulate how the message about the cross, which Paul claims was derided as "foolishness" by some, could be considered "the power of God" (1 Cor 1:18). What was rather embarrassing in the beginning quickly became a place of pride. It is an often-observed peculiarity that both the Apostles' Creed and the Nicene Creed emphasize the death of Jesus while omitting details of his earthly life, apart from his birth. Interpretive efforts to construe this death on the cross as salvific are often considered center to atonement in early Christian discourse. Along with the cross, connections to concepts of Jewish sacrifice often infuse atonement discourse with reflections on vicarious punishment, suffering, blood, and death. For instance, after Tyndale, Anselm of Canterbury developed the popular theory of atonement as vicarious "satisfaction."[11] These types of theories, however, are often debated and rejected by other Christian communities. N. T. Wright was certainly right

---

denominations, including Greek and Russian Orthodoxy, and on modern Bible editions, hymnals, and liturgical gowns. While ministers and congregants of Christian worship services make the sign of the cross (the practice of which has been attested since approx. 200 CE; cf. Volker Leppin, "Cross: B. Medieval Times and Reformation Era," *EBR* 5:1047), the crucifix, a cross featuring a representation of the tortured body of Jesus, is especially popular in the Roman Catholic tradition. However, the cross itself was preceded by a stylized fish as a characteristic symbol of Christianity; this symbol renders one of its oldest creedal formulas, the acronym ΙΧΘΥΣ "*ichthys*," conveying that "Jesus is the Christ, the son of God, the savior."

8. Christoph Auffarth and Marvin Döbler, "Cross: II. Christianity. C. Modern Europe and America," *EBR* 5:1050–53, here 1050, with reference to Navid Kermani's criticism of the crucifixion scene in Christian churches (Navid Kermani. *Gott ist schön: Das ästhetische Erleben des Koran* [Munich: C. H. Beck, 1999]).

9. For detailed and comprehensive information on the crucifixion, see Heinz-Wolfgang Kuhn, "Die Kreuzesstrafe während der frühen Kaiserzeit: Ihre Wirklichkeit und Wertung in der Umwelt des Urchristentums," *Aufstieg und Niedergang der Römischen Welt* 2/25/1 (Berlin: De Gruyter, 1982), 648–793; Martin Hengel, *Crucifixion in the Ancient World and the Folly of the Message of the Cross*, trans. John Bowden (London: SCM Press, 1977), 51–63.

10. Dale C. Allison, Jr., "Cross: I. New Testament," *EBR* 5:1042.

11. I further discuss this point in subsequent paragraphs.

when he noted, "To put it crudely, the Eastern Orthodox churches never had 'an Anselm.'"[12]

The concept of atonement is neither unique to the Western Church nor even to Christianity more broadly. It was and remains an important concept within Judaism. It was a particularly important interpretive term in the context of regulations for sacrificial rituals. The corporate identity of Judaism gravitated around the First and Second Temple in Jerusalem, the site of almost continuous worship and sacrifice for a millennium. One of the key religious festivals of Judaism was and remains the Day of Atonement, celebrated on the tenth day of the month of Tishri. It featured the archaic "scapegoat" ritual and required the application of sacrificial blood to effect purification (cf. Lev 16).[13] The destruction of the Herodian Temple in 70 CE put an end to the offering of animal sacrifices in the Jerusalem Temple. Today, Jews obtain atonement for their sins on Yom Kippur with repeated prayer services, private and public confessions of sins, and fasting.

These brief observations show that atonement was not just an ancient concern. The concept is still relevant in religious practice and remains a popular topic in academic discourse. Atonement is central to the question of how salvation is imagined and communicated and is not limited to some marginal or irrelevant aspect of Jewish and Christian dialogue. I will revisit the concept of atonement below and place it in specific relation to sin, sacrifice, and forgiveness.

## General Remarks on Sacrificial Rituals in the Hebrew Bible

The Hebrew root כפר is usually translated "to atone." This term occurs in the Hebrew Bible to capture the result of sacrificial rituals, elimination rites, and various noncultic phenomena. Atonement was a central aspect of the cultic sphere, although other aspects remain central to sacrificial discourse. For example, an important celebration in Israel's annual calendar is the Day of Atonement

---

12. N. T. Wright, *The Day the Revolution Began: Reconsidering the Meaning of Jesus's Crucifixion* (New York: Harper One, 2016), 26.

13. The importance of atonement for Judaism is manifest in the fact that the first book Jewish boys learn in the Rabbinic system of education is Leviticus. It features regulations about sacrificial rituals to obtain atonement and also happens to provide the only definition of cultic atonement in the Bible (Lev 17:11). The importance of Leviticus for Jewish legislation is, in turn, evidenced by the fact two midrashim are dedicated to it (*Sifra*, a halakic book, and *Vayikra Rabbah*, a haggadic text).

(יום הכפרים / ἡμέρα ἐξιλασμοῦ, Lev 16; 23:26–32; Num 29:7–11), as previously mentioned. During this festival, atonement is obtained for the sanctuary and for the Israelites. The meaning of both sacrificial rituals and atonement itself, however, is the subject of ongoing scholarly debates. In what follows, I shall offer a short summary of recent developments in scholarship on Israel's cult.[14]

First, a consensus emerged in the second half of the twentieth century that strongly associated sacrifice with killing. As a result, ritual slaughter became the key to understanding atonement. Based partially on studies in anthropology and classics, some scholars even claimed that sacrifice could be considered as collective murder.[15] However, Kathryn McClymond has rightly countered that animal slaughter has been overrated in the interpretation of sacrifice. Blood application rites and sacrificial rituals consist of a variety of elements, and thus require a polythetic approach.[16] This shift in perspective is necessary for properly interpreting the most comprehensive and informative description of sacrificial rituals in the Hebrew Bible: Leviticus 1–7. In the canonical sequence of the Torah, these chapters follow the construction and installation of Israel's portable sanctuary, the tabernacle (Exod 25–40). The opening chapters of Leviticus outline five different types of sacrifice: the burnt offering (עלה/ὁλοκαύτωμα), cereal offering (מנחה/θυσία), communion sacrifice (שלמים/זבח/θυσία σωτηρίου), sin offering (חטאת/περὶ τῆς ἁμαρτίας), and guilt offering (אשם/περὶ τῆς πλημμελείας). All of these five types are explicitly labeled an "offering" (קרבן) for Yhwh.

Further, Lev 1–7 contains precise instructions about the correct performance of ritual activities. Almost two millennia after the cessation of sacrifice in the Second Temple, these texts still enable scholars to distinguish the specific profile of each type of sacrifice. Yet these regulations do not contain any definition of how exactly these sacrifices "work." Is it then possible to claim that sac-

---

14. A more detailed overview of the history of research on sacrifice is available in Eberhart, "Introduction," 2–12.

15. Cf. Walter Burkert, *Homo Necans: The Anthropology of Ancient Greek Sacrificial Ritual and Myth*, trans. Peter Bing (Berkeley: University of California Press, 1983). See also Walter Burkert, *Kulte des Altertums: Biologische Grundlagen der Religion* (Munich: Beck, 1998), 181: "Die zentrale Handlung im antiken Opfer ist das, 'heilige' Schlachten eines Tieres . . ." ("The central activity in antique sacrifice is the 'sacred' slaughter of an animal . . ."). Similar to Burkert's theory of sacrifice is that of René Girard, *Violence and the Sacred*, trans. Patrick Gregory (Baltimore: Johns Hopkins University Press, 1977), 19, 93. Cf. Raymond Schwager, "Christ's Death and the Prophetic Critique of Sacrifice," in *René Girard and Biblical Studies*, ed. Andrew J. McKenna, Semeia 33 (Baltimore: SBL, 1985), 109–23.

16. Kathryn McClymond, *Beyond Sacred Violence: A Comparative Study of Sacrifice* (Baltimore: Johns Hopkins University Press, 2008).

rifice is fundamentally about slaughter, or even ritually sanctioned "murder"? To be sure, all types of animal sacrifice require that an animal be slaughtered (שׁחט/σφάζω, Lev 1:5, 11; 3:2; 4:4 etc.).[17] However, even a cursory reading of the descriptions of sacrificial rituals in Lev 1–7 shows that an act of slaughter is not always required. For instance, Lev 2 features the ritual of the cereal offering (sometimes called the "grain offering" or "meal offering"). Although this type of sacrifice only consists of wheat, oil, and frankincense, it is nevertheless included in the list and labeled a קרבן for YHWH.[18] Hence, ritualized killing cannot be the sole purpose of cultic sacrifices in Lev 1–7 or elsewhere in the Hebrew Bible. One might say that ritual sacrifices in early Judaism were instituted in part to deal with sin, but their operative paradigm is not killing.[19]

Second, the regulations about the five types of sacrifice feature comments about the intended outcome or result of particular ritual activities, along with instructions about accurate performance. One of these results is atonement (כפר *piel*) (cf. Lev 1:4; 4:26, 31; etc.). The regulations for the Day of Atonement make an explicit connection between this result and the blood application rites of the required sin offerings (cf. Lev 16:14–15, 18–19). Multiple theories have been proposed to explain this connection. Some interpreters posit that atonement is the requisite feature of the human encounter with God, which happens vicariously after a process of existential substitution through the ritual activities of hand-leaning and blood application.[20] However, Lev 16 features

17. According to the Lev 1:5 MT, the offerer is the subject of animal slaughter. Leviticus 1:5 LXX reads the plural σφάξουσι and thus relates the activity to the priests. Later Ibn Ezra (actually Abraham ben Meir Ibn Ezra, 1089–ca.1167) also assigns this task to the priests, while Rashi (actually Shlomo Yitzchaki, 1040–1105 CE) and Nachmanides (actually Moses ben Nahman, 1194–1270 CE) see the offerer in charge of it; see Michael Carasik, *The Commentator's Bible: The Rubin JPS Miqra'ot Gedolot. Leviticus* ויקרא (Philadelphia: Jewish Publication Society, 2009), 7.

18. According to Rashi, the cereal offering was a type of sacrifice instituted especially for the poor (Carasik, *Commentator's Bible*, 13).

19. The scriptural basis for the notion that sacrifice requires killing is, in my opinion, only to be found in early Christian texts of the late first century CE. It is the so-called Letter to the Hebrews that adopts cultic imagery as christological and soteriological metaphors and, in the process, creatively changes their content to use the terms θυσία and προσφορά with reference to the death of Jesus (Heb 7:27; 10:10, 12, 14), suggesting specifically that Christ accomplished salvation in this way (2:14; cf. Christian A. Eberhart and Don Schweitzer, "The Unique Sacrifice of Christ According to Hebrews 9: A Study in Theological Creativity," *Religions* 10/1 [2019], online at: https://www.mdpi.com/2077-1444/10/1/47). This creative license in employing cultic concepts has had much influence on later attempts of understanding sacrificial rituals as such.

20. Cf. Karl C. W. F. Bähr, *Symbolik des Mosaischen Cultus*, 2 vols. (Heidelberg: Mohr,

further interpretive comments, according to which the modus operandi of blood application rites and the result of atonement is purification and consecration. Sacrificial blood actually purifies the sanctuary from sin and impurities (Lev 16:16, 19, 20; cf. 8:15). Likewise, it purifies and/or consecrates humans (Lev 8:23–24, 30; 14:14). According to Lev 17:11, sacrificial blood "is" or "represents" the life of the animal, not the lives of humans. Atonement has to do with this life. No biblical text warrants the interpretation that existential substitution for a human life occurs in sacrificial rituals of the Hebrew Bible.[21] One could say that atonement in early Judaism was often (though not always) the result of blood application rites in the context of sacrificial rituals; yet their modus operandi of how these rites eliminate sin and impurity is conceived of as purification and consecration.

Third, exploration of the sacrificial cult in Lev 1–7 reveals that the burning rite on the main altar is the only ritual element that occurs in all five types of sacrifice. Through the altar fire, material offerings are sublimated into an ethereal quality. The interpretive term אִשֶּׁה, "fire offering," conveys this process.[22] With the smoke of the altar fire, the offerings ascend to the heavenly sphere

---

1839), 190–202; Henri Hubert and Marcel Mauss, "Essai sur la nature et la fonction du sacrifice," *Année Sociologique* 2 (1899): 29–138; Hartmut Gese, "Die Sühne," in *Zur biblischen Theologie: Alttestamentliche Vorträge*, 2nd ed. (Tübingen: Mohr Siebeck, 1983), 85–106. It is worth mentioning that already the medieval Jewish philosopher and biblical commentator Nachmanides suggested that the spilling of sacrificial blood and the burning of the animal's body happened vicariously for the blood and flesh of the offerer who deserves to die because of sin (Nachmanides, *Commentary on the Torah: Leviticus* [New York: Shilo Publishing House, 1974], 1:9, 21; for a comprehensive description of this interpretation see Thomas Ryba, "Bloody Logic: The Biblical Economy of Sacrificial Substitution and Some of Its Eucharistic Implications," in *Sacrifice, Scripture, and Substitution: Readings in Ancient Judaism and Christianity*, ed. Ann W. Astell and Sandor Goodhart [Notre Dame, IN: University of Notre Dame Press, 2011], 90–92).

21. For a more comprehensive discussion, see Christian Eberhart, *Studien zur Bedeutung der Opfer im Alten Testament: Die Signifikanz von Blut- und Verbrennungsriten im kultischen Rahmen*, WMANT 94 (Neukirchen: Neukirchener, 2002), 222–88; Friedhelm Hartenstein, "Zur symbolischen Bedeutung des Blutes im Alten Testament," in *Deutungen des Todes Jesu im Neuen Testament*, ed. Jörg Frey and Jens Schröter, WUNT 181 (Tübingen: Mohr Siebeck, 2005), 119–37.

22. Cf. Eberhart, *Studien*, 40–48; James W. Watts, *Leviticus 1–10*, HCOT (Leuven: Peeters, 2013), 209–11; Matthias Ederer, *Identitätsstiftende Begegnung: Die theologische Deutung des regelmäßigen Kultes Israels in der Tora*, FAT 121 (Tübingen: Mohr Siebeck, 2018), 483. Commenting on the purpose of sacrifices, Nachmanides remarks: "[Lev] 3:16 says explicitly that the sacrifices are 'food—an offering by fire, of pleasing aroma'" (Carasik, *Commentator's Bible*, 9, italics original).

where they are accepted by Yʜwʜ. Interpretive terms such as "to atone," "to forgive," "to make acceptable," "fire offering," "pleasing odor," and "offering for Yʜwʜ" provide important insights into how sacrifices function and should thus be taken into consideration by those theorizing on sacrifice. All sacrificial rituals feature this burning rite and are therefore called an "offering for Yʜwʜ," which is why the burning rite can be seen as the constitutive element of sacrifice. In the priestly cultic system, all ritual sequences that feature the burning of materials on the altar of burnt offering are considered sacrifices. Sacrifices should therefore be construed as spatial processes and approaches toward the holy, as conveyed in the Hebrew term for sacrifice, קרבן.[23] Furthermore, sacrifices were tokens for the human encounter with Israel's God that could happen in response to distress, suffering, and sin, as well as in situations of joy and happiness. Atonement and pleas for forgiveness were juxtaposed with celebrations of gratitude and recognition of divine blessing.

## The Hand-Leaning Gesture in the Context of Sacrificial Rituals

David Calabro has recently provided fresh insight into one specific aspect of sacrifice: the hand-leaning gesture.[24] In priestly regulations for sacrificial rituals in Lev 1–7, the hand-leaning gesture is instituted for the four types of animal sacrifice. For example, the rule for the burnt offering stipulates: וסמך ידו על ראש העלה, "and he shall lay his hand on the head of the burnt offering" (Lev 1:4). The Masoretic text (MT) vocalizes the Hebrew consonants of ידו as the singular יד ("hand") with a third person singular masculine suffix. In recent scholarly literature, a difference has been recognized between this hand-leaning rite and the one for the famous "Azazel goat" or "scapegoat" in the Day of Atonement ritual. In this ritual, Aaron is said to impose שתי ידו, "his two

23. With this particular focus, early Jewish sacrifice can be integrated into the larger framework of the ancient Mediterranean cults. In his recent book, F. S. Naiden demonstrates that for the ancient Greeks, the burning of the sacrificial substance was important. In addition, modern interpreters who want to understand these rituals need to pay attention to the deities to whom the sacrifices were addressed (F. S. Naiden, *Smoke Signals for the Gods: Ancient Greek Sacrifice from the Archaic through Roman Periods* [Oxford: Oxford University Press, 2013]).

24. David Calabro, "A Reexamination of the Ancient Israelite Gesture of Hand Placement," in *Sacrifice, Cult, and Atonement in Early Judaism and Christianity: Constituents and Critique*, ed. Henrietta L. Wiley and Christian A. Eberhart, RBS 85 (Atlanta: Society of Biblical Literature Press, 2017), 99–124.

hands," on the head of the second goat (16:21). In the MT, the Hebrew consonants are vocalized as a defective dual form. But the unvocalized consonants are ידו, which means they are identical to the terminology of the hand-leaning gesture in the burnt offering ritual of Lev 1. So, is the noun ידו singular or dual? The text in Lev 16:21 is unambiguous: it explicitly mentions שׁתי ידיו, "his two hands." As a result, Lev 1:4 needs to be revisited in order to assess whether the singular interpretation proposed above is correct.

A look at the Septuagint tradition is instructive. Recent research suggests that the Greek translation of Leviticus was produced by the Jewish diaspora community of Lower Egypt, most likely in Alexandria and in its neighboring military outpost Leontopolis.[25] It utilizes cultic terminology from the Greek Exodus, which was also translated in this region. Leviticus 1:4 appears in the Old Greek as follows: καὶ ἐπιθήσει τὴν χεῖρα ἐπὶ τὴν κεφαλὴν τοῦ καρπώματος, "and he will lay the hand upon the head of the offering." Thus, the Old Greek agrees with the MT by reading the singular "hand," but it omits the personal pronoun. But the case is not resolved. The regulation for the well-being/communion offering (or "peace" offering, זבח שׁלמים) also features a hand-leaning gesture (Lev 3). Although the MT reads וסמך ידו, "and he shall lean his hand" (3:2), the Old Greek translates as follows: καὶ ἐπιθήσει τὰς χεῖρας, "and he will lean the hands." The plural "hands" appears without the personal pronoun. Another contemporary witness from the Jewish com-

---

25. Cf. Peter Schwagmeier, "1.2 Exodos / Exodos / Das zweite Buch Mose," in *Einleitung in die Septuaginta* (LXX.H 1), ed. Siegfried Kreuzer (Gütersloh: Gütersloher, 2016), 120–36, at 134; Martin Vahrenhorst, "1.3 Levitikon / Levitikus / Das dritte Buch Mose," in *Einleitung in die Septuaginta* (LXX.H 1), ed. Siegfried Kreuzer, (Gütersloh: Gütersloher, 2016), 137–45, at 141–42. Founded by Alexander the Great in 332/331 BCE, the city of Alexandria became an important commercial and intellectual center. It was cosmopolitan and had a large Jewish diaspora community (cf. Siegfried Kreuzer, "Die Septuaginta im Kontext alexandrinischer Kultur und Bildung," in *Im Brennpunkt: Die Septuaginta*, vol. 3 of *Studien zur Theologie, Anthropologie, Ekklesiologie, Eschatologie und Liturgie der Griechischen Bibel*, ed. Heinz-Josef Fabry and Dieter Böhler, BWA(N)T 14 [Stuttgart: Kohlhammer, 2007], 33–36; Joan Taylor, "Alexandria," EBR 1 [2009], 760–62; Marjorie S. Venit, "Alexandria," in *The Oxford Handbook of Roman Egypt*, ed. Christina Riggs [Oxford: Oxford University Press, 2012], 103–21, esp. 104, 108, 119). The military outpost in Leontopolis was located approximately 120 miles southeast of Alexandria. It had its own temple including a sacrificial cult according to Jewish customs (Jos. *Ant.* 13:72), which makes it even more interesting for studies of sacrificial rituals and atonement (cf. John J. Collins, *Between Athens and Jerusalem: Jewish Identity in the Hellenistic Diaspora*, 2nd ed. [Grand Rapids: Eerdmans, 2000], 68–73; Livia Capponi, *Il tempio di Leontopoli in Egitto: Identità politica e religiosa dei Giudei di Onia (c. 150 a.C – 73 d.C.)* [Pubblicazioni della Facoltà di Lettere e Filosofia dell'Università di Pavia 118], Pisa: Edizione ETS, 2007).

munity of Alexandria is Philo Judaeus (ca. 15 BCE–40 CE), who relates the following details in his *Special Laws*: ἔπειτα δ᾽ ἀπονιψάμενος ὁ προσάγων τὰς χεῖρας ἐπιφερέτω τῇ τοῦ ἱερείου κεφαλῇ, "then the offerer has to wash his hands and lay them on the head of the offering" (*Spec.* 1:198). In a similar fashion, the Mishnah, Tosefta, and Babylonian Talmud mention a two-handed hand-leaning gesture (m. Men. 9:8; t. Men. 10:12; b. Yom. 36a). As Calabro has noted, the development toward the singular reading in Lev 1:4 MT, which is later adopted by Ibn Ezra, was "occasioned by loss of the actual rite and by linguistic changes that obscured the meaning of the biblical phrases."[26] This demonstrates the importance of listening to ancient interpreters of the biblical texts who discuss sacrificial processes, particularly those of the Jewish diaspora in and around Alexandria.

While this discussion may seem like academic hair-splitting—after all, it concerns the vocalization of a singular Hebrew consonant (or one letter in the English translation!)—it has ramifications for theories of atonement that are rooted in particular interpretations of the hand-leaning gesture. This gesture has often been interpreted as the moment when the offerer "identifies" himself or herself with the sacrificial animal; as such it has been construed as the prerequisite for existential substitution.[27] In the context of the scapegoat ritual, this gesture has the effect of transferring Israel's iniquities and sins onto the head of the goat (stated explicitly in Lev 16:21). As a result, a fundamental difference between the one-handed and two-handed gesture may need to be recognized. According to Calabro, only one interpretation is suitable for this gesture, "appointing a person or animal to a particular status or role."[28] With this in mind, many modern scholarly theories of sacrifice and atonement might need to be readjusted.

## The Reception of Isaiah 52:13–53:12

Before discussing the reception of atonement in select early Christian texts, I would like to briefly consider a text that has loomed large in atonement debates: Isa 52:13–53:12. Why consider Isaiah's fourth Servant Song? Indeed, the passage does not contain the root כפר, and Hebrew Bible scholars have

26. So Calabro, "Reexamination," 116.

27. Cf. Hubert and Mauss, "Essai," 66–67, 76; Gese, "Die Sühne," 97.

28. Calabro, "Reexamination," 123. Calabro also points out that "this interpretation avoids the potential pitfalls of using modern Western philosophical terms, like *identification*, *designation*, and *attribution*, to describe ancient Israelite ritual practices" (124).

recently suggested that the term אָשָׁם in Isa 53:10 does not refer to the guilt offering but to something more generic—for example, debt redemption. As a result, Hebrew Bible scholars might not consider the fourth Servant Song as an exemplar of atonement discourse.

Scholars of the Hebrew Bible, however, often approach the topic of atonement rather differently than scholars of early Christian literature. The former typically use the term "atonement" to render the Hebrew root כפר and concepts related thereto, as I have done in the previous section of this essay. Scholars of early Christian literature, by contrast, usually employ the term in a broader sense, one that encompasses salvation and its many different facets. As such, one can claim that atonement occupies the core of Paul's Christology and soteriology and remains a central concern for other New Testament writings as well. As a theological-conceptual abstraction, the term "atonement" functions as a comprehensive interpretive category that expresses the meaning of the death of Jesus Christ in light of his resurrection.[29] It is in this sense that I approach Isa 52:13–53:12 and its reception in early Christianity.

The Suffering Servant Song (Isa 52:13–53:12) has often been considered a central feature of christological atonement discourse in early Christian literature, specifically with regard to the notion that the servant of the Lord gave his life vicariously for others. Some even posit its influence on the words of institution at the Last Supper/Eucharist.[30] In response to these positions, Wolfgang Kraus has recently published a thought-provoking study in which he explores quotations of Isa 52:13–53:12 in the New Testament. In particular, Kraus makes the following two points. First, New Testament texts contain

---

29. Cf. Christian A. Eberhart, "Atonement. II. New Testament," *EBR* 3:32.

30. Cf. Peter Stuhlmacher, "Jes 53 in den Evangelien und in der Apostelgeschichte," in *Der leidende Gottesknecht: Jesaja 53 und seine Wirkungsgeschichte*, ed. Peter Stuhlmacher and Bernd Janowski, FAT 14 (Tübingen: Mohr Siebeck, 1996), 93–106, at 94, 97 [English: "Isaiah 53 in the Gospels and Acts," in *The Suffering Servant: Isaiah 53 in Jewish and Christian Sources*, ed. Peter Stuhlmacher and Bernd Janowski, trans. Daniel P. Bailey (Grand Rapids: Eerdmans, 2004), 147–62]; Ulrich Wilckens, *Theologie des Neuen Testaments 1/2: Jesu Tod und Auferstehung und die Entstehung der Kirche aus Juden und Heiden* (Neukirchen-Vluyn: Neukirchener, 2003), 75; Hermann Lichtenberger, "'Bund' in der Abendmahlsüberlieferung," in *Bund und Tora: Zur theologischen Begriffsgeschichte in alttestamentlicher, frühjüdischer und urchristlicher Tradition*, ed. Hermann Lichtenberger and Friedrich Avemarie, WUNT 92 (Tübingen: Mohr Siebeck, 1996), 217–28, at 225. Critical of such theories is Gerhard Barth, *Der Tod Jesu Christi im Verständnis des Neuen Testaments* (Neukirchen-Vluyn: Neukirchener, 1992), 56–59. For a history of research, see Marie-Louise Gubler, *Die frühesten Deutungen des Todes Jesu: Eine motivgeschichtliche Darstellung aufgrund der neueren exegetischen Forschung* (Göttingen: Vandenhoeck & Ruprecht, 1977), 259–311.

fewer explicit quotations of Isa 52:13–53:12 than we typically assume. If 1 Pet 2 is counted twice, only eight quotations of Isa 52:13–53:12 appear in the New Testament: Matthew 8:17 (referring to the activity of Jesus), Luke 22:37 (a christological context, with reference to the crucifixion), John 12:38 (concerning Israel's disbelief), Acts 8:32–33 (christological context, with reference to the passion), Rom 10:16 (concerning Paul's mission and Israel's disbelief), Rom 15:21 (concerning Paul's mission and apostolate), and 1 Pet 2:24–25 (a christological confession in an ethical context).[31] None of these citations depict Jesus giving his life vicariously for others. Paul, for example, cites Isa 52:15 and 53:1 with reference to his own mission as an apostle to the gentiles, not for christological or soteriological purposes (Rom 10:16; 15:21).[32]

Second, with the exception of Matt 8:17, all New Testament quotations of Isa 52:13–53:12 are drawn from the Septuagint.[33] Recently, Arie van der Kooij proposed that the book of Isaiah was translated into Greek in Leontopolis in the second century BCE.[34] The Greek version of Isaiah appears to differ from its Hebrew *Vorlage* at several points. This applies particularly to Isa 52:13–53:12. For instance, Isa 53:10a MT reads:

ויהוה חפץ דכאו החלי אם־תשים אשם נפשו יראה זרע יאריך ימים

Yet Yʜᴡʜ, whose will it was to beat him, healed the one who gave his life as a redemption of debt. He will see his offspring and live many days, . . .[35]

31. Wolfgang Kraus, "Jesaja 53 LXX im frühen Christentum—eine Überprüfung," in *Beiträge zur urchristlichen Theologiegeschichte*, ed. Wolfgang Kraus, BZNW 163 (Berlin: De Gruyter, 2009), 149–82, at 150–51. See also Arie van der Kooij and Florian Wilk, "Esaias / Isaias / das Buch Jesaja," in *Septuaginta Deutsch: Erklärungen und Kommentare zum griechischen Alten Testament*, vol. 2: *Psalmen bis Daniel*, ed. Martin Karrer and Wolfgang Kraus (Stuttgart: Deutsche Bibelgesellschaft, 2011), 2484–2505, at 2493–98.

32. Kraus, "Jesaja 53 LXX," 151.

33. In this regard, see the comment by Emanuel Tov: "In the first century of the Common Era, when the NT writers quoted the early Scripture, they used the wording of the LXX. That was a natural development since the NT was written in Greek, and under normal circumstances its authors would quote from earlier Scripture written in the same language" (Emanuel Tov, "The Septuagint Between Judaism and Christianity," in *Die Septuaginta und das frühe Christentum—The Septuagint and Christian Origins*, ed. Thomas Scott Caulley and Hermann Lichtenberger, WUNT 277 [Tübingen: Mohr Siebeck, 2011], 3–25, at 4).

34. Arie van der Kooij, "6.2 Esaias / Isaias / Jesaja," in *Einleitung in die Septuaginta* (LXX.H 1), ed. Siegfried Kreuzer (Gütersloh: Gütersloher, 2016), 559–76, at 566.

35. English translation according to the German rendering in Kraus, "Jesaja 53 LXX," 156 (which in turn is based on the translation in Hans-Jürgen Hermisson, "Das vierte Gottes-

Kraus rightly notes that this passage contains the concept, unique in the Hebrew Bible, of someone vicariously giving his life for others.[36] It is all the more surprising, then, that the Old Greek reads:

καὶ κύριος βούλεται καθαρίσαι αὐτὸν τῆς πληγῆς, ἐὰν δῶτε περὶ ἁμαρτίας, ἡ ψυχὴ ὑμῶν ὄψεται σπέρμα μακρόβιον, . . .

And/Yet the Lord wanted to cleanse him from the blow; if you offer sin offerings, then your souls will see eternal offspring.

In the Septuagint, the sentence becomes a statement that conveys the rewards of offering a particular type of cultic sacrifice. Subsequent sentences differ as well. For example, Isa 53:11 LXX omits the comment that many others have attained righteousness as a result of the servant's sacrifice. Rather, it states that the servant himself has attained righteousness. The Greek text, therefore, suppresses the concept of substitution that is important in the MT.[37]

This point is significant for the interpretation of those New Testament texts that feature scriptural quotations of Isa 52:13–53:12 LXX. It is methodologically inappropriate to make soteriological claims about New Testament passages that reference Isa 52:13–53:12 LXX when the MT alone seems to depict vicarious substitution. Likewise, Isa 52:13–53:12 does not appear to influence the words of institution over the cup of the Eucharist, as is occasionally suggested.[38] Instead, the words of institution rely on the famous words of Moses in the covenant ratification ceremony in Exod 24:8: "See the blood of the covenant (דם־הברית/τὸ αἷμα τῆς διαθήκης) that YHWH has made with you in accor-

---

knechtslied im deuterojesajanischen Kontext," in *Der leidende Gottesknecht*, ed. Janowski and Stuhlmacher, 1–26, here 8: "Aber JHWH, dessen Plan es war, ihn zu schlagen, heilte den, der sein Leben als Schuldausgleich/Ersatzleistung einsetzte. Er wird Nachkommenschaft sehen, lange leben, . . .").

36. Kraus, "Jesaja 53 LXX," 157: "Damit liegt in Jes 53,10 insofern eine Spitzenaussage alttestamentlicher Tradition vor, als hier singulär einer für andere stellvertretend sein Leben hingibt."

37. Ibid.: "Diese Stellvertretungsaussage in V.10 bietet die LXX nicht." See also Klaus Baltzer and Jürgen Kabiersch, "Esaias / Isaias / das Buch Jesaja," in *Septuaginta Deutsch*, ed. Karrer and Kraus, 2640. It is possible that the translators of the book of Isaiah in second-century BCE Leontopolis identified the suffering servant either with the high priest Onias IV, who founded the local Jewish temple, or with the Jewish diaspora community (oral communication with Wolfgang Kraus and Arie van der Kooij). This might have occasioned the text modification.

38. See the literature above, n. 30.

dance with all these words." But linguistic evidence does not evince any connection to Isa 52:13–53:12.

## The Death and Resurrection of Jesus (Romans 4:25)

How might these exegetical observations reshape our understanding of atonement in early Christianity? To answer this question, I turn to a passage that appears to be central to Paul's atonement theology, Rom 4:25:

> ὃς παρεδόθη διὰ τὰ παραπτώματα ἡμῶν καὶ ἠγέρθη διὰ τὴν δικαί-
> ωσιν ἡμῶν

> . . . who [Jesus] was handed over to death for our trespasses and was raised for our justification.

First, this is often thought to evoke Isa 52:13–53:12. Contemporary scholarship has reached near-unanimous agreement on this point. Thus, discussions tend to be concerned with the precise nature of the reference, not with whether it is, in fact, present.[39] Based on this scriptural background, Paul's statement is understood to articulate the redemption in Jesus, a redemption that is comprised of both his vicarious death on the cross and his resurrection. But Kraus recognizes methodological difficulties in many of the arguments in support of the reference to Isa 52:13–53:12. For example, scholars adduce linguistic evidence from the Septuagint, while at the same time importing theological concepts from the MT.[40] If the MT alone conveys the notion of the suffering servant's

---

39. Kraus lists, for example, James D. G. Dunn (*Romans 1–8*, WBC 38A [Grand Rapids: Zondervan, 1988], 224–25), Joseph A. Fitzmyer (*Romans: A New Translation with Introduction and Commentary*, AYB 33 [New York: Doubleday, 1993], 389), and Robert Jewett (*Romans: A Commentary*, Hermeneia [Minneapolis: Fortress, 2007], 342) in support of this opinion, while Daniel G. Powers (*Salvation through Participation: An Examination of the Notion of the Believers' Corporate Unity with Christ in Early Christian Soteriology*, CBET 29 [Leuven: Peeters, 2001], 128–30) remains critical of any reference to Isa 52:13–53:12. Further support of this opinion is found in, for example, Volker Hampel, *Menschensohn und historischer Jesus: Ein Rätselwort als Schlüssel zum messianischen Selbstverständnis Jesu* (Neukirchen-Vluyn: Neukirchener, 1990), 291–92; Barth, *Tod Jesu Christi*, 45; Michael Wolter, *Der Brief an die Römer*, 2 vols., EKKNT 6 (Neukirchen-Vluyn: Neukirchener, 2014), 1:311–12.

40. Kraus, "Jesaja 53 LXX," 176: "Die Vermischung von Bezügen zu MT und LXX scheint mir, wie gesagt, vor allem methodisch problematisch. Lexikalisch wird Bezug genommen auf Jes 53 LXX, theologisch jedoch auf den MT."

*vicarious* death, then we should question whether a statement about a vicarious death in Rom 4:25 can indeed be derived from Isa 52:13–53:12 LXX.[41]

Second, current atonement debates must also consider the significant connection between the death of Jesus and his resurrection. Some recent studies emphasize this very point. The earliest Christians believed and proclaimed that the crucifixion of Jesus was more than just a tragedy or an accident. As soon as the message of the resurrection began to spread, the cross was understood as a key symbol of salvation. Thus, the New Testament Gospels present the life, passion, death, and resurrection of Jesus of Nazareth as one continuous narrative. Romans 4:25 shows that, for early Christians, the death and resurrection of Jesus belong together. Without the latter, it is unlikely that early Christians would have described Jesus's death on the cross as a salvific event—nor would they have formulated atonement theologies around it. The resurrection of Jesus further validated his death on the cross. Without the resurrection, the death of Jesus would have been as remarkable, soteriologically speaking, as the decapitation of John the Baptist. While death had appeared to defeat Jesus, his resurrection became the moment of his vindication from and victory over the power of death. Paul makes this point when he writes, "Death has been swallowed up in victory" (1 Cor 15:54, alluding to Isa 25:8 and Hos 13:14). Paul's point, however, was difficult for future readers to conceptualize, which resulted in the ongoing development of atonement concepts.

The Alamo is a fitting metaphor for this phenomenon. On the one hand, "the Alamo" in what is nowadays San Antonio, Texas, has little to do with atonement. At most, it was the location of the Texans' defeat that later came to be included in a battle cry on the road to victory. During the Texas Revolution (1835–1836), an old Spanish mission building was occupied by Texan soldiers, who were attacked by the Mexican army during the Battle of the Alamo. Most of the Texans were killed. Had the defeat alone been recorded in the history books, nobody today would remember the Alamo. But a few weeks later, at San Jacinto, the victorious Mexican army was now attacked by Texans, who repeatedly shouted, "Remember the Alamo! Remember the Alamo!" Commenting on these events, the anthropologist Michel-Rolph Trouillot notes the following about the Mexican general: "Santa Anna . . . was doubly defeated at San Jacinto. He lost the battle of the day, but he also lost the battle he had won at the Alamo . . . The military loss of March was no longer the end point of the narrative but a necessary turn in the plot, the trial of the heroes, which, in turn,

---

41. Cf. Kraus, "Jesaja 53 LXX," 177.

made final victory both inevitable and grandiose."[42] A victory for the Mexicans had retroactively turned into a crushing defeat. By contrast, the defeat of the Texans had turned into victory. A shameful event became a powerful symbol that has, and continues to be, remembered with pride. "The Alamo," a location of defeat that was destroyed, has since been rebuilt and is celebrated today as a "Shrine of Texas Liberty."

Similar insights emerge when Jesus's crucifixion and resurrection are conjoined, as they are in Paul's letters. Atonement has to do with the retroactive validation of the death of Jesus. As such, atonement is a central theme in New Testament writings and remained relevant to early Christians. But the question remains: do the past images deployed in service of this task remain intelligible for us today? Many of the negative connotations associated with atonement theology have to do with the theory of vicarious satisfaction developed by Anselm of Canterbury (ca. 1033–1109). Anselm starts with Augustine's doctrine of original sin and with Paul's anthropological axiom of the all-encompassing sinfulness of humanity. Anselm therefore argues that humans cannot give God, their creator, the obedience and veneration that are his due. Humans, in other words, are left with a duty of recompense that can never be fulfilled. And since God is bound by his own justice, he cannot simply repeal the punishment humanity deserves. Within this dilemma, the only possibility for salvation is an "external agent." Jesus, a divine being, came to obtain what humans could not. As a human, he suffered vicariously the punishment of death due to humanity, thus earning humanity's redemption.

While crafting his theory of atonement and vicarious satisfaction, Anselm adopted images and concepts from Roman legal conventions and political structures that his contemporaries readily understood. But these are not universally valid. Rather, every generation in every locale needs to do the creative work of adopting and developing its own atonement imagery and terminology. Simple repetition of images found in the New Testament or later church history may be insufficient, since these too were employed with reference to contemporary and local exigencies, ideas, and language.

The New Testament's concept of the Son's incarnation may remain a particularly fruitful avenue for further reflection. While considered outdated by some, the concept of "incarnation" has been included in recent films with much success. One example is the eponymous 2009 epic film *Avatar*, directed

---

42. Michel-Rolph Trouillot, *Silencing the Past: Power and the Production of History* (Boston: Beacon Press, 1995), 2.

by James Cameron.[43] Similarly, even first-century CE atonement concepts and theories, like those of Paul, need "avatars" to be efficaciously communicated. Indeed, Paul's participatory atonement paradigms are, in their own right, reminiscent of avatar representation, when he attributes crucial events in the life of Jesus to believers: "For if we have been united with him in a death like his, we will certainly be united with him in a resurrection like his" (Rom 6:5).

New Testament writings already feature a creative development of atonement concepts and terminology. Some thirty or forty years after Paul penned the earliest New Testament text, the anonymous author of the Letter to the Hebrews deployed cultic imagery with great virtuosity and poetic license.[44] In his interpretation of Hebrews, David M. Moffitt has argued that Christ's bodily resurrection, rather than being passed over or transformed into a spiritual concept, remains central to its cultic construal of the Christ-event. Moffitt specifically proposes that Christ is appointed high priest at his ascension and enthronement, at which point Christ offers himself to God in the holy of holies of the heavenly tabernacle, just as the Levitical high priest offered blood when he entered the inner sanctum of the earthly tabernacle.[45] Space limitations prevent me from assessing the merits of his approach, but it is clear that Moffitt's proposal connects what is already connected in the New Testament Gospels. Such a view is instrumental to understanding atonement concepts that remain "at-one" within larger redemptive frameworks.[46]

43. The term "avatar," which is derived from Sanskrit, refers to the phenomenon of embodiment or appearance. Vedic literature relates embodiments of deities like Indra or Vishnu on earth (cf. Geoffrey Parrinder, *Avatar and Incarnation: The Divine in Human Form in the World's Religions* [Oxford: Oneworld, 1997], 19–20).

44. On the date of composition of Hebrews, see Craig R. Koester, *Hebrews: A New Translation with Introduction and Commentary*, AYB 36 (New York: Doubleday, 2001), 50–54; Martin Karrer, "Hebrews, Epistle to the," *EBR* 11:681; Mary Ann Beavis and HyeRan Kim-Cragg, *Hebrews*, Wisdom Commentary 54 (Collegeville, MN: Liturgical Press, 2015), lxii–lxiv.

45. Cf. David M. Moffitt, "Blood, Life, and Atonement: Reassessing Hebrews' Christological Appropriation of Yom Kippur," in *The Day of Atonement: Its Interpretations in Early Jewish and Christian Traditions*, ed. Thomas Hieke and Tobias Nicklas, TBN 15 (Leiden: Brill, 2012), 211–24, esp. 220–22.

46. I am grateful to Ms. Peace A. Cowen, for her careful proof-reading of, and helpful comments on, this chapter. All remaining errors are, of course, my own responsibility.

# CHAPTER TWO

# Sin, Sacrifice, but No Salvation

## When the Circle Cannot Be Completed

DEBORAH W. ROOKE

> Can the circle be unbroken
> By and by, Lord, by and by?
> There's a better home awaiting
> In the sky, Lord, in the sky.

So thought Johnny Cash, one of the many country and Western singers who recorded this particular version of an early-twentieth-century Christian hymn.[1] Unfortunately, his (and their) optimism is not shared by the Priestly writers at whose hand we have received much of the legislative material in Exodus, Leviticus, and Numbers. Despite the apparent abundance of atonement opportunities for which P legislates, there is nevertheless a hard core of cases in which nothing can be done to complete the circle from sin through sacrifice to salvation, and the end result in these cases is that of *karet*, or cutting off.[2] This paper will consider these cases in an effort to understand why these particular sins lead to such negative consequences. I should stipulate that this is primarily a final-form investigation of the text, and although I have no doubt that what we conveniently call "P" is a multi-faceted, multi-stranded and many-layered work, my concern is with the effect of those layers as we now encounter them, rather than with what they are and how or when they got there.

---

1. The hymn in its original version was written by Ada R. Habershon in 1907. The hymn was reworked into a country music song by the singer A. P. Carter and recorded in 1935 by The Carter Family, a country music group of which A. P. was a founding member. The chorus given here is from Carter's version.

2. The term *karet*, from the Hebrew verb כרת, "to cut (off)," is used in the Mishnah to denote the penalty (m. Ker. 1:1).

## The *Karet* Penalty

The penalty of *karet*, or cutting off, is characteristic of the Priestly writings, broadly conceived.[3] *Karet* is usually understood to be a divine penalty inflicted without recourse to human agency, consisting of premature or unnatural death and/or lack of descendants. The most detailed discussion of *karet* in modern times is in an unpublished doctoral thesis and an SBL seminar paper by Donald Wold from 1979.[4] Wold's position was summed up by Jacob Milgrom in his own 1991 commentary on Leviticus 1–16.[5] Traditional exegesis agreed that *karet* was some sort of untimely death with lack of descendants, with some exegetes suggesting that the cutting off meant no access to the afterlife in addition to cutting off from earthly life.[6] More recently there has been a tendency to view *karet* as excommunication, an idea that was explored at length by Thomas Hobson in a 2010 dissertation arguing for *karet* as punitive expulsion.[7] That said, the majority view is still the one that sees *karet* as associated with end-of-life punishment, both for the offender and by implication for the offender's family, thereby cutting off the offender's future existence via descendants. (The idea that *karet* denies the offender any position in a metaphysical afterlife is not one that can be validated from the Priestly materials as we have them, whatever religious convictions may have developed subsequently.)

The penalty of *karet* is stipulated for the following offenses:

---

3. As indicated above, for these purposes no distinction is being made between the texts assigned to the Priestly substratum known as the Holiness school (H) and those regarded more broadly as P. Interestingly, Israel Knohl (*The Sanctuary of Silence: The Priestly Torah and the Holiness School* [Minneapolis: Fortress, 1995], 104–105), attributes to H all but four of the instances of *karet* discussed below, which would make the distinction between P and H in this area rather less significant than it might otherwise be thought. In Knohl's view, Exod 30:33, 38 and Lev 7:20–21 originate from P, Gen 17:14 is uncertain, and all the other references are in H.

4. Donald J. Wold, "The *Kareth* Penalty in P: Rationale and Cases," in *SBL Seminar Papers 1979*, vol. 1, ed. Paul J. Achtemeier (Missoula, MT: Scholars Press, 1979), 1–45.

5. See the excursus on *karet* in Jacob Milgrom, *Leviticus 1–16: A New Translation with Introduction and Commentary*, AYB 3 (New York: Doubleday, 1991), 457–60.

6. Milgrom, *Leviticus 1–16*, 457.

7. Thomas Hobson's 2009 SBL paper, "'Cut Off from (One's) People': Punitive Expulsion in the Torah and in the Ancient Near East," is available online at https://biblicallaw.files.wordpress.com/2013/07/hobson.pdf. A version of the material was subsequently published as "Punitive Expulsion in the Ancient Near East," *ZABR* 17 (2011): 15–32.

1. Failure to be circumcised (Gen 17:14)
2. Eating leaven or leavened material during the feast of Unleavened Bread (Exod 12:15, 19)
3. Making or using imitation holy anointing oil or incense (Exod 30:33, 38)
4. Working on the Sabbath (Exod 31:14)
5. Eating meat from sacrifices of well-being when in a state of uncleanness (Lev 7:20, 21)
6. Eating the suet of animals that are sacrificeable (i.e., sheep, goat, bovine) (Lev 7:25)
7. Eating blood (Lev 7:27; 17:10, 14)
8. Profane slaughter of a sacrificeable animal (i.e., sheep, goat, bovine) (Lev 17:4)
9. Making burnt offerings elsewhere apart from at the tabernacle (Lev 17:9)
10. Committing incest, bestiality, adultery, male-male intercourse (Lev 18:29)
11. Eating meat from sacrifices of well-being on the third day after the sacrifice (Lev 19:8)
12. Sacrificing to Molek (Lev 20:3–5)
13. Following wizards or mediums (Lev 20:6)
14. Sleeping with one's sister (Lev 20:17)
15. Sleeping with a menstruating woman (Lev 20:18)
16. Priest approaching holy donations while unclean (Lev 22:3)
17. Failing to afflict oneself on the Day of Atonement (Lev 23:29)
18. Working on the Day of Atonement (Lev 23:30)
19. Neglecting, without cause, to celebrate the Passover (Num 9:13)
20. Deliberate sins (Num 15:30–31)
21. Failing to cleanse oneself from corpse impurity (Num 19:13, 20)

Milgrom, following Wold, puts these offenses into five different groups: offenses against sacred time, offenses against sacred substance, offenses against purification rituals, illicit worship, and illicit sex;[8] in this way they are all seen as being sacral offenses, which accounts for the Deity's ire being aroused against those who commit them. Another feature they have in common is

8. Milgrom, *Leviticus 1–16*, 458.

that they are hard to police,[9] particularly in the case of the sexual offenses, which could well take place without witnesses other than the participants. As such, their punishment has to be left to Yahweh who sees everything. But they also have an ideological dimension. On the assumption that the penalties associated with offenses are an indicator of the offenses' gravity and thus of their significance in the worldview of those who compiled the law codes, these offenses are grave because many of them can be seen as compromising the identity of the people of Israel as the holy people of a holy God, an identity that requires them to separate themselves from the nations and gods round about and from customs that are seen as unholy. Being holy people of a holy God requires total dedication to that God; and so, many of the sacral sins that lead to being cut off are those that compromise the people's sole dedication to their God: sacrificing to Molek (Lev 20:3–5); following wizards or mediums (Lev 20:6); and making burnt offerings other than at the shrine of their God (Lev 17:9). Other offenses threaten to undermine the boundaries that are put up by God in order to preserve his own holiness as he consents to inhabit the tabernacle among his people: making and using imitation holy oil or incense (Exod 30:33, 38), which cheapens and thus profanes the special fragrances of the tabernacle; eating suet and blood from sacrificial animals (Lev 7:25, 27; 17:10, 14), which are given sacral significance; eating sacrificial meat when in a state of uncleanness (Lev 7:20, 21) or when its "eat by" date has passed (i.e., it is deemed to have become abominable) (Lev 19:8), which profanes the sacrifices; profane slaughter of animals that are reserved for cultic use (Lev 17:4); and approaching holy donations in a state of uncleanness (Lev 22:3). Still other offenses show a disrespect toward the structures that shape and constitute the community, thereby undermining its separate and holy identity: failure to circumcise (Gen 17:14); eating leaven during the festival of Unleavened Bread (Exod 12:15, 19); failure to observe the Sabbath (Exod 31:14) or the Passover (Num 9:13); failure to self-afflict or abstain from work on the Day of Atonement (Lev 23:29, 30). So it is little wonder that these fall into the class of "unforgivable sins," because they threaten to undermine what might be referred to as the "Yahweh-Israel enterprise" as construed in Priestly terms.

But the *karet* penalty does not simply describe the consequences of certain actions. In all but four instances the penalty is declared using the *niphal* form of כרת, "to cut (off)." As the *niphal* is the simple passive form, it results in translations such as "the person who does such and such *will be cut off*" (and

---

9. Noted by Gordon Wenham, *The Book of Leviticus*, NICOT (Grand Rapids: Eerdmans, 1979), 242, 285–86.

we will consider from what they are to be cut off in a moment). Given that no agent is specified as doing the cutting off, the *niphal* form is usually taken as what might be called a divine passive, in other words, as a periphrastic means of describing God's action. This idea is also supported by the fact that in some of the instances given above the *hiphil* form, that is, the active causal form, is used, with Yahweh as the subject; this results in translations such as "Yahweh *will cause x to be cut off*," and clearly suggests that Yahweh is likewise the instrument of cutting off when the *niphal* forms are used.

But I think there are also other nuances in the use of the *niphal* form. One of the functions of any law code is to actualize or to inculcate societal values, whether by enshrining in law the values to which a given society subscribes or by prescribing values that are not currently widespread in an effort to change practice and ultimately attitudes. It is difficult to tell whether P is descriptive or prescriptive, though James Watts has argued for the rhetorical force of Leviticus as a plea for priestly privileges,[10] and elsewhere I have argued for P as prescriptive rather than descriptive, not least because it is far from being a complete treatment of every issue that would be required for it to be a workable code as it stands.[11] On the basis, then, that P's legal scheme is a manifesto rather than a constitution, the *niphal* form that is used in describing the *karet* penalty can be understood as part of the rhetorical effort to inculcate a particular set of values among the people of Israel by expressing how the community should respond toward those who commit these offenses.[12] In other words, not only will God cut them off (whatever that means), but the community too are to shun them, and this can be expressed by translating the *niphal* form as "the person who does such and such a thing *is to be cut off*"—or, we might say, by translating it prescriptively rather than descriptively. As already noted, one of the suggestions made for defining the *karet* penalty as such is excommunication or punitive expulsion, but what I am suggesting is something more subtle: given that some of the offenses at least may well be hard to police, there

---

10. James W. Watts, *Ritual and Rhetoric in Leviticus: From Sacrifice to Scripture* (Cambridge: Cambridge University Press, 2007), esp. chs. 3–7.

11. See, e.g., the discussion of Lev 17–26 in Deborah W. Rooke, "The Blasphemer (Leviticus 24): Gender, Identity and Boundary Construction," in *Text, Time and Temple: Literary, Historical and Ritual Studies in Leviticus*, ed. Francis Landy et al., Hebrew Bible Monographs 64 (Sheffield: Sheffield Phoenix Press, 2015), 154–55.

12. This may sound tautologous, given the earlier comment that the *karet* penalty often comes into play for offenses that are likely to be hidden from human view. Nevertheless, it is possible for people to learn of an offense being committed even though there are no witnesses and therefore no basis for any formal judicial process.

is instead an attempt to inculcate the values to which the lawmakers subscribe into the minds of the populace by encouraging them to reject such offenders. It can be read as a kind of stigmatization which goes alongside the idea that offenders will be cut off by or from the Deity and which draws its power from precisely that thought. If God is cutting them off, so should you!

There is also a further possible nuance in the use of the *niphal*, arising from the fact that it can have a reflexive significance in some contexts. It is true that the *niphal* of כרת is not used in such a sense elsewhere in the Hebrew Bible, but about half the *niphal* forms of כרת in the Hebrew Bible are those that come in P's declarations of the *karet* penalty, which is a distinctive and technical usage and which might therefore be argued to have a nuance that is not present in other uses of כרת in the *niphal*. In particular, it is tempting to see in this usage a declaration that those who commit the offenses leading to *karet* are effectively cutting *themselves* off, putting *themselves* beyond the boundaries of the community or outside the relationship with the Deity by their wilful disregard of stipulations that are seen as fundamental to maintaining that relationship and community.

## Cut Off–But from What?

We noted earlier that most interpretations of the *karet* penalty assume a cutting off from life in some sense, whether prematurely, suddenly, or after death. The exception to this is the idea that *karet* refers to excommunication, which is a spatial rather than a temporal cutting off—in other words, the offender is sent away from the community without necessarily being deprived of life. It is not possible to say definitively on the basis of the biblical text whether the cutting off is spatial or temporal in terms of its destination (exile or death),[13] but there are some indications of the context from which the offender is cut off, and these again can be seen to add to the picture of how the offenses were viewed by the legislators. Indeed, rather than employing a fivefold categorization of the offenses based on the area of life against which they are seen to offend, I would offer a categorization based on how precisely the cutting off is defined, which seems to me to indicate a kind of hierarchy of offenses and contribute

13. James Watts (*Leviticus 1–10*, HCOT [Leuven: Peeters, 2013], 418) comments that the rhetorical force of the *karet* penalty is evident despite—and indeed, even because of—its vague, indefinite nature: "For purposes of persuasion, the uncertain implications of being 'cut off from their people' heighten the sense of danger in order to motivate compliance with the regulations."

to the ideological rhetoric of the Priestly legislation.[14] It would be dishonest of me to say that this is as clear in every case as in every other case, but it seems to me that it is sufficiently clear to be worth considering. The variations on the formulaic declaration of being cut off are as follows.

## *"I Will Cut Off from the Midst of Their People"*

The fiercest declarations are those in which Yahweh says, "I will cut off such and such a person from the midst of their people (מקרב עמו/עמה)."[15] These refer to the sins of eating blood, Molek-worship ("giving one's seed to Molek"), and following wizards and mediums. There is also a related declaration that Yahweh will *destroy* (rather than cut off) from the midst of their people anyone working on the Day of Atonement. All of these matters can be seen to be fundamental violations of the Israelite identity as "holy to the Lord" (cf. Lev 19:2):

1. *The ingestion of blood (Lev 17:10)* is a fundamental taboo incumbent on all humankind, which according to the Priestly schema was given to Noah after the flood (cf. Gen 9:3–4), well before the rest of the law. In Lev 17 blood is said to have been given for sacral use only, and in particular for atonement, because "the blood is the life" (Lev 17:11); so to eat it is a complete rejection of Yahweh's scheme of holiness as P sees it.[16]

2. *Worshipping the god Molek (Lev 20:3–5)* is gross idolatry, whether we understand "giving one's seed to Molek" as child sacrifice or as some

---

14. Nobuyoshi Kiuchi (*Leviticus*, AOTC 3 [Nottingham: Apollos, 2007], 140) claims that in Leviticus "the term *krt* is always followed by *mēʿammāyw* (from one's people), where ʿam *[sic]* is pl. (except 22:3)." The plural, thinks Kiuchi, refers to the many individuals making up a group of people. As the present paper will show, however, this significantly misrepresents the actual situation regarding how the *karet* formulae are structured.

15. Elsewhere, the same formula appears but using the plural noun עמים, "peoples," i.e., "kin." Milgrom (*Leviticus 17–22: A New Translation with Introduction and Commentary*, AYB 3A [New York: Doubleday, 2000], 1471–72) regards the two variants as interchangeable and as reflecting the differences between P and H sources; his argument, however, is based on usage in contexts other than as part of the *karet* formula (e.g., Gen 25:8), evidence which is of questionable relevance for a discussion of the *karet* formulae. The present study offers a different way of reading the variants. The use of the plural עמים is discussed below.

16. Kiuchi (*Leviticus*, 142, 320) makes a similar point about the significance of ingesting blood. The *karet* penalty for consuming blood also appears in Lev 7:27, though with a different formulation. See section below entitled "The Offender Is Cut Off from Their Peoples (pl.)" for further details and discussion.

kind of sexual rite.[17] Clearly worship of such a rival deity to Yahweh cannot be tolerated. Indeed, this particular offense is given the death penalty in addition to the declaration that Yahweh will cut off the offender (Lev 20:2), so either way offenders will be eliminated from the community—if the death penalty doesn't get you then Yahweh will! There is also here a strong anti-Molek warning for the community: failure to carry out the death penalty for the Molek-worshipper will lead to Yahweh also cutting off those who let the offender live, as being complicit in the idolatry (vv. 4–5), so there is an appeal to self-interest in the formulation in order to increase its rhetorical force. The Priestly legislators were clearly very exercised about this particular matter.

3. *Following wizards and mediums (Lev 20:6)* is likewise to be outlawed, since it implies getting spiritual guidance from sources other than Yahweh, again contradicting the idea that Israel should be holy or separated off to Yahweh.

---

17. Most modern scholars view the sin as child sacrifice; see, for example, Baruch A. Levine, *Leviticus*, JPS Torah Commentary Series (Philadelphia: JPS, 1989), 258–59; John E. Hartley, *Leviticus*, WBC 4 (Grand Rapids: Zondervan, 1992), 333–37; Milgrom, *Leviticus 17–22*, 1729–30; Adrian Schenker, "What Connects the Incest Prohibitions with the Other Prohibitions Listed in Leviticus 18 and 20?," in *The Book of Leviticus: Composition and Reception*, ed. Rolf Rendtorff and Robert Kugler, VTSup 93 (Leiden: Brill, 2003), 162–85, here 169–70. Milgrom (*Leviticus 17–22*, 1551–55) has an extensive review of interpretations. The idea that the crime in view involves illicit sex originates in antiquity and arises from the notion that condemnation of Molek-worship in both Lev 18 and Lev 20, which are included amidst multiple condemnations of illicit sexual activity, are out of place if Molek-worship does not also involve illicit sex. For a survey of ancient sexual interpretations of Molek-worship, which equate it with exogamy resulting in the raising of children who become idolaters, see Geza Vermes, "Leviticus 18:21 in Ancient Jewish Bible Exegesis," in *Studies in Aggadah, Targum and Jewish Liturgy in Memory of Joseph Heinemann*, ed. Jakob J. Petuchowski and Ezra Fleischer (Jerusalem: Magnes Press, 1981), 108–124, here 113–117. Though never a majority position in modern scholarship, a sexual interpretation of Molek-worship has been revived periodically; thus, N. H. Snaith ("The Cult of Molech," *VT* 16 [1966]: 123–24) argued that giving one's seed to Molek meant dedicating one's offspring to Molek to be trained as temple prostitutes; Walter Zimmerli (*Ezekiel 1: A Commentary on the Book of the Prophet, Chapters 1–24*, trans. R. Clements, Hermeneia [Philadelphia: Fortress, 1979], 344) followed a conjecture made by Karl Elliger ("Das Gesetz Leviticus 18," *ZAW* 67 [1955]: 1–25, here 17, and repeated in Elliger's commentary *Leviticus*, HAT 4 [Tübingen: Mohr Siebeck, 1966], 241) that the Molek cult involved sacrificing to the god Molek newborns who were conceived from cultic intercourse; and E. J. Wiesenberg ("Exogamy or Moloch Worship?," in *Jewish Law Association Studies II: The Jerusalem Conference Volume*, ed. B. S. Jackson [Atlanta: Scholars Press, 1986], 193–95) argued in favor of the ancient interpretation of "giving seed to Molek" as exogamy.

4.  *Working on the Day of Atonement (Lev 23:30)* when it is declared a holy
    day of complete rest and solemn assembly to Yahweh is to cut oneself
    off from the opportunity for renewal of the relationship with Yahweh
    by cleansing from accumulated sins. Such disregard gives the sense of
    "I'm not interested at all in being a part of this—I'm ignoring both
    the regulations and the means of making up for ignoring the regula-
    tions." So it is hardly surprising that this should be portrayed as among
    the most serious offenses, and that the text uses the terminology of
    Yahweh *destroying* rather than *cutting off* the person from the midst of
    their people.[18]

It is notable, too, that in all four of these cases the individuals concerned are
to be cut off or destroyed מקרב עמו/עמה, "from the midst of their people."
There are two observations to make here. First, the sense given by the term
קרב is of being at the very heart of the people, since קרב also has the physical
meaning of entrails or inner parts.[19] So the picture is of eradicating something
no matter how deeply seated it may be, or how high a status the offender may
have. Second, by contrast with other instances of the *karet* penalty formula, the
term "people" here is singular, which gives the sense of a unitary people or a
nation. In other words, the body from which the offender is being removed is
not just his or her own family, but the nation to which he or she belongs, that is,
the nation of Israel. These offenses are of national significance: they are so elemental that they threaten to destabilize the nation and the self-understanding
on which it is built, and so the offenders are removed actively and directly by
God *from* the nation, from the body against which they have offended. This
is radical surgery indeed.

## X Will Be Cut Off from the Midst of the People

This is the second most severe "cutting off" category. Though the declaration
of penalty using the *niphal* form of כרת ("will be cut off") lacks the same
immediacy and directness as the active verb forms ("I will cut off") used to
declare the penalty for the previous four sins, the cutting off is likewise from

---

18. A similar point about the seriousness of the offense was made by Julian Morgenstern
in "The Book of the Covenant. Part III – The Ḥuqqim," *HUCA* 8–9 (1931–32): 1–151, at 36 n. 43.

19. Milgrom claims that the use of קרב ("midst") here is indicative of the H version of
the *karet* formula (*Leviticus 17–22*, 1471); however, not all the *karet* formulae that appear in
material attributed to H—even assuming a minimal definition of H as Lev 17–26—use קרב
in their construction, as will be seen below.

the midst of the singular "people," implying that once again these sins have significance on a national scale. The offenses in question here are as follows:

1.  *Non-sacrificial slaughter of potential sacrificial victims (Lev 17:4)* threatens to profane the means of atonement set in place by Yahweh by appropriating that means for common use, as well as depriving the priests of their subsistence by failing to provide them with the appropriate parts of the sacrificial animal (e.g., Lev 7:1–10, 28–36). Once again, therefore, it cocks a snook at an aspect of the system that both makes and maintains the people's holiness,[20] and it does so in a fashion that could be seen as a kind of (un)holy tax evasion. Indeed, Lev 17:5–7 also expresses a concern that permitting slaughter apart from at the tabernacle is tantamount to encouraging idolatry, which as we have already seen is incompatible with membership of the holy people of Yahweh.

2.  *Sexual sins (Lev 18:29)*—i.e., adultery, incest, bestiality, and male-male intercourse—are put under a generic ban in Lev 18 (though elsewhere in Leviticus there are different penalties for them).[21] As I have argued previously,[22] the sanction in Lev 18 is in a context where the identity of Israelites is being constructed in deliberate contrast to that of Egyptians and Canaanites, who are characterized as thoroughly sexually depraved and as given to the types of sexual practice that are proscribed for the Israelites. The chapter's message is that such depravity is incompatible with an Israelite identity, so it is not surprising that those who engage in it should be cut off even from the very heart of the people.

3.  *Sleeping with a menstruating woman (Lev 20:18)* is also included among

20. As Hartley, *Leviticus*, 272, comments, "Misappropriation of the means of expiation . . . abuses the only means of finding forgiveness from the holy God."

21. Leviticus 20:10–16 prescribes the (humanly inflicted) death penalty for adultery, male-male intercourse, and male and female bestiality, along with certain kinds of incest (intercourse with a stepmother or daughter-in-law, and sleeping with a woman as well as her mother). Other forbidden sexual liaisons in Lev 20 attract *karet*-type penalties, as in Lev 18; the offenses in question are sleeping with a sister, a menstruant, an aunt by blood or marriage, and a sister-in-law (Lev 20:17–21). These differences raise the question of how Lev 18 and 20 relate to each other. Alfred Marx (*Lévitique 17–27*, CAT 3b [Geneva: Labor et Fides, 2011]) describes Lev 18 and 20 as two panels of the same diptych (100), and suggests that individual penalties for the misdemeanors in 18 are given on a case-by-case basis in 20 (74).

22. Deborah W. Rooke, "The Bare Facts: Gender and Nakedness in Leviticus 18," in *A Question of Sex? Gender and Difference in the Hebrew Bible and Beyond*, ed. Deborah W. Rooke (Sheffield: Sheffield Phoenix Press, 2007), 20–38, at 23–24.

the sexual activities that are banned collectively on pain of *karet* in Lev 18, though here it is apparently deemed worthy of receiving its own *karet* penalty, and for both parties.[23] Lee Trevaskis suggests that the menstruant here symbolizes sin and impurity in general, and that her temporary inability to conceive enhances her symbolic value as representing abominable customs such as those in Lev 18 that lead to being cut off.[24] Elsewhere in Leviticus, the consequence of sleeping with a menstruating woman is temporary uncleanness rather than permanent *karet* (Lev 15:24), a discrepancy that is most reasonably explained by understanding the act in 15:24 as inadvertent but that in 20:18 (and 18:19) as deliberate.[25] Thus, in Trevaskis's reading, the deliberate embrace of such women was like deliberately pursuing abominable customs and would lead to the same consequence of being cut off.[26] Deliberate flouting of the rules on sex is construed as blurring the boundaries between holy Israel and unholy others, and so cannot be tolerated; hence the penalty of cutting off from the people as a whole. That said, repeated menstrual sex will indeed result in *karet* for both parties on the grounds that no offspring will be conceived from such liaisons, and so in that sense it is its own punishment.

4. *Deliberate sins (Num 15:30–31)* is rather a catch-all designation, but seems intended to make the point that whatever system of atonement or forgiveness or expiation is in place it cannot be taken as an automatic or mechanistic system that simply operates regardless of the offender's attitude or state of mind.[27] The kind of cynical abuse of the system whereby one offends blatantly out of total disregard for anything beyond one's own desires or self-interest does indeed result in offenders putting themselves outside the system's reach and so outside the people of Israel, regardless of whereabouts in the people they may have begun.

---

23. Milgrom, *Leviticus 17–22*, 1754, argues that the prohibition here is more wide-ranging than in 18:29 and includes women with any kind of discharge rather than simply menstruants.

24. Lee Trevaskis, "Dangerous Liaisons: Sex and the Menstruating Woman in Leviticus," in *Text, Time and Temple: Literary, Historical and Ritual Studies in Leviticus*, ed. Francis Landy et al., Hebrew Bible Monographs 64 (Sheffield: Sheffield Phoenix Press, 2015), 131–52.

25. Trevaskis ("Dangerous Liaisons," 133) has a good discussion of this point of view, defending it against Milgrom's critique (Milgrom, *Leviticus 17–22*, 1755–56).

26. Trevaskis, "Dangerous Liaisons," 150–51.

27. In the words of Timothy R. Ashley (*The Book of Numbers*, NICOT [Grand Rapids: Eerdmans, 1993], 288), "The sinner with a high hand feels no guilt; therefore the offense is not sacrificially expiable."

5.  *Working on the Sabbath (Exod 31:14–15; cf. 35:2; Num 15:35)* is presented
    very early on in P's legislative programme as completely unacceptable,
    an offense against the holiness of the day set apart particularly for the
    Israelites to reflect on and rest in God's holiness. Working on it therefore
    implies disrespect of a basic aspect of what it is to be an Israelite. Like
    Molek-worship, this too is to be punished by what we might call the
    human death penalty (Exod 35:2; Num 15:35),[28] which indicates a high
    degree of Priestly anxiety about its effects, and the desire to inculcate
    respect for the Sabbath deeply into the Israelites' consciousness. Unusu-
    ally, this offense is punished with cutting off "from the midst of one's
    *peoples* (pl.)," an expression which seems elsewhere to have overtones
    of kinship rather than national identity. This may reflect the inclusion
    of slaves and resident aliens in the Decalogue version of the command-
    ment (Exod 20:8–10; Deut 5:12–14), who in an Israelite context might
    have kin but would have no nation from which to be cut off.[29]

## *X Will Be Cut Off from Israel, the Congregation of Israel, or the Assembly*

Somewhat surprisingly, only two offenses include the specific designation *Israel* in the penalty clause:

1.  *Eating leaven, or leavened goods, during the festival of Unleavened Bread
    (Exod 12:15, 19)*: in terms of its place in the narrative, this is a very early
    prohibition, given in the context of instructions for the first Passover in
    Exod 12. The context is foundational for the nation of Israel, describing
    as it does the events that will mark off Israel definitively from the Egyp-
    tians and enable them to be constituted independently. Little surprise,
    then, that in also giving instructions for the annual commemoration
    of these events with the feasts of Passover and Unleavened Bread, the
    legislator deems that those who fail to adhere scrupulously to the fes-
    tival instructions cannot remain a part of "Israel"—the entity whose

---

28. Cornelis Houtman, *Exodus Volume 1*, HCOT (Kampen: Kok, 1993), 436–37, apparently takes this double penalty in Exod 31:14–15 to indicate that the *karet* penalty is one of
execution by human hand, although commenting on Exod 12:15 (*Exodus Volume 2*, HCOT
[Kampen: Kok, 1996], 187) he says that כרת is "usually taken to mean expulsion from the
civic and cultic community."

29. Other such examples are considered in the next section.

foundation the festivals recall.[30] The inclusion of the גֵר, "resident alien," in the penalty in Exod 12:19 is no bar to this understanding of the text, since in 12:48–49 resident aliens who wish to celebrate the Passover may do so on condition of being circumcised. This implies their virtual assimilation to the people of Israel, and their corresponding liability to the penalty of being cut off from Israel if they fail to observe the instructions.

2. *Failing to cleanse oneself from corpse impurity (Num 19:13, 20):* if eating leaven during the feast of Unleavened Bread is almost the first "cutting off" offense, and comes in the context of the nation's birth, the stipulation about cleansing from corpse impurity, together with the penalty of being cut off from the nation if cleansing is neglected, is the last "cutting off" offense that appears in the Priestly law code. Located in Num 19, it stipulates that anyone touching a corpse, or entering a tent where a corpse is present, incurs impurity for seven days, and must be aspersed with ritually prepared "water of impurity" on the third and seventh days of their impurity. If such purifying actions are not undertaken the subject will be cut off from the assembly of Israel.[31] Corpse-related impurity is clearly more serious than other types of impurity, which tend to require some combination of bathing, laundering of clothes, and a waiting period, but not necessarily all of these and certainly no extra asperging with a special purifying water that was ritually concocted for this sole purpose.[32] The additional requirement may tempt those affected by the impurity to neglect the cleansing ceremonial, and so the law attempts to incentivize the people by spelling out the dire consequences of such neglect. Precisely why corpse-generated impurity is regarded as so fearsome is not addressed in the laws, but given the various other provisions about not consulting mediums and the strictures on mourning rites, particularly for priests (e.g., Lev 21:1–6), we might surmise that the concern once again was to discourage the Israelites from engaging with any kind of alternative religious observances—in this case, worship of the dead, which would be incompatible with their

---

30. As Nahum M. Sarna (*Exodus*, JPS Torah Commentary [Philadelphia: JPS, 1991], 58) comments of the *karet* penalty in Exod 12:15: "[O]ne who deliberately excludes himself from the religious community of Israel cannot be a beneficiary of the covenantal blessings and thereby dooms himself and his line to extinction."

31. Eryl W. Davies (*Numbers*, NCB [London: Marshall Pickering, 1995], 83–84, 158) thinks that the cutting off here is probably excommunication.

32. Details of how to prepare the water of impurity are given in Num 19:1–10.

identity as Yahweh's holy people. Yahweh is the God of life, so anything to do with the realm of the dead is his complete antithesis.

## The Offender Is Cut Off from Their Peoples (pl.)

Whereas the previous three formulae have used phrases implying that the *karet* penalties for those particular offenses are aimed at protecting the people of Israel as a whole, this last group speaks in more familial tones. The reference to "peoples" probably indicates kin rather than nation, a usage that elsewhere is attested in the marriage restrictions for the high priest, who has to marry a virgin of his own "peoples" (Lev 21:14). The logical interpretation of this is that he has to marry within his own tribe, by contrast with the ordinary priests who according to Ezek 44:22 must marry within Israel but are not required to marry from among "their own peoples."

These are the offenses that lead to cutting off "from one's peoples":

1. *Neglecting circumcision (Gen 17:14).* This is rather a difficult punishment to understand at first sight, since it requires every male to be circumcised on the eighth day of his life and declares that the uncut male will be cut off from his kin. Surely if a child is not circumcised it is not the child's fault, but the parents'. So why should the son be punished for the sin of the father? There are a number of considerations here. First, it seems clear that there is an ideological connection between circumcision and fertility, as implied by the narrative of Abraham in Gen 17, where it is only post-circumcision that Abraham and Sarah together are enabled to conceive.[33] So it seems that fertility is contingent upon circumcision, both for the parents and for the child, and that their failure to circumcise their child prejudices both his fertility and their own— their own to the extent that their child may not survive unless circumcised, and his in that if he does not survive to adulthood (or even if he does) he himself will die without issue.[34] Second, if a male does survive to adulthood without being circumcised he then becomes responsible for his own circumcision, and that may require some incentivization.

33. For a discussion of the link between circumcision and fertility, see Howard Eilberg-Schwartz, *The Savage in Judaism: An Anthropology of Israelite Religion and Ancient Judaism* (Bloomington: Indiana University Press, 1990), 141–76.

34. Eilberg-Schwartz (*The Savage*, 148) similarly associates the penalty of being cut off in Gen 17:14 with infertility.

But the first scenario, whereby an uncircumcised male child does not survive to adulthood, is aptly connoted by the picture that he will be cut off from his kin. This is a penalty that bites most at the family level. It is an acknowledgment by the Israelites of the God through whom alone generation of offspring is made possible, a dedication of the male generators to Yahweh and thus by implication the repudiation of the need for other fertility deities. It also indicates that the uncircumcised male can only be cut off from his kin, rather than from the people as a whole, because in effect he never becomes a member of the people of Israel.

2. *Making and using imitation holy oil or incense (Exod 30:33, 38)* is something that will once again diminish the holiness of Yahweh by profaning his special aroma. Those who do this are to be held in contempt and shunned by their fellows to discourage them from their cynical devaluation of the special things of Yahweh.[35] It will also serve to protect the prerogative of the priesthood, on whom the oil of anointing is poured and who alone have the right to use the incense when they approach the presence of Yahweh. That this is one of the motivations for the penalty is suggested by the phraseology of the prohibition: those who are warned against this particular offense are not designated by the generic term נֶפֶשׁ, "person" or "soul," as is the case in many other instances, but by the term אִישׁ, "man," that is, "adult male." This suggests that those liable to commit this offense might be men who are trying to increase their own status by inveigling their way into another family—the priestly family; but by so doing they will end up being cut off from even the non-priestly family that they have.

3. *Eating the fat of sacrificeable animals (Lev 7:25)*, including when they have died by non-sacrificial means (i.e., natural causes or killed by predators), appropriates for human ingestion what may only be "ingested" by Yahweh in the form of smoke from a sacrifice. It is an offense that may be known only among the offender's family because they are the ones with whom the offender eats. It is thus fitting that they are the ones from whom the offender is regarded as being cut off.

4. The same penalty of being cut off from one's kin is decreed two verses later for *eating blood (Lev 7:27)*, in a provision that functions as a continuation of the prohibition on eating fat. Here the domestic context

---

35. As Cornelis Houtman (*Exodus, Volume III*, HCOT [Leuven: Peeters, 2000], 578) comments, "Anyone who [does this] thereby erases the boundary between the holy and the profane, the divine and the human, and upsets the order and balance of the world."

is definitely in view, as the prohibition forbids eating blood "in any of your dwelling places" (Lev 7:26); hence again the familial-level penalty, which contrasts with the fierce declaration in Lev 17:10 that Yahweh will actively cut off "from the midst of the people" those who eat blood. This is the only offense for which two different levels of being cut off are explicitly prescribed, indicating that it is a sin at both a personal and a national level.

5. *Offering sacrifices elsewhere than the tabernacle (Lev 17:8–9)* is forbidden for both native Israelites and resident aliens, which might account for why this is said to result in being cut off from one's kin rather than one's singular people—resident aliens can have kin from which to be cut off but not (in their alien context) a people. This prohibition can be compared with the prohibition against non-sacrificial slaughter in Lev 17:4 discussed above, which has an anti-idolatry thrust, is addressed only to members of the house of Israel, and is punished by excision from the midst of one's people. Leviticus 17:8–9 could likewise be referring to idolatrous sacrifices, in which case the Israelites who carry them out are subject to being cut off at both national (17:4) and personal (17:9) levels. If, on the other hand, Lev 17:8–9 is referring to ostensibly Yahwistic worship taking place away from the tabernacle and carried out without any priests,[36] the slightly more muted expression of penalty as being cut off from one's immediate circle makes sense. It is a local rather than a national scandal that, in offering worship, an Israelite would choose to circumvent the priests whom Yahweh has put in place to facilitate worship—but a scandal nevertheless, and one that needs to be prevented from happening again.

6. *Eating the meat of well-being offerings when unclean (Lev 7:21), or on the third day after the sacrifice (Lev 19:8)* are offenses which disrespect the conventions of the sacrificial offering. It is notable that the well-being offerings are the only ones from which the people are allowed to eat, and so these seem to be stipulations as much for the laity as for the priesthood (who have their own portions from the sacrifices and accompanying strictures as to consuming them; see below). The well-being offering allows individuals to feast with their kin as they consume the meat, and so it seems appropriate that the ones from whom they will

---

36. Philip J. Budd, *Leviticus*, NCB (London: Marshall Pickering, 1996), 245, suggests that the text here evidences a desire not necessarily for centralization of worship, but to bring sanctuaries under priestly control.

be cut off if they eat inappropriately are precisely their kin rather than the nation at large. What should therefore be a means of strengthening kinship becomes a means of destroying it.

7. *Failing to afflict oneself on the Day of Atonement (Lev 23:29)* is the lesser of two evils that might be committed on Yom Kippur, the other one being working. We saw earlier that those doing any kind of work on the Day of Atonement incur the fiercest version of the *karet* penalty: Yahweh will actively destroy them from the midst of the people. Here, those who do not afflict themselves will "merely" be passively cut off from their kin. The difference between the penalties for these two related offenses seems to me to be confirmation that the different phraseology is indicative of the severity with which the offenses are to be viewed, not just here but wherever the *karet* penalty is prescribed. In this instance the two penalties indicate that failing to afflict oneself on Yom Kippur is bad enough, but going so far as to actually work is unspeakably bad. We should also note that no other festival in the festival calendar in Lev 23 has the penalty of being cut off for those who do not observe it, so this particular observance is clearly central to the system constructed by P for maintaining holiness among the people.

8. *Neglecting to celebrate the Passover at its appointed time, without good cause (Num 9:13):* having just stated that no festival in the calendar in Lev 23 other than Yom Kippur carries the *karet* penalty for those who fail to observe it, I now find myself constrained to point out that Num 9 declares *karet* for those who do not celebrate the Passover when they have no good reason not to. Nevertheless, this does not contradict what I said about the Day of Atonement, because this *karet* penalty in Num 9 is not expressed in Lev 23, and because it is not a blanket condemnation of those who do not celebrate the Passover. Instead, it comes at the end of a provision for those who are unclean or who are on a journey at the date when the Passover sacrifice and meal should be celebrated; the provision allows such individuals to observe the rite a month later than everyone else. But this should not be used as an excuse *not* to celebrate Passover at the appointed time, and those who are not afflicted by uncleanness or journeyings must celebrate at the due time or be cut off.[37] Presumably this is to discourage the idea that a second-month

---

37. Milgrom (*Numbers*, JPS Torah Commentary [Philadelphia: JPS, 1990], 70) considers this is the only prescriptive festival observance whose neglect is punishable by *karet* (taking the failure to self-afflict on Yom Kippur noted above as a detail of the mode of observance

Passover is an optional alternative, a position that could result in a loss of solidarity in the community by engendering a sense of laxity toward the observance.[38] Interestingly, though, the penalty is "local" rather than "national" *karet*, that is, cutting off from one's kin rather than from one's nation; this is in line with P's conception of the Passover sacrifice as a family event, to be offered household by household (cf. Exod 12:1–8).

## Unique Formulations

1. *The priest who approaches holy portions from offerings while in a state of uncleanness (Lev 22:3)* is to be cut off from before Yahweh. This is a characteristically Priestly penalty, since the priests are those whose job it is to come before Yahweh, so it is logical that those who offend against the conditions under which that job is to be carried out should be excluded from such access.[39] In effect it denies the priest his priesthood.[40] It is also followed in Lev 22:9 by the declaration that priests who eat from the holy portions when unclean will die; so the implication here is that being cut off from before Yahweh consists of being struck dead for profaning the holy offerings.

2. *When a man marries his (half-)sister they will both be cut off before the eyes of the sons of their people (Lev 20:17).* This does not sound like a death penalty but more like the declaration of "no descendants" that accompanies other such disapproved liaisons in Lev 20, although no other such declaration is so phrased.[41] The idea is that the sons of the present generation will not see the descendants of this unhappy couple because they will have no descendants to be seen by the next generation.

---

rather than as out-and-out failure to observe the occasion). Philip J. Budd (*Numbers*, WBC 5 [Grand Rapids: Zondervan, 1984], 99) views the probable penalty here as "excommunication—an appropriate fate for one who values his identity within the community so slightly."

38. So Davies, *Numbers*, 80.

39. As Levine, *Leviticus*, 147, comments, "The idea is that God directly objects to the nearness of impure priests and does not wish them to stand in His presence."

40. So Marx, *Lévitique 17–27*, 128.

41. Levine, *Leviticus*, 138, understands the phrasing of the *karet* penalty here as an expression of banishment.

## Conclusion

There is more to understanding the *karet* penalty, then, than working out what *karet* represents. The overall point of the penalty is that to benefit from the Priestly system of holiness and sacrifice one must be a part of it and abide by its values, and there are certain actions that put perpetrators outside of the system and therefore render them ineligible for its benefits. But in the wording of the penalty there is a sense of the level at which the offense operates—in other words, just how serious an offense it is—and equally significant, an attempt to inculcate the values of the Priestly legislators into the minds of the community for whom they were writing. Indeed, these penalties that indicate what is beyond the bounds of permissibility in the hierarchically structured holy society constructed by P are essential to maintaining its stability. Little wonder, then, that for those who commit these offenses, in the eyes of P the circle cannot remain unbroken.

x

# CHAPTER THREE

# ATONEMENT BEYOND ISRAEL

*The Holiness School's Amendment to Priestly Legislation on the Sin Sacrifice (ḥaṭṭāʾt)*

DAVID P. WRIGHT

Of the various sacrifices prescribed by the Priestly (P) corpus of the Pentateuch, or as I refer to it, the Priestly-Holiness (PH) corpus (explained in a moment), the most prominent is the חטאת (*ḥaṭṭāʾt*), i.e., the sin or purgation offering.[1] Its function, according to these prescriptions, was to purify the sanctuary from impurities arising from various causes. The sacrifice may have come from adapting non-sacrificial purification rites that used animal blood to the schema of sacrifices proper, which traditionally included the burnt and well-being offerings and whose basic symbolic function was as food gifts to the deity, to praise and thank him, solicit his help, or appease his anger.[2] In the PH

---

1. I use transliterations (like *ḥaṭṭāʾt*) for some technical terms whose meanings are unclear or for which translations are cumbersome or misleading. The *ḥaṭṭāʾt* has been interpreted as a noun with a privative *piel* connotation of "sin removal" or "purgation" (see Jacob Milgrom, "Sin-offering or Purification-offering?" *VT* 21 [1971]: 237–39). In the passage this essay studies, H renders P's phrase על־חטאתו אשר חטא "for the sin that he sinned" (Lev 4:28) as לחטאת, "for a sin/as a sin offering" (Num 15:27). This may mean H understood the offering to mean "sin offering."

2. The blood rites of the *ḥaṭṭāʾt* are different from other sacrifices and distinctively purify the sancta (Lev 4; 16; see below). A carcass of one type of *ḥaṭṭāʾt* is burned outside the habitation (Lev 4:12, 21; 6:23; 16:27). A similar blood purification rite that was never incorporated into the *ḥaṭṭāʾt* system and thus shows the type of ritual the *ḥaṭṭāʾt* may develop from is the bird rite performed for a person or house recovered from scale-disease (Lev 14:4-7, 49-53). P also incorporated other purification rites under the rubric of the *ḥaṭṭāʾt*, which were not sacrificial and fit only imperfectly, i.e., the red cow ritual in Num 19 (see v. 9) and the scapegoat in Lev 16 (see vv. 5, 8, 20-22). The *ḥaṭṭāʾt* was assimilated to

corpus the *ḥaṭṭāʾt* sacrifice was particularly well suited to its story about the revelation and institution of Israel's first national sanctuary, the place where the Deity manifested himself among the people and which, accordingly, had to be kept uncontaminated.[3]

But though the *ḥaṭṭāʾt* works aptly in that narrative, the various prescriptions about the sacrifice do not all belong to the same redactional level. A major difference in this regard appears between P and H, the two major strata of the work. In the corpus broadly, P is the earlier, foundational stratum. The later H stratum includes not only the so-called Holiness Code of Lev 17–26, but also material elsewhere that is often assigned to the P corpus, including some passages in the first half of Leviticus and parts of Exodus, Numbers, and even Genesis.[4] H preserves P for the most part and usually appears as an addition to or an insertion into a base P text. It is reasonable to think of H as the next generation of the P scribal school, which supplemented and completed the P work. Though the immediate heir of P, the H school had a distinctive ideology that shaped its reaction to P. A chief difference is that, while P had a narrow cultic focus—on the ritual procedures associated with the wilderness

---

the sacrificial system by having it offered at the altar by priests, having its fat pieces burned on the altar (similar to the well-being offering), listing it with the other sacrifices (see Lev 4:1–35; 5:1–13; and 6:17–23 in the context of Lev 1–7), and allowing priests to consume the flesh of one type of *ḥaṭṭāʾt* as a sacrificial prebend (Lev 6:22). On sacrifices broadly, the best introduction is Jacob Milgrom, "Sacrifices and Offerings," *IDBSup* (1976): 763–770. On the analogy of sacrifices as food gifts, see David Wright, "The Study of Ritual in the Hebrew Bible," in *Jewish Studies in the 21st Century*, ed. Frederick E. Greenspahn (New York: New York University Press, 2008), 120–38.

3. For the scope and purpose of the PH narrative, see David Wright, "Law and Creation in the Priestly-Holiness Writings of the Pentateuch," in *Laws of Heaven—Laws of Nature: Legal Interpretations of Cosmic Phenomena in the Ancient World*, ed. Konrad Schmid and Christoph Uehlinger, OBO 276 (Fribourg: Academic Press; Göttingen: Vandenhoeck & Ruprecht, 2016), 71–101.

4. See Israel Knohl, *The Sanctuary of Silence: The Priestly Torah and the Holiness School* (Minneapolis: Fortress, 1995); Jacob Milgrom, *Leviticus 17–22*, AYB 3A (New York: Doubleday, 2000), 1319–1364. I agree with these studies that H includes more than just the Holiness Code and that H is chronologically later than and supplementary to P. I do not agree, however, with their early dating of P and much of H. I also argue H is dependent on D and later than it (see n. 22). For more recent considerations, see the analyses and bibliographies in Christophe Nihan, *From Priestly Torah to Pentateuch: A Study in the Composition of the Book of Leviticus*, FAT 25 (Tübingen: Mohr Siebeck, 2007); Jeffrey Stackert, *Rewriting the Torah: Literary Revision in Deuteronomy and the Holiness Legislation*, FAT 52 (Tübingen: Mohr Siebeck, 2007); David M. Carr, *The Formation of the Hebrew Bible: A New Reconstruction* (Oxford: Oxford University Press, 2011), 292–303.

tabernacle—H broadened the perspective to deal with legal matters beyond the cult, the people in general and the land that they are about to acquire. This led H to recontextualize and augment P's legislation, including the laws on the *ḥaṭṭā't*. This paper explores H's revision or recasting of these laws. It first provides an overview of P's legislation then turns to a section-by-section analysis of H's amendment in Num 15:22–31. H's primary concern was to broaden the application of the scope of atonement (as indicated by the *piel* of the root כפר) to non-Israelites living in the Israelites' newly acquired land.

## P's *ḥaṭṭā't* System

P's main passages on the *ḥaṭṭā't* sacrifice display a rather coherent system, visible mainly in the breadth of cases covered and complementary features between the cases.[5] Its basic legislation appears in Lev 4.[6] The sacrifice is brought for inadvertent sins committed by various members of society. The sin is ex-

5. My view of the *ḥaṭṭā't* is based on that of Jacob Milgrom. See, for example, his classic statement in "Israel's Sanctuary: The Priestly 'Picture of Dorian Gray,'" *RB* 83 (1976): 390–399 and the later detailed analysis in his *Leviticus 1–16*, AYB 3 (New York: Doubleday, 1991), 226–318, 1009–1084. For some other studies, see Roy Gane, *Cult and Character: Purification Offerings, Day of Atonement, and Theodicy* (Winona Lake, IN: Eisenbrauns, 2005); Bernd Janowski, *Sühne als Heilsgeschehen: Studien zur Sühnetheologie der Priesterschrift und der Wurzel* KPR *im Alten Orient und im Alten Testament*, WMANT 55 (Neukirchen: Neukirchener Verlag, 1982); Nobuyoshi Kiuchi, *The Purification Offering in the Priestly Literature: Its Meaning and Function*, LHBOTS 56 (Sheffield Academic Press, 1987); Nobuyoshi Kiuchi, *A Study of* Ḥāṭā' *and* Ḥaṭṭā't *in Leviticus 4–5* (Tübingen: Mohr Siebeck, 2003); Jay Sklar, *Sin, Impurity, Sacrifice, and Atonement: the Priestly Conceptions*, Hebrew Bible Monographs 2 (Sheffield: Sheffield Phoenix Press, 2005); and the essays in Baruch J. Schwartz et al., eds., *Perspectives on Purity and Purification in the Bible*, LHBOTS 474 (New York: T&T Clark International, 2008).

6. The chapter may not belong to the first stages of P, having been created, for example, in the image of and, hence, after the more fundamental sacrificial legislation of Lev 1 and 3. But Lev 4 belongs to P. The chapter does not show signs of H formulation; it has textual priority over the (dependent) P texts of Lev 5:1–13, 5:14–26, and 6:17–23; and Lev 16:16b appears to presume the rituals of 4:5–7, 16–18. Therefore Lev 4, which features the incense altar (vv. 5–7, 16–18), has to be prior to the H-influenced passage about the incense altar in Exod 30:1–10. In this regard, it should be noted that Exod 30:1–10 has signs of composite P and H formulation. The H elements appear primarily in vv. 6aβ–10, whereas vv. 1–6aα are consistent with the 2nd person singular formulation found in the basic architectural prescriptions attributable to P in Exod 25–27. Though textual reconstruction is extremely difficult, H's addition of rites performed by Aaron in vv. 6aβ–10 may have been responsible for moving the passage about the incense altar from a more original context around the end

pressly the transgression of prohibitions, not omissions of positive commands. The cases are socially graded. The chapter begins with the sin of a high priest (4:2–12), next the whole community (vv. 13–21), then the chieftain (vv. 22–26), and finally a lay Israelite, including two options for the animal offered (vv. 27–31 and 32–35). The animals brought for all these cases descend in species and gender commensurate with the gradations in human social status: respectively, a bull (v. 3), a bull (v. 14), a male goat (v. 23), and a female goat or sheep (vv. 28, 32). Blood rites are performed in graded fashion. For a sin by the high priest or community, the blood of the animal is brought into the outer room of the tabernacle tent and sprinkled seven times before the curtain separating this room from the most holy place, where the ark is located. The blood is then also applied to the horns of the incense altar which stands before the curtain (vv. 5–7, 16–18). For the chieftain and lay Israelite, the blood is placed only on the horns of the altar in the courtyard, outside the tent (vv. 25, 30, 34). Whatever the location involved, these various blood rites purify the sancta to or around which the blood is applied. This purification is sometimes explicitly described with language referring to purification or the removal of impurity.[7] Often the effect is described with the *piel* of כפר, which entails a notion of purification (of the sancta) as well as appeasement (of the Deity).[8] No single English word

---

of Exod 25 to its present location in the MT. For discussion and other evidence to consider, see Nihan, *Priestly Torah*, 31–33, 195–197.

7. Some passages use the *piel* stem verb חטא, "to purify," with the altar as direct object or with the preposition על, "upon" (Exod 29:36; Lev 8:15; cf. the use of the verb in Lev 14:49, 52 and Num 19:19 the impure person as direct object). The verb טהר, "purify" (also *piel*) is also used to describe the effect of the blood rite (with the courtyard altar as direct object, Lev 16:19; cf. Lev 14:7, 11).

8. In PH, the *piel* of כפר is used mainly for (or inclusive of) the חטאת (Exod 29:33, 36–37; 30:10; Lev 4:20, 26, 31, 35; 5:6, 10, 13; 6:23; 8:15, 34; 9:7; 10:17; 12:7, 8; 14:19–20, 31; 15:15, 30; 16:6, 11, 16–18, 20, 27, 30, 32–34; 23:8; Num 6:11; 8:12, [21]; 15:25, 28; 28:22, 30; 29:5, 11; for the scapegoat see Lev 16:10), though it is used separately for the אשם ("reparation sacrifice"; Lev 5:16, 18, 26; 7:7; 14:18, 21, 28–29; 19:22; Num 5:8) and less frequently for the עלה ("burnt offering"; Lev 1:4; 16:24; cf. 12:7–8; 14:20, 31; 15:15, 30; Num 6:11; 8:12). In some cases the verb must be translated "to purify" (Exod 29:36; 30:10; Lev 16:16; see also Lev 4:20, 26, 31, 35; 16:17, 20, 27). The use of the verb to describe the purification of a house cleansed from scale-disease (Lev 14:53)—not a sacrifice and otherwise lacking an appeasement context—also points to a meaning of "purify." This usage parallels the use of the verb חטא elsewhere in the prescription (vv. 49, 52; see n. 7). That כפר entails a meaning of "purify" is supported by the Akkadian cognate, D-stem (i.e., *piel*) *kuppuru* "to purify (by wiping)" (cf. David Wright, *Disposal of Impurity* [SBLDS 101; Atlanta: SBL, 1987], 291–299). Nonetheless, appeasement is evident in the use of the verb for cases of plague prevention, described in cases other than sacrifice (Num 8:19; 17:11–12; 25:8, 13). Appeasement is also seen in the use of the noun

provides a suitable translation. *Atone* or *atonement* may be used if it is kept in mind that is just a placeholder, as it functions in the title of this essay. One may render the verb as "to effect *kippûrîm*," a circumlocution that employs a transliteration of a biblically attested noun derived from the root כפר.⁹

P's ritual legislation in Lev 16:1–28 for what in H becomes the annual Day of Atonement (see below) complements this system to treat the effect of intentional sins by expanding the area and sancta purified and using multiple sacrifices. It calls specifically for two *ḥaṭṭāʾt* sacrifices, a bull for the priests and a male goat for the people (vv. 3, 5–11, 15). The blood from these animals is used in two parallel and identical rites (vv. 11–16). Uniquely in this ceremony, the high priest goes into the most holy place and sprinkles blood over the ark cover and then seven times in front of the ark (vv. 14–16a). This is said to remove the impurity of the Israelites, the cause of which includes "their crimes/rebellions" (ומפשעיהם). This term points to the inclusion of the effect of intentional sins as an object of purification. After purifying the most holy place, the high priest performs blood purification in the outer tent room (v. 16b), presumably using the procedure of Lev 4. Finally, he places blood on the horns of the courtyard altar and sprinkles blood on it seven times (vv. 17b–19). It is explicitly said that the blood rites both purify the altar (טהר) and sanctify (קדש) it from Israelite impurities (v. 19). After this purification is performed, the scapegoat is sent away having been laden with the people's sins, which is artificially included as part of the *ḥaṭṭāʾt* offering (vv. 20–22). The high priest also performs two burnt offerings, one for the priests and one for the people. These augment the atonement effect (v. 24–25).

P also prescribes *ḥaṭṭāʾt* sacrifices for persons recovered from long-term impurities, including a parturient (Lev 12; see vv. 6–8), a leper (Lev 14:8–32; see vv. 10, 19, 22, 30–31), and males and females with irregular sexual discharges (Lev 15:13–15, 28–30). P also requires a *ḥaṭṭāʾt* sacrifice for a nazirite who has suffered

---

כפר ("ransom") in contexts with the verb (Exod 30:12, 15–16; Num 35:31–33). The meaning of כפר as "to ransom" (in the semantic range of "appease") appears when accompanied by adverbial object "for your/our lives" (Lev 17:11 [see n. 33, below]; Num 31:50; cf. Num 35:31). One wonders if the complex meaning of the verb in PH sacrificial contexts is the result of *semantic blending*, i.e., a traditional notion of ransom/appeasement overlaid with the meaning "purify" from rites of purification (perhaps from international influence; cf. Wright, *Disposal*, 62–65; Kenton Sparks, "Enūma Elish and Priestly Mimesis: Elite Emulation in Nascent Judaism," *JBL* 126 [2007]: 625–648).

9. This noun, a *plurale tantum*, appears in the name for the "Day of Atonement" (Lev 23:27, 28; 25:9; יום הכפרים) and in reference to the primary offering on that occasion, the "*ḥaṭṭāʾt* of atonement" (חטאת הכפרים; Exod 30:10; Num 29:11). The noun is also used to describe the expiation effect in other, less ceremonial contexts (Exod 29:36; 30:16; Num 5:8).

corpse contamination or is fulfilling his vow (Num 6:10–11, 14, 16).[10] While there are variations in the types of animals brought depending on the case, these prescriptions share the requirement of bringing two animals (quadrupeds or birds), one as a *ḥaṭṭā't* and one as a burnt offering. The latter augments the efficaciousness of the former, especially its symbolism as a food gift, like the burnt offerings in the Day of Atonement ritual. This complementarity is also found in the prescriptions for the economically graduated *ḥaṭṭā't* in Lev 5:1–13, where a person offering the sacrifice may bring two birds, one as a *ḥaṭṭā't* and one as a burnt offering, instead of a single *ḥaṭṭā't* quadruped (v. 7). In these instances of combined *ḥaṭṭā't* and burnt offerings, however, it is the *ḥaṭṭā't* offering that purifies the sancta.[11]

In these various cases, the sins or severe impurities appear to have polluted the sanctuary from a distance or at least have concurrently generated impurity there in a more abstract phenomenological manner. The sinners or impure persons do not have to be in or near the tabernacle to pollute it. P never explains how this works. Perhaps it has to do with the idea that the tabernacle is the divine abode or palace, an analogy that informs P's cultic system broadly. The behavior and symptomatology of the overlord's subjects, even out in the larger realm, has the power to impugn or defame him or his concerns. This is characterized concretely as pollution of the divine residence. This pollution must be removed to ensure the overlord's, i.e., deity's, continuing presence.

## H's *ḥaṭṭā't* in Numbers 15:22–31

The Holiness prescriptions for the *ḥaṭṭā't* appear in Num 15:22–31 (cited in portions over the course of the discussion below), quite a distance from P's basic legislation in Lev 4. This passage is part of a larger legal miscellany in that chapter on a variety of topics. This miscellany is inserted between P (or PH) narrative scenes: the story of spies being sent to the land before in Num 13–14* and the story of Korah's rebellion in Num 16*.[12] Its specific contextual anchor may have disappeared in the later editing that created the Pentateuch. P's story

10. Knohl, *Sanctuary*, 89 (and 105), ascribes Num 6:1–21a to P.

11. Other passages have a sin offering and burnt offering that work in a complementary fashion (e.g., Lev 9:2–3, 7).

12. The P spy story includes Num 13:1–17a, 21, 25–26bα*, 32; 14:1a, 2–10, 26–39. The Korah story includes Num 16:1a, 2aβ [starting אנשים]–11, 16–24, 26–27a, 35 (see Joel Baden, *The Composition of the Pentateuch*, AYBRL [New Haven: Yale University, 2012], 149–168; a base P story may have been expanded by H).

about the granting of quail and manna, found in Exod 16, probably had its original location near the P spy and Korah stories.[13] P's quail and manna story certainly does not make contextual sense back in the environment of Exod 16. It fits better near the wilderness rebellions of PH found in the book of Numbers and after the Sabbath regulations of Exod 31:12–17; 35:2–3; and the chapters on the tabernacle in Exod 25–31, 35–40. If P's manna and quail story originally appeared near Numbers 15, it would have provided the contextual motivation for H's inclusion of a legal novella about the Sabbath-breaker in that chapter (vv. 32–36), which exemplifies the intentional sin of vv. 30–31—part of H's *ḥaṭṭāʾt* pericope (vv. 22–31; discussed below).

That the passage about the *ḥaṭṭāʾt* in Num 15:22–31 and all the laws in Num 15 broadly are attributable to H is clear from a variety of evidence: the application of law to the גר (*gēr*) "immigrant" (vv. 13–16, 26, 29, 30–31, discussed below); the adverbial לדרתיכם, "through your succeeding generations" (vv. 15, 21, 23); the motif of besmirching Yʜwʜ (v. 30), which parallels H's interest in the desecration of the divine name and the sanctification of the Deity elsewhere (see n. 31); the punishment of "cutting off" (vv. 30–31, discussed later); the theme of national holiness (v. 41, discussed later); the motif of law applying in the land to which the people will come (vv. 2, 18; e.g., Exod 12:25; Lev 14:34; 19:23; 25:2; see the conclusion); repetition of language, a feature of H's rhetoric (see vv. 23–24, 25–26, 27–28, 30–31); and the pronominal numerical preference for the second-person plural for the people and the first-person singular for the Deity. Furthermore, the novella about the Sabbath-breaker (מקשש עצים; vv. 32–36), which follows the passage about the *ḥaṭṭāʾt* in Num 15 and is contextually tied to it, is clearly H, being fashioned in the image of H's novella about blasphemy in Lev 24:10–23.[14]

Thus the passage on the *ḥaṭṭāʾt* in Num 15:22–31 belongs to H and is thereby a scribal product subsequent to P and P's *ḥaṭṭāʾt* legislation. A contextual analysis shows further that H's passage responds to and develops P's legislation on the *ḥaṭṭāʾt* for inadvertent sins from Lev 4.[15] In this elaboration, H does not

---

13. PH is Exod 16:1–3, 6–20, 21a*, 21b, 22a*, 22b–25, 31–35a, 36. The rest of the chapter is J. See Joel Baden, "The Original Place of the Priestly Manna Story in Exodus 16," *ZAW* 122 (2010): 491–504.

14. Of the two, the novella in Lev 24 is primary, having been crafted directly from the legal motifs of the Covenant Code and Deuteronomy. See David Wright, "Source Dependence and the Development of the Pentateuch: The Case of Leviticus 24," in *The Formation of the Pentateuch: Bridging the Academic Cultures of Europe, Israel, and North America*, ed. Jan Gertz, et al., FAT 111 (Tübingen: Mohr Siebeck, 2016), 651–82.

15. For earlier discussions of the dependence of the Numbers passage on Leviticus 4,

take up every element of Lev 4. Rather, it responds selectively to elements in that chapter for a particular purpose. This revision of material from Lev 4 also folds in motifs from or modifications to P's Day of Atonement prescriptions in Lev 16:1–28. The following discussion looks at contrasts in H's legislative passage section by section: (1) an introduction with the description of the sin as inadvertent (vv. 22–23), (2) a case in which the whole community thus sins (vv. 24–26), (3) a case in which an individual sins (vv. 27–29), and (4) the contrasting case of intentional sin (vv. 30–31).

## Introduction (Numbers 15:22–23)

H's introduction in vv. 22–23 expands the range of sins covered. As noted earlier, P's *ḥaṭṭā't* is brought for inadvertent transgression of *prohibitions*, as the following verses introducing each case in Lev 4 indicate:

Lev 4:2, 13, 22, 27 (P):

[2] . . . When anyone sins inadvertently in regard to any of YHWH's commandments that are not to be done. . . .

[13]If the whole community of Israel errs inadvertently and the matter is hidden from the eyes of the group, and they do one of any of YHWH's commands that are not to be done and they then realize their guilt. . . .

[22]If a chieftain sins and inadvertently does one of any of the commands of YHWH, your God, that are not to be done, and then realizes his guilt [23]or is informed of the sin he committed. . . .

[27]If a person from the general populace sins inadvertently by doing one of any of YHWH's commands that are not to be done and then realizes guilt. . . .

[2]. . . כי־תחטא בשגגה מכל מצות יהוה אשר לא תעשינה ועשה
מאחת מהנה: . . .

see Israel Knohl, "The Sin Offering Law in the 'Holiness School,'" in *Priesthood and Cult in Ancient Israel*, ed. Saul M. Olyan and Gary A. Anderson, JSOTSup 125 (Sheffield: Sheffield Academic, 1991), 192–203; Aryeh Toeg, "מדרש הלכה—לא-במדבר טו כב" ("A Halakhic Midrash in Num. xv: 22–31"), *Tarbiz* 43 (1973–74): 1–20.

<sup>13</sup>וְאִם כָּל־עֲדַת יִשְׂרָאֵל יִשְׁגּוּ וְנֶעְלַם דָּבָר מֵעֵינֵי הַקָּהָל וְעָשׂוּ אַחַת
מִכָּל־מִצְוֹת יהוה אֲשֶׁר לֹא־תֵעָשֶׂינָה וְאָשֵׁמוּ: . . .
<sup>22</sup>אֲשֶׁר נָשִׂיא יֶחֱטָא וְעָשָׂה אַחַת מִכָּל־מִצְוֹת יהוה אֱלֹהָיו אֲשֶׁר לֹא־
תֵעָשֶׂינָה בִּשְׁגָגָה וְאָשֵׁם:
<sup>23</sup>אוֹ־הוֹדַע אֵלָיו חַטָּאתוֹ אֲשֶׁר חָטָא . . .
<sup>27</sup>וְאִם־נֶפֶשׁ אַחַת תֶּחֱטָא בִשְׁגָגָה מֵעַם הָאָרֶץ בַּעֲשֹׂתָהּ אַחַת מִמִּצְוֹת
יהוה אֲשֶׁר לֹא־תֵעָשֶׂינָה וְאָשֵׁם:

These describe the transgression as "sinning inadvertently" (חטא בשגגה, v. 2, 27; cf. v. 22), "acting inadvertently" (עשׂה בשגגה; v. 22), or just "committing an error" (with the verb שׁגה, v. 13). Inadvertence is further described by saying that the sin is hidden from the eyes of the perpetrator (v. 13), that the sinner is informed about it after the fact (v. 23), or that the person feels guilt after the fact (v. 22). The violation is specifically described as doing "(one of) all the commands of Yhwh (your God) *which are not to be done*" (often with the governing verb עשׂה in addition to the statement of inadvertent sin; vv. 2, 13, 22, 27).

H's language imitates P's language but alters the meaning.

Num 15:22–23 (H):

<sup>22</sup>When you inadvertently err and do not perform all these commandments that Yhwh has spoken to Moses, <sup>23</sup>all that Yhwh commanded by Moses from the time that Yhwh gave the commandments and onward through all your generations . . .

<sup>22</sup>וְכִי תִשְׁגּוּ וְלֹא תַעֲשׂוּ אֵת כָּל־הַמִּצְוֹת הָאֵלֶּה אֲשֶׁר־דִּבֶּר יהוה אֶל־
מֹשֶׁה:
<sup>23</sup>אֵת כָּל־אֲשֶׁר צִוָּה יהוה אֲלֵיכֶם בְּיַד־מֹשֶׁה מִן־הַיּוֹם אֲשֶׁר צִוָּה יהוה
וָהָלְאָה לְדֹרֹתֵיכֶם:

This states that *all sins* require a ḥaṭṭā't, including omissions of positive commands. This change of meaning is achieved with minimal legislative surgery, mainly by moving the negative particle from a modifying relative clause to the main clause, i.e., from P's wording of "doing any of all the commandments that should <u>not be done</u>" to H's "<u>not doing</u> all of the commandments." This expansion of scope is emphasized rhetorically by the adverbial modifier that looks backward and forward in time: "all these commandments that Yhwh has spoken to Moses, all that Yhwh commanded by Moses *from the time that Yhwh gave the commandments and onward through all your generations.*"

The amplification of sins covered can be partly explained by H's different orientation toward cultic categories and ontology. P's view of impurity is concrete, even physically so. Certain bodily discharges, diseases, and the bodies of humans and carcasses of many animals cause pollution, and a person suffers or contacts these impurities to become impure. Similarly, P's impurity from sin arises from acts of commission rather than mere omission. While H did not deny P's basic perspective in this regard, it had a broader legislative goal. As will be shown in more detail later, H supplemented P's narrow cultic orientation with wider-ranging legislation addressing communal life beyond the tabernacle. H did this in part by drawing on some of the broader legal ideas in the Covenant Code and Deuteronomy and transforming them to fit the collective PH ideological context. One of the motifs developed from these earlier sources is the notion of national holiness, discussed later. Here it can be briefly noted that for H, national holiness was exemplified, indeed achieved, by obedience to all of YHWH's commands. Thus for H, inadvertent omission of positive commands would obviously require a *ḥaṭṭāʾt*.

### Specific Cases (vv. 24–26, 27–29)

The middle sections of H's passage, which prescribe the specific occasions for offering the *ḥaṭṭāʾt*, have conspicuous omissions compared to P. Recall that P's *ḥaṭṭāʾt* legislation in Lev 4 dealt with four socially graded cases, from high to low status: high priest, whole community, chieftain, and lay Israelite. H's prescription deals with only the second and fourth of these: the community (Num 15:24–26) and an individual (vv. 27–29). The compared texts are provided below. Underlining points to exact or synonymous correlations:

| Lev 4:13–21, 27–31 (P) | Num 15:24–26, 27–29 (H) |
|---|---|
| [13]If the <u>whole community</u> of Israel <u>errs inadvertently</u> in that a matter is hid <u>from the eyes of the group,</u> such that <u>they do</u> any of the commands of Yhwh which should not <u>be done</u> and then they realize their guilt, [14]or the sin they committed becomes known, <u>the group</u> <u>shall bring</u> | [24]If it <u>is done</u> <u>from the eyes of</u> the <u>community</u> (sic) inadvertently, <u>the</u> <u>whole community</u> <u>shall do</u> |

a bull from the herd

> one bull from the herd
> as a burnt offering for a pleasing
> aroma for Yhwh, along with its
> cereal offering and libation following
> the rule, and also one male goat

for a *ḥaṭṭāʾt* offering.
They shall bring it before the Tent of Meeting. ¹⁵The elders of the community shall impose their hands on the head of the bull before Yhwh. The bull shall then be slaughtered before Yhwh. ¹⁶The anointed priest shall take some of the blood of the bull into the Tent of Meeting. ¹⁷The priest shall dip his finger (taking) some of the blood and sprinkle seven times before Yhwh in front of the partition curtain. ¹⁸Then he shall put some of the blood on the horns of the altar that is before Yhwh, which is in the Tent of Meeting. The rest of the blood he shall pour out at the base of the burnt offering altar, which is near the entrance to the Tent of Meeting. ¹⁹He shall remove all the fat from it and burn it on the altar. ²⁰He shall do with the bull exactly as he did with the (previous) *ḥaṭṭāʾt* [described in vv. 2– 12].
Thus the priest shall effect *kippūrîm* for them, and they will be forgiven.

> for a *ḥaṭṭāʾt* offering.

> ²⁵The priest shall effect *kippūrîm* for the whole community of the Israelites and they will be forgiven

²¹He shall take [the rest of] the bull outside the camp and burn it, just as he burned the first bull.

| | |
|---|---|
| It is a *ḥaṭṭā't* offering for the group. | because it was an inadvertent error, they having brought their (burnt) offering as an oblation to Yhwh along with their *ḥaṭṭā't* before Yhwh for their inadvertent error. |
| | ²⁶*The whole community of the Israelites will be forgiven, including the immigrant that resides in their midst, because it involves the entire population for the case of inadvertent sin.* |
| ²⁷If a single individual sins inadvertently from the general population by doing one of the commands of Yhwh which should not be done and then realizes his guilt ²⁸or is informed about the sin he committed, | ²⁷If a single individual sins inadvertently |
| he shall bring as his offering an unblemished female she-goat for the sin he committed. | he shall offer a year-old she-goat as a *ḥaṭṭā't* ("sin") offering. |
| ²⁹He shall impose his hand on the head of the *ḥaṭṭā't* offering. The *ḥaṭṭā't* shall then be slaughtered, in the place of the burnt offering. ³⁰The priest shall then take some of its blood with his finger and place it on the horns of the burnt offering altar. He shall pour out the rest of its blood at the base of the altar. ³¹He shall remove its fat, just as the fat of the well-being offering was removed, and the priest shall burn it on the altar as a pleasing aroma for Yhwh. The priest shall thus effect *kippūrîm* for him | |
| | ²⁸The priest shall effect *kippūrîm* for the individual that inadvertently errs |

and he (the offerer) will be forgiven.

by committing an inadvertent sin
before Yhwh, effecting *kippūrîm*
and he will be forgiven.
²⁹*For the hereditary native among
the Israelites and the immigrant that
resides in their midst you have a
single law pertaining to one who acts
inadvertently.*

²⁴ והיה אם מעיני העדה נעשתה
לשגגה
ועשו


כל־העדה פר בן־בקר אחד
לעלה לריח ניחח ליהוה
ומנחתו ונסכו כמשפט
ושעיר־עזים אחד
לחטת:

¹³ואם כל־עדת ישראל ישגו ונעלם
דבר מעיני הקהל
ועשו אחת מכל־מצות יהוה אשר
לא־ תעשינה ואשמו:
¹⁴ונודעה החטאת אשר חטאו עליה
והקריבו הקהל פר בן־בקר


לחטאת
והביאו אתו לפני אהל מועד:
¹⁵וסמכו זקני העדה את־ידיהם על־
ראש הפר לפני יהוה ושחט את־הפר
לפני יהוה: ¹⁶והביא הכהן המשיח
מדם הפר אל־אהל מועד: ¹⁷וטבל
הכהן אצבעו מן־הדם והזה שבע
פעמים לפני יהוה את פני הפרכת:
¹⁸ומן־הדם יתן על־קרנת המזבח אשר
לפני יהוה אשר באהל מועד ואת־כל־
הדם ישפך אל־יסוד מזבח העלה א
שר־פתח אהל מועד: ¹⁹ואת כל־
חלבו ירים ממנו והקטיר המזבחה:
²⁰ועשה לפר כאשר עשה לפר
החטאת כן יעשה־לו
וכפר עלהם הכהן
ונסלח להם:
²¹והוציא את־הפר אל־מחוץ למחנה
ושרף אתו כאשר שרף את הפר
הראשון

²⁵וכפר הכהן על־כל־עדת בני ישראל
ונסלח להם

כי־שגגה הוא והם הביאו את־קרבנם
אשה ליהוה
וחטאתם לפני יהוה על־שגגתם:
26ונסלח לכל־עדת בני ישראל ולגר
הגר בתוכם כי לכל־העם בשגגה:

27ואם־נפש אחת תחטא בשגגה

והקריבה עז בת־שנתה

לחטאת:

28וכפר הכהן על־הנפש השגגת
בחטאה בשגגה לפני יהוה
לכפר עליו
ונסלח לו:
29האזרח בבני ישראל ולגר הגר
בתוכם
תורה אחת יהיה לכם לעשה בשגגה:

חטאת הקהל הוא: ...

27ואם־נפש אחת תחטא בשגגה מעם
הארץ
בעשתה אחת ממצות יהוה אשר לא־
תעשינה ואשם: 28או הודע אליו
חטאתו אשר חטא
והביא קרבנו שעירת עזים תמימה
נקבה
על־חטאתו אשר חטא:
29וסמך את־ידו על ראש החטאת
ושחט את־החטאת במקום העלה:
30ולקח הכהן מדמה באצבעו
ונתן על־קרנת מזבח העלה ואת־
כל־דמה ישפך אל־יסוד המזבח:
31ואת־כל־חלבה
יסיר כאשר הוסר חלב מעל זבח
השלמים והקטיר הכהן המזבחה
לריח ניחח ליהוה
וכפר עליו הכהן

ונסלח לו:

The reason for the omission of the cases about the high priest and the chieftain must be the addition of the social category גר (*gēr*) to the legislation (cf. Num 15:26, 29; verses italicized in the translation). This term is often rendered "resident alien," though I render it "immigrant" for convenience. In H a person of this status contrasts with an אזרח, often rendered "citizen." The latter is the primary audience of legislation and hence those who are genetically Israelite. This term is sometimes defined as אזרח הארץ, which carries a geographical orientation. The term אזרח might therefore be rendered "hereditary native" or just "native." Obviously in the PH narrative a "native" would be relative to the exodus and acquisition of the land. The *gēr* is distinct from the hereditary native geographically and genealogically: this person comes in from the outside and is not part of the Israelite line.[16]

Important for understanding H's motivation for adding the immigrant is that, of P and H, only the latter is concerned with the immigrant. Neither גר nor אזרח appears in P. In the foundational corpus of P, the Israelites are just the בני ישראל, "Israelites," or the like, and P does not speak of immigrants or foreigners.[17]

H's concern about the immigrant is specifically motivated from its use of earlier non-P law collections, the Covenant Code (CC), and Deuteronomy (D). These corpora treat the *gēr* sporadically and mainly in regard to ethical obligations due a person of this status. CC prohibits oppressing the *gēr* (Exod 22:20; 23:9), along with the widow and orphan. The *gēr* is to benefit from the rest observed by the Israelites on the seventh day (23:12).[18]

Deuteronomy develops CC's regulations about the *gēr* in various ways. Besides requiring the *gēr* to rest on the Sabbath it its Decalogue (Deut 5:14), several laws in Deuteronomy are oriented toward CC's trio of *gēr*, widow, and orphan, sometimes with mention of other poor people.[19] Deut 10, part of D's introduction, folds together motifs from CC's injunctions on the poor and justice, and describes the Deity as one who maintains the justice of the orphan and widow and who loves the *gēr*. Therefore, the people should love the *gēr*

---

16. For the *gēr* in H, see the recent discussion by Christophe Nihan, "Resident Aliens and Natives in the Holiness Legislation," in *The Foreigner and the Law: Perspectives from the Hebrew Bible and the Ancient Near East*, ed. Reinhard Achenbach et al., BZABR 16 (Wiesbaden: Harrassowitz, 2011), 111–34. He discusses the *gēr* in Num 15:22–31 on p. 126. See the older but valuable close analysis of Jacob Milgrom, "Religious Conversion and the Revolt Model for the Formation of Israel," *JBL* 101 (1982): 169–76. While Nihan (and Milgrom) provides ultimately a social-historical analysis, it is not clear to what extent the legal texts reflect real social circumstances or are academic or ideological constructs. The pseudoarchaeographic contextualization of the law texts (whether CC, D, or PH) as well as an ideological and academic orientation obscures social reality. See Wright, "Law and Creation," 76; David P. Wright, "Ritual Theory, Ritual Texts, and the Priestly-Holiness Writings of the Pentateuch," in *Social Theory and the Study of Israelite Religion*, ed. Saul M. Olyan, RBS 71 (Atlanta: SBL, 2012), 195–216.

17. H also uses the term תושב (Exod 12:45; Lev 22:10; 25:6, 23, 35, 40, 45, 47; Num 35:15), related to the *gēr* (on the distinction, see Nihan, "Resident Aliens," 118–119). H has בן־נכר, "(son of) a foreigner," in Lev 22:25 (also in Gen 17:12, 27, which may be part of an H expansion).

18. Exodus 20:10 prescribes rest for the *gēr* on the Sabbath. Though the Decalogue in Exod 20:1–17 is part of CC's legal and narrative context, it is not clear if or to what extent the list of rest beneficiaries in v. 10 is influenced by D (cf. Deut 5:14 and 12:12, 18; 16:11, 14).

19. For the three together, see Deut 14:29; 16:11, 14; 24:17, 19–21; 26:12 (cf. 10:18; 27:19).

because they themselves were immigrants in Egypt (Deut 10:18–19; cf. Exod 22:20–23; 23:9). D's legislation proper prohibits economic exploitation of the *gēr* and other poor persons (Deut 23:14–15; cf. Exod 22:20–22) and forbids prejudice against these persons in court (Deut 24:17; 27:19; cf. Exod 23:1–8). The *gēr* along with the widow and orphan may glean fields for sustenance (Deut 24:19–22), a law that correlates functionally with CC's seventh year law (Exod 23:10–11).[20] D also rewrote CC's laws on impure animal carcasses for the benefit of the *gēr* (Deut 14:21; cf. Exod 22:30). Instead of throwing the meat to the dogs, as advocated in CC, D gives it to the immigrant. D also goes beyond CC's limited rules about the immigrant to say something about the participation of this individual in cultic activities. The *gēr* may join joyous celebrations at the chosen cult place on, for example, the Feast of Weeks and Feast of Booths (Deut 16:11, 14), and the person may share in the bounty of Israelite first fruits (26:11) and the third-year tithe (26:12–13). While the body of D's laws portray the *gēr* as standing somewhat apart from the Israelite community in terms of ritual and cultic obligations (e.g., Deut 14:21), a supplement portrays this individual as having a measure of communal religious obligation. Every seven years, at the seventh-year debt release on the Feast of Booths, all the people, including women, children, and immigrants, are to be gathered to hear the reading of the law so that they may learn to fear Yʜᴡʜ (31:10–13).[21]

H appears to have reacted to these earlier and somewhat fuzzy portrayals, seeking specifically to clarify the legal and religious status of the *gēr*.[22] Four examples illustrate that H knew and revised D's and CC's rules: (1) H's command to love the *gēr* in Lev 19:33–34 builds on the command of Deut 10:18–19 along with CC's prohibition against oppressing him (Exod 22:20–23; 23:9).[23] (2) H's gleaning law in Lev 19:9–10 boils the corresponding law from Deuteronomy (Deut 24:19–22) down to a single streamlined rule, turning D's gift to the poor, an *accident* of imperfect harvesting, into something due *to be intentionally left for the poor*.[24] (3) H's carrion law in Lev 17:15–16 solves the legal problem created

20. D kept CC's cycle of *seven years* in Deut 15:1–11, but turned it into a release of debt, not the release of plant and tree produce. The gleaning law of Deut 24:19–22 nevertheless maintained an agricultural benefit for the poor similar to Exod 23:10–11, but made it an annual affair.

21. In D, the *gēr* appears also in Deut 23:8 (of Israelites in Egypt) and 28:43–44 (in a curse about inversion of status).

22. That H knew CC is not in dispute (see, e.g., Milgrom, *Leviticus 17–22*, 1355–56, 1370; Milgrom, *Leviticus 23–27*, AYB 3B [New York: Doubleday, 2001], 2154–55). For H's knowledge and use of D, see Wright, "Source Dependence"; Stackert, *Rewriting*; Nihan, "Resident Aliens," 112 (in contrast to, for example, Milgrom, *Leviticus 17–22*, 1357–1361).

23. For some discussion, see Nihan, "Resident Aliens," 121–122.

24. The logic of what H is doing here is connected with its seventh year and jubilee laws in Lev 25, which take elements from CC's and D's seventh year and debt-slave legislation

in Deut 14:21, which allows the *gēr* to consume carrion, in contrast to D's broader legislation, which allows the *gēr* to participate in the cult. H has the *gēr* perform ablutions like Israelites to regain a cultically pure status. (4) Related to the foregoing, H's emphasis on national holiness builds on D's notions of national holiness (cf. Deut 7:6; 14:2, 21; cf. 10:15; 18:13).[25] H's most comprehensive statement on the topic is found in Lev 20:24–26. This imitates the language of Deut 14:21 and other similar passages, with a call to be holy, a notice of divine election from among the nations (H uses the Priestly verb for separating and discerning, בדל "to separate, divide" for this), and the people as the Deity's possession.

An odd thing about H's treatment of the *gēr* throughout its legislation is that, apart from the laws in Lev 19:9–10, 33–34 (and 23:22 which reiterates 19:9–10), H's prescriptions are not concerned with the ethical treatment of this individual, in contrast to the emphasis in D and CC. A correlate of this is that, in contrast to D and CC, H does not take up the orphan and widow as objects of ethical concern.[26] It appears that H's interest in the *gēr* is a matter of legal technicality, determining the extent to which a person of that status has the same obligations as Israelites. For H, the *gēr* is more of a concept than a person in society—a borderline test case that clarifies the application of law.

Table 1 summarizes H's laws about the *gēr*. These indicate that the *gēr* is obligated to follow rules about transgression and impurity, especially prohibitions. He does not have to celebrate festivals of national identity, like the Passover, though he may do this if he is circumcised. Nonetheless, even during such festivals and related occasions, the individual must follow prohibitions, such as not consuming leavened bread during the feast of Unleavened Bread and fasting and resting on the Day of Atonement. The inclusion of the immigrant in the *ḥaṭṭāʾt* law fits this scheme of responsibility for sin, impurity, and controlled behaviors. To that extent the immigrant is part of the larger Israelite national community, the עדה or קהל.

---

(Exod 23:10–11; Deut 15:1–11, 12–18) and reformulate them into a complex cycle of agricultural and debt release. See David Wright, "'She Shall Not Go Free as Male Slaves Do': Developing Views About Slavery and Gender in the Laws of the Hebrew Bible," in *Beyond Slavery: Overcoming Its Religious and Sexual Legacy*, ed. Bernadette Brooten et al. (New York: Palgrave Macmillan, 2010), 125–42.

25. D for its part builds on the motif of national holiness in CC and its narrative (Exod 22:30 and 19:5–6).

26. The widow appears only in Lev 21:14; 22:13; Num 30:9, in contexts other than ethical treatment. The orphan does not appear. Nihan, "Resident Aliens," 113, 117–18, notes that in CC and D the *gēr* is economically dependent whereas in H he is rather independent. Much of his essay is devoted to fleshing out H's conception of the *gēr*.

| H Passage | Topic |
|---|---|
| *Festivals* | |
| Exod 12:48–49; Num 9:14 | May observe Passover, if circumcised |
| Exod 12:19 | Must not consume leaven during feast of Unleavened Bread |
| Lev 16:29 | Must fast and rest on Day of Atonement |
| | |
| *Sacrifice and Blood* | |
| Lev 17:8 | Must offer animal at tabernacle (if offering) |
| Lev 17:10, 12, 13 | Must not consume blood |
| Lev 22:18 | Must offer unblemished animals (if offering) |
| Num 15:13–16 | Must offer auxiliary cereal and libation offerings |
| Num 15:26, 29 | Must bring *ḥaṭṭāʾt* for inadvertent sins |
| | |
| *Purity Rules* | |
| Lev 17:15; Num 19:10 | Must purify after eating carrion or corpse contamination |
| | |
| *Other Sins* | |
| Lev 18:26; 20:2 | Must avoid sexual and related abominations and Molech worship |
| | |
| Lev 24:16, 22 | Must not blaspheme the Deity |
| Num 15:30 | Is liable for intentional sins |
| Num 35:15 | Is liable for homicide |
| | |
| *Economic Rules* | |
| Lev 25:47, 53 | Must not treat enslaved Israelite harshly |
| | |
| *Ethical Treatment of* Gēr | |
| Lev 19:10; 23:22 | Beneficiary of gleanings (along with other poor persons) |
| Lev 19:33–34 | Object of love by Israelites |

*Table 1. The* גֵר *(gēr) "immigrant" in H*

The rationale for H's inclusion of the immigrant in its *ḥaṭṭā't* laws and its systematic thinking about this matter will become clearer as the essay turns now to the final verses of its pericope on the intentional sin. This will, in the end, provide an explanation for a novel feature in H's communal *ḥaṭṭā't* unmentioned to this point: the requirement that the community bring a burnt offering in addition to a *ḥaṭṭā't* for its inadvertent sin (Num 15:24).

## Intentional Sin (vv. 30–31)

The final verses of H's *ḥaṭṭā't* law (vv. 30–31) deal with intentional sin, a topic not included in P's *ḥaṭṭā't* legislation in Lev 4:

Num 15:30–31 (H):

[30](But) the individual who acts with a high hand (i.e., sins intentionally), whether a hereditary native or an immigrant, thus disparages Yʜᴡʜ; that individual will be cut off from the midst of his people, [31]because he has despised Yʜᴡʜ's word and has broken his commandment—that individual shall be cut off; his sin is on him.

‏30 וְהַנֶּפֶשׁ אֲשֶׁר־תַּעֲשֶׂה בְּיָד רָמָה מִן־הָאֶזְרָח וּמִן־הַגֵּר אֶת־יהוה הוּא
מְגַדֵּף וְנִכְרְתָה הַנֶּפֶשׁ הַהִוא מִקֶּרֶב עַמָּהּ:
‏31 כִּי דְבַר־יהוה בָּזָה וְאֶת־מִצְוָתוֹ הֵפַר הִכָּרֵת תִּכָּרֵת הַנֶּפֶשׁ הַהִוא
עֲוֹנָה בָהּ:

H's verses are only incidentally inspired by Lev 4.[27] P's prescriptions for the Day of Atonement in Lev 16 are of greater influence, conceptually. As noted earlier in this essay, P's Day of Atonement prescriptions are part of its larger *ḥaṭṭā't* sacrificial legislation. The rites on this occasion rectify the impurity of intentional sins (Lev 16:16) and thus complement the sacrifices of Lev 4, which rectify the impurity of inadvertent sins. H's attachment of the topic of intentional sin to its *ḥaṭṭā't* law hermeneutically brings together the two types of sins that are systematically complementary but separately treated in P.

27. H's designation of the legal subject as a נֶפֶשׁ, "person," in Num 15:30–31 builds on the previous verses (vv. 27, 28), which themselves build on the terminology of P's *ḥaṭṭā't* law (Lev 4:2, 27; the term נֶפֶשׁ appears elsewhere in P and H). The adverbial that describes intent בְּיָד רָמָה, "with a high hand," parallels the adverbial בִּשְׁגָגָה, "inadvertently," found in P (Lev 4:2, 22, 27). The latter is used six times earlier in H's *ḥaṭṭā't* law (Num 15:24, 25, 26, 27, 28, 29).

But though they take up the topic of intentional sins, H's verses do not summarize P's Day of Atonement sacrificial rites. Rather, H goes in a different direction and fills a legislative gap left by P. H sets out the personal liability that obtains for these sins. Those sinning brazenly will suffer the penalty of excision, literally, being "cut off" (described with the root כרת). This penalty is generally found in the H materials in the PH corpus (mostly in the *niphal* verbal stem, but sometimes *hiphil*). The few passages with this penalty that are not clearly H still appear to be secondary to a more basic P text.[28] The penalty is imposed by deity and involves two dimensions: the untimely death of the individual and, more broadly, the extinction of his or her family line.[29] The transgressions for which this punishment is prescribed are emblematic and cover violations of cultic and ritual rules and also various taboos. The liability for intentional sins in general entails cases otherwise not specified.

Part of the motivation for H's description of personal liability for intentional sins may be P's story of the sin and death of Aaron's sons, Nadab and Abihu in Lev 10. The first verse of P's Day of Atonement passage (16:1) refers back to this. P's Day of Atonement ritual, which takes place soon after setting up the tabernacle on the first day of the first month a year after the exodus (Exod 40:2), and dedicating it (Lev 8–10), may have been an emergency rite prescribed for egregious sins such as the sin committed by these priestly novices. In any case, YHWH's execution of Aaron's sons is an example of the sort of penalty that H would include under the umbrella of excision.

H's story about the Sabbath-breaker (Num 15:32–36), which immediately follows the verses on intentional transgression, presumably seeks to exemplify H's verses on intentional sins. According to this, the Israelites find a man gath-

---

28. General categories of sins with the excision penalty include the following: improper sacrificial consumption (Lev 7:20–21*, 25, 27; 17:10, 14; 19:8); other cultic and purity transgressions (Exod 30:33, 38; Num 4:18; 19:13, 20); violating Sabbath and festival requirements (Exod 12:15, 19; 31:14; Lev 23:29; Num 9:13); and various sins (Gen 17:14*; Lev 18:29; 20:17, 18; 20:3, 5, 6; Num 15:30–31). Almost all the passages are H or arguably so (see Knohl, *Sanctuary*). Those marked with asterisks might be questioned, but still appear to be intermediate between P and H. See Deborah Rooke's paper in this volume for a different analysis of the excision penalty.

29. Milgrom, *Leviticus 1–16*, 457–460; Milgrom, *Leviticus 17–22*, 1420–23; D. J. Wold, "The Kareth Penalty in P: Rationale and Cases," in *Society of Biblical Literature 1979 Seminar Papers*, vol. 1 (Missoula: Scholars Press, 1979), 1–45. On the related ambiguous penalty of bearing sin, see Baruch Schwartz, "The Bearing of Sin in the Priestly Literature," in *Pomegranates and Golden Bells: Studies in Biblical, Jewish, and Near Eastern Ritual, Law, and Literature in Honor of Jacob Milgrom*, ed. D. P. Wright et al. (Winona Lake, IN: Eisenbrauns, 1995), 3–21; Wright, "Source Dependence," 668–69.

ering wood. Yʜwʜ instructs Moses to have the man executed: "The man shall be put to death; the whole community shall stone him with stones outside the camp." The Israelites then perform the execution. Some other laws in H portray execution by human agency as a possible complement to excision by the Deity, since excision goes further to include genealogical extinction, something only the Deity can impose.[30]

H rationalizes the excision penalty at the end of its *ḥaṭṭā't* law by describing it as an abuse of the Deity: "he (the sinner) thus disparages (גדף) Yʜwʜ; that individual will be cut off from the midst of his/her people, because he has despised (בזה) Yʜwʜ's word and has broken his commandment" (vv. 30b–31). The verbs used here are not found elsewhere in H (or P), but are nonetheless consistent with H's perspective that various sins are an affront to the Deity's person. It is an act of reviling, even blaspheming, Yʜwʜ. It parallels H's concept of desecrating the Deity or his name and not upholding his sanctity, developed elsewhere.[31] If the Sabbath-breaker novella in vv. 32–36 contextually relates to H's *ḥaṭṭā't* law as an illustration of a case of intentional sin (vv. 30–31), then it parallels H's legal novella about a blasphemer in Lev 24, who also defames the Deity by cursing him (קלל) and disparagingly enunciating his name (נקב). Contextually and similarly, the Sabbath-breaker has denigrated the Deity twofold, by disparaging (גדף) and scorning (בזה) him.

H's verses in Num 15 about intentional sins include the *gēr* as did the preceding rules about the *ḥaṭṭā't* sacrifices brought for communal and individual inadvertent sins. This is also a function of H's preoccupation with P's Day of Atonement legislation. Indeed, H significantly altered P's Day of Atonement. It changed P's rite from what seems to be an ad hoc emergency rite for sanctuary purification into a performance done just once a year on the tenth day of the seventh month. It also added the requirement that the people fast and rest from work.[32] In the context of Lev 16, H made these changes by appending

---

30. Both capital punishment and excision are prescribed for Sabbath violation in Exod 31:12–17 (on PH textual strata, see Jeffrey Stackert, "The Composition of Exodus 31:12–17 and 35:1–3 and the Question of Method in Identifying Priestly Strata in the Torah," in *Current Issues in Priestly and Related Literature: The Legacy of Jacob Milgrom and Beyond*, ed. Roy E. Gane and Ada Taggar-Cohen, RBS 82 (Atlanta: SBL, 2015], 175–96) and H's law on Molech worship (Lev 20:2–5).

31. See Lev 18:21; 19:12; 20:3; 21:6; 22:2, 32; 24:10–23; cf. Exod 29:43; Lev 10:3; 11:44–45; 19:2; 20:7, 26; Num 20:10–12; 27:14. For the meaning of the root גדף, see 2 Kings 19:6, 22 // Isa 37:6, 23; Isa 43:28; 51:7; Ezek 5:15; Zeph 2:8; Ps 44:17.

32. For this argument, see Knohl, *Sanctuary*, 27–34.

six verses at the end (vv. 29–34). This addition explicitly includes the *gēr* in the requirements for fasting and resting (v. 29):

Lev 16:29 (H):

> It will be a permanent statute for you in the seventh month on the tenth day of the month you shall afflict yourselves (i.e., practice abstinence) and shall not do any work, both the hereditary native and the immigrant that dwells in your midst.

והיתה לכם לחקת עולם בחדש השביעי בעשור לחדש תענו את־
נפשתיכם וכל־מלאכה לא תעשו האזרח והגר הגר בתוככם:

This has significant contextual ramifications. The *gēr* is not simply practicing self-denial out of solidarity with the Israelite community. Rather, H views those of this class as now covered by the rites on the Day of Atonement. That is, for H, the intentional sins of immigrants can pollute the sanctuary and the impurity of these sins must be expunged. This is fully consistent with H's inclusion of the *gēr* in the *ḥaṭṭā't* sacrifices for inadvertent sins in Num 15:26 and 29, discussed above. And it is consistent with the inclusion of the *gēr* in the law about intentional sins in Num 15:30–31. All of these H passages are part of the same scribal system of thought even though they have been inserted at different points in the base P text.[33]

Recognizing that H took up elements from P's Day of Atonement ritual allows the explanation of an innovation in its prescription for the communal *ḥaṭṭā't* in Num 15:24–26 (see the text cited above). H's law requires the community to bring a burnt offering in addition to a *ḥaṭṭā't*. This can be explained as blending features from P's communal *ḥaṭṭā't* in Lev 4 and its communal *ḥaṭṭā't* on the Day of Atonement in Lev 16. Lev 4 requires the community to bring just a bull of the herd (פר בן־בקר) for a *ḥaṭṭā't* (v. 14). Lev 16 requires the community to provide for slaughter both a male goat (v. 5 called a שְׂעִיר־עִזִּים)

---

33. Nihan, "Resident Aliens," 127, briefly notes the appearance of the *gēr* in the legislation of Lev 17 (vv. 8, 10, 12, 13). This means that the individual derives the benefits entailed by the verb כפר there (v. 11). This, however, is not specifically part of the *ḥaṭṭā't* system. The sacrifices in this chapter do not expressly include the *ḥaṭṭā't* (vv. 5, 7, 8), the rite of blood throwing (זרק, v. 6) does not belong to *ḥaṭṭā't* ceremonial (see n. 2, above), and the concern about blood consumption in vv. 11–14, precisely where כפר appears, is also inconsistent with the context of the *ḥaṭṭā't*, but fits the well-being sacrifice (cf. Lev 7:26–27). The verbal idiom in v. 11 also carries more the meaning of "to ransom" (see v. 8, above).

for a *ḥaṭṭā't* and a ram for a burnt offering (v. 5, 9, 15, 24–25). Num 15 keeps the bull of the herd from Lev 4, using the same terminology (פר בן־בקר), but turns this into a burnt offering, parallel to Lev 16. It then adds a male goat (termed שְׂעִיר־עִזִּים), consistent with Lev 16. The community's *ḥaṭṭā't* in Num 15 thereby becomes a rite with more pageantry than the individual *ḥaṭṭā't* that is prescribed next, which requires only a single she-goat.[34] The addition of the burnt offering fortifies the efficacy of the *ḥaṭṭā't*, particularly its function as a food gift (distinctively an אִשֶּׁה, "fire offering" or "gift," in v. 25), as also found in the case of the combination of *ḥaṭṭā't* and burnt offering in several performances in P (see the discussion of P's *ḥaṭṭā't* system, above).

## Conclusion

H's revision of P's *ḥaṭṭā't* legislation is consonant with its legislative agenda and ideology. As noted at the outset, H's overall body of legislation goes beyond P's focus on the cult to deal with the people in general and the land that they are about to conquer. The context of the land is presupposed contextually in H's *ḥaṭṭā't* law in the inclusion of the *gēr* along with the hereditary native. The category of *gēr* does not fit the context envisaged for the wilderness, but rather a context where the native and immigrant live together in symbiosis. The mixed parentage of the blasphemer in H's legal novella of Lev 24:10–23 is as close as one might get to a *gēr* in the wilderness context.[35]

The context of the land is also apparent from the larger legislative context of Numbers 15. Some of the laws in Num 15 are written to apply to the land to which the Israelites are coming. These include the first section on cereal offerings and libations that are accompaniments to animal sacrifices (vv. 1–16, see v. 2) and the next section on the hulled grain offering (vv. 17–21, see v. 18).

---

34. For pageantry in ritual see Robert N. McCauley and E. Thomas Lawson, *Bringing Ritual to Mind* (Cambridge: Cambridge University Press, 2002), which builds on E. Thomas Lawson and Robert N. McCauley, *Rethinking Religion: Connecting Cognition and Culture* (Cambridge: Cambridge University Press, 1990).

35. The verse about the עֵרֶב רַב, "mixed multitude," in Exod 12:38 may belong to PH, see Baden, *Composition*, 199 (contrast 76 and Baden, *J, E, and the Redaction of the Pentateuch*, FAT 68 [Tübingen: Mohr Siebeck, 2009], 107, n. 25; cf. Num 11:4). For discussion of the term as referring to non-Israelites, see William Propp, *Exodus 1–18: A New Translation with Introduction and Commentary*, AYB 2 (New York: Doubleday, 1999), 414–415. One wonders if H's law on the *gēr* and the Passover in Exod 12:43–49 (see Knohl, *Sanctuary*, 20–21, 62, 104) is in part a reaction to 12:38, if the latter belongs to P.

From a strict literary point of view, H's *ḥaṭṭāʾt* law is part of the latter context. Its introduction reads: "Yhwh spoke to Moses: speak to the Israelites and say to them, When you come to the land to which I am bringing you" (vv. 17–18). The *ḥaṭṭāʾt* law immediately follows vv. 17–21 without a new introduction. One may assume that the circumstance of "when you enter the land" in v. 18 also applies to H's *ḥaṭṭāʾt*.

This focus on laws in the land fits H's view that, in addition to maintaining the purity and holiness of the sanctuary as set out in P, the integrity of the land must be maintained. According to H, sins pollute the land, though its legislation describes this only emblematically through examples. For example, the sexual abominations listed in Lev 18 pollute the land, with the result that the land will vomit out the transgressors (Lev 18:24–28). The *gēr* is liable for these transgressions. Moreover, H's homicide law of Num 35 says that the crime pollutes the land (vv. 33–34). The *gēr* is also liable for this crime. H's inclusion of the immigrant in P's *ḥaṭṭāʾt* system is one element that keeps the sanctuary pure, following P, and serves to keep the land pure.

Thus H's extension of atonement beyond Israel to include the immigrant is not a means of enlarging the religious community by conversion or adoption,[36] but of ensuring the vitality of Israel in its land. A stranger who comes to live in the land must abide by the moral and ritual requirements that preserve its sanctity.[37]

---

36. For discussion of this view in older literature, see Nihan, "Resident Aliens," 113–19.

37. I thank my students Justin Huguenin, for helping me with some of the bibliography, and Eileen Xing, for proofreading the manuscript and offering critique.

## PART TWO

*Anthropology, Cosmology, and Mediators in*
*Early Jewish and Christian Atonement Theologies*

# WHEN THE PROBLEM IS NOT WHAT YOU HAVE DONE BUT WHO YOU ARE

*The Changing Focus of Atonement in Second Temple Prayer and Poetry*

CAROL A. NEWSOM

*Atonement* is a word so dense with overlapping layers of meaning and significance that one sometimes hesitates to use it at all. And yet, the problem it seeks to address—a relationship ruptured by a sense of culpable injury—is one that is fundamental not just to human societies but also to other highly social primates.[1] It is similar to the legal term "tort," which connotes "a wrongful act ... that results in injury to another's person, property, reputation, or the like, and for which the injured party is entitled to compensation."[2] In social terms the wrongful act creates a social estrangement that, when remedied, allows for reconciliation. The dynamics are present in the narrative of the meeting of Jacob and Esau in Genesis 32. Jacob is aware that his actions toward Esau, deceiving their father Isaac into giving him the blessing intended for Esau (Gen 27), have caused a material and social injury to Esau. Thus Jacob seeks to "propitiate him" with gifts (אכפרה פניו) that he hopes will result in a gesture of acceptance of Jacob by Esau ("perhaps he will lift up my face," Gen 32:21), signaling the restored social balance. In political contexts, too, a sense of unjust

---

1. Frans B. M. de Waal and Angeline van Roosmalen, "Reconciliation and Consolation among Chimpanzees," *Behavioral Ecology and Sociobiology* 5 (1979): 55–66; Signe Preuschaft, Zin Wang, Filippo Aureli, and Frans B. M. de Waal, "Reconciliation in Captive Chimpanzees: A Reevaluation with Controlled Methods," *International Journal of Primatology* 23 (2002): 29–50.

2. Dictionary.com.

imbalance must be addressed in order to restore not only proper relationships but also the very order of things. In 2 Samuel 21 a severe famine during David's reign is discovered to be the result of bloodguilt incurred by Saul's execution of a number of Gibeonites (v. 1). David asks the Gibeonites what he should do to "make expiation" (אכפר, v. 3). Here the injured party defines the appropriate compensation (the lives of seven of Saul's male offspring [v. 6]).

In the religious realm the same basic logic operates, though, of course, only in one direction, given the hierarchical and ontological difference between God and humans. The problem of actions offensive to the deity and how to remedy them is the subject of several different but overlapping discourses. The cultic discourse found in priestly writings exhibits a highly developed system of classification of offenses according to the status of the offender and the intentionality of the offense, with the cultic system primarily designed to address inadvertent or unintentional sins, of which the perpetrator may not even be aware at the time.[3] Sins committed with arrogant intentionality and particularly heinous sins have no cultic remedy except that the perpetrator is to be "cut off," presumably referring to the extirpation of the family line.[4]

Outside of priestly compositions, however, other discussions concerning sin and atonement, rupture and reconciliation, occur in narrative, hortatory, prophetic, and psalmic texts. These treatments testify to a more fluid and complex system for negotiating breaches of relationship and their repair, including

---

3. The literature on the cultic system of atonement and the theology (or theologies) attached to it is voluminous. Scholars often disagree, however, on the relative significance of cleansing, ransoming, reconciling, and related concepts in the way sacrificial atonement was understood to function. The fundamental work on cultic atonement is the commentary on Leviticus by Jacob Milgrom, *Leviticus 1–16: A New Translation with Introduction and Commentary*, AYB 3 (New York: Doubleday, 1991); Jacob Milgrom, *Leviticus 17–22: A New Translation with Introduction and Commentary*, AYB 3A (New York: Doubleday, 2000); Jacob Milgrom, *Leviticus 23–27: A New Translation with Introduction and Commentary*, AYB 3B (New York: Doubleday, 2001). Other studies of significance, some of which take issue with aspects of Milgrom's interpretation, include Nobuyoshi Kiuchi, *The Purification Offering in the Priestly Literature: Its Meaning and Function*, JSOTSup 56 (Sheffield: JSOT Press, 1987); Bernd Janowski, *Sühne als Heilsgeschehen: Traditions- und religionsgeschichtliche Studien zur Sühnetheologie der Priesterschrift*, 2nd ed., WMANT 55 (Neukirchen-Vluyn: Neukirchener, 2000); Jonathan Klawans, *Purity, Sacrifice, and the Temple: Symbolism and Supersessionism in the Study of Ancient Judaism* (New York: Oxford University Press, 2006); Daniel Stökl Ben Ezra, "Atonement III: Judaism," in *EBR* 3:43–50; Jay Sklar, *Sin, Impurity, Sacrifice, Atonement: The Priestly Conceptions*, Hebrew Bible Monographs 2 (Sheffield: Sheffield Phoenix Press, 2015).

4. See the discussion of "moral impurity" in Jonathan Klawans, *Impurity and Sin in Ancient Judaism* (New York: Oxford University Press, 2000), 26–31.

those that are committed consciously and arrogantly. Though the means may differ, the social transactional nature of the ways in which people attempt to restore a ruptured relationship with the deity are foregrounded. In place of material or sacrificial "compensation" the offending party may offer acts of contrition or self-humiliation (e.g., 1 Kgs 21:27–29; Jonah 3:5–10; Dan 9:4–19). In some instances, petitioners may seek reconciliation simply as a gracious act of God, in which God foregoes ritual compensation or the satisfaction of punishment and simply forgives the people (e.g., Ps 78:38). There may, of course, be a bit of passive-aggressive manipulation. David Lambert argues that certain rites of repentance, like fasting and wearing sackcloth, are designed, rather like hunger strikes, to make the deity so uncomfortable that he forgives the people.[5] But even these actions are a kind of public offering of self-humiliation that acknowledges the distress of the people at the breach with God.

All of these practices are based on the common-sense assumptions that the members of the society are functional and free moral agents. But what if those assumptions about moral agency are challenged? What if the problem is not what you have done but who you are? Consider the description of human nature in certain passages from the Hodayot:

> What is one born of woman . . . He is a thing constructed of dust and kneaded with water. Sin[ful gui]lt is his foundation, obscene shame, and a so[urce of im]purity. And a perverted spirit rules him. If he acts wickedly, he becomes [a sign for]ever, and a portent for dis[ta]nt generations of flesh. (1QH^a 5:31–33).[6]

> As for me, from dust [you] took [me, and from clay] I was [pin]ched off, as a source of impurity and obscene shame, a heap of dust and a thing kneaded [with water, a council of magg]ots, a dwelling of darkness. And there is a return to dust for the vessel of clay at the time of [your] anger [. . .]dust returns to that from which it was taken. What can dust and ashes reply [concerning your judgment? And ho]w can it understand its [d]eeds? How can it stand before the one who reproves it? (1QH^a 20:27–31).

This is a problem that the system of cultic atonement and the social practices of reconciliation are not designed to address. In one sense, of course, the

5. David Lambert, *How Repentance Became Biblical: Judaism, Christianity, and the Interpretation of Scripture* (New York: Oxford University Press, 2016), 17.
6. All translations are my own unless otherwise noted.

problem remains "what one has done," in that the abysmal creature described in the Hodayot literally cannot do anything except what is offensive to God, thus ensuring God's disgust and judgment. But the problem is compounded by the fact that this miserable being cannot even grasp that what it does is sinful ("how can it understand its deeds?"). And even if it could, it would not have the moral capacity to offer any gesture of recompense or contrition or repentance. The origin of the problem is not to be traced to some lack of moral formation, inner conflict, or other failure over which it might have putative control. Neither is there a "fall" or a problem to be traced to the consequences of angelic misbehavior or demonic deception.[7] Rather, as 1QH$^a$ 20:27–28 (cited above) attests, this being was *created without* moral capacity—from the moment it was pinched off from clay. The fact that a person has no agency does not avert the consequences. Sin and impurity are objective conditions. Thus the individual is utterly trapped—it is in its very *being* an offense against God despite having no capacity to be or do otherwise.

Although the radical anthropology represented in the passage in the Hodayot appears to be developed through a complex exegetical practice that brings together a variety of biblical claims,[8] the issue of innate and intractable human moral deficiency was already an issue of considerable concern in earlier Second Temple Judaism.[9] In order to understand better why this issue was of such importance and what its implications might have been, I wish to pursue three questions in this essay. First, is it possible to locate the origins and context of the emergence of the framing of the problem of sin as a radical defect in the person rather than simply a matter of bad deeds? Second, when the problem is framed as an ontological problem, how is the solution to the problem envisioned—if, indeed, there is a solution? Third, how does changing the discourse about sin in a way that seems quite negative paradoxically open up new forms of spiritual intimacy and even ecstasy?

---

7. Contra Stephen J. Hultgren, *From the Damascus Covenant to the Covenant of the Community: Literary, Historical, and Theological Studies in the Dead Sea Scrolls*, STDJ 66 (Leiden: Brill, 2007), 436–37. His argument suggesting a connection with the angelic sin of the Enochic traditions is refuted by Nicholas A. Meyer (*Adam's Dust and Adam's Glory in the Hodayot and the Letters of Paul: Rethinking Anthropology and Theology*, NovTSup 168 [Leiden: Brill, 2016], 38).

8. See n. 40 below.

9. See the careful and informative study by Miryam T. Brand, *Evil Within and Without: The Source of Sin and Its Nature as Portrayed in Second Temple Literature*, JAJSup 9 (Göttingen: Vandenhoeck & Ruprecht, 2013).

## The Origins of the Shift

While one must be careful not to oversimplify, one important point of origin in the development of doubt about the assumption of free moral agency emerges historically in the attempt to grapple with the traumatic events of the destruction of the kingdom of Judah in 586 BCE. The prevailing mode of understanding political success or failure—a model attested in prophetic discourse as well as in Deuteronomic covenantal and historiographical discourse—was that it was a consequence of obedience or disobedience to the commands of God (e.g., Deut 28:1, 15; 2 Kgs 17:7–20; 21:1–15; Jer 11:1–8; Ezek 7:1–4). The destruction, when it came, was thus inevitably understood as a catastrophic failure of moral agency. That the nation, despite clear warnings of the consequences of disobedience, had done so anyway, suggested that the problem was more radical than simply a sequence of bad choices. It pointed to a defect in the fundamental moral equipment of the people. If that is the case, then what one has done is perceived as a symptom of a problem with what one is. Given the body-based moral psychology of ancient Israel, the problem is often expressed in physical images. The trope of the uncircumcised heart, which appears in numerous texts from this era (Deut 10:16; 30:6; Jer 4:4; 9:26; cf. Ezek 44:7–9; Lev 26:41) uses the imagery of a physical impediment that must be removed before the heart can function properly as a moral organ.[10] The image may have been employed initially simply as an emphatic rhetorical gesture rather than as a claim about anthropology per se, but tropes, once introduced, have a potential that may exceed the intent of their original crafters. Significantly, the image implies that obedience and even reconciliation after disobedience are blocked unless and until there is a fundamental moral transformation of the people. In what are likely the earliest uses of the trope in Jer 4:4 and Deut 10:16, this transformation is one that can be accomplished by the agency of the people themselves. Thus it presents only a modest shift in the model of moral anthropology.

In the post-exilic redaction of Deut 30:1–10, however, the agency for the circumcision of the heart shifts from the people to God. This passage is a complex one and subject to different interpretations. Verses 1–2, which describe an act of returning (שׁוּב) by Israel, are often read as the protasis of a

---

10. Werner Lemke ("Circumcision of the Heart: The Journey of a Biblical Metaphor," in *A God So Near: Essays on Old Testament Theology in Honor of Patrick D. Miller*, ed. Brent A. Strawn and Nancy R. Bowen [Winona Lake, IN: Eisenbrauns, 2003], 306–7), argues cogently that Jeremiah may have been the source of the trope.

long sentence, the apodosis of which occurs in verses 3–9. If so, then Israel's prior act of "return" evokes the divine response of the circumcision of the heart. Read in this fashion, repentance is not precluded by the uncircumcised heart, and God's act of circumcising the heart is rather a prophylactic action that enables the people in the future "to love the Lord your God . . . and to obey all his commandments" (vv. 6, 8), and so avoid future disaster. As Marc Brettler has shown, however, it is also possible syntactically to construe the apodosis as beginning in v. 1b, so that Israel's repentance is not a precondition of God's response but is itself an effect of God's action on the people.[11] This more deterministic reading, which shifts all of the agency to God, is in fact the way the passage was interpreted in later Second Temple texts, such as the Words of the Luminaries (4Q504 18:12–19) and Bar 2:27–35. Whether that is the proper interpretation of Deuteronomy itself is less clear, but one can find other instances of the shift of agency to God in contemporaneous texts.

In Jeremiah, for example, the problem of moral failure is frequently framed as a failure of understanding (Jer 5:4–5, 13, 21; 6:10; 8:4–9; 9:3; etc.), the inexplicable inability of the heart to receive and internalize torah. But the problem seems to be more than a functional failure, since the solution involves the physical placement of the teaching into the body (קרב) and the writing or inscribing of it onto the heart itself (31:33–34; cf. 32:39–40). This physical intervention draws attention to the heart as an objectified, problematic *thing*. The divine action explicitly replaces the failed human process of teaching and learning ("No longer will they teach one another . . . ," v. 34) and creates the desired knowledge of the Lord, thus allowing God to forgive the people. Indeed, the imagery suggests that the people will henceforth never again sin, since the teaching is inscribed on their hearts indelibly. Problem solved.

The most radical depiction of failed moral agency and divine intervention is, of course, in Ezekiel. To be sure, some passages in Ezekiel speak as though moral agency is still a real possibility (notably, ch. 18). It is, in fact, quite difficult to abandon such a way of speaking, which is deeply grounded in the inherited discourse. But whether one should understand these passages as inconsistencies, contextually motivated, or indications of a gradual shift in perspective on Ezekiel's part, there is no doubt, as Jacqueline Lapsley has persuasively demonstrated, that the overall conclusion of the book of Ezekiel is a radical claim that Israel's massive failures of obedience can only be explained

---

11. Marc Zvi Brettler, "Predestination in Deuteronomy 30:1–10," in *Those Elusive Deuteronomists: The Phenomenon of Pan-Deuteronomism*, ed. Linda S. Schearing and Steven L. McKenzie, JSOTSup 268 (Sheffield: Sheffield Academic Press, 1999), 171–88.

on the assumption that the people never, ever possessed functional moral agency.[12] Both the allegories in Ezekiel 16 and 23 and the historical retrospective in Ezekiel 20 depict Israel as "predeterminedly possessed of a depraved nature from birth."[13] Most succinctly, the problem is summed up in the image of the heart of stone that the people possess. *What they are* is the problem. Thus the solution is articulated in God's assertion that he will "remove the heart of stone from your body and give you a heart of flesh; and I will put my spirit into you" (36:26b–27a; cf. 11:19). The result of the transformation is stated as follows: "Thus I will cause you to follow my laws and faithfully to observe my rules" (36:27b; NJPS). In a manner similar to Jeremiah, it appears that the presence of the divine spirit in the people ensures that their future actions will be completely faithful. Problem solved.

Clearly, the formulations regarding the defect in human agency were motivated by a specific contextual crisis—the need to account for the destruction of the kingdom of Judah and to envision a future that would not be merely a repetition of the failures of the past. Thus one may ask whether, as these events receded into the past, the formulations of Deuteronomy, Jeremiah, and Ezekiel were forgotten or had lasting effect on the moral imagination of Second Temple Judaism. Evidence certainly exists for a robust continuation of the discourse of individual and collective moral agency in the Second Temple period. The books of Chronicles develop an understanding of moral responsibility that is more comprehensive and individualized than one finds in the Deuteronomistic History. A new genre of communal penitential psalms (e.g., Neh 1:4–11; 9:6–37; Ezra 9:3–15; Dan 9:4–19; Bar 2:10–3:8) develops a model for acknowledging ancestral and present sin and seeking God's forgiveness and restoration of the people. Narratives of arrogant and sinful kings, such as Manasseh (2 Chr 33:10–17; Pr. Man.) and Nebuchadnezzar (Dan 4) vividly describe their humiliation, acknowledgment of sin, and restoration, presenting them as role models of repentance. Psalms such as Psalm 32 extol the healing power of confession of sin to God. In all of these cases the focus is on what the persons or their ancestors have *done* to displease God. Alongside of these texts, however, one can trace an alternative discourse that demonstrates the continuing power of Jeremiah and Ezekiel's more radical analysis of human sinfulness.

---

12. Jacqueline E. Lapsley, *Can These Bones Live? The Problem of the Moral Self in the Book of Ezekiel*, BZAW 301 (Berlin: de Gruyter, 2000). See especially Ch. 4, "The Shift in the Origin of Moral Selfhood from Intrinsic in Human Beings to Gift from God," 67–107.

13. Lapsley, *Can These Bones Live?* 78.

Before exploring that legacy, however, a second, apparently independent formulation of human moral incapacity that is fully as radical as Ezekiel needs to be introduced into the discussion. This account occurs in the speeches of Eliphaz and Bildad in the book of Job. Although the date of Job is uncertain, most scholars would place it in the early Second Temple period.[14] An immensely learned book, Job draws on international traditions of wisdom literature, but especially those from Mesopotamia.[15] The radically negative anthropology that appears in three passages, however, is without close parallel either within earlier Israelite or Mesopotamian literature. In chapter 4 Eliphaz reports the words of a mysterious voice from a dream-vision: "Can a mortal be righteous before God or a man be pure before his maker? Truly, he does not trust his own servants and attributes fault to his angels. How much less those who dwell in houses of clay, whose foundation is in the dust" (vv. 17-19a). Eliphaz recapitulates this perspective in chapter 15: "What is a mortal that he could be pure, or that one born of woman could be righteous. Truly [God] does not trust his holy ones, and the heavens are not pure in his eyes. How much less one who is loathsome and foul, a human who drinks iniquity like water" (vv. 14-16). And finally, in chapter 25 Bildad adds, "How can a mortal be righteous before God, or how can one born of woman be pure? Truly even the moon is not bright and the stars are not pure in his eyes. How much less a mortal—a worm, a human—a maggot" (vv. 4-6).

In contrast to the texts in Deuteronomy, Jeremiah, and Ezekiel, which served a dual purpose of explanation for disaster and a means of envisioning a solution to the problem, these texts from Job are not interested in constructing a solution but are offered solely as a grim theodicy. They explain human moral corruption as a natural correlate of physical corruption. Indeed, there can be no solution, since the logic is ontological, sketching a chain of being from God, to heavenly beings, to humans and maggots.

It should be noted that this radical perspective is not characteristic of the friends' views in general. Elsewhere in their advice to Job they readily distinguish between the righteous and the wicked among humankind and assume that Job, like other humans, possesses full and free moral agency (e.g., 4:7-8; 8:4-7, 20-22; 11:13-16; 22:21-27). The variety of the friends' arguments is a

14. See Choon Leong Seow, *Job 1-21: Interpretation and Commentary* (Grand Rapids: Eerdmans, 2013), 39-45.

15. For a discussion, see Moshe Weinfeld, "Job and Its Mesopotamian Parallels—A Typological Analysis," in *Text and Context: Old Testament and Semitic Studies for F. C. Fensham*, ed. W. Classen, JSOTS 48 (Sheffield: JSOT, 1988), 217-26; Carol A. Newsom, *The Book of Job: A Contest of Moral Imaginations* (New York: Oxford University Press, 2003), 72-89.

helpful reminder that individuals and cultures often hold a spectrum of beliefs as true that are logically inconsistent with and even contradictory to one another.[16] The divergent models do not create a sense of cognitive dissonance because they are employed in logically different frames of reference. Thus, when the friends construct what one might call a "horizontal" argument, comparing righteous persons with wicked persons, they easily distinguish between good and bad moral agency and treat persons as capable of exercising free moral agency. Even a person who has acted in egregiously immoral ways, as Eliphaz assumes Job has in 22:2–11, can be restored to God's good favor by attending to God's instruction and reforming his desires and conduct accordingly (22:21–27). But when the friends construct a "vertical" argument, comparing humans qua humans with God's righteousness, then all humans are viewed as morally abysmal (4:17–19; 15:14–16; 25:4–6).

As striking as the topos of morally disgusting humanity is in the book of Job, it is largely an isolate within the biblical tradition. Only Ps 90:3–9 suggests a possibly similar connection between human materiality, mortality, and iniquity. In the psalm, however, the language of moral disgust is lacking, and there appears to be a possibility of achieving humility, a "wise heart" (v. 12), and a return of God's favor (v. 17). The Priestly tradition does direct attention to the ontological differences between the divine in its purity and holiness and the human with its inevitable impurities. These inescapable impurities of everyday life, however, are not considered to be moral offenses and are easily addressed by ritual practices.[17] Grave sins, however, including certain sexual sins, bloodshed, and idolatry, create moral impurity that is difficult, if not impossible, to remedy and can even defile the land itself.[18] Such moral sins do evoke disgust, as indicated both by the term "abomination" (תועבה), frequently used to describe them, and the warning that the land may "vomit out" (תקיא) the sinful people (Lev 18:25, 28) as a consequence of these sins. Yet both the Priestly and Holiness traditions in the Pentateuch assume that people are capable of

---

16. Cognitive anthropologist Claudia Strauss, "Analyzing Discourse for Cultural Complexity," in *Finding Culture in Talk: A Collection of Methods*, ed. Naomi Quinn (New York: Palgrave Macmillan, 2005), 203–42, has examined competing inconsistent and incompatible cultural models within informants' discourse. She finds that compartmentalization is the dominant strategy by which persons hold inconsistent ideas, being largely unaware of the inconsistency. Less frequently, informants who are aware of inconsistencies exhibit ambivalence about the inconsistencies. The third strategy involves attempts to integrate ideas into a more complex model (223).

17. Klawans, *Impurity and Sin*, 22–26.

18. Klawans, *Impurity and Sin*, 26–31.

refraining from such immoral behavior. They do not conflate the ontological and moral as do the passages from Job. Indeed, the Holiness Code robustly admonishes obedience by reminding the people that "you shall be holy, for I, Yhwh your God, am holy" (Lev 19:2). Only Ezekiel, whose intellectual horizon is deeply indebted to the Holiness Tradition,[19] draws the conclusion that Israel has been morally incapacitated from its origins. Although his exploration of a radically negative anthropology is motivated by the trauma of the fall of Judah, the concepts and vocabulary with which he explores this idea are drawn from the cultic traditions.

Are there any other negative anthropologies? The Primeval History, which, like Job, shows traces of wisdom elements and familiarity with Mesopotamian traditions, also reflects thoughtfully on issues of anthropology. But the Yahwist (or, better, "non-P") creation narrative in Gen 2–3,[20] though it later comes to play a central role in Christian negative anthropologies, is actually more plausibly read as an etiology for the origin of moral capacity itself, rather than as articulating a negative anthropology.[21] The tree that is off limits to the first humans is described as the tree of the knowledge of good and bad (טוב ורע,

---

19. Michael A. Lyons, *From Law to Prophecy: Ezekiel's Use of the Holiness Code*, LHBOTS 507 (New York: T & T Clark, 2009), makes a strong case for Ezekiel's intentional use of the Holiness Code. Although most scholars recognize some relationship between the two corpora, debate continues as to the nature and direction of the relationship.

20. There is reasonably widespread consensus on the division of sources in the primeval history. David M. Carr, *The Formation of the Hebrew Bible: A New Reconstruction* (New York: Oxford University Press, 2011), 461, concludes that "an early form of the non-P primeval history probably comprised some form of the following narratives: the Eden story of creation and expulsion (Gen 2:4b–3:23 [minus 2:9b; 3:22]); the Cain-Abel story and Cainite genealogy (Gen 4:1–24); the non-P flood story (Gen 6:5–8 [minus 6:6abβ]; 7:1–2, 3b–5, 7, 16b, 10, 12, 17, 22–23aα, 23b; 8:2b–3a, 6–13, 20–22); the story of Noah and his sons (Gen *9:20–27) and a genealogical overview of the descendants of Noah's sons (Gen 10:1b, 8–15, 21, 24–30)." The date of the non-P narrative remains somewhat elusive. Although Carr dates the narrative to the early monarchy (463–69), I find more persuasive those who argue for an early Second Temple date. See, e.g., Terje Stordalen, *Echoes of Eden: Genesis 2–3 and Symbolism of the Eden Garden in Biblical Hebrew Literature*, CBET 25 (Leuven: Peeters, 2000), 206–10; Jean-Louis Ska, "Genesis 2–3: Some Fundamental Questions," in *Beyond Eden: The Biblical Story of Paradise (Genesis 2–3) and Its Reception History*, ed. Konrad Schmid and Christoph Riedweg, FAT 2/34 (Tübingen: Mohr Siebeck, 2008), 1–27; Mark S. Smith, *The Genesis of Good and Evil: The Fall(out) and Original Sin in the Bible* (Louisville: Westminster John Knox, 2019), 45–48.

21. As Smith (*Genesis*, 40) observes, "Genesis 3 dramatizes how [humans] disregard a divine prohibition and thereby acquire the very moral knowledge that makes them morally accountable agents." Smith's analysis of Gen 2–3 is nuanced and thoughtful throughout.

2:17). As often noted, these are very broad terms, encompassing all kinds of valuations, not just moral ones, and the capacity to "know" or discriminate between them is the mark of judicious cognitive maturity (cf. Deut 1:39; 1 Kgs 3:9; Isa 7:15–16), which may decline, along with other capacities, in advanced old age (2 Sam 19:36).[22] Far from forming an ontological contrast with the divine, eating from the tree of knowledge represents the acquisition of a capacity that makes one "like God/the gods" (Gen 3:5, 22). Humans, however, created from the "dust of the earth" (2:7), are not divine beings. Nevertheless, the non-P narrative appears to conclude that humans do not have the capacity to use this ability well, prefacing and concluding its account of the flood narrative with the judgment that "the whole tendency of the plans devised by their mind was nothing but bad, all the time" (כל־יצר מחשבת לבו רק רע כל־היום, 6:5). Even the flood does nothing to change this state of affairs (8:21). Although it will be several centuries before the expression *yēṣer ra'* (יצר רע) is formulated and treated as an objectified aspect of moral psychology, the narrative's pessimism about human ingenuity may point to some sense of structural defect related to our unplanned combination of animal and divine characteristics. In contrast to Deuteronomy, Jeremiah, and Ezekiel, but similar to Job, the non-P narratives do not envision a solution to the problem. Nevertheless, the problem is ultimately treated with some irony, as the only conclusion that God draws is that there is no point in attempting a wholesale cleansing of the earth. With an apparent sense of resignation, God simply promises to ensure the stability of the diurnal and agricultural cycles that support human life (8:22).

## Later Second Temple Developments

One of the consequences of the traumatic events surrounding the destruction of the kingdom of Judah was a greater preoccupation with sin, both at the corporate and at the personal level, and the extant texts demonstrate a variety of ways of thinking about moral agency. As noted above, numerous narratives and prayer texts continue to reflect the classic view of human moral agency and so seek reconciliation with God through the traditional means of confession, repentance, and reminders to God of God's tendency to gracious-

22. Ben Sira thinks so highly of the capacity and its necessity for obedience to God that he engages in a creative rewriting of Gen 2–3 to insist that when God "created human beings out of the earth . . . he filled them with knowledge and understanding, and showed them good and evil" (Sir 17:1a, 7). See Shane Berg, "Ben Sira, the Genesis Creation Accounts, and the Knowledge of God's Will," *JBL* 132 (2013): 139–57.

ness and forgiveness. But what, if anything, becomes of the distinctive model developed by Ezekiel?

Even though Ezekiel was largely concerned with the problem of the sin of the people as a national entity, the first evidence of the influence of Ezekiel's representation of a fundamentally defective moral self occurs not in a communal prayer but in a prayer of the individual—Psalm 51.[23] Variously described as a penitential or a petitionary prayer, this psalm begins with traditional representation of sin as wrongful actions, referring to "my transgressions" (פשעי), "my iniquity" (עוני), and "my sin" (חטאתי) as things "done" (עשיתי) against God. The first suggestion of a more radical view comes in verse 7 where the speaker describes his iniquity and sin as congenital, echoing the perspectives, if not the language of Ezekiel. The invocation of priestly categories of purgation and purity in verse 9 also evokes the conceptual frameworks of Ezekiel. Actual intertextual allusions to Ezekiel occur in verses 12–13, where the creation of a "pure heart" (לב טהור) and the renewal (חדש) of a "steadfast spirit in my body (בקרבי)" echo the "one heart" (לב אחד) and "new spirit" (רוח חדשה) of Ezek 11:19, and the request that God not take away "your holy spirit" (רוח קדשך) alludes to the placement of "My spirit in your body" (רוחי ... בקרבכם) in Ezek 36:27. Thus the fundamental problem is not simply "sins" but a "sinful condition," and the resolution is not merely forgiveness of specific sins but a transformation of the moral being that the speaker is unable to accomplish for himself.[24]

The appropriation of Ezekiel's imagery in a petitionary psalm, however, requires a significant change in perspective. For Ezekiel, Israel was so depraved that it had no awareness of its radically sinful condition until *after* God's intervention. It is only after Israel is transformed that it has sufficient moral understanding so that "you will remember your evil ways . . . and you will loathe yourselves for your iniquities and abhorrent practices" (36:31). Self-directed moral disgust is actually the *result* of the gracious gift of a moral self.[25]

---

23. The majority opinion appears to be that Ps 51 is a post-exilic composition that reflects the influence of Ezekiel (see, e.g., Frank-Lothar Hossfeld and Erich Zenger, *Psalms 2: A Commentary on Psalms 51–100*, trans. Linda M. Maloney [Minneapolis: Fortress, 2005], 18), though some scholars note the similarity but are cautious about defining directions of influence (see, e.g., Lesley R. DiFransico, *Washing Away Sin: An Analysis of the Metaphor in the Hebrew Bible and Its Influence*, BTS 23 [Leuven: Peeters, 2016], 136–42). In my opinion the pattern of verbal similarities and the way in which Psalm 51 employs them makes its dependence on Ezek 36 the most likely reading of the evidence.

24. Brand, *Evil Within*, 40.

25. Lapsley, *Can These Bones Live?*, 139–42.

In order to utter a petitionary prayer about his defective heart and spirit, however, the psalmist of Psalm 51 has to be already aware of and anxious about his sinful condition. In this way a more complex subjectivity is constructed. The speaker is aware of his profound offensiveness to God and yet is powerless to do anything about it—except to appeal to the very God who is offended by his sinfulness.

The speaker's position of helpless vulnerability is, of course, structurally similar to that of earlier lament psalms in which the fearful opponents are the psalmist's human enemies or other threatening forces.[26] This rhetorical parallel will be exploited in various ways in later psalms and prayers as the speaker's sinful condition is depicted as a hostile alien will, either internal or external to the speaker. Thus Psalm 51, which is probably a relatively early Second Temple composition, signals an important new development in thinking about sin and the moral predicament of the individual.

Unfortunately, the literary record of Second Temple Judaism is spotty, and only a small number of petitionary prayers are extant. Miryam Brand has analyzed these, noting a shift from a concern with sins as actions to the problem of an intractable sinful condition.[27] In 11QPs^a 24 (Syr. Ps 155), as in Psalm 51, the speaker begins with traditional language but then introduces novel images of sin as disease and as a parasitic plant:

> The sins of my youth cast far from me, and let my transgressions not be remembered against me. Purify me, O Lord, from (the) evil affliction, and let it not return again to me. Dry up its roots from me, and let its le[av]es not flourish within me. . . . (ll. 11–13a; trans. Brand).

Although "evil affliction" sometimes refers to a pain or disease that is a consequence of sin (cf. 2 Sam 7:14; Isa 53:8; Ps 89:33), Brand rightly concludes that here it refers instead to a sinful condition or the inherent propensity to sin, since the following image of sin as a plant growing within the speaker

---

26. Claus Westermann, *Praise and Lament in the Psalms*, trans. Keith R. Crim and Richard Soulen (Atlanta: John Knox Press, 1981), 193–94. Amy C. Cottrill, *Language, Power, and Identity in the Lament Psalms of the Individual*, LHBOTS 493 (New York: T&T Clark, 2008), 29–57, provides an insightful analysis of the language of bodily helplessness in lament psalms and the ways in which it both establishes an identity for the speaker and constructs "a bid for some degree of relational power" (53) by enlisting God in his support.

27. Brand, *Evil Within*, 37.

refers back to the affliction.[28] The image metaphorizes sin as an objectified, alien entity within the individual. And yet, it is his *own* sin. As in Psalm 51, the speaker's only agency is in recognizing and recoiling from this aspect of himself and pleading with God to transform him by destroying this alien aspect of the self.

Not surprisingly, the depiction of the propensity to sin as an alien element of the self facilitates the assimilation of the newly developing understanding of demonic powers as spirits that not only bring misfortune, disease, and sudden death, but that also create moral blindness and lead persons astray (see Jub 1:20; 7:27; 10:1–2; 12:20).[29] Psalm 119, in which the speaker frequently seeks divine agency for moral strengthening, requests in verse 133, "let not any iniquity (אָוֶן) rule over me (אַל־תַּשְׁלֶט־בִּי)." In an exegetical reinterpretation of this verse in the Aramaic Levi Document, Levi prays, "And let not any satan (שָׂטָן) rule over me, to make me stray from your path" (3:9), recasting iniquity as a demonic spirit. But the difference between sin as an external alien power and as an alien aspect of oneself is quite fluid. In 11QPsᵃ 19 (Plea for Deliverance) the speaker asks for purification from sin and for positive qualities ("a spirit of faithfulness and knowledge") and then prays, "Let not a satan (שָׂטָן) rule over me, or an impure spirit; let pain and evil inclination (יֵצֶר רַע) not have control over me" (lit. "in my bones," ll. 15–16). The parallelism between "satan" and "evil inclination" and between the verbs "rule over" and "have control" implies at least a functional similarity between the two sources of the alien sinful will. This is scarcely surprising, since as demons become active in causing moral harm they operate on the thoughts and moral will of a person, as Abraham observes in his prayer in Jub 12:20–21.

---

28. Brand, *Evil Within*, 39.

29. Traditionally, both in Israel and in the rest of the ancient Near East, demons were associated with causing illness, misfortune, and death. They were not concerned with the moral behavior of persons. The extension of their area of activity appears to be a development of the traditions associated with the Watchers, their mating with human women, and the birth and death of their offspring, the giants. Although 1 En. 19:1 alludes to such a view (in 15:11 the text is uncertain), the major development is found in Jubilees. The sins with which Jubilees is primarily concerned are the "big three" of early Judaism: sexual sins, bloodshed and, especially, idolatry. As James VanderKam has argued, Jubilees is concerned to differentiate between gentiles (who are completely under the sway of demons) and Jews (who are at risk of being misled by demons but who can resist them, with God's help). See his essay "The Demons in the 'Book of Jubilees,'" in *Die Dämonen: Die Dämonologie der israelitisch-jüdischen und frühchristlichen Literatur im Kontext ihrer Umwelt*, ed. Armin Lange, Hermann Lichtenberger, and Diethard Römheld (Tübingen: Mohr Siebeck, 2003), 339–64, at 346–47.

The Plea for Deliverance is perhaps the earliest attestation of the objectification of the *yēṣer ra'* as an aspect of anthropology (cf. also CD 2:16), though in Second Temple Judaism the term never achieves the central role that it has in later rabbinic moral thought.[30] But its assimilation to imagery of the demonic is also attested in another text, likely from the second-century BCE, Barkhi Nafshi. These are thanksgiving psalms, and so, in contrast to the petitionary prayers, the speaker is one who has already experienced divine transformation. In one remarkable passage the author exploits the ancient Israelite anthropology that distributes moral proclivities and actions to various body parts.[31] But whereas such references are largely made unselfconsciously in older literature, here the author constructs a veritable catalog of parts of the body and the ways in which each has been transformed through the agency of God from being morally problematic to being morally positive. Behind this elaborate development stand the key tropes from Deuteronomy, Jeremiah, Ezekiel, and Psalm 51 for the transformation of the moral body.

> (. . .) You have commanded my heart, and my kidneys you have taught well, lest they forget your statutes. [On my heart] you [have enjoined] your law, on my kidneys you have engraved it; and you have prevailed upon me, so that I pursue after you[r] ways (. . .) 10 [the heart of stone] you have [re]buked out of me, and have set a pure heart in its place. The evil inclination [you] have rebuked [out of my kidneys] [. . .] *vacat* [and the spirit of ho]liness you have set in my heart. Lechery of the eyes you have removed from me, and they (lit. it) gazed upon [all] [your ways. The s]tiffness of neck you have expelled from me, and you have made it into humility. A wrathful nose you have removed [from me, and have set] [in me a spirit of lo]ng suffering. (4Q436 1i 5b–6, 10–1ii 4; par. 4Q435 2i 1–5; trans. Brand, adapted).

This passage constructs something of a spiritual exercise in which the various parts of the body (heart, kidneys, mouth, tongue, foot, hand, eyes, neck, nose)

30. Ishay Rosen-Zvi, *Demonic Desires: Yetzer Hara and the Problem of Evil in Late Antiquity* (Philadelphia: University of Pennsylvania Press, 2011), 44–64, reviews the development of ideas about the *yēṣer ra'* in Second Temple Judaism.

31. For an overview of the body-based anthropology of ancient Israel, see Hans Walter Wolff, *Anthropology of the Old Testament*, trans. Margaret Kohl (Philadelphia: Fortress, 1974); and Thomas Staubli and Sylvia Schroer, *Body Symbolism in the Bible*, trans. Linda M. Maloney (Collegeville, MN: Liturgical Press, 2001).

are objectified as loci of moral concern. The evil inclination, too, is placed among other moral deficits and given a place within the body. The divine agency over the speaker is expressed through a series of forceful verbs, but the use of "rebuke" (גער) is especially noteworthy, since it is the verb used for the expelling of demons.[32] Even if used metaphorically, the verb aptly configures the heart of stone and the evil inclination as internal alien wills from which the speaker seeks to be freed.

In the series of texts that I have examined so far, what I have been attempting to trace is a shift in how the problem of sin and its solution are framed. The classic model presents sin as an offense creating a breach that requires resolution through social practices of atonement and reconciliation. But the texts from the exilic and Second Temple period to which I have drawn attention present sin as a problem that first and foremost requires transformation of a human who is posited as in some way structurally morally defective and thus continually and consistently offensive to God. Consequently, this transformation cannot be effected by the human for himself but must be a gift from God. At most the human can recognize and be appalled by the structural defect in himself, sometimes distancing himself from it by envisioning it as a kind of alien force or will within himself. This new stance of piety is characterized by the moral pathos of a being who is a victim of sin as much as a perpetrator of it. But, as is apparent in Barkhi Nafshi, as each site of the body is a locus for anxiety-producing moral flaws, so each is also a site for God's intimate act of repair and moral healing.[33] Reducing the scope of human agency and magnifying the negative representation of oneself becomes a means of enhancing and experiencing the compassion and power of the divine.

One might note, however, that these texts create their moral vision by deliberately avoiding the more radical critiques of moral agency found in Ezekiel and in Job. Ezekiel had no place for the appealing moral subject painfully aware of his defects and seeking divine aid—Ezekiel's view is of the human as

---

32. Brand (*Evil Within*, 46–48) and Eibert J. C. Tigchelaar ("The Evil inclination in the Dead Sea Scrolls, with a Re-Edition of 4Q468i [4QSectarian Text?]," in *Empsychoi Logoi: Religious Innovations in Antiquity; Studies in Honour of Pieter Willem van der Horst*, ed. A. Houtman, A. de Jong, and M. Misset-van de Weg, AJEC 73 [Leiden: Brill, 2009], 351–52) disagree about whether the *yēṣer raʿ* is an external or an internal entity but both agree that the language casts it in demonic terms.

33. Menahem Kister ("'Inclination of the Heart of Man,' the Body and Purification from Evil," in *Meghillot: Studies in the Dead Sea Scrolls VIII*, ed. Moshe Bar-Asher and Devorah Dimant [Jerusalem: Bialik Institute and Haifa University Press, 2010], 243–84 [Hebrew]) emphasizes the therapeutic nature of the transformation.

morally abject. Only after transformation is any moral consciousness possible, and then only as a form of self-loathing (6:9; 20:43; 36:31).[34] Eliphaz and Bildad's human is morally disgusting in the way that a maggot is viscerally disgusting. One might not think these radically negative depictions provide particularly promising material for exploring the potentialities of the spiritual life. But in fact, the opposite is the case. The authors of the Qumran Hodayot perceived that paradox which has intrigued ascetic religious virtuosos in many traditions—the close connection between degradation and exaltation. Drawing on Peter Berger's analysis, I have referred to this phenomenon as the cultivation of the "masochistic sublime."[35] Indeed, self-denigration can become a kind of engine for creating an experience of transformation and elevation. As I discuss below, the Hodayot construct a hyper-negative anthropology, drawing on previously unexploited texts from Job to establish exegetically potent intertextual connections with creation traditions from Genesis, resulting in the extraordinary claim that human moral depravity is implicit in the very materiality of human existence. Moreover, humans are morally depraved because God created them to be so. This is a condition that exceeds the logic of traditional forms of atonement and reconciliation. Such a shocking anthropology, however, proves to be the precondition for God's wondrous action in transforming certain elect humans through an act of second creation, envisioned via an interpretation of Ezek 36:25–27 as the implantation of God's spirit. But in contrast to Ezekiel, where the result is simply the creation of a functioning human moral agent who can now fulfill God's commandments, the Hodayot exploit the undeveloped potential of Ezekiel's imagery. By exploring what it means for God's holy spirit to be placed in elect humans, the Hodayot conclude that the result is a purified and proleptically divinized subject. Though still a bodily being, the human who now bears within himself the divine spirit has been endowed with a purity that enables him to be united with the angels themselves in a congregation of praise and to take up his station with the divine beings.[36] That is to say, although the Hodayot are certainly interested in

---

34. Lapsley, *Can These Bones Live?*, 139–42.

35. The classic study of Peter Berger, *The Sacred Canopy: Elements of a Sociological Theory of Religion* (Garden City, NY: Doubleday, 1967), 64, 75, discusses the logic of religious masochism (though I disagree with his analysis of the book of Job). My discussion occurs in Carol A. Newsom, *The Self as Symbolic Space: Constructing Identity and Community at Qumran*, STDJ 52 (Leiden: Brill, 2004), 219–21.

36. Esther Chazon, "Lowly to Lofty: The Hodayot's Use of Liturgical Traditions to Shape Sectarian Identity and Religious Experience," *RevQ* 26 (2013): 3–19; Philip Alexander, *The*

the moral aspects of the transformation (e.g., 1QHᵃ 8:22–23), their distinctive contribution is to explore its spiritual and indeed ontological aspects.

But how do they reach these extraordinary conclusions? If one collects and sorts the imagery associated with negative anthropology in the Hodayot, it quickly appears that the negative imagery is largely associated with the mortal and material aspect of humanity—most frequently dust, clay, and flesh, with occasional references to corpses, worms, and maggots.[37] This materiality is correlated with immorality ("guilt" [אשמה], "sin" [חטאה], "iniquity" [עולה])[38] and with "impurity" (most often נדה).[39] Though נדה can sometimes be a generalized term for impurity, in the Hodayot its explicitly gendered nature is underscored by other sexualized or feminized imagery.

Elsewhere I have given a more detailed account of the intertextual allusions that the Hodayot employ to generate this extraordinary depiction of human nature, but here I can only give an abbreviated account.[40] One of the most common designations of the human is a "vessel (יצר)" of dust" and "a vessel of clay, kneaded with water" (9:23; cf. 11:24–25; 21:10–11; 1QS 11:21), apparent allusions to Gen 2:7 where God "formed" (וייצר) the first human out of "dust (עפר) of the soil." That the allusion is specifically to Genesis and not simply to a common image is indicated by ten clear intertextual allusions in the Hodayot to Gen 3:19 ("until you return to the soil from which you were taken; for you are dust and to dust you will return").[41] In Genesis, however, these images connote mortality but not immorality. Similarly, though Genesis 3 gives an etiology of sexual reproduction, naming Eve as mother of all the living, nei-

---

*Mystical Texts: Songs of the Sabbath Sacrifice and Related Manuscripts* (London: T&T Clark International, 2006), 101–10.

37. In the Hodayot the term "dust" (עפר) occurs 35 times, "clay" (חמר) some 17 times, and "dirt" (אדמה) 1 time. "Flesh" (בשר) occurs 22 times. As Jörg Frey has demonstrated, "flesh" takes on a negative connotation in the Hodayot that is distinct from the neutral use that predominates in the Hebrew Bible. See his essay, "Flesh and Spirit in the Palestinian Jewish Sapiential Tradition and in the Qumran Texts: An Inquiry into the Background of Pauline Usage," in *The Wisdom Texts from Qumran and the Development of Sapiential Thought*, ed. Charlotte Hempel, Armin Lange, and Hermann Lichtenberger, BETL 159 (Leuven: Leuven University Press, 2002), 367–404.

38. For אשמה, see 1QHᵃ 5:32; 22:8–9; 23:13; for חטאה, see 5:32; 9:24; 19:23; for עולה, see 21:30, 35.

39. Cf. 1QHᵃ 5:32; 9:24; 19:14–15; 20:28.

40. Carol A. Newsom, "Deriving Negative Anthropology through Exegetical Activity: The Hodayot as Case Study," in *Is There a Text in This Cave? Studies in the Textuality of the Dead Sea Scrolls in Honour of George J. Brooke*, ed. Ariel Feldman, Maria Cioată, and Charlotte Hempel, STDJ 119 (Leiden: Brill, 2017), 258–74.

41. Newsom, "Deriving Negative Anthropology through Exegetical Activity," 265.

ther Genesis nor the Priestly tradition draws the conclusion that humans are therefore rendered essentially impure.

What allows the authors of the Hodayot to reinterpret the creation traditions in such a radical fashion? Interpretive practices in Second Temple Judaism were not arbitrary. But there was a sense that the meaning of a text did not lie exclusively in its surface features. New dimensions of meaning could be unlocked by juxtaposing texts that used the same or similar words and concepts. For the Hodayot, the key texts that unlock the negative anthropology of the creation traditions lie in Job. That book contains a surprising number of references to human creation, most of which, however, are not in themselves negative. That the Hodayot is specifically drawing on Job is demonstrated from its citation of a series of unique or highly distinctive phrases from that book, such as "pinched off from clay" (Job 33:6—unique to Job),[42] "dust and ashes" (Job 30:19; 42:6; elsewhere, only Gen 18:27),[43] and "born of woman" (Job 14:1; 15:14; 25:4—also unique to Job).[44]

The phrase "born of woman" allows one to trace the exegetical connections that the Hodayot forge to use Job to unlock the hidden meaning of Genesis 2–3. First of all, two of the three occurrences of "born of woman" in Job are in the negative anthropologies of Eliphaz (15:14) and Bildad (25:4)[45] where the human is described as "abhorrent" (נתעב), "foul" (נאלח) and "impure" or "guilty" (לא זכו). The other occurrence in 14:1 introduces the passage in verse 4 in which Job protests that no one can make "a clean thing (טהר) from an unclean one (טמא)," referring to humankind. This proximity facilitates the transfer of a negative valence to the phrase "born of woman" and allows for a link to references to female impurity that can contaminate men who come in contact with it (e.g., Lev 20:18). Although the extant Hodayot do not clearly allude to Ps 51:7 ("in sin my mother conceived me"), it is likely that they understood the physical aspects of birth render all persons congenitally sinful and thus impure.[46] Second, the book of Job also makes other references to birth from the female body that link to creation accounts, as in Job 1:21 where birth from the mother's womb and the return to earth's womb are paralleled, thus facilitating a connection with the creation account

---

42. Cf. 1QHᵃ 18:6, 20:27; cf. the similar Maśkil hymn in 1QS 11:22.

43. Cf. 1QHᵃ 18:7; 20:30.

44. Cf. 1QHᵃ 5:31; 21:9–10; 23:13–14.

45. It is possible that Bildad's reference to "worm" (רמה) and "maggot" (תולעה) is the source for these terms in the Hodayot (4:31; 19:15; 20:28), though the evidence is indecisive.

46. Klawans, *Impurity and Sin*, 75–88, demonstrates that the systems of ritual and moral impurity are no longer distinguished at Qumran as they are in earlier biblical texts.

in Genesis 2–3 and especially to 3:19 ("until you return to the ground, for from it you were taken; for dust you are, and to dust you shall return"). Job 10:8–15 describes the formation of the human fetus, using the poetic pair dust and clay to describe the being whom God watches and judges for its inevitable sinfulness ("Consider that you fashioned me like clay; will you then turn me back into dust?" Job 10:9, NJPS). The final piece of evidence that the book of Job plays a pivotal role in the development of this negative anthropology is the *Niedrigkeitsdoxologie* from the Songs of the Maśkil, which refers to "my foundation of dust" (סוד עפרי; 4Q511 Frags. 28–29 l. 4),[47] a clear allusion to Eliphaz's speech in Job 4:19 ("whose foundation is in the dust," [אשר־בעפר יסודם]). Thus the Joban texts become the exegetical linchpins for a radical reinterpretation of the creation "from the dust" in Gen 2:7 and the means for an equally radical association of birth from a woman with congenital sinfulness and impurity. How complexly these allusions are woven together in the Hodayot is evident in the text from col. 20:27–30, with intertextual allusions indicated.[48]

> As for me, from dust [you] took [me (*Gen 3:19*), and from clay] I was pinched off (*Job 33:6*), as a source of impurity and obscene shame (*~Lev 20:18*), a heap of dust and a thing kneaded [with water (*~Gen 2:7*), a council of magg]ots, a dwelling of darkness. And there is a return to dust (*Gen 3:19; cf. Job 10:9; 34:15*) for the vessel of clay (*~Jer 18:3–6; Isa 29:16; 45:9*) at the time of [your] anger [. . .] dust returns to that from which it was taken (*Gen 3:19*). What can dust and ashes (*Job 30:19; 42:6; cf. Gen 18:27*) reply [concerning your judgment?. . . .]

47. The Songs of the Maśkil is a Qumran sectarian text that includes passages strikingly similar to the Songs of the Sabbath Sacrifice and the Hodayot. Given the fragmentary remains of all three compositions, it is not possible to say whether the Songs of the Maśkil borrow directly from these other texts or simply imitate characteristic passages. Only the Hodayot and the Songs of the Maśkil contain *Niedrigkeitsdoxologien*. Given the number and distribution of these passages in the Hodayot, it is clear that they are originally developed as a feature of these compositions and borrowed or imitated by the Songs of the Maśkil. For the original identification and description of these passages, see Heinz-Wolfgang Kuhn, *Enderwartung und gegenwärtiges Heil: Untersuchungen zu den Gemeindeliedern von Qumran*, SUNT 3 (Göttingen: Vandenhoeck & Ruprecht, 1966), 27–29.

48. The symbol ~ indicates a textual similarity that points to a biblical text but is not strictly an intertextual allusion. See the criteria established by Julie A. Hughes, *Scriptural Allusions and Exegesis in the Hodayot*, STDJ 59 (Leiden: Brill, 2006), 41–55.

The abject creature described in the Hodayot would, of course, not have this knowledge about himself. But since the Hodayot are, generically, thanksgiving psalms, they are the utterances of a being who has already been transformed by God. The capacity for understanding the profound mysteries of existence, including the nature of human existence and its role in the divine plan, is explained in a phrase repeated some six times in the Hodayot.[49] Such understanding comes from "the spirit that you have placed in me" (see 4:29; 5:36; 8:20, 29; 20:15; 21:34). As John Levison, among others, has demonstrated, the phrase is an adaptation of Ezek 36:27 ("I will place my spirit into you").[50] Several times the spirit is referred to as "your holy spirit" (e.g., 8:20; 20:15) and is both the source of the speaker's moral agency (8:29) and his knowledge of divine mysteries (20:15). The "purifying waters" that God sprinkles on Israel in Ezek 36:25 are interpreted here as the sprinkling of "your holy spirit" on the elect to purify them (15:10; 23:29, 34).

The purpose and result of this transformation, however, far exceeds what Ezekiel envisions and explicitly reverses the negative anthropology of Job:

> For the sake of your glory you have purified a mortal from sin, so that he may sanctify himself for you from all impure abominations and from faithless guilt, so that he might be united with the children of your truth and in the lot with your holy ones, so that a corpse-infesting maggot might be raised up from the dust to the council of [your] t[ruth], and from a spirit of perversion to the understanding that comes from you, and so that he may take (his) place before your face with the everlasting host and the [eternal] spirit[s], and so that he may be renewed together with all that i[s] and will be and with those who have knowledge in a community of jubilation (19:13–17).

This form of liturgical union with the worshipping congregation of the angels has rightly been identified as a form of mystical praxis.[51] Thus the benefits conveyed through the divine transformation of the formerly abhorrent human are not simply a reconciliation with God but access to a realized eschatological joy.

---

49. These passages occur in compositions that are either explicitly associated with the Maśkil or, where the incipit is missing, show other characteristic features of those texts.

50. John R. Levison, *Filled with the Spirit* (Grand Rapids: Eerdmans, 2009), 188–89.

51. Chazon, "Lowly to Lofty," 15; Alexander, *Mystical Texts*, 101–10.

## Conclusion

Although traditional formulations of moral agency, sin, and atonement continued robustly throughout the Second Temple period, alongside of them there developed alternative discourses that shifted concern away from the commission of specific sins to the problem of an innate sinful condition. Although one could consider these developments simply as the creation of highly negative views of human nature and treat them as a kind of religious pessimism, they were also employed to highlight the transforming power of God's spirit and to construct new forms of religious experience that promised a sense of moral transformation, intimacy with God, and even mystical acts of liturgical communion with the angels themselves. These developments explored the religious paradox that it is only by immersing oneself in deep abjection that one is prepared for exaltation.

# CHAPTER FIVE

# THE HIGH PRIEST IN BEN SIRA 50

*The High Priest Is an Incorporative Divine Messiah and
At-One-Ment Takes Place through Worship in the Microcosm*

CRISPIN FLETCHER-LOUIS

In a paper delivered at a 2016 conference in Saint Andrews I proposed that in 1 Kgs 3–4 Solomon functions as a representative, incorporative king.[1] He represents God, is exalted as a new Adam, and sums up God's people by taking their interests on his heart. If my reading of 1 Kgs 3–4 is anywhere near the mark, those chapters pose a question: Why are there not more texts that depict Israel's king as a representative of God and of God's people? The sophisticated theology of kingship in 1 Kgs 3–4 is exceptional. The king's Adamic and representative character does not figure prominently in the Hebrew Bible. Also, there is a striking paucity of evidence for a widely shared interest in a coming royal messiah at the turn of the eras. Such evidence as there is lacks the density of symbolic or mythological meaning invested in Solomon in 1 Kgs 3–4.[2]

One likely reason for the lack of hope for a royal messiah points also to an answer to the puzzle of the absence of a widespread interest in the king's symbolic and representative functions: after the exile the priesthood played roles that kings played at other times and in other nations.[3] Israel's Scriptures parcel out the prerogatives of kingship to others: to all humanity (Gen 1:26–28; Ps 8), to Israel (Isa 55:3) (who is truly God's "son" [Exod 4:22–23], against the claims of

---

1. Published as Crispin H. T. Fletcher-Louis, "King Solomon, a New Adam and Incorporative Representative of God's People (1 Kings 3–4): A Text That Supports N. T. Wright on Paul and the Messiah," in *One God, One People, One Future: Essays in Honour of N. T. Wright*, ed. John Anthony Dunne and Eric Lewellen (London: SPCK, 2018), 126–47.

2. Crispin Fletcher-Louis, *Christological Origins: The Emerging Consensus and Beyond*, vol. 1 in *Jesus Monotheism* (Eugene, OR: Wipf & Stock, 2015), 220–30.

3. Fletcher-Louis, *Jesus Monotheism*, 220–30.

the Pharaoh), and to the high priest. From the introduction of the office (Exod 28–29) onwards, the high priest is given the paraphernalia, and some of the responsibilities and privileges that belonged to kings in the ancient world.[4] At the same time, Torah either has no place for a king, or it permits one but denies him many of the rights typically granted to royal persons (Deut 17:14–20).

The combination of such scriptural evidence and historical data leads to a hypothesis. If the high priest often functioned as a royal figure, then perhaps the Deuteronomistic History's incorporative, representative vision of kingship was transferred to the priesthood in other texts. Preliminary confirmation of this hypothesis can be found in Exodus 28, where Aaron carries the names of the twelve tribes on his breast piece and shoulders, engraved on the stones of the ephod (28:9–12, 21). The panel of twelve stones of the breast piece was placed over Aaron's heart in order that he might "continually bear the judgment of the sons of Israel *on his heart* before the LORD" (v. 30). That prescription is evocative of the way Solomon had a "listening heart" (1 Kgs 3:9), which meant he was able to exercise wise judgment of his people (1 Kgs 3:16–25). In 1 Kings 4 the king is given a "largeness of heart like the sand of the seashore" (v. 29) that is coextensive with the Israel that had become as "many, as the sand by the sea in multitude" (4:20a), thereby acting as their empathic, incorporative figurehead.[5] In a similar way, Aaron's garments may be designed to visualize the notion that the nation's ruler is to have the people on his heart: their interests are to be his interests.

If it is legitimate to interpret the position and function of the high priest's breast piece in this way, we would expect the high priest's *representative* role to feature more widely in Second Temple traditions. And we should not be surprised to find that other features of the portrayal of Solomon in 1 Kings crop up in priestly material. That is precisely what we find in the Wisdom of Ben Sira, a text that shows that, at least by the third century BCE, if not long before, the deep well of symbolism that had sometimes been used to water imaginative portrayals of Israel's king had been directed to the irrigation of the garden of priestly theology.

## Ben Sira 50

The Hebrew wisdom collection known as Ben Sira, which was written in the early decades of the second century BCE (ca. 195–175), builds to a climax in a long praise of the high priest Simeon ben Johanan in its fiftieth chapter

---

4. Fletcher-Louis, *Jesus Monotheism*, 224–27.
5. Fletcher-Louis, "King Solomon," esp. 129–35, 139–45.

(50:1–21). For Ben Sira it is priests—Simeon, Aaron (45:6–22, 25), Phinehas (45:23–25)—who, more than any other, deserve devotion and imaginative, literary attention (cf. 7:27–31). The hymnic praise of Simeon follows six chapters of praise of the pious men of old (chs. 44–49), which include briefer treatments of the best of the kings—David (47:2–11) and Solomon (47:12–23). As figures of a God-ordained history, Israel's kings are celebrated for their exemplary piety (cf. 48:16–17, 22; 49:1–4).[6] But Ben Sira knows that Solomon went astray in his later years (Sir 47:19–21, cf. 1 Kgs 10–11), according to the Deuteronomist, by his wanton behavior sowing seeds of disunity that led to the division of the kingdom (Sir 47:20–21, cf. 47:23–25; 48:15–16; 49:4).

As is now well known, Ben Sira not only takes a dim view of the majority of Israel's kings, he also transfers royal privileges and responsibilities to the high priest. The evidence for that appears most strikingly in his treatment of Aaron (using the language of kingship in 45:12, 15, 25) and of Simeon's royal responsibilities in 50:1–4.[7] In a close study of Ben Sira's treatment of Solomon, Pancratius C. Beentjes has also suggested that the description of Solomon's wise heart in 1 Kgs 3:9 is used in Ben Sira's prayers for the high priesthood (Sir 45:26; 50:23).[8] Solomon's prayer for a listening heart (1 Kgs 3:9) is central to the presentation of him as an ideal, representative and empathic king. And there are reasons to think that the connection Beentjes has made is but the tip of a larger conceptual and literary iceberg.

For Ben Sira, it is the priesthood and the divinely appointed temple service that provides unity—*at-one-ment*—on a truly cosmic scale. And in his praise of Simeon, Ben Sira says that the true high priest possesses all the symbolic, representative identities that characterized the early reign of Solomon. Simeon, as exemplary performer of his office, is a true Adam and representative of the nation. But he is a representative of much more besides, holding together all of creation in mysterious unity through a civil and temple service that entails multiple representative functions. The remainder of this essay explores how this is so. First, I consider the ways in which Ben Sira 50 places all creation in

---

6. Ben Sira/Sirach 47:15 might allude to 1 Kgs 4:29 ET (Heb. 5:9). See Patrick W. Skehan and Alexander A. DiLella, *The Wisdom of Ben Sira*, AYB 39 (New York: Doubleday, 1987), 524.

7. For recent discussions see Fletcher-Louis, *Jesus Monotheism*, vol. 1, 220–25; Pancratius Cornelis Beentjes, "The Book of Ben Sira: Some New Perspectives at the Dawn of the 21st Century," in *Goochem in Mokum, Wisdom in Amsterdam*, ed. Pancratius Cornelis Beentjes, OtSt 68 (Leiden: Brill, 2016), 1–19, at 6–11.

8. Pancratius Cornelis Beentjes, "'The Countries Marveled at You': King Solomon in Ben Sira 47:12–22," in *"Happy the One who Meditates on Wisdom" (Sir. 14.20). Collected Essays on the Book of Ben Sira*, CEBT 43 (Leuven: Peeters, 2006), 135–44, at 143.

the Jerusalem temple and its liturgy. Second, I explore several ways in which the high priest is symbolically, or ritually, identified with the lead characters in the drama of creation and history.

## Hebrew Ben Sira 49:16–50:21

Ben Sira 49:16–50:21 is a rich and complex text, attested in one Hebrew manuscript (HB) and in Greek (G) and Syriac (S) translations that, in several places, testify to an older, more original Hebrew.[9] The case for thinking it a profound statement of at-one-ment through temple worship and priestly representation can be made on the basis of the Hebrew (with occasional help from G), which is the basis for the following translation.[10]

> [16] Shem, Seth and Enosh were cared for,
> and above all the living creatures
> is/was the beauty of a human/of Adam.
> [50:1] Greatest of his brothers, beauty of his people,
> (was) Simeon ben Johanan, the priest,
> In whose generation the house was taken care of/visited,
> and in whose days the palace-sanctuary was strengthened,
> [2] In whose days the wall was built,
> the corners of the habitation in the King's palace-sanctuary,
> [3] In whose generation the water-pool was dug,
> a cistern like the sea in its tumult.
> [4] Who was concerned for his people (to preserve them) from
> robbery,
> and who strengthened his city against the enemy.
> [5] How adorned he was as he gazed forth from the tent,
> and as he went forth from the house of the veil.
> [6] As a star of light from among the clouds,
> and a full moon bringing understanding in/
> determining the festival days.
> [7] And as the crimson sun lighting up the King's
> palace-sanctuary,

9. For reasons beyond the scope of this essay I consider 49:16 an integral part of the literary unit that runs to 50:21, though I shall sometimes refer to the passage simply as Ben Sira 50.

10. For the Hebrew, see Pancratius Cornelis Beentjes, *The Book of Ben Sira in Hebrew*, VTSup 68 (Leiden: Brill, 1997).

and as a bow appears in the cloud.

⁸ As blossom on branches in their season/in festival days,

and as a lily in streams of water.

As a shoot of Lebanon on summer days.

⁹ And as fire of incense upon the offering,

as vessels of gold [. . . . .]

which is held in place on delightful stones.

¹⁰ As a green olive full of berries,

as an oil tree laden with branches.

¹¹ When he wrapped himself in the garments of glory,

and clothed himself in garments of beauty,

When he ascended upon the altar there was majesty,

and he made splendid the court of the holy place.

¹² When he received the sacrificial portions from his brothers'
hands,

and he himself stood over the arranged pieces/ordered
assembly.

Around him was the crown of his sons,

As saplings of cedar trees in Lebanon,

and as willows of the brook they encircled him.

¹³ All the sons of Aaron in their glory

and the fire offerings of the LORD in their hands

in front of all the congregation of Israel.

¹⁴ Until he finished ministering at the altar,

and set in order the arrangements of the Most High,

¹⁵ [And stretched out his hand over the flagon,

and poured a drink offering from the blood of the grape.

He poured it out to the foundation of the altar,

a pleasing odor to the Most High, the King of all.]¹¹

¹⁶ Then the sons of Aaron, the priests, sounded forth

on trumpets of turned metal-work.

So they blasted and made heard the majestic sound,

to make remembrance before the Most High.

¹⁷ *"All flesh together"* (Isa 40:5) were hastened,

and fell on their faces, to the earth,

To worship before the Most High,

before the Holy One of Israel.

¹⁸ And he raised his voice, the song,

---

11. Verse 15 is missing in the Hebrew, but should be restored on the basis of the G and S.

and over the tumult sweet strains of praise resounded.[12]
[19] And all the people of the earth/land gave a ringing shout
in prayer before the Merciful One,
Until he finished ministering at the altar,
and with his judgments he touched him.
[20] Then he went down and raised his hands
over all the congregation of Israel,
And the blessing of the LORD was on his lips,
and in the Name of the LORD he beautified himself,
[21] and they fell down (in worship) again a second time,
to r[eceive a blessing] from his face.

## Priestly and Temple Service Makes All Present to God

Ben Sira likes to think of the Deity as "God of (the) all (אלהי הכל)" (36:1; 45:23, cf. Gk. 18:1; 24:8a; 50:22; Heb. 51:12d), and the praise of Simeon brings into view the whole panoply of creation in a dramatic procession that climaxes with a collective act of worship of "the Most High" (50:14-21). There is mention of "the sea" (v. 3), "the earth" (vv. 17, 19), elemental realities ("light," "fire" and "stones," vv. 6, 9), creation's fecundity (vv. 8, 10, 12: "blossom on branches, a lily, a shoot of Lebanon, a green olive, an oil tree laden with branches, seedlings of cedar trees, willows of the brook"), the fat of the land (in the sacrificial portions at the altar; v. 12a), and the sun, moon, and stars of the heavens (vv. 6-7).

There are human beings. To begin with, there is a lineage from "Shem, Seth, and Enosh," and Adam, whose beauty is "over all the living creatures" (49:16). There are priests: one who serves as the nation's political (50:1-4) and liturgical head (vv. 5-13) in sacrificial (vv. 11-13) and musical worship (vv. 16-19), and in prayer (v. 19). In response to his leadership, the one is joined by the many; first a college of fellow priests, his "sons" (vv. 12-14, 16), and then by the whole congregation of Israel (vv. 17-21, cf. v. 4a). And there is the one God: "the King," "the Most High," the "Holy One of Israel," the "Merciful One," "Yahweh" (vv. 2, 7, 14, 16, 17, 19, 20). The movement from the one (high priest) to the many priests and people worshipping in the presence of God gives the impression that Sir 50 is a great literary procession, recalling the grand civic

12. Heb. has ועל המון העריכו נרו which is almost certainly an error. For my translation (following G), see Skehan and Di Lella, *Wisdom,* 547, 549.

processions that marked the Hellenistic age. It is a procession that builds, like a musical score for many parts, to a harmonious crescendo. At its climax, in verses 14–20, there are trumpets blasting, there are people genuflecting, there is a raised voice over the tumult, a ringing shout in prayer, a dramatic final blessing and a second prostration. The "tumult" (המון, v. 18b) is not a disordered one. On the contrary, the pageant Ben Sira paints is a beautiful and glorious "ordering of the arrangements of the Most High" (v. 14a). The repetition of the word "all" encourages the perception that here heaven and earth and all their host are before the readers' eyes (49:16b, כל חי; 50:13a, כל בני אהרן, v. 13b; כל קהל ישראל; v. 17, כל בשר; v. 19a, כל עם הארץ; v. 20b, על כל קהל ישראל). The statement in verse 17 that "all flesh *together* were hastened and fell on their faces to the earth to worship," with its adverbial יחדו "together, as *one*," is a signature moment that underscores the point of it all. Here is *all of heaven and earth and its people experiencing at-one-ment, unity, in worship of the one God*.

The ways in which the passage presents all of creation in unified worship of the one God emerge fully when we examine carefully the author's choice of language and his arrangement of his material. The passage is a poetic totality, gathering up, by means of subtle symbolic references, all creation.

The praise of the high priest can be laid out according to theme and language in distinct literary blocks:

- Sir 49:16–50:4—Simeon's civil and political position as servant of his own people and in relation to all humanity;
- 50:5–7—the high priest's likeness to the heavenly bodies as he comes out of the sanctuary;
- 50:8–10—his likeness to vegetation and incense;
- 50:11–13—his service at the bronze altar, surrounded by his brothers the priests;
- 50:14–19—the worship of the whole congregation, led by the priests, in response to Simeon's completion of his ministry;
- 50:20–21—his blessing of the congregation (Num 6:22–25) and their final worshipful prostration.

On careful examination, the whole of 49:16–50:21 is further organized according to the heptadic structure that governs the two literary high points of the Priestly material in the Pentateuch: the seven days of creation (Gen 1) and the reflex of those seven days, at Sinai, in seven speeches to Moses, which contain the instructions for the setting up of the tabernacle in Exodus 25–31.

Scholars have long noted connections between the seven days of Genesis 1 and the seven divine speeches that Moses hears atop Sinai. In another study, I have presented reasons to think that Ben Sira knew there was a complex heptadic intratextuality between Genesis 1 and Exodus 25–31 and that it provided him a thematic and theological framework both for his praise of the high priest in chapter 50 and for the self-praise of Wisdom in Sir 24:1–23.[13]

Some of the ways in which 49:16–50:21 correspond to the details of the Priestly heptameron can be readily identified in the translation of the Hebrew as laid out above. Ben Sira 50:3 says that in the days of Simeon "a water-pool (מקוה) was dug . . . like the sea (כים)."[14] This corresponds both to the third day of creation (Gen 1:9–10), when a gathering of waters (מקוה המים) was gathered together in one place to be called "the seas (ימים)," and to the third speech to Moses (Exod 30:17–21) wherein the lawgiver is told to make a bronze laver for the temple forecourt. (The temple version of that basin is called the "sea" in 1 Kgs 7:23–26.) In Ben Sira 50:5–7 a series of similes compares Simeon's appearance from the sanctuary to "a star of light," "a full moon," "the crimson sun," and a rainbow. So, following on the making of a sea-like structure, verses 5–7 evoke the *fourth* day of creation (Gen 1:14–19) when God made the sun, moon and stars (cf. Sir 43:1–12).

At a glance, it is not hard to see how days six and seven might be evoked in the distinct blocks at vv. 11–13 and 14–19. In the former case, there are multiple echoes of Psalm 8, the psalm whose idealized vision for humanity parallels both linguistically and conceptually the description of the creation of the image and likeness of God on day six. Simeon and his fellow ministers have the glory (כבוד) and splendor (הדר) of the perfect humanity (Ps 8:6: "crowned with glory and honor [כבוד והדר]"), and the majesty (הוד) of God himself (v. 11c, cf. v. 2). They are his crown (עטרת, v. 12c, cf. v. 6 תעטרהו), and as he stands over "the cut-up sacrificial portions (נתחים)," he represents a humanity that is properly installed with authority over creation, all things under its feet (Ps 8:7, cf. Gen 1:26–29; Sir 17:3–4), including the butchered joints of "sheep and oxen" that sometimes furnished the Lord's barbecue. Day six.

13. Crispin H. T. Fletcher-Louis, "The Temple Cosmology of P and Theological Anthropology in the Wisdom of Jesus ben Sira," in *Of Scribes and Sages: Early Jewish Interpretation and Transmission of Scripture*, ed. C. A. Evans, LSTS 50/SSEJC 9 (Sheffield: Sheffield Academic Press, 2004), 69–113, revised edition in Crispin Fletcher-Louis, *The Image-Idol of God, the Priesthood, Apocalyptic and Jewish Mysticism*, vol. 1 in *Collected Works* (Eugene, OR: Wipf & Stock, forthcoming).

14. HB is corrupt at 50:3, reading אשיח בם בהמונו, which makes no sense. A reference to the sea is restored by most commentators, in line with G.

The inclusio around verses 14–19, with its repeated "until he finished (עד
כלותו)...," echoes the distinctive and repeated statement of divine completion
in Gen 2:1–2, where the heavens and the earth—"the ordered arrangements of
the Most High" (Sir 50:14b)—were finished (יכלו) because God finished (יכל)
his work. A similar echo of the seventh day appears at the climax of the account of the setting up of the tabernacle in Exod 31:18a, 39:32a and 40:33b. The
connection in Hebrew Ben Sira is recognized by the author's grandson, who
in his Greek translation accentuates the point with the words ἕως συντελεσθῇ
κόσμος κυρίου in verse 19b and another allusion to the cosmos in verse 14b,
κοσμῆσαι προσφορὰν ὑψίστου παντοκράτορος.[15] Day seven.

Those are the simplest and most obvious arguments for the connections between days three, four, six and seven, and successive blocks of material in Ben
Sira 50. The case is confirmed on fuller analysis provided the reader is mindful
of all the ways Israel's Scriptures speak about the cosmos and human origins,
the literary connections between Genesis 1 and Exodus 25–40 and their possibilities, the place of Ben Sira 50 as the climax of the foregoing 49 chapters, and
the carefully worked out symmetry between the praise of the high priest in Ben
Sira 50 and Wisdom's self-praise in chapter 24. Those considerations confirm
the case for days three, four, six and seven, and they bring to the surface the
correspondences between Sir 49:16–50:1 and day one, Sir 50:1c–2 and day two,
and Sir 50:8–10 and day five that are far from obvious to the modern reader.
*The ways in which our chapter uses the Pentateuch's heptameron as a canvas
are obvious when Ben Sira's text is held in one hand and Israel's scriptural and
liturgical encyclopedia is held open in the other.*

They are obvious, too, when the reader bears in mind a notion that goes back
to the first, Solomonic temple and that appears prominently in later first-century
CE authors, namely that the temple is a microcosm of the universe. One primary
point of the Priestly intratextuality between Genesis and Exodus 25–40 is to say
that tabernacle construction and what then takes place there are reenactments
of the original order of creation. By structuring his material according to that
intratextuality in chapter 50 (and in ch. 24), Ben Sira says the same about the
temple service in Simeon's day. Indeed, in three places the poem expresses a
specific connection between temple architecture and the cosmos.

In verse 2b the word מעון ("habitation") in the phrase פנות מעון בהיכל מלך
("the corners of the habitation in the King's palace-sanctuary") for the roofed
part of the temple signals the *hekhal*'s function as a symbol, or sacramental

---

15. C. T. R. Hayward, *The Jewish Temple: A non-biblical sourcebook* (London: Routledge,
1996), 79–80.

manifestation, of the heavens. In a description of the place where God "the King" dwells, the word מעון implies its usual sense of God's heavenly dwelling (Deut 26:15; Ps 68:6 [Eng. v. 5]; Jer 25:30; Zech 2:13; 2 Chr 30:27).[16]

Similarly, it is fitting that Simeon brings with him the light and splendor of the sun, moon, stars and a rainbow "when he gazed forth" from the sanctuary—"house of the veil" (v. 5b)—because that is the place that symbolizes the heavens (wherein the sun, moon and stars were placed on day four). There has been much scholarly discussion about the precise identity of Ben Sira's "veil (הפרכת)," whether it hung at the entrance to the holy of holies or at the boundary between sanctuary and forecourt. Whichever is in view, what should not be missed is the likelihood that the word is included here to evoke a veil on which was depicted the whole panorama of the heavens.[17] In the temple-as-microcosm, the high priest's stage directions correspond to those of the heavenly bodies in their daily, annual and seasonal movements through the sky.

The third instance of the narrative's cosmic staging is the location of the scene that corresponds to day six. The priesthood fulfills the vision of humanity ruling over the earth (Gen 1:26, 28) *at the forecourt altar* (vv. 11–13). In the Solomonic temple there was an altar of uncut stone that tradition identified with the earth, or a cosmic mountain: "the mountain of God (ההראל)" (Ezek 43:13–17, cf. 1 Kgs 8:64).[18] How fitting that humanity *in nuce* should rule over the earth *here*; at this point on the cultic stage that tradition identified with the middle layer of the three-tiered cosmos.

Jerusalem, the temple and its liturgy recall the original order of creation. The whole world is here, in all its divinely ordered beauty: creation is brought to God's remembrance (cf. v. 16d).

### Priesthood as a Representative Office Summing Up All Reality

In the Praise of the Fathers, chapters 44–49, Ben Sira praises the nation's devout fathers; the names, divinely bestowed gifts, and powerful deeds of thirty individuals (from Enoch in 44:16 to Nehemiah in 49:13) are singled out for their exemplary glory and memory. Commentators have been divided on the

---

16. Skehan and Di Lella, *Wisdom*, 548–49.

17. For the veil and the heavens see Josephus, *J. W.* 5:213.

18. Jon D. Levenson, *Creation and the Persistence of Evil. The Jewish Drama of Divine Omnipotence* (San Francisco: Harper & Row, 1988), 92–94; Jacob Milgrom and Daniel I. Block, *Ezekiel's Hope: A Commentary on Ezekiel 38–48* (Eugene, OR: Cascade, 2012), 120.

question as to whether or not the praise of Simeon belongs with those chapters, or if it should be viewed as a separate appendix.[19]

Arguments can be made for both positions. As praise of the individual Simeon, Sir 50:1–21 is obviously similar in kind to the praise of the men of chapters 44–49. There are words and themes in those chapters that continue in chapter 50, especially glory, memory and beauty. The praise of Simeon is tied to what immediately precedes by the catchwords פקד (in *niphal*: 49:15, 16; 50:1c) and תפארת (49:16; 50:1). And the literary and numerical structure of 44–50 has patterns that imply 50:1–24 is a part of the whole.[20]

However, a straight historical sequence from the pious in 44–49 to Simeon in 50:1 is broken by 49:14–16. Those verses jump back from Zerubbabel, Joshua son of Jozadak and Nehemiah in 49:11–13 to Enoch (who is contrasted with Joseph) in 49:14, along with Shem, Seth, Enosh and Adam in 49:16. Mention of these primeval figures creates an inclusio with 44:16–17, where the sequence of heroes begins with Enoch and Noah, in a way that makes 44:1–49:16 a discrete unit, separate from what follows. There are also features of 50:1–21 which set it apart from everything else in 44–49. The praise of Simeon is so much more than anything in those chapters. It tells the story of creation, bringing the whole world to God in worship. The passage praises Simeon, together with his fellow priests (vv. 12–13, 16) and the whole people (vv. 17–19, 21), in a way unparalleled by anything in chapters 44–49. The catchword connection between 49:15–16 and 50:1 is not a literary technique that is used to bind together other sections within chapters 44–49, which suggests it is a device that signals 50:1–21 is as much a separate piece as it is a part of what precedes.[21] Both those

19. The appendix view: Skehan and Di Lella, *Wisdom,* 499, 550; Alon Goshen-Gottstein, "Ben Sira's Praise of the Fathers," in *Ben Sira's God: Proceedings of the International Ben Sira Conference,* ed. Renate Egger-Wenzel, BZAW 321 (Berlin: de Gruyter, 2002), 260–61. The continuity view: T. R. Lee, *Studies in the Form of Sirach 44–50,* SBLDS 75 (Atlanta: Scholars Press, 1986), 10–21; Otto Mulder, *Simon the High Priest in Sirach 50: An Exegetical Study of the Significance of Simon the High Priest as Climax to the Praise of the Fathers in Ben Sira's Concept of the History of Israel,* JSJSup 49 (Leiden: Brill, 2003), 47.

20. Jeremy Corley, "A Numerical Structure in Sirach 44:1–50:24," *CBQ* 69 (2007): 43–63; and Jeremy Corley, "Sirach 44:1–15 as Introduction to the Praise of the Ancestors," in *Studies in the Book of Ben Sira: Papers of the Third International Conference on the Deuterocanonical Books, Shime'on Centre, Pápa, Hungary, 18–20 May 2006,* ed. Géza G. Xeravits and Józsee Zsengellér, JSJSup 127 (Leiden: Brill, 2008), 151–81, at 156, 179.

21. If there is a catchword bond between 45:26 (where the text is uncertain) and 46:1 (Goshen-Gottstein, "Ben Sira's Praise," 240–41) it is an exception that is fitting for a major section transition within the Praise of the Fathers.

connections and the many ways that chapters 44–49 anticipate the description of the high priest are best explained in another way.

The relationship between the Praise of the Fathers and the praise of Simeon is best explained if Simeon is Israel's representative high priest. Ben Sira 50:1–21 is literarily tied to the figures in 44–49 by catchwords and thematic repetition, *not because Simeon is the last in a series of pious persons, but because he is their cultic representative.* He is praised as the priest messiah, that is, an incorporative office.[22] He is not the last among equals, but their sum. There are both continuity and discontinuity between 50:1–21 and what precedes because Simeon is praised for what he does and all that he is *as the bearer of a representative office* (not simply for his own person). And 49:16–50:21 looks back not just to the Praise of the Fathers but to the rest of Ben Sira 1–43, since the high priest is representative of all wise and righteous actors in the drama of history and creation.

It is not just that all of creation is present in chapter 50. It is also that God, humanity, and the wider created order *are present in, and held together in, the (high) priesthood.* The high priest serves *in persona domini* (or, *in gloriam dei*—בכבודו HB 45:7), *in persona homini, in persona Israhel,* and as the beauty of the earth and the heavens.[23] He is a multiple personality order, enacting and leading humanity's, Israel's, and creation's praise of the Creator.

## The High Priest as Representative of Israel

In four ways Simeon recalls the people who have gone before him.

### "Beauty of His People"

First, there are the opening words תפארת עמו "beauty of his people" (50:1). "For ben Sira . . . Simon represents the people of Israel . . . who in a sense find their 'modern' realization and culmination in him as the *tip'eret* of his people."[24]

---

22. For the high priest "anointed," see 45:15; cf. Exod 28:41; Lev 4:5.

23. My approach to Ben Sira 50 is anticipated by Enno Janssen, *Das Gottesvolk und seine Geschichte: Geschichtsbild und Selbstverständnis im palästinensischen Schrifttum von Jesus Sirach bis Jehuda ha-Nasi* (Neukirchen-Vluyn: Neukirchener, 1971), 28–30; Hayward, *Temple,* 44–72; Johannes Marböck, "Der Hohepriester Simon in Sir 50: Ein Beitrag zur Bedeutung von Priestertum und Kult im Sirachbuch," in *Treasures of Wisdom: Studies in Ben Sira and the Book of Wisdom,* FS M. Gilbert, ed. N. Calduch-Benages and J. Vermeylen, BETL 143 (Leuven: Leuven University Press, 1999), 215–29, at 220–26; Georg Sauer, *Jesus Sirach/Ben Sira,* ATD –Apokryphen 1 (Göttingen: Vandenhoeck & Ruprecht, 2000), 338–340.

24. Hayward, *Temple,* 46.

The word תפארת comes from Exodus 28, where it appears at the beginning and the end of the description of Aaron's garments that are said to be "for glory and for beauty (לכבוד ולתפארת)" (vv. 2, 40). The word pair, which is used nowhere else in the Hebrew Bible, appears in Sir 45:8 for the garments of Aaron and in 50:11 for those worn by Simeon. Given the firm linguistic association with the pentateuchal chapter that describes the high priest's apparel, the expression תפארת עמו "beauty of *his people*" likely recalls the fact that those garments include beautiful, multi-colored stones upon which are inscribed the names of the twelve tribes (Exod 28:9–12, 17–21, 28–30).

In 45:11 those precious stones, which were first given to Aaron "on the breast piece" and are said to have engraved on them a memorial for the number of the tribes of Israel, are called "stones of delight (אבני חפץ)" (using an expression from Isa 54:12). The same expression occurs in 50:9c, at a point where our only Hebrew manuscript (HB) is damaged. There is no explicit mention of the inscribed names of the twelve tribes in 50:9, but we can be confident that the words of 50:9c helped to spell out the identification of high priest with the people of God that is signaled in verse 1. The striking expression "stones of delight (אבני חפץ)" in verse 9c is a hook back to 45:11 where the stones memorialize God's people. Also, as we shall see, a poetic reference to the high priest's role as the one who wears over his heart the names of the twelve tribes in verse 9 fits the context very well, since his role as representative of the people is the theme of the immediately surrounding verses (vv. 8, 10).

## Simeon Sums Up the Wise and Righteous Heroes of the Previous Chapters

Reading chapter 50 after a patient study of the rest of Ben Sira's wisdom collection we find that, time and again, the high priest is portrayed in ways that recall memorable descriptions of righteous individuals, ideal types and Israel's heroes of old.

The section on the good wife (26:1–18) ends with a poetic combination of the cosmological and the cultic that anticipates the praise of Simeon. The ideal housewife is likened to "the sun rising in the heights" (v. 16) and to "a light burning on the holy menorah" (v. 17) that illuminates the sanctuary. A similar image is used in chapter 50:5–7. She lights up her home; the high priest lights up God's. She is a menorah in her private world; he the heavenly lights of Israel's model world.

Judging by the Greek, where the Hebrew is missing, two times Ben Sira had used the language of heavenly bodies to describe the sage's instruction. He determined "to shine forth instruction like the dawn" (24:32), as one full of things to say, like the full moon (39:12). Again, these verses anticipate 50:5–7, and in the second case the lunar comparison is immediately followed by language that is parallel to the praise of Simeon in 50:8–10, 12. That is, the young sages are to listen to the author "and blossom, like a rose growing by a stream of water" and "put forth blossoms like a lily" (39:13, cf. 50:8a–b, 12e). They are to "give out a fragrant aroma as incense," just as the high priest lights incense and is, himself, "as fire of incense" (50:9a). In his ministry, the high priest brings to mind the life-enhancing aroma of the wise in Israel's midst.

The attentive reader is bound to notice that "in the high priest Simon all the lines of the praise of the fathers come together. Whatever positive thing was said of individual Israelites, finds its fulfillment and embodiment in Simon."[25] In his beauty (תפארת) and his beautifying himself (התפאר) by God's name (50:1, 11, 20), Simeon reminds us of Aaron (45:7–23, esp. v. 8). Both have glory (כבוד) and splendor (הוד) by virtue of their garments (45:7–8, 12, 20; 50:11, cf. 50:13a), which include "delightful stones (אבני חפץ)" (45:11; 50:9).[26] Ben Sira marvels at the appearance of Simeon from the sanctuary ("how adorned he was [מה נהדר]"—50:5), echoing his earlier comment on Joshua: "how adorned he was (מה נהדר)" when he stretched out his hand to take the city of Ai (46:2). The coming of Elijah is likened to fire (48:1) and Ben Sira asks, "Who like you beautifies himself (יתפאר)?"—a question answered in chapter 50, when Simeon, who is "as a fire (כאש) of incense (לבונה)" (50:9), "beautified himself (התפאר) in the name of the LORD." Simeon's aromatic appearance recalls Josiah whose name "is like incense (קטרת) spices, salted—work of a perfumer" (49:1).

In 50:1–4 Simeon oversees the kind of good works that were expected of ancient rulers who cared for their people and their cities. He dug a "water-pool (מקוה)," "made his city stronger (מחזק עירו) than the enemy (מצר)," and in his days "the palace-sanctuary (היכל) was strengthened (חֻזַּק)" (v. 1d). He built a wall, "the corners of the habitation in the King's palace-sanctuary (היכל)" (v. 2d). In so doing, as high priest, he takes up the activities that in days past had been the responsibility of Israel's kings. He is a contemporary reincarnation of Hezekiah, who "strengthened his city (חזקיהו חזק עירו) by channeling water into its midst . . . (and) cut with bronze the rocks (צורים) and damned up mountains for a water-pool (מקוה)" (48:17). In these great public works Simeon adorns the memory of Nehemiah who had been a healer, restorer, and

---

25. Janssen, *Das Gottesvolk,* 28.
26. For more on Aaron and Simon, see Marböck, "Der Hohepriester Simon," 220–222.

rebuilder of doors and bars in Israel's capital (49:13). And his achievements recapitulate those of Zerubbabel and Josiah who "built the house and raised up the holy palace-sanctuary (היכל)" (49:11–12).

## Simeon's Glory and Greatness

Besides all those ways in which Simeon memorializes specific individuals or types of wise and virtuous people, the theme of glory and honor (and beauty and splendor) that runs through chapters 44–50 reinforces the point that, in the drama of Israel's liturgy, the priesthood gathers up and makes present to God all that is good and praiseworthy in his people. There is no simple equation: high priest-equals-Israel without remainder. Rather, Simeon is "*the beauty* of his people" (v. 1a). He is, in his representative capacity, all that there is in Israel that renders them worthy of the divine presence.

The opening lines of the hymn in praise of the fathers make "glory," "greatness" and "beauty" its major theme: to the pious men, the fathers of the nation, the Most High apportioned "abundance of glory (רב כבוד)" and "(his) greatness from days of old (גדלה/גדלו מימות עולם)" (44:2, cf. v. 7).[27] "Their descendants will stand forever and their glory (כבודם) will never be blotted [out]" (44:13 HM; HB, "their righteousness"). Eight times in the chapters that follow the ancestors are praised for their glory (44:2, 7, 13, 19; 45:7–8, 12, 20; 49:5). So, when in 50:11, 13 and 21 Ben Sira describes the glory and beauty and splendor of Simeon and his brothers it once again makes the priests representatives of the virtue and achievements of the nation.

## Arboreal Symbolism in the Psalms

In Psalms and the Prophets the righteous are described as fruitful trees in God's presence and house. The portrayal of Simeon in verses 8 and 10 and his brothers, the priests, in verse 12, is a pastiche of echoes of those passages (Pss 52:10; 92:13–15; Hos 14:5–7) and of similar ones where explicitly temple language is lacking (e.g., Ps 128:3; Isa 44:4).

In Ps 52:10 (Eng. v. 8) David proclaims, "I am as a green olive tree in the house of God (כזית רענן בבית אלהים)." Simeon in God's temple is "as a green olive (כזית רענן) full of berries" (50:10).[28] In Ps 92:13–15 (Eng. vv. 12–14) the "righteous sprout forth (יפרח) like the palm tree and grow like a cedar in

---

27. HM has גדלה and HB has גדלו.

28. Cf. Hayward, *Temple*, 53; Mulder, *Simon*, 142–43.

Lebanon (כארז בלבנון). Plantings (שתולים) in the house of the LORD; they sprout forth (יפריחו) in the courts of our God. . . . they are ever full of sap and green (רעננים)." Similarly, Simeon is "as a shoot of Lebanon (כפרח לבנון)" (v. 8c), "as a green (רענן) olive" (v. 10a), and his fellow priests are "as saplings of cedar trees in Lebanon (כשתילי ארזים בלבנון)" (v. 12d).

Hosea prophesied that God's people would "sprout forth (יפרח) as the lily (כשושנה)," their splendor would be "like the olive," their fragrance like Lebanon (כלבנון) (the cypress-tree-covered mountain range) (14:6–7 [Eng. vv. 5–7]). This will be possible because they will return and "dwell beneath my shadow" (v. 7 [Eng. v. 8])—language evocative of the temple and the protective wings of the cherub throne in the *devir* (Pss 36:8–9; 63:3, 8, cf. Sir 49:16). After his exit from the sanctuary, Simeon is "as a lily (כשושן) . . . as a shoot (כפרח) of Lebanon (לבנון)," and "as a green olive" (50:8b–c, 10a). "Thus ben Sira seems to attribute to Simeon the same qualities as the Israel of Hosea's prophecy."[29] And between verses 8 and 10, that employ this traditional vegetative language, Ben Sira refers, fittingly, to the "stones of delight" (v. 9) on which there are engraved the names of the twelve tribes (45:11).

In a similar vein, the vision of the chief priest serving at the altar, God's table, "around him (סביב לו) . . . his sons (בנים), as saplings (כשתילי) of cedar trees . . . ," is indebted to Ps 128:3: ". . . within your house; your sons (בניך) will be like olive shoots (כשתלי זיתים) around your table (סביב לשלחנך)." That Psalm blesses "everyone who fears the LORD" (vv. 1, 4), which is a posture that is dear to Ben Sira (cf. Sir 1:11–20, 27–30; 2:7–17; 7:29–31; 50:29; inter alia).

Psalm 128 does not place the arboreal righteous in the temple, but for Ben Sira the allusion to v. 3 is surely metaleptic: it invites the reader to consider the ways the rest of Ps 128 interprets the scene in vv. 11–13. The God-fearer in the Psalm eats the fruit of the labor of their hands (Ps 128:2). Their flourishing children (lit. "sons") encircle *the domestic table*, like seedlings or cuttings (v. 3). This is a blessing that comes, ultimately, from the LORD in Zion (v. 5). In Ben Sira 50 there is also a table, so to speak: the altar at which Simeon's "*sons*" serve and from which they eat. The priests eat, then, as paragons of those who fear God. But they also dine as representatives of the nation; the people whose hands have provided the food for God's table. The temple altar is a national hearth for the high table of the capital's banqueting hall. And the high priest is paterfamilias-in-chief, standing in, before God, for every blessed and God-fearing head of the houses of Israel (cf. 7:27–31).

One point of all the talk of arboreal abundance, of course, is to say that

---

29. Hayward, *Temple*, 53; cf. Mulder, *Simon*, 142.

this place—and this worship—offers the reality of life in all its fullness. The passage is a Hellenistic-era example of the centuries-old theme of the temple as paradise or Eden (cf. Sir 24:25–29). But the biblical allusions by which Ben Sira expresses that theme show that he has gone out of his way to make another, related, point.

Whereas older texts describing the tabernacle and the temple (in Exod 25–31 and 1 Kgs 6–7) employ vegetative symbolism for the buildings' *structures* (the lampstand, paneled walls, doors, bronze laver, and bronze pillars; Exod 25:31–36; 1 Kgs 6:18, 29, 32, 35; 7:18–19, 22, 26) for Ben Sira it is *people*, specifically *priests*, who represent or actualize the botanical beauty and arboreal fruitfulness of God's creation. The reason for this difference is now not hard to see. In our text *it is priests who play this role because in Israel's Scriptures righteous individuals are like trees and for Ben Sira it is the true high priest (with his colleagues) who sums up, in his office, the people of God.*

By the same rationale, no doubt, Ben Sira avoids any reference to the actual vegetative symbolism of the high priest's garments. He does not mention here the golden flower (ציץ) on the turban on the priest's forehead (Exod 28:36, cf. Sir 45:12), or the pomegranates hanging from the hem of his garments (Exod 28:34; 39:26, cf. 45:9). Other authors made much of these.[30] But in Ben Sira 50 they are ignored because they offer no opportunity to say, by means of scriptural allusion, that the priests play the role of righteous Israelites in the temple drama.

## The High Priest Is Adam, God's Image and Likeness, a True Humanity

In 1 Kings 3–4 Solomon is a new Adam. For Ben Sira that representative role is played by the high priest, who in other respects, as we have seen, takes over functions that were traditionally played by the king (esp. in 50:1–4). The point is made in two places.

In 50:1a the epithet "beauty of his people (תפארת עמו)" parallels "above all the living creatures is the beauty of Adam" (על כל חי תפארת אדם) of the preceding line (49:16b). Somehow, the priest, we are invited to conclude, has an Adamic beauty. Hayward has suggested that 50:1a reflects the rabbinic-era tradition that the high priest's garments were those worn by Adam.[31] That is a possibility, though his grandson apparently either did not know or rejected the idea, since in his Greek translation at 45:13 he says that before Aaron was

---

30. Philo, *Mos.* 2:119–121, 133; *Spec.* 1:93–94; Josephus, *Ant.* 3:172–78, 184.
31. Hayward, *Temple*, 45.

given his garments "such beautiful things did not exist" (Heb. missing). In any case, there are other, more straightforward observations, that explain the parallelism between 49:16b and 50:1a.

The fact that 50:1a does not say Simeon is, or has, "the beauty *of Adam*," is understandable because in two places our author has already signaled that Israel fulfills the God-intended identity of Adam. In chapter 17 (for which we rely on the G and S), Ben Sira moves seamlessly from the first human beings (vv. 1–8) to Israel, to whom God gave "the law of life" (v. 11b, cf. Lev 18:5) and with whom he established "an eternal covenant" (v. 12a) at Sinai (v. 13). Israel is the people that fulfills the God-intended role for Adam and Eve. Second, in 44:1–15, the prologue to the praise of the ancestors opens with another allusion to Gen 1:26–28 that identifies the pious as a true humanity. Those to be praised, to whom God has given a portion of glory (v. 2), are "the rulers of the earth in their kingdoms (רודי ארץ במלכותם)," an obvious echo of the command in Gen 1:26 that humanity exercise regal "rule (וירדו)" over the creatures "in all the earth (בכל־הארץ)."[32]

If, for Ben Sira, God's purposes for Adam have found fulfillment in Israel then it is understandable that 50:1a should identify the high priest with both those parties. The expression תפארת עמו ("beauty of his people"), coming, as it does, straight after the one about Adam's תפארת ("beauty") over all the creatures (another allusion to Gen 1:26–28?) does double duty, signaling the high priest's summing up of *both* his people *and* Adam.[33]

We can be confident that Ben Sira thinks that, at times, the priesthood is Adamic because of the way he weaves allusions to Ps 8 into the passage. These were noted earlier, in the discussion of 50:11–13, where Simeon and his fellow priests fulfill that Psalm's vision for an exalted humanity. The central role played by the vision of Psalm 8 is signaled already in 49:16, in the words "Shem, Seth and *Enosh* (אנוש) *were cared for* (נפקדו) . . . above all the living creatures is the beauty of *a human/of Adam* (תפארת אדם)." This is an unmistakable reference to Ps 8:5: "What/who is a human (מה־אנוש) that you remember them, the son of man (בן־אדם) that you care for them (תפקדנו)?" By recalling Ps 8:5 in the introduction to the praise of Simeon, Ben Sira offers answers to the psalmist's question. First, 49:16 says that the *enosh* (אנוש) of the psalmist's question is Enosh, the man of primeval lineage remembered here in poetic

---

32. Corley, "44:1–15," 165n52. Although רודי is the marginal reading in HB (and the main text has דודי "dwellers"), it is confirmed by G: κυριεύοντες ἐν ταῖς βασιλείαις αὐτῶν.

33. Cf. Hayward, *Temple*, 45: "Ben Sira seems to imply that the privileges granted to the first man, and thus to all humankind, are also peculiarly summed up in Israel whose representative is Simon in his function as sacrificing high priest."

praise that is heard in the congregation of Israel (44:15). Second, the vignette in Sir 50:11–13, drawn with lines from Ps 8:6–9, answers the psalmist's question "who, or what, is the son of man (בן אדם) whom God cares for and exalts in creation?" (Ps 8:6–9). The high priest, in his college, is that "son of Adam."

Ordinarily, in fractured, quotidian space and time, we do not see "all things subjected" to humanity (Ps 8:7). But here, in a pristine sacramental space–time, we see him who sums up a perfected humanity "crowned with glory," distributing splendor to those around him (v. 11d), bringing his many sons to the same glory (v. 13a) which he himself possesses (v. 11a), as one to whom, like his progenitor Adam, God has delegated dominion in creation.

So, when the Hebrew at verse 19 says "כל עם הארץ gave a ringing shout," the word ארץ is intentionally ambiguous. On the one hand, it means "all the people of the *land* of Israel," who have gathered here to worship. On the other hand, it means "all humanity—all the peoples of the *earth*—who are represented by this people, this priestly kingdom."[34] Just as the priests represent Israel, so the Israelites themselves are taken up into the drama of creation and history, representing humanity in its fullness. Israel's priesthood is made possible by the Aaronic priesthood.

## *The High Priest as Wisdom*

The structure, language, and imagery of the praise of Simeon maps point for point onto the praise of Wisdom in 24:1–23. The high priest is Wisdom in human form.[35] So he is all that she is in the spheres that Ben Sira explores in his wisdom collection. The universal presence of the wise and the understanding path is present in this particular place and its people. Wisdom's self-praise in chapter 24 roughly bisects the work. It not only looks forward to chapter 50, it also recalls the praise of wisdom in chapter 1 that introduces the themes of glory, boasting, growth, vegetative abundance, festival plenty and "an eternal foundation" that come to their fullest expression in chapter 50.[36] Everything in this wisdom anthology moves toward this point: the activities of Israel's high priest, the perfect human instantiation of Wisdom wherever she may be found. A universal condensed to a particular.

34. Marböck, "Der Hohepriester Simon," 222; cf. Janssen, *Das Gottesvolk*, 29–30.

35. Fletcher-Louis, "Cosmology of P," cf. Hayward, *Temple*, 52, 78; Marböck, "Der Hohepriester Simon," 224.

36. For literary connections between chs. 1 and 24, see Johannes Marböck, *Weisheit im Wandel: Untersuchungen zur Weisheitstheologie bei Ben Sira*, BBB 37 (Bonn: Peter Hanstein, 1971), 43, 56–57.

## The High Priest as God the Creator in Human Form

By organizing the chapter according to the seven days of creation Ben Sira not only dresses the high priest in Wisdom's costume, he also gives him the part of Creator in the temple drama. This is especially clear in the sections that fulfill the second, third and seventh days of creation. Simeon's provision of a water-pool and cistern "like the sea" echoes God's work in Gen 1:9–10. Because the *hekhal* is heaven in the temple's symbolic system, by strengthening it (v. 1d) Simeon maintains the boundary established on day two, when God created the firmament and called it "heaven." Above all, in 50:14, 19 his finishing his ministry at the altar reenacts God's completion of the making of heaven and earth. When he "finished ministering at the altar and set in order the arrangements of the Most High" (v. 14a–b, cf. v. 19c), he does in liturgical space and time what God did for the whole cosmos. The two parts of v. 14 sum up Simeon's achievements, just as Gen 2:1 summarizes Gen 1 in its statement that God "completed the heavens and the earth and all their host."

All Simeon's activities provide a visual testimony to God's works in creation, thereby answering the prayer in 36:14–15a: "Fill Zion with your majesty (Gk. ἀρεταλογίας σου, 'a celebration of your wondrous deeds') and your palace-sanctuary (היכלך) from your glory. Provide testimony to the first/chief of your works (עדות למראש מעשיך)." As a sacramental retelling, in word and deed, of God's seven-day creation, Ben Sira 50 is that aretalogy—a "testimony" to the first and most important of God's works.

Perhaps the most obvious way in which the high priest represents God is through a series of references and allusions to scriptural theophanies. These combine to suggest that in the liturgy the high priest narrates historic movements of the divine glory. In 50:7b "as a bow appears in a cloud (כקשת נראתה בענן)" likens the high priest to the human-like form of God's glory atop the four living creatures of Ezekiel's call vision (Ezek 1:26–28). A reference to Ezekiel's vision of the glory of God is encouraged by the fact that passages in Exodus and Numbers also speak of the divine glory appearing (*niphal* ראה) in a cloud (Exod 16:10; Num 17:7 [Eng. 16:42]; cf. Isa 60:1–3). Ben Sira had referred to Ezekiel's vision "of the *merkavah*" in the previous chapter (49:8) and 50:7 is the first of three scriptural references that identify the high priest with the glorious, visible form of God.[37]

---

37. 50:7b also recalls Gen 9:14, a fitting echo after Simeon's works of authority over the waters in 50:3.

The second comes in 50:11, "when he wrapped himself (בעטותו) in the garments of glory (בגדי כבוד), and clothed himself (והתלבשו) in garments of beauty (בגדי תפארת), . . . there was majesty (הוד), and he made splendid (ויהדר) the court of the holy place." This combines the language of "glory and beauty" from Exod 28:2, 40 with the opening of Ps 104: "You are clothed with majesty and splendor (הוד והדר לבשת), wrapped in light (עסה־אור) as with a garment" (Ps 104:1c–2a; cf. Isa 59:17). Standing at the altar Simeon is the visible image of the light-clothed Creator.

After passages from the Prophets (Ezek 1) and the Psalms (Ps 104), the divine glory theme continues with another from Isaiah and one from Exodus. From the focus on the priesthood at the altar in vv. 11–12, the camera pans back to the whole worshipping community in vv. 14–21, where there is a fulfillment of the narrative adumbrated in Isa 40:5: "Then the glory of the LORD shall be revealed (נגלה כבוד יהוה), and all flesh together shall see it (ראו כל־בשר יחדו)." In the liturgical story Ben Sira tells, the glory of the Lord has been revealed *by the high priest who is clothed in and so makes manifest that glory* (vv. 7b, 11) when he appears from the sanctuary and ministers at the forecourt altar. When the action turns to the whole liturgical community it is the people who play the role of Isaiah's *all flesh together* beholding that glory: "All flesh together (כל בשר יחדו) were hastened (נמהרו), and fell on their faces, to the earth (ויפלו על פניהם ארצה), to worship before the Most High (להשתחות לפני עליון). . . . And all the people of the earth/land gave a ringing shout in prayer before the Merciful One (רחום)" (vv. 17, 19). Isaiah's contribution to Israel's history was celebrated in Sir 48:20 and the words כל בשר יחדו appear in Isa 40:5 but nowhere else in Israel's Scriptures. The message is clear: in the high priest's appearance from the sanctuary and at the forecourt altar the people have experienced the theophany Isaiah predicted—at least, that is, a sacramental dress rehearsal or a reenactment of it.[38]

The rest of the verse and verse 19b pick up another theophany, namely the one at Exod 34. There God descends in the cloud (again), passes before Moses and reveals himself as the LORD, a God merciful and gracious. The divine self-disclosure provokes a prostration (Exod 34:8): "And Moses *hurried* (וימהר), bowed his head towards the ground and worshipped (ויקד ארצה וישתחו)." In Ben Sira, the whole community plays the role of Moses: they "were hastened (נמהרו), and fell on their faces, to the ground (פניהם ארצה), and worshipped

---

38. The phrase ויפלו על פניהם in v. 17b appears three times in the Hebrew Bible (Num 16.22; 20:6; Judg 13:20) and, as Mulder (*Simon*, 177) points out, in each case the prostration is a response to a theophany.

the Most High (להשתחות לפני עליון)." Moses encountered the Lord as אל רחום (Exod 34:6), so it is fitting that Ben Sira 50:19 should call the one to whom the people prostrate "the Merciful One" (רחום) (v. 19b).[39]

The principal storyline that organizes chapter 50 is the one about creation in Gen 1. In addition, and in keeping with the high priest's role as Creator, a subplot says he manifests the glory of God in a way that recalls the great events of Israel's history in the Pentateuch (Exod 34), in moments of past crisis (Ezek 1) and in the prophesied future (in Isa 40). The combination of 50:5–7, where the high priest comes out from the holy place revealing the glory of the Lord, with 50:11, where he appears as the light-clothed image of God at the temple altar that symbolizes the earth or a cosmic mountain, evokes the traditional storyline in which the Lord appears from his holy place with the power and authority of the divine warrior and his effects are felt on the earth, the hills and the mountains (see Isa 26:21–27:1; Mic 1:2–4; Hab 2:20–3:6).

## The High Priest Is the Cosmos

Last, the "whole creation is present when the high priest appears."[40] In Sir 50:5–7 he represents the heavenly bodies—stars, the moon, the sun and a rainbow—that were praised in the Praise of Creation in 43:1–12. In 50:8, 10 and 12 he manifests the earth's arboreal and botanical beauty. In 50:17 the people now represent "all flesh," an expression that in other places denotes all creatures, not just human beings (Sir 13:15–16; 14:17–18; 44:18 [cf. Gen 9:11], cf. 39:19). Perhaps, too, the expressions "as a lily in streams of water" (v. 8b) and "as willows of the brook they encircled him" (v. 12e) are meant to suggest that Simeon and the other priests are, or that they have, life-giving water. His sons are "willows of the brook" around him.[41] Ergo, he is that brook?

Other Jewish writers found cosmic symbolism in temple furniture (see Philo, *Mos.* 2:71–145; Josephus, *J. W.* 5:212–13, 217; *Ant.* 3:179–187). As we have noted, our chapter assumes and sometimes articulates the old Israelite view that the principal structures of the temple map out a microcosm. However, for Ben Sira the cosmic symbolic nexus comes to its fullest expression in the high priest, his colleagues and the whole people of Israel.

---

39. For Exod 34:6–7 in Ben Sira see 2:11, 18c–d; 5:4–6.
40. G. Sauer, *Jesus Sirach/Ben Sira*, 339.
41. Cf. the oxen "encompassing (מקיפים)" the molten sea, "in two rows" in 2 Chr 4:3.

## Conclusion

Everything is present there. All creation. Every part of Israel's Scriptures (law, history, prophecy, psalms, wisdom literature). Temple and temple city (v. 2) are creation writ small. But more than that, *people* represent or contain all space, all persons and all God's creation. Everyone and everything are summed up and find their properly ordered place in God's presence, in and through this office and this people-at-worship. Priests and people reflect back to the one God, who is enthroned on high (1:8), the glorious *oneness* of all creation (50:17): *atonement in worship*.

So, Ben Sira 50 confirms the hypothesis with which we began. In the Second Temple period the high priest played the representative role that older tradition ascribed to the ideal king. But it would be a mistake to speak of a simple transference of an incorporative identity from king to priest. There are marked differences. Ben Sira 50 presents a far richer vision of the high priest's incorporative identity that includes a cosmological dimension lacking in 1 Kgs 3–4. Where Solomon's representative identity is worked out in the political and civil spheres, for the high priest it is manifest not just in the realms of national government (Sir 50:1–4), but also temple liturgy (50:5–21). Also, where Solomon's incorporative identity is the result of personal piety (1 Kgs 3:3–15), Simeon the priest is an incorporative messiah in the fulfillment of a preexisting script. Everything he does, both in the temple and the civil administration, conforms to Torah's heptadic structure for world-making and worship. Solomon was a royal *person*; Simeon perfectly fulfills a high priestly *office*.

# CHAPTER SIX

# GET THE STORY RIGHT AND THE MODELS WILL FIT

*Victory through Substitution in "Atonement Theology"*

N. T. WRIGHT

It has become increasingly clear to me that in discussions between exegetes and theologians the latter regularly approach theological topics by means of the different *models* which they see being explored. This at least has the benefit of allowing different emphases to be put on the table rather than trying to pretend that one of the models is the *correct* one and that all the others must be subsumed within it. But I frequently find myself reflecting that the model which is absent from such discussions is the biblical one itself, which is always couched in terms of a *story*. I know that some theologians are allergic to this suggestion, but anyone who professes to regard the Bible as in some way the ultimate source, or even *an* ultimate source, for theological knowledge and understanding, cannot ignore the fact that the Bible—both the Jewish Bible, in its way, and the Christian Bible, in its subtly different way—presents an overarching narrative which is more than simply a loose frame in which abstract theological teaching happens to be embedded. Israel's Scriptures in themselves, and the Christian Scriptures which (because of their view that Jesus was and is Israel's long-awaited Messiah) saw Israel's Scriptures as the necessary foundation for the story they now had to tell, had to do with the Creator God and his people, and with the story of creation and covenant which that involved. This is not an incidental framework. It is what the story is about.

Within that story, the question of *atonement* has routinely loomed large. I have addressed this in various places over the years, particularly in a recent book and one or two related articles.[1] The present essay continues the discussion, going beyond my earlier attempts not least by trying to integrate into the same picture the themes of temple and cosmology which have occupied me more recently.[2]

## Introduction: The Distorted Story

I begin with an analogy. When Albert Schweitzer, aged 23, was studying the organ in Paris with Charles-Marie Widor in 1899 (between writing his first two books on Jesus, and for that matter between his first two hearings of Wagner's Ring Cycle at Bayreuth), Widor asked him to explain the chorale preludes of J. S. Bach.[3] Widor could play them, of course, but he didn't understand why Bach had written them or what they were really about. Schweitzer replied that this was because Widor and his French Catholic tradition didn't know the words of the Lutheran Chorales for which these were the music, and Schweitzer illustrated the point by quoting the texts and translating them into French. Widor was fascinated, and asked Schweitzer to write a little essay explaining all this for other French pupils. Schweitzer did so—and the pamphlet grew into his famous two-volume work on Bach, which he published in 1904, between his second and third books on Jesus (and for that matter during his early medical studies). The reason Widor couldn't quite understand the chorale preludes was that he didn't know the words, the underlying narrative which made sense of the music.

My proposal in the present article is that something similar has happened within what we think of as Western atonement theology as a whole. We have forgotten the story which makes sense of the music. When we play the music,

1. See my *The Day the Revolution Began: Reconsidering the Meaning of Jesus's Crucifixion* (London: SPCK; San Francisco: HarperOne, 2016); "Redemption from the New Perspective? Towards a Multi-Layered Pauline Theology of the Cross" and "Reading Paul, Thinking Scripture: 'Atonement' as a Special Study," in *Pauline Perspectives: Essays on Paul, 1978–2013* (London: SPCK; Minneapolis: Fortress Press, 2013), chs. 19, 22.

2. See particularly my Gifford Lectures, *History and Eschatology: Jesus and the Promise of Natural Theology* (London: SPCK; Waco, TX: Baylor University Press, 2019), ch. 5. I am grateful to Simon Dürr for his help in editing this essay for publication.

3. On Schweitzer and Wagner, see *History and Eschatology*, ch. 2. Widor himself tells the story of his conversation with Schweitzer in his Preface to the German edition (1908) of Schweitzer's two-volume book on Bach (in English translation, *J. S. Bach*, trans. Ernest Newman [London: A & C Black, 1923 (1911)], vii–xii). See, too, N. O. Oermann, *Albert Schweitzer: A Biography* (Oxford: Oxford University Press, 2016), 46–59.

repeating words like *redemption, sacrifice, reconciliation* and indeed *atonement* itself, we hear them (as many readers have pointed out) as basically saying the same thing, reducing their specific content to the status of metaphors or models which can be explored or even played off against one another—distant and somewhat vague gestures to a single but fuzzy reality.

Actually, it's worse than that. The analogy doesn't go far enough. In the case of Western atonement theology, we are more in the position Widor would have been had some French theologian written different words to the chorales, words which didn't quite fit either metrically or theologically, thus making it look as though Bach hadn't quite written the right music. We have got the story wrong, and so have reduced its various themes to a miscellany of motifs or models or metaphors.[4] While of course every language-field is planted thick with bushy metaphors, in biblical atonement theology they mean what they mean within the story: the story to which they belong.

How does this work out? In *The Day the Revolution Began* I have outlined three wrong moves in the dominant Western atonement narrative. First, we have *Platonized our eschatology*; second, we have *moralized our anthropology*; third, we have *paganized our soteriology*.[5]

First, most Western theology (and particularly popular preaching) has taught that we humans have souls which are exiled from their true home, which is heaven, and that we are looking forward to going back there one day, leaving behind this shabby and shadowy old world. But in the first century this is precisely the teaching of the Middle Platonist Plutarch; not of Jesus, or Paul, or the early Christians.[6] The early Christians were robust creational monotheists who, like the Psalms and Isaiah, were looking for the renewal, not the abandonment, of heaven and earth.[7]

Second, if our *souls* are the key thing, and getting them into heaven the key challenge, the problem is *sin*. This is not to say that sin is unimportant. But Western theology both in the academy and the church has moralized our anthropology, supposing that the *only* thing that matters is whether or not we have kept the rules (or, if not, how we can get round the problem). The early Christians, however, retrieving all sorts of bits of classic Israelite thinking, saw the human vocation as far more than merely rule-keeping. Being made "in the image of

---

4. See Wright, *Revolution*, 93–94.

5. Eschatology: Wright, *Revolution*, 28–34; moralizing, 74–87; paganized soteriology, 38–46; summarized at e.g., 94.

6. See, e.g., Plutarch, *On Exile* 607A–F.

7. See my *Paul and the Faithfulness of God* (London: SPCK; Minneapolis: Fortress Press, 2013), ch. 9.

God" had to do with the purpose for which humans were made, which cannot be reduced to "fellowship with God," vital though that remains. The rules matter; the *role* matters far more. The Creator had a purpose for his whole creation, and image-bearing humans had a vital part to play within that creation.

Third, if the problem is getting sinful souls into heaven, the solution has been to take certain key passages, particularly in Paul, and to construct from them a form of penal substitution in which God so hated the world that he killed Jesus. No preacher ever says it like that, of course, but that is what many generations of Catholics, as well as Protestants, have heard; and many have rejected it. Once more it is important not to misunderstand. There *is* such a thing as a biblical doctrine of penal substitution. I'll come to that. But it doesn't function within that narrative, and the key texts normally invoked in its support do not say exactly what the theory demands. (A good example would be Gal 3:10–14, where Paul doesn't say that Christ became a curse for us to free us from the guilt, penalty and power of sin but that he became a curse so that the blessing of Abraham might come on the gentiles and that "we [Jewish Jesus-believers, it seems] might receive the promised Spirit through faith."[8]) We have forgotten the true biblical story; we have substituted a different (albeit distantly related) story instead; and we have then had to cope with the key strands in the true story collapsing into a disparate little heap of models or themes, all appearing to be imprecise ways of saying the same thing: that sinners can go to heaven after all.

## Contours of the Biblical Narrative

### *The Unfinished Project*

So what is the true story? No doubt we all have our own ways of answering that question; here is mine. There are five interlocking strands to this narrative, which then set the scene for what I take to be the New Testament's theological portrayal of the significance of Jesus's death. There are of course many differences of emphases and imagery, particularly relating to this theme, among the early Christian writings. The narratival strands I present here underlie not only the Pauline letters but also, in various ways, all four gospels. This seems to be a good start. The exercise I am undertaking here is a form of *biblical theology*, though that phrase means many different things to many different people.[9] My

8. See the discussions in Wright, *Paul and the Faithfulness of God*, 863–68 and elsewhere.

9. See, e.g., Scott J. Hafemann, ed., *Biblical Theology: Retrospect and Prospect* (Downers Grove: InterVarsity Press, 2002).

construct here depends at every point on the detailed exegesis of many texts which I have offered elsewhere and now am pulling together as best I can into a larger picture. This is an explicitly Jesus-based reading of Israel's Scriptures, following the New Testament writers in their retrieval of many ancient themes, some of which were prominent in some Second Temple circles and some of which—so far as our evidence allows—seem not to have been.

It should be noted that I am not saying that "all Jews of the time" believed this or that.[10] Rather, the story the early Christians tell is emphatically a story of *how the creation-project was reaching its goal.* It is, to repeat, the story of creational monotheism: of how the good and wise Creator God made a world, how this God made it to work and move forward in a particular way, namely through the work of his image-bearing humans, and how this project, though tragically derailed by human non-cooperation, was to be put back on track.[11] The Psalms, and many passages in Isaiah, speak not of humans rescued from creation but of creation itself restored, often under the rule of the ultimate human being, the Davidic king.[12] The puzzle that the early Christians thought had been solved by the events concerning Jesus, including centrally though not exclusively his death, was the puzzle of how the divine project would reach its goal.

## The Unquiet Sea

This puzzle was given depth, in Israel's Scriptures, by a second theme, going back all the way to Gen 1:2 but emerging in the Psalms, Isaiah and notoriously Dan 7: *the unquiet sea.*[13] Woven into many biblical texts is a theme familiar from wider cultures: that within creation as it stands, albeit for Gen 1 tamed by the Creator's act of making heaven and earth, there is a dark, wild force of chaos that might threaten to destroy it all—and that indeed, under severe provocation in Noah's day, was used by the Creator himself to destroy all but

10. I have sketched something of the diversity of Jewish views in the period in *The New Testament and the People of God* (London: SPCK; Minneapolis: Fortress Press, 1992), Part III. It is now commonplace to make sharp distinctions between the contexts and contents of different Jewish traditions, e.g., ben Sirach from Qumran, *4 Ezra* from the Rabbis, etc.

11. See Gen 1:26–28; Ps 8; for a study of "image" in its ancient context, see e.g., J. R. Middleton, *The Liberating Image: The* Imago Dei *in Genesis 1* (Grand Rapids: Brazos Press, 2005); in the first century Jewish world, George van Kooten, *Paul's Anthropology in Context: The Image of God, Assimilation to God, and Tripartite Man in Ancient Judaism,* WUNT 232 (Tübingen: Mohr Siebeck, 2008), 1–91.

12. See, e.g., Pss 2; 72; 89; 96; 98; Isa 11:1–10; 35; 55:12–13; 65–66.

13. See, for a start, B. Alster, "Tiamat," in the *Dictionary of Deities and Demons,* ed. K. van der Toorn, 2nd ed. (Leiden: Brill, 1999), 867–69.

a tiny remnant.[14] The question of responsibility, as between Adam, Eve and the serpent, is not resolved; all are implicated. The ancient world, whether of Moses's day or Jesus's day, doesn't seem to have had very good language for the dark forces of evil and chaos, any more than we do. But to suggest that such ideas are therefore outdated or dispensable is dangerously naïve. Jesus, making the vindication of the Son of Man thematic for his own vocation, certainly saw the dark powers, operating through political powers but not reducible to them alone, as a vital element in a cosmos yet to be rescued.[15] Paul saw the present creation as still enslaved to corruption and decay.[16] He used language for its coming liberation which borrows rather obviously from the foundational narrative of Passover and Exodus, to which I shall soon return. This ties together my first two strands of forgotten narrative: as at the Red Sea, when the chaos-monsters thwart the Creator's purposes by enslaving and destroying his creation, they will themselves be defeated and destroyed. Once we put the Creator's purpose at the top of the narrative line, it is clear that, though we must recognize the vital positive role humans are called to play as image-bearers within that purpose, we must equally take into account the role of the powers of chaos. When Jesus, in the parable, says "an enemy has done this," he is gesturing toward the same overall theme.[17]

## *The Idolatrous Humans*

Once we have recognized the role played by the dark powers, however, human responsibility comes back with a bang. But the human failure cannot be reduced simply to *sin*, as though the point of Genesis 1 and 2 were that the Creator was setting humans a moral examination to see if they were fit for his presence or if he would have to kill them after all. No: the point, again, is *image bearing*, which I, like others, have expounded in terms of the "royal priesthood": humans are to reflect the wise stewardship of the Creator into his world, and they are to do this not least by summing up the worship of all creation.[18] The image is like an angled mirror—not simply reflecting the Creator back to the Creator, but reflecting God into the world and the world, in worship, back

14. Gen 7:7.

15. On the question of the "powers" in relation to human vocation, see Wright, *Revolution*, ch. 4. For Jesus's view see, e.g., Luke 10:18; 22:53.

16. Rom 8:19–22.

17. Matt 13:28.

18. The "royal priesthood" is reflected explicitly in Exod 19:6; 1 Pet 2:9; Rev 1:6; 5:10. One might compare the royal motif in Rom 5:21.

to God.[19] The human problem is then to be seen in terms, not simply of moral failure, but of *idolatry*. If you worship anything other than the one true God, your image-bearing humanness will deconstruct, and will drag down with it all those bits of the world into which you ought to be reflecting God's love and creative purposes but into which you will reflect instead whatever aspect of creation you have chosen as your alternative object of worship.[20] *Hinc Illae Lacrimae*, as Terence put it.[21] Idolatry results directly in sin; or, if you like, sin is the outward and visible sign of the inward and spiritual false worship. That is the ultimate human problem to which the gospel, if it is to be gospel, must be the solution. But we must never forget that the problem about dysfunctional humans isn't just that they are in danger of self-destruction. The problem is that humans were assigned a central role in God's purposes for creation. The purpose of putting humans right is so that, as restored image-bearers, they can take up that vocation once more.

## The Unrealized Hope

The combination of the dark forces of chaos and human idolatry means that not only is the creational project unfinished, the hope at its heart remains unrealized. As many writers have stressed, Gen 1 echoes the theme of temple-building, reaching its climax with the insertion into this new heaven-and-earth reality of the image of the Creator; and, when all is done, God comes to dwell in this new house, to take his rest, his ease, in the house which he has built and which he wishes to share with his human creatures. I have explored this theme at much more length, noting its turns and twists and the range of scholarship which has taken different sides on the relevant issues, in the fifth chapter of *History and Eschatology*. Rather than repeat the arguments, I am here cutting long corners and will simply say that I see an initial narrative arc running from Genesis 1 to Exodus 40: with the construction of the tabernacle, a small working model of heaven and earth has come into being, with Aaron the priest standing in for the image-bearing humans. The construction of this Tabernacle, and the inauguration of its worship and liturgy, then appears to be the main purpose of the Exodus. It is a sign of the Creator's intention for

19. I first employed this image in my interpretation of 2 Cor 3:18; see *The Climax of the Covenant: Christ and the Law in Pauline Theology* (Edinburgh: T&T Clark, 1991), 185.

20. G. K. Beale explores this theme in *We Become What We Worship: A Biblical Theology of Idolatry* (Downers Grove: IVP Academic, 2008).

21. "Hence these tears," cf. *Andria* 126, though the text there reads *lacrumae*; in allusions to this by Cicero (*Pro Caelio* 61.12) and Horace (*Epistulae* 1.19.41) it is spelled *lacrimae*.

the whole cosmos; Israel is to be the bearer of this purpose. One might think, reading Moses's repeated request to Pharaoh that he should let Israel go so that they might serve their God in the desert, that this was just a ruse, covering up the ultimate intention which was to reach the promised land.[22] But the purpose seems to be, rather, rooted in the belief that Israel would not be able to worship the covenant God in Egypt, a country full of idolatry and—as it later appeared, for instance in some Psalms—guarded by the watery chaos-monster in the form of the Red Sea, which had to be overcome by superior divine force before Israel could escape.[23] Likewise, if one reads through the book of Exodus quickly, it is easy to feel that the story runs out of steam after chapter 20 (with the giving of Torah). But the detailed commandments in the chapters immediately following constitute only a momentary pause. It soon becomes clear that the purpose of the plagues in Egypt, of Passover itself, of freeing the slaves, of overcoming the Red Sea, and even of giving Torah, was to prepare Israel to be the Tent-Bearers, the people in whose midst the living God would come to dwell. And if that was to become a reality there would need to be a stringent theological health-and-safety code, which is what Leviticus then supplies. (As it turned out, of course, the making of the golden calf in Exod 32 meant a further hiatus, after which, as a compromise, the tabernacle was placed, not in the middle of the camp, but just outside the gate.)

But this purpose—for God to dwell in the midst of his people, or at least alongside them—is more complicated than just setting up the tabernacle and watching it be filled with the glorious divine presence. Whoever edited the Pentateuch was, we assume, very much aware that the golden calf had been just the start of a long history of rebellion on Israel's part. Deuteronomy, particularly chapters 28, 29 and 32, says just this. Despite great and glorious days, particularly under David and Solomon, and particularly with Solomon's Temple—the tabernacle's replacement, similarly filled with glory (1 Kgs 8)—Israel had failed again and again, from David's adultery to Solomon's corrupted heart to the calves at Bethel and Dan, to the multiple idolatries even in the temple itself, as in the great indictment in Ezekiel 8. Exile was a new slavery, requiring a new exodus. And as Ezekiel insists, in parallel with Isa 40 and 52 (and picked up by Zechariah and Malachi even after the return from Babylon), the new exodus, the real return from exile, would not have happened, would not be complete—however much the temple might be cleansed by the Maccabees or

22. On the request, see Exod 3:12; 4:23; 7:16, 26; 8:16; 9:1, 13; 10:3, 7, 8, 11, 24, 26; 12:31. See, too, Exod 20:5.

23. E.g., Ps 77:16, 19; 106:9; 114:3, 5; Isa 43:16; 51:9–11. For the story, cf. Exod 14:21–22; 15:7–8.

rebuilt by Herod—until Israel's God returned in power and glory, with Jerusalem's watchmen shouting with joy and all enemies being put to flight.[24] The theme of the divine return to Zion has been downplayed or even ignored in much scholarship, and I think it's time to put it back where it belongs. I have become increasingly convinced that it is central to New Testament Christology.[25] I believe it is also vital for both eschatology and (our present theme) atonement theology itself. The New Testament writers, in different ways, tell the story of Jesus's crucifixion as the story of how Israel's God came back in person to do for Israel and the world what Israel and the world could not do for themselves. Up to that point, so Jesus's followers believed, the hope had remained unrealized.

## The Unkept Covenant

All this was taken by many to indicate that the covenant God had made with Abraham, the promises of family and land, remained unkept on Israel's side and therefore unfulfilled on God's side. We may assume that almost all first-century Jews, except perhaps the Sadducees, would have agreed on this point. In particular, some of the great promises of an extension to the family and the land—we may think of Psalms like 2 and 72, where the "inheritance" is spread out widely to reach to the ends of the earth, or Ps 87, where the other great nations are included in the divine blessing, or 47, where the princes of the people are joined to the people of the God of Abraham—had likewise remained unfulfilled. There was no Davidic king ruling over the world from a high throne in Jerusalem. There is a reason why Jesus, using the shepherd imagery associated with royalty, said cryptically that all who came before him were thieves and brigands.[26] So much the worse, his hearers might have thought, for the Maccabees,[27] for the Hasmoneans, and for the Herodians. Jesus has in mind a different kind of victory, one which will fulfill Ps 2 at last: when the Greeks come to the feast and ask to see him, he declares (John 12:23) that now is the time for the Son of Man to be glorified; that now is the moment of victory when "the ruler of this world" is to be cast out (12:31), so that then he, Jesus,

---

24. See, e.g., Isa 40:3–11; 52:7–12; Ezek 43; Zech 1:16–17; 8:3; Mal 3:1. For the larger issue of an extended "exile" and a long-awaited "return," see now James M. Scott, ed., *Exile: A Conversation with N. T. Wright* (Downers Grove: IVP Academic, 2017).

25. See Wright, *Paul and the Faithfulness of God*, ch. 9.

26. John 10:1, 8.

27. The Maccabees will have been in mind in John 10 because the scene is dated to Hannukah (10:22).

will draw all people to himself. At the center of John's theology of the cross is the victory through which the dark power is overthrown and the nations of the world are summoned to give allegiance to Israel's Messiah. John's reader knows that this is because he is the Word-Made-Flesh, the new and ultimate *tabernacle* where the divine glory is displayed at last (1:14).

These five narrative strands—the unfinished project of creation, the unquiet sea which is the source of chaos and all evils which lead to it, the idolatrous humans who have failed as image-bearers, the unrealized hope of the Creator coming to dwell in the midst of his people, and the unkept covenant which meant that the promises associated with Abraham and David had yet to be realized—these strands are brought together in many rich and mutually illuminating ways as the New Testament writers tell, or allude to, or evoke, the story of Jesus and particularly his death.

## Contours of Jesus's Saving Death

### Jesus's Chosen Symbol

As is well known, the New Testament and the Christian tradition developed many ways of speaking about the meaning and effects of Jesus's death. It is equally common knowledge that, unlike doctrines such as the Trinity and incarnation, the atonement (as some, though not all, Christians refer to it) has never officially been defined—until, that is, the sixteenth-century controversies made it important for various Protestant groups to do so. Among many reasons for this there is one which sometimes gets overlooked, and which I wish to highlight: that the central point of it all for Jesus was not a *theory* but an *action*. When Jesus wanted to explain to his disciples what his forthcoming death was all about, he didn't give them a set of ideas. He gave them a meal. And the meal is more than a mere visual aid, because the reality to which it points (and in which it partakes rather as the grapes brought back from the promised land in Num 13 partook of the reality which they symbolized) is not a set of true beliefs or—back to Plato again!—an abstract *spiritual* reality. The reality to which the eucharistic bread and wine point is the reality of *new creation*, creation set free from its slavery to decay.

This is where the Platonizing of our eschatology has led not only to bad atonement theology but to the twin dangers of rationalism (imagining that being Christian is a matter of figuring out and then believing a true set of ideas) and romanticism (supposing that being a Christian is about people having their hearts strangely warmed). I have nothing against figuring out true ideas; and I am certainly in favor of the strange warming of the heart. But in the New Testament these are in service to the larger goal of new creation, the new creation which is launched in the resurrection of Jesus after the defeat of all hostile powers including death itself. This new creation will finally include the resurrection of all Jesus's people. In the meantime it already includes their revivification by the power of the Spirit.

But this is to run somewhat ahead of ourselves. We may display the point in a sequence of three further features of the New Testament, before then summing it up in five complex but coherent propositions which correspond to the puzzles of my earlier section.

### Jesus Chose Passover as the Kingdom-moment

First, Jesus chose Passover to do what had to be done. He did not choose the Day of Atonement. It is striking, indeed, that though the Gospels, particularly John, mention many of the Jewish holy days, Yom Kippur is conspicuously absent. This relates to something my colleague David Moffitt has stressed in various places: when in the grip of exile—as many Jews believed they still were—what is required is not another regular sacrifice, but a fresh, rescuing, divine action. And the obvious model for that is not the Day of Atonement but the rescue from Egypt: Passover, in other words.

For Jesus, the final Passover was the kingdom-moment, the royal moment *par excellence*. Remarkably, the four Gospels are normally all but ignored in discussions of atonement, precisely because they don't fit the normal, and I have suggested inappropriate, narrative that Western theology has wanted to tell. They are simply not about how sinful souls go to heaven when they die—though some people still try to squash them into that thoroughly inappropriate mold. They are about God's kingdom coming on earth as in heaven. Here we meet the well-known problem, which I have seen all over the place in church life as well as theology: what has Jesus's kingdom-proclamation got to do with his cross, and vice versa? In the Gospels, the two are intricately bound up together. If that is hard for us to grasp, it shows how deeply we have misread the whole tradition. God's kingdom (according to Isa 52 and many Psalms, and also of course Daniel, which are all invoked in this sense in the New Testament) means that God is returning at last to take charge, to put things right, to make all things new. As we might have anticipated, the Gospels tell the story of how, when Jesus announced God's kingdom, at once the forces of chaos seemed to strike back: shrieking demons in the synagogue, plotting

Pharisees in the cornfields, malicious accusations from detractors, malevolent despots in the background, treachery among his own followers, and finally the symbolic and actual power of Rome. The Gospels describe how, after his initial victory over the satan, Jesus drew all these strands of evil onto himself in order to exhaust them in his own death.

The dominant note of the Gospels at this point is that of victory. That is where you arrive if you take the Gospels' kingdom-theme seriously all the way to the cross. That is why, when I have highlighted it, those who see things through the lens of Gustav Aulen's famous book assume that I am playing his game, which is to oppose a supposed *Christus Victor* motif to that of *substitution* or some equivalent.[28] That, I might add, is exactly the same spurious theological either/or as the one advanced by J. Louis Martyn and his followers; but I have dealt with that elsewhere.[29] The point is that, for the Gospel writers, the cross is seen as the moment when Israel's God, in and through the Emmanuel, the Word Made Flesh, wins the victory over all the forces of evil. This victory does not mean that saved souls can now ascend to a Platonic heaven. It means that new creation can at last be launched.

The means by which the victory is won (as indicated in the subtitle to this paper) is through substitution: through Jesus *taking the place of sinners*, dying in their stead. This is woven into the Gospel narratives at point after point, without any statement of a grand theory but simply in the course of events. Jesus identifies with the tax collectors and sinners; he is betrayed into the hands of sinners; he is handed over to sinners.[30] Barabbas is guilty, but Jesus dies in his place.[31] The brigands crucified beside him are guilty, but he has done nothing wrong.[32] He was officially condemned, but he was in fact innocent.[33] Thus, whether on the large scale—where Jesus as Messiah stands in for Israel, and hence (because of Israel's representative status in God's purposes) for the world—or on the small scale, with individual moments, the point is rammed home by all four Gospels. It is not *either* victory *or* substitution. The victory is won by Jesus dying the death of the unrighteous.

How does this work theologically? When you worship an idol, you give

---

28. Gustav Aulén, *Christus Victor: An Historical Study of the Three Main Types of the Idea of the Atonement* (London: SPCK, 1931 [and frequently reprinted]).

29. See my *Paul and His Recent Interpreters: Some Contemporary Debates* (London: SPCK; Minneapolis: Fortress Press, 2015), 135–218.

30. E.g., Luke 5:30; 7:34; Mark 14:41; Luke 24:7.

31. Mark 15:6–15 parr.

32. Luke 23:39–43.

33. Luke 23:47.

that idol power over you; the idol's grip is tightened by the sin which you commit as a result. Thus, if God is to win the victory over the idols which have usurped his rightful rule over his creation, he must deal with the human sins through which the idols consolidate and maintain their power. *Victory through substitution* is thus the name of the game; just as substitution itself is based on Jesus's representative messiahship, as he stands in for Israel and thence for the whole world. That is how Jesus's Passover-project, his kingdom-project, is implemented. All this of course needs much more filling in, as I've tried to do in *The Day the Revolution Began*; but this must suffice for now.

### Paul Saw Jesus's Death as the Defeat of the Powers through Messianic Substitution

The second point about the New Testament is that for Paul all the lines of Gospel narrative run through the cross, but those lines can by no means be reduced to the normal formulae of Protestant dogma or preaching. We are not talking about how sinful souls go to heaven. Again and again—not least in Gal 3 which I mentioned before—the death of Jesus is for Paul the means by which the divine purposes for the world can go forward. Abraham's promise-bearing family were stuck in the Deuteronomic curse because of sin, so that the promise could not get out to the nations; now, with the curse borne, the gentiles can come in. This applies particularly to the great scene in Galatians 2, with Paul's confrontation with Peter at Antioch. Perhaps the main reason why Jews wouldn't share table-fellowship with gentiles was that all pagans were assumed to be fatally tainted with idolatry.[34] But Paul insists that with the death of the Messiah the grip of the pagan idols has been broken. When someone is in the Messiah, as evidenced by faith, then they can and must be treated as full members of the messianic family, because the Messiah's death has dealt precisely with the power of the idols. Not to welcome gentile Jesus-believers is thus to deny the victory of the cross.

So, too, in 2 Cor 5:21, Paul's famous statement about God making the Messiah to be sin is part of his long discussion of his own apostolic ministry, which had been challenged by the Corinthians. Paul applies to himself what he would say of every Christian, that God made the Messiah, who knew no sin, to be sin for us; but the specific purpose is not the normal forensic one of Protestant dogma (that we might have something called "the righteousness of God" imputed to us), but rather that we—apostles in particular, though

34. Cf. e.g., Jub 22:16–17.

no doubt others as well if we'd asked Paul that—might *embody* the divine covenant faithfulness. That is why he goes on at once to quote Isa 49, where the servant is given as the covenant to the peoples. The death of Jesus wins the victory which enables the gospel to go out and fulfill the Isaianic as well as the Abrahamic promises.[35]

We could follow this up in Romans in particular, where the cultic imagery of Rom 3, with the glory and the mercy seat, needs to be brought to the fore instead of being displaced by the heavy-handed post-Anselmic attempts at an imputed legalism.[36] And in Rom 8 we find, at last, the true location of something we can properly call "penal substitution," where there is "no condemnation for those in Messiah Jesus," since God has, on the cross, condemned sin in the flesh of the Messiah, so that the Spirit may do in and through the Messiah's people the life-giving work which the law had all along wanted to do but could not.

That is the point, too—though there is no space here to develop this— where Paul gives his own version of the narrative of the Gospels. Torah was given, he says in Rom 5 and develops in Rom 7, in order "that sin might be exceedingly sinful": in other words, Torah was given paradoxically in order to draw sin—the dark power that had enslaved the world—onto the one place, the single spot, where it could at last be condemned. Sin did its worst in Israel, in the idolatry and rebellion even among those who officially delighted in Torah, leading to the extended exile of Deuteronomy and Daniel, alluded to here in the image of imprisonment.[37] But this was all in the service of the divine purpose in which the Messiah would come, as the focal point of Israel, to take upon himself the weight of Israel's rebellion and with it the idolatry and catastrophe of the whole human race. That is the overall argument of Rom 7 and 8, summed up densely already in Rom 5:20–21.[38]

All this, once more, is in the service, not of a Platonic gospel in which souls make their way to heaven, but the biblical gospel in which the new-temple people (those in whom the Spirit dwells) are on their way to the promised in-

---

35. See the discussion of the passage, with other references, in Wright, *Paul and the Faithfulness of God*, 881–85.

36. See my "God Put Jesus Forth: Reflections on Romans 3:24–26," in *In the Fullness of Time: Essays in Honor of Richard Bauckham*, ed. Daniel Gurtner, Grant Macaskill, and Jonathan T. Pennington (Grand Rapids: Eerdmans, 2016), 135–61.

37. See Rom 7:23: the root αἰχμαλωτίζω resonates with the regular term for "exile," particularly that in Babylon, in e.g., Pss 13:7; 125:1 (both LXX); Neh 1:2–3 [= 2 Esdr. 11:2–3]; Jer 1:3; Ezek 1:1–2; 3:11, 15.

38. I have discussed this in considerable detail in various places including my commentary on Romans in *New Interpreters Bible*, vol. 10 (Nashville: Abingdon, 2003).

heritance which is now the whole redeemed creation. The Spirit here plays the role of the glorious divine presence in the Exodus narrative. The whole world is now God's holy land; Rom 8 celebrates the paradoxical arrival, through suffering and prayer, of the long-awaited kingdom of God on earth as in heaven. There is no time to look wider, except to note that in the climactic passage in 1 Cor 15 Paul offers his own "apocalyptic" scenario of the divine victory, through the Messiah, over all forces of evil, in order that, exactly in line with scriptural promise, the cosmic temple might be filled with the divine presence: so that God may be "all in all."

Thus, exactly as in the Gospels, Paul holds together what many have wanted to split apart. The Messiah, he says at the start of his earliest letter, "gave himself for our sins in order to set us free from the present evil age." Victory through substitution. These are not alternative models or schemes, though people have tried to make them so. They are interlocking features of the one story.

## Revelation Highlights the Victory of the Lamb

The third point, more briefly, is found in Revelation. There, as in John's Gospel (1:29, 36), Jesus is the Lamb who was slain (Rev 5:12). That Passover motif resonates through much of the complex symbolic narrative, as the plagues mirror those in Egypt, as the monster comes up out of the sea but is defeated, as the people sing the song of Moses and the Lamb, and as—the equivalent of Exod 40!—the new Jerusalem comes down from heaven as a bride adorned for her husband.[39] The dimensions of the New Jerusalem mark it out as the great holy of holies in a new creation which, holding heaven and earth together, is the new temple itself.[40] There is no more sea, because in the new creation there is no threat of a resurgent evil. There is no snake in the garden city. And all is achieved through the victory of the Lamb: the scene in chapter 5 says it all. The Creator's purposes, the scroll waiting to be unrolled, cannot be taken forward because no human is capable of it—except the Lamb himself, and then only in virtue of his victorious death. But with that death humans are rescued from their plight of sin and death, not so that they may "go to heaven," but so that, when heaven comes to earth, and even in advance of that ultimate promised reality, they may be the "royal priesthood," the kings and priests in the new temple, the genuine humans in the ultimate heaven-and-earth creation.

---

39. Rev 8–9 (plagues); 13 (beast); 15:3–4 (song); 21:1–5 (New Jerusalem).

40. See, e.g., G. K. Beale, *The Book of Revelation: A Commentary on the Greek Text*, NIGTC (Grand Rapids: Eerdmans, 1999), 1075–76.

## The Cross in Its Narrative Framework

We may now draw the threads together in five propositions, working back up the five points with which I began and showing how the different *models* or *metaphors* or *images* cohere within the larger narrative framework we find in the New Testament—but only once we give up the Platonic hope, and the false trains of thought into which it has led us.

### Covenant Renewed

First, the covenant has been renewed. Jesus's words at the Last Supper, however tricky they are to reconstruct exactly, are clearly meant to carry the connotations, within the carefully staged quasi-Passover celebration, of Moses's inauguration of the original covenant and Jeremiah's prophecy of its renewal. The creator God has been faithful to his promises to Abraham and David. That faithfulness, embodied in the faithfulness of the Messiah, becomes the badge which distinguishes the Messiah's people, whatever their ancestry. *God is faithful to the covenant, renewing it through Jesus's death and resurrection and the gift of the Spirit, so that those who come to belong to the renewed family may be faithful stewards of the covenant purposes.*

### Hope Realized

Second, what Paul calls "the hope of the glory of God" has been realized. That hope, as in Isa 40 and 52, was for the divine glory to return to Zion in public, visible, redeeming action. That action, in Isa 40–55, was focused poetically and theologically on the work of the servant, which, when complete, resulted precisely in the renewal of the covenant (Isa 54) and the renewal of creation (Isa 55). All four Gospels, albeit in very different ways, indicate clearly that they see Jesus as the fulfillment of this hope for the victorious and liberating return of Israel's God.[41] Paul develops the same point in various ways. Thus, as in Exodus, God always intended to dwell with his people, and he does this in Jesus, the Emmanuel, the Word who tabernacles in the midst but who, like the original tabernacle, is placed outside the camp.[42] If the God of life is to dwell with humans, this can

---

41. See Richard B. Hays, *Echoes of Scripture in the Gospels* (Waco, TX: Baylor University Press, 2016); and my discussion in "Pictures, Stories, and the Cross: Where Do the Echoes Lead?," *JTI* 11 (2017): 53–73.

42. Matt 1:23 (Emmanuel); Heb 13:12 (outside the camp).

only be through the removal of the pollution which would prevent his being there, and the New Testament, at precisely this point in the argument, draws upon Israel's sacrificial traditions to explain how that has now happened. I did not develop the sacrificial theme in *The Day the Revolution Began*, but this is where I think it belongs. *God intends to dwell with his people, and he does this in and as Jesus the Emmanuel, thereby also dealing with the problem of pollution; he now dwells in his people by his Spirit so that they can be both the foretaste and the agents of his plan to fill the whole creation with his glory.*

## The Royal Priesthood

Third, formerly idolatrous humans are transformed by the gospel into the royal priesthood—the ancient Israelite designation of God's people, indicating their vocation to be genuine humans, image-bearers, idolaters no longer. It is striking that in Revelation 5 this is seen as the aim and the result of the Lamb's victorious death: "You were slain, and by your blood you ransomed humans for God, from every tribe, tongue, people and nation, and made them a kingdom, priests to our God."[43] As such, the ransomed—the people of the new exodus, in other words—are to be people of prayer and worship, as well as people who bear witness to the gospel with their own suffering and testimony. Their worship, exactly in line with the democratization of the sacrificial system which was taking place in the Jewish world already in the synagogue communities and then much more after the destruction of the temple, was expressed in sacrificial terms, as in Heb 13 or Rom 12. No doubt this sounded strange to pagan neighbors for whom life without animal sacrifice was unusual to say the least. And to get to this point these renewed humans must be liberated from the sins because of which they have been in thrall to the idols they have worshipped, a situation which has allowed the idols to gain a wrongful power not only *over* them but *through* them in the wider world. That is where all the usual questions about God dealing with human sin on the cross come in, as I have already indicated. But as in Revelation, so in Paul and the Gospels, sinners are forgiven not simply so that they can "go to heaven" or have "restored fellowship with God," but so that they can be part of his ongoing purposes as genuine humans. Thus, in Rom 8, sinners are to be "glorified" in the sense of Ps 8, that is, set in authority over the world and thereby renewing it into its original purpose.[44] And in the resurrection narratives in the Gospels, particu-

43. Rev 5:9–10.
44. See Haley G. Jacob, *Conformed to the Image of His Son: Reconsidering Paul's Theology of Glory in Romans* (Downers Grove: InterVarsity, 2018), esp. 233–51.

larly in Luke and John, the result of Jesus's crucifixion and resurrection is that the disciples are commissioned to be for the world what Jesus was for Israel.[45] *God intends to work, as from the start, through obedient, worshipping, image-bearing humans; so he deals with their sin to liberate them from idols and set them free for his service once more.*

## No More Sea

The last two points can be made more briefly. Fourth, in the new creation there is "no more sea"; that is, no more dark chaos-monster threatening to rise up again and attack the fulfilled new creation.[46] Once sins are dealt with, the idols have lost their power. *God intends to overthrow the power of chaos and evil, in order to establish the new world as the ultimate house where he will live. He does this in the death of Jesus, establishing his new house through the resurrection and the Spirit. Now, in the lives of those who believe, he defeats chaos and evil through their mortification, suffering and obedience, so that they may be part of his defeating-evil plan for the world.*

## New Heavens, New Earth

Fifth and finally, God has always intended to put the world right. This is what is meant by *justice* or *justification*; in the Psalms and Isaiah the justice of God is God's determination, like a good judge, to put right what has gone wrong. But this is far wider than simply the "putting right" or justification of individuals, though that remains vital.[47] We could say it like this: *God intends to put the whole world right at last; he accomplished this through the death and resurrection of Jesus, and will complete it at Jesus's return; and, in the meantime, he puts people right through the gospel and Spirit, so that they can themselves be part of his project to put the world right.*

## Conclusion

Thus at every point the larger, more complex but still rigorously coherent biblical narrative finds its dramatic focus on the crucifixion of Jesus. Once that is put at the center, however, it works its way out into the areas of creation and

45. See esp. John 20:19–23, focusing on v. 21: As the Father has sent me, so I'm sending you.
46. Rev 21:1.
47. See Wright, *Paul and the Faithfulness of God*, ch. 10.

new creation, covenant and renewed covenant, the defeat and overthrow of evil, the rescue of idolaters from the grip and consequence of their sin, and the establishment of the new heaven and new earth in which "the dwelling of God is with humans." That, after all, is the ultimate biblical goal, and it is brought about by the victory of the Lamb. The final scene in the Bible is not of saved souls going up to heaven—that would make no sense in terms of Israel's Scriptures, either—but of God's kingship expressed in his rescuing sovereignty, of the great cosmic holy of holies established "on earth as in heaven." The narrative arc from Gen 1 to Exod 40 is the foretaste of the larger arc that reaches all the way to Rev 21. And in the center, presented in the New Testament as the shocking but authentic fulfillment of the Scriptures of Israel, is Israel's Messiah doing what (according to Ps 72) Israel's king should do—rescuing the helpless, so that the world might be filled with the glory of God. The early Christians, then, were not merely ransacking miscellaneous metaphors or models, throwing random items like the law-court, the slave-market, human relationships and the sacrificial cult into a melting-pot where they would all end up meaning more or less the same thing. They were reflecting the coherent interlocking themes of the biblical narrative and affirming their fulfillment in Jesus and the Spirit. If we get the story right, the models will fit.

Ironically perhaps, the word *atonement* has not featured very much in this essay. It has become, as has often been said, too awkwardly polyvalent, too redolent of narratives which have slipped their biblical moorings and drifted off on other philosophical or cultural tides. But if we may use the word heuristically, so that atonement in a Christian context simply means "what the death of Jesus achieves so that the Creator's purposes may be accomplished through the rescue of humans," then it should be clear that this essay has been about nothing else. Perhaps the best reason for not defining what we mean by atonement in one quick formula is that, when rightly understood, the word points to the entire biblical narrative, without losing the centrality of the cross; points, too, to the real world, the world of creation renewed—of flesh and blood, of laughter and tears, of bread and wine.

# CHAPTER SEVEN

# "Seeing," Salvation, and the Use of Scripture in the Gospel of John

*Intertextual Perspectives on the Johannine Understanding of Jesus's Death*

CATRIN H. WILLIAMS

As is true of most, if not all, New Testament writings, the Gospel of John seeks to articulate its understanding of the death of Jesus with reference to, and drawing support from, Scripture. It would indeed be virtually impossible to explore John's contribution to the overarching theme of this volume without taking into account its reception of the Jewish Scriptures and also developments in the study of that reception in recent Johannine scholarship. It is the textual form and function of John's explicit quotations that have hitherto tended to be the focus of scholarly attention, but there is increasing interest in how those quotations relate to the Gospel's ubiquitous allusive modes of scriptural reference—not only in an attempt to plumb the depths of John's engagement with Scripture but in order to determine how that engagement functions within the text. How, then, do scriptural quotations and allusions operate as part of John's narrative design, particularly with regard to their rhetorical, christological, and—we may add—soteriological functions?

## Composite Citations

One notable feature in this respect is John's fondness for composite citations, defined in a recently published two-volume study of this intertextual phenomenon as cases where "literary borrowing occurs in a manner that includes two or more passages (from the same or different authors) fused together and conveyed as though they are only one."[1] In my own contribution to the second of these volumes, I have argued that eight of John's fifteen explicit quotations draw on two or more scriptural source texts to form a single composite citation (John 6:31; 7:38; 12:13; 12:15; 12:40; 13:18; 19:36; 19:37),[2] and that, in most cases, they fit the category of "conflated" citation because they are "characterized by the insertion of a word or phrase from one passage into a quotation from another passage with no signal to the audience that such a commingling of texts has taken place."[3] Shared themes or common vocabulary between two or more *distant* texts have, in all of these cases, played a decisive role in the formation of composite citations, thereby bringing discrete elements into a new interpretative dialogue with one another. The application of such techniques is widely attested in late Second Temple Jewish texts (including the writings of Philo and the Dead Sea Scrolls), although the closest parallels to John's exegetical operations are to be found in various books of the Septuagint, where translational decisions involving verbal modifications, additions or omissions are often dictated by the presence of an identical, or sometimes similar, Greek word or phrase in a separate but analogous context.[4] Such catchword associations or analogical exegesis (linked, to some degree, to what the rabbis later described as *gezerah shawah*) more often than not provides the exegetical legitimation for John's fusion of discrete scriptural verses, even if the impetus—christological or otherwise—for the composite character of a quotation lies elsewhere.[5]

Among the distinguishing features of John's composite citations is that they

1. Sean A. Adams and Seth M. Ehorn, "What Is a Composite Citation? An Introduction," in *Composite Citations in Antiquity: Volume One: Jewish, Graeco-Roman, and Early Christian Uses*, ed. Sean A. Adams and Seth M. Ehorn, LNTS 525 (London: Bloomsbury T&T Clark, 2016), 4.

2. Catrin H. Williams, "Composite Citations in the Gospel of John," in *Composite Citations in Antiquity: Volume Two: New Testament Uses*, ed. Sean A. Adams and Seth M. Ehorn, LNTS 593 (London: Bloomsbury T&T Clark, 2018), 94–127. The "non-composite" direct quotations in John are to be found in 1:23; 2:17; 6:45; 10:34; 12:38; 15:25; 19:24.

3. Christopher D. Stanley, "Composite Citations: Retrospect and Prospect," *Composite Citations in Antiquity: Volume One*, ed. Adams and Ehorn, 204.

4. See, e.g., Jan Joosten, "The Impact of the Septuagint Pentateuch on the Greek Psalms," in *Collected Studies on the Septuagint: From Language to Interpretation and Beyond*, FAT 83 (Tübingen: Mohr Siebeck, 2012), 153–54; Myrto Theocharous, *Lexical Dependence and Intertextual Allusion in the Septuagint of the Twelve Prophets: Studies in Hosea, Amos and Micah*, LHBOTS 570 (London: Bloomsbury, 2012), 107–48.

5. Maarten J. J. Menken, *Old Testament Quotations in the Fourth Gospel: Studies in Textual Form*, CBET 15 (Kampen: Kok Pharos, 1996), convincingly argues that the fusion of analogous passages is an underpinning principle for John's composite citations. See further Catrin H. Williams, "John, Judaism, and 'Searching the Scriptures,'" in *John and Judaism:*

have been deliberately shaped to align closely with the distinctively Johannine presentation of Jesus. *New* scriptural elements are introduced precisely for this purpose, while John limits the scope of the citations to words and phrases that are integral to their new narrative context. Thus, to explain the significance of the unbroken bones of Jesus's crucified body, the second explicit quotation in John's passion narrative takes the form of a tightly phrased composite citation: "Not one of his bones shall be broken" (19:36). Two clusters of sources are generally proposed for this quotation: a configuration of pentateuchal stipulations for eating the Passover lamb, including the prohibition against breaking the animal's bones (Exod 12:46; cf. 12:10 LXX; Num 9:12) and the description in Ps 34:20 (33:21 LXX) of how the bones of the righteous ones will remain intact after death as a sign of God's deliverance: "He [the Lord] will guard all their bones; not one of them shall be broken." The Septuagintal versions of all these passages exhibit close verbal parallels to John 19:36:

| John 19:36 | Exod 12:10 (LXX), 46 |
|---|---|
| ὀστοῦν οὐ συντριβήσεται αὐτοῦ. | καὶ ὀστοῦν οὐ συντρίψετε ἀπ᾽ αὐτοῦ. |
| | **Num 9:12 LXX** |
| | καὶ ὀστοῦν οὐ συντρίψουσιν ἀπ᾽ αὐτοῦ. |
| | **Ps 33:21 LXX** |
| | κύριος φυλάσσει πάντα τὰ ὀστᾶ αὐτῶν, |
| | ἓν ἐξ αὐτῶν οὐ συντριβήσεται. |

A quotation that centers on pentateuchal regulations about the Passover lamb certainly aligns well with the prominence of Passover motifs in John 18–19, including the timing of Jesus's death to coincide with the slaughtering of the lambs (18:28; 19:14, 31) and the intriguing reference to hyssop as the carrier of the sour wine (19:29; cf. Exod 12:22).[6] The pentateuchal passages in question have a high proportion of words in common with John 19:36, but the verbal form συντριβήσεται ("shall be broken") is only found in the Septuagint version of the psalm text to describe how the bones of the righteous ones (plural in the

---

A *Contested Relationship in Context*, ed. R. Alan Culpepper and Paul N. Anderson, RBS 87 (Atlanta: Society of Biblical Literature, 2017), 77–100.

6. See, e.g., Christine Schlund, *"Kein Knochen soll gebrochen werden": Studien zu Bedeutung und Funktion des Pesachfests in Texten des frühen Judentums und im Johannesevangelium*, WMANT 107 (Neukirchen-Vluyn: Neukirchener, 2005), 120–31.

LXX, though singular in the Hebrew text) will remain unbroken after death to demonstrate how God can offer them deliverance. The most likely explanation is that elements from both (sets of) scriptural sources have, on the basis of their analogous lexical features, been fused together by John to form the precisely worded composite citation required for christological purposes. Whereas the psalm refers to the bones of many (τὰ ὀστᾶ αὐτῶν), only the pentateuchal texts focus on a single figure (αὐτοῦ) lending itself directly for application to Jesus. And although all of the passages in question contain συντρίβω in the future tense, the verbal form in the psalm highlights the *divine* passive ("shall be broken"); ultimately, for John, it belongs to God's eschatological plan as to whether Jesus's bones remain unbroken. In its entirety, the citation signals a deliberately *composite portrayal* of Jesus underpinned by catchword association: he is the righteous one of the Psalms who is protected and vindicated by God and, at the same time, he is the true Passover Lamb whose bones will not be broken.

## Composite Allusions

The interpretative maneuvers identifiable in John's composite citations also serve as a helpful guide, even template, for mapping out some of the mechanisms and controls at work in its composite allusions. Thus, one can account for the composite character of some of John's allusions on the basis that if certain elements required for their new Johannine context are absent from one (sometimes primary) source, elements drawn from additional scriptural passages may also be incorporated or are being evoked. It is therefore often unnecessary to pin down John's rich deposit of scriptural allusions to individual references and single meanings. Some motifs bear traces of several sources, evoking not one but a network of associations from the Jewish Scriptures. So, in the case of figurative images like the shepherd (John 10:1–18) and the vine (15:1–10), catchword assimilation between two or more scriptural passages provides the exegetical lever for allusions to act as metonymic scriptural markers with the capacity to fulfill an innovative and multilayered function within the new text.[7] The clustering together of metaphorical images from a variety of scriptural sources is similarly attested, for example, in the Qumran Hodayot,[8] again situating John's exegetical techniques firmly within a Jewish environment.

7. Catrin H. Williams, "Persuasion through Allusion: Evocations of Shepherd(s) and their Rhetorical Impact in John 10," in *Come and Read: Interpretive Approaches to the Gospel of John*, ed. Alicia Myers and Lindsey Trozzo (Lanham: Fortress Academic, 2020), 111–24.

8. Cf. Julie Hughes, *Scriptural Allusions and Exegesis in the Hodayot*, STDJ 59 (Leiden: Brill, 2006), 150–73; see also Gary T. Manning Jr., *Echoes of a Prophet: The Use of Ezekiel in*

## "Lamb of God" (John 1:29, 36) as a Composite Allusion

Taking into account these principles and techniques of exegetical engagement can contribute much to the discussion of what is frequently noted as one of John's foremost contributions to New Testament interpretations of Jesus's death as a form of *atonement,* namely John the Baptist's initial testimony to Jesus as "the Lamb of God who takes away the sin of the world" (1:29; cf. 1:36). Atonement terminology, in the strict sense of cultic-sacrificial categories linked to the Day of Atonement as attested in the Hebrew Bible (Lev 16) and later Jewish traditions, is of course absent from John's Gospel. Neither can it be assumed that references to ἱλασμός in 1 John (2:2; 4:10) should function as an interpretative lens for the Gospel's presentation of Jesus and his mission. All the same, it is not uncommon for the description of Jesus as "the Lamb of God" to be regarded as denoting his atoning death, and this on the basis of one of two principles: either because the term atonement is used by scholars in a more generalized (including noncultic) soteriological sense,[9] or, more commonly, because the acclamation of Jesus as "the Lamb of God" is said to be linked to evocations of lambs as atoning sacrifices in the Hebrew Bible, including—some have argued—the lamb of the Passover ritual.

The Book of Leviticus and other pentateuchal texts frequently refer to young lambs being sacrificed as whole burnt offerings (Lev 9:3), either for the purpose of purification (12:6) or reparation (14:12–13, 21), and often in relation to individual festivals (cf. Num 28–29). However, there are numerous obstacles to associating the Lamb of John 1:29 and 36 with ritual sin offerings, especially in connection with the Day of Atonement.[10] Neither the sacrificial animal

---

the Gospel of John and the Literature of the Second Temple, LNTS 270 (London: T&T Clark International, 2004), 52–59.

9. As noted by Christian Eberhart, "Introduction: Constituents and Critique of Sacrifice, Cult, and Atonement in Early Judaism and Christianity," in *Sacrifice, Cult, and Atonement in Early Judaism and Christianity: Constituents and Critique,* ed. Henrietta L. Wiley and Christian A. Eberhart, RBS 85 (Atlanta: Society of Biblical Literature Press, 2017), 12, 16–17, 22. Cf. Jörg Frey, "Probleme der Deutung des Todes Jesu in der neutestamentlichen Wissenschaft: Streiflichter zur exegetischen Diskussion," in *Deutungen des Todes Jesu im Neuen Testament,* ed. Jörg Frey and Jens Schröter, UTB 2953 (Tübingen: Mohr Siebeck, 2007), 8. For a broad(er) definition, see, e.g., Thomas Knöppler, *Die theologia crucis des Johannesevangeliums: Das Verständnis des Todes Jesu im Rahmen der johanneischen Inkarnations- und Erhöhungschristologie,* WMANT 69 (Neukirchen-Vluyn: Neukirchener, 1994), 91: "ein Heilshandeln Gottes, das die aufgrund von Schuld verwirkte Existenz des Menschen dem verdienten Tod entreißt."

10. Cf. Jörg Frey, "Die Deutung des Todes Jesu als Stellvertretung: Neutestamentliche Perspektiven," in *Stellvertretung: Theologische, philosophische und kulturelle Aspekte,* ed.

of the sin offering (Lev 4:3) nor that of the elimination ritual on the Day of Atonement (16:20–22) is identified as a lamb, and even the evocative notion of the scapegoat "bearing" (Hebrew: נשׂא), thus taking away, the people's sins is expressed in the Septuagint not with the aid of αἴρω, as in John 1:29, but with the verbs λαμβάνω and ἐξαποστέλλω (Lev 16:22 LXX: "And the goat shall bear [λήμψεται] on itself their offenses to an untrodden region, and he [Aaron, the high priest] shall send off [ἐξαποστελεῖ] the goat into the wilderness").[11]

There are several other interpretative possibilities for linking together "the Lamb of God" and the taking away of sin, particularly if John 1:29 is categorized as a composite allusion marked by some degree of indeterminacy.[12] John's fondness for fusing diverse source texts in explicit composite quotations, as well as a growing scholarly awareness of the polyvalent significance of Johannine metaphors in terms of their origin and evocation, support the notion that composite elements linked to a/the lamb in the Jewish Scriptures are consciously being presented in the Baptist's opening witness to Jesus. Polyvalence can open the door to much "semantic creativity,"[13] with the result that the designation of Jesus as "the Lamb of God" has prompted the search for

---

J. Christine Janowski, Bernd Janowski, and Hans P. Lichtenberger (Neukirchen-Vluyn: Neukirchener, 2006), 118–19: "der Sachverhalt, daß Jesus als das wahre Passalamm stirbt, bietet keinen eindeutigen Hinweis auf ein Verständnis seines Todes im Horizont kultischer Sühne."

11. Echoes of the scapegoat ritual (Lev 16:20–22) in John 1:29 are suggested, for example, by Dorothy Lee, "Paschal Imagery in the Gospel of John: A Narrative and Symbolic Reading," *Pacifica* 24 (2011): 16. It can be noted, in this respect, that נשׂא, the first of the two verbs in the Hebrew text of Lev 16:22, is predominantly rendered as αἴρω in the Septuagint, on which see further below.

12. See Jörg Frey, "Edler Tod – wirksamer Tod – stellvertretender Tod – heilschaffender Tod: Zur narrativen und theologischen Deutung des Todes Jesu im Johannesevangelium," in *The Death of Jesus in the Fourth Gospel*, ed. Gilbert Van Belle, BETL 200 (Leuven: Peeters, 2006), 86n89: "eine offene Chiffre."

13. Jesper Tang Nielsen, "The Lamb of God: The Cognitive Structure of a Johannine Metaphor," in *Imagery in the Gospel of John*, ed. Jörg Frey, Jan G. van der Watt, and Ruben Zimmermann, WUNT 200 (Tübingen: Mohr Siebeck, 2006), 226. Nielsen uses conceptual blending theory to examine "the metaphorical construction" through "conceptual integration" of Jesus's description as "the Lamb of God." See further Jesper Tang Nielsen, *Die kognitive Dimension des Kreuzes: Zur Deutung des Todes Jesu im Johannesevangelium*, WUNT 2/263 (Tübingen: Mohr Siebeck, 2009). Nielsen affirms the significant role played by the Jewish Scriptures in this construction but does not examine the contribution of Jewish exegetical techniques such as catchword association (identifiable in John's direct citations) to the *composite* character of the "Lamb of God" acclamation.

several possible scriptural contenders,[14] including the daily offerings of the *tamid* sacrifice in the Jerusalem Temple (Exod 29:38-41 and Num 28:3-10 [Hebrew: כבש, LXX: ἀμνός]) and the Aqedah traditions relating to Abraham's offering of Isaac (Gen 22:7, 8 [Hebrew: שה; LXX: πρόβατον]). Three important considerations must, in this respect, be noted. First, the kind of catchword association identifiable in John's composite citations stems from the use of the same vocabulary (usually Greek but sometimes Hebrew lexemes and phrases) in separate scriptural sources. Second, in the composite quotations, as well as in John's composite allusions, analogical exegesis must be legitimated on *intratextual* as well as intertextual grounds: that is, the identification of possible source texts must be controlled on the basis of their fit with Johannine themes actualized either in the immediate or the wider narrative context.[15] And third, particularly with reference to John 1:29 and 36, "Metaphors remind in order to say something new, they are 'tradition,' but also at the same time 'innovation.'"[16]

Given, as I noted earlier, the prominence of Passover imagery in John's passion narrative, the Passover lamb is a strong contender for the status of primary referent in the case of the figurative statement in John 1:29 and 36.[17] In the Exodus narrative, of course, the lamb[18] does not remove sin(s); rather, its blood—with the aid of hyssop (12:22; cf. John 19:29)—is smeared on the doorposts of the houses as an apotropaic ritual protecting the Hebrews from

14. E.g., Ruben Zimmermann, "Jesus – the Lamb of God (John 1:29 and 1:36): Metaphorical Christology in the Fourth Gospel," in *The Opening of John's Narrative (John 1:19-2:22): Historical, Literary, and Theological Readings from the Colloquium Ioanneum 2015 in Ephesus,* ed. R. Alan Culpepper and Jörg Frey, WUNT 385 (Tübingen: Mohr Siebeck, 2017), 83-90; William Loader, *Jesus in John's Gospel: Structure and Issues in Johannine Christology* (Grand Rapids: Eerdmans, 2017), 158-68.

15. As noted by Lee ("Paschal Imagery," 17-18) with reference to the identification of the likely scriptural elements in the Baptist's statement in John 1:29: "they need to be justified on the basis of their consonance with wider Johannine themes and symbols." See also Sandra M. Schneiders, "The Lamb of God and the Forgiveness of Sin(s) in the Fourth Gospel," *CBQ* 73 (2011): 16-29.

16. Zimmermann, "Jesus – the Lamb of God," 90.

17. See, e.g., Rainer Metzner, *Das Verständnis der Sünde im Johannesevangelium,* WUNT 122 (Tübingen: Mohr Siebeck, 2000), 143-56. For a contrary view, see Reimund Bieringer, "Das Lamm Gottes, das die Sünde der Welt hinwegnimmt (Joh 1,29): Eine kontextorientierte und redaktionsgeschichtliche Untersuchung auf dem Hintergrund der Passatradition als Deutung des Todes Jesu im Johannesevangelium," in *The Death of Jesus in the Fourth Gospel,* ed. Gilbert Van Belle, BETL 200 (Leuven: Peeters, 2006), 207-13.

18. Exod 12:3-5 (MT: שה; LXX: πρόβατον); 12:6 LXX (ἀρνίον); cf. 12:21, 27, 43 (MT: פסח; LXX: πάσχα).

the angel of death (Exod 12:2–7, 23). The blood, rather, is said to be a sign (12:13; Hebrew: אֹת; LXX: ἐν σημείῳ) that will be *seen* by God (LXX: ὄψομαι; cf. 12:23 LXX: καὶ ὄψεται τὸ αἷμα), thus leading to Israel's liberation. This ritual, in turn, is to be repeated annually to commemorate the deliverance of the Israelites from servitude and death in Egypt (12:14, 17, 25–27). Some scholars have attempted to interpret the blood of the lambs in the Passover ritual as a way of atoning for sins,[19] although there is no conclusive evidence in biblical and late Second Temple Jewish traditions to support this view.[20] The interpretation of Passover in Jubilees 49 refers to the lamb being slaughtered before evening (49:1, 12, 19) and its blood being offered on the altar (49:20); it also states that the breaking of the bones of the lamb in the ritual is prohibited on the basis that "not a single bone of the Israelites will be broken" (49:13; cf. John 19:36).[21] The emphasis in Jubilees is not upon the expiatory significance of the Passover lamb as a way of dealing with sin,[22] but on commemorating Passover as a sign of God's deliverance from Mastema and of protection from death (49:2, 7).

The Passover ritual, as described in Jewish Scripture and tradition, may have sacrificial connotations, but it does not establish a clear link between the lamb and the elimination of sin. The Johannine connection between the one and the other can be explained instead on the basis that the Baptist's pronouncement also evokes the description of the Isaianic servant as "like a lamb before its shearer" (Isa 53:7). In this respect, and as Richard Bauckham has convincingly argued,[23] the exegetical legitimation for the composite character of the Johannine Lamb is much stronger if based on the Hebrew text of the scriptural sources in question, since they use the same lexeme (שֶׂה) with reference to both the Passover lamb (Exod 12:3–5; cf. LXX: πρόβατον) and the servant (Isa 53:7; cf. LXX: ὡς ἀμνός). Admittedly, the Isaianic servant is only

19. E.g., Knöppler, *Die theologia crucis des Johannesevangeliums*, 84–85.

20. See, e.g., Hans-Ulrich Weidemann, *Der Tod Jesu im Johannesevangelium. Die erste Abschiedsrede als Schlüsseltext für den Passions- und Osterbericht*, BZNW 122 (Berlin: de Gruyter, 2004), 426–40; Nielsen, " Lamb of God," 237–39. Discussions focus largely on Ezek 45:18–20, 21–25; 2 Chr 30:15–20; Josephus, *Ant.* 2.312; and, for rabbinic evidence, on Exod. Rab. 15:13; 17:3; Mek., on Exod. 12:6.

21. On the apotropaic effect on the community of the non-breaking of the lamb's bones, see also Wis 18:5–9; Ezek. Trag. 184–87. On Jub. 49:13 and its relevance for the interpretation of the scriptural quotation in John 19:36, see Menken, *Old Testament Quotations in the Fourth Gospel*, 161–64.

22. "Sin" in Jub. 49:9 refers to the state of someone who is purified but does not bring an offering to God in its appointed time.

23. Richard Bauckham, *Gospel of Glory: Major Themes in Johannine Theology* (Grand Rapids: Baker Academic, 2015), 154–56, also with reference to the Aqedah tradition in Gen 22.

*likened* to a lamb,[24] but to cite this as a reason for rejecting a possible connection with John 1:29 is to play down the metaphorical force of the acclamation of Jesus as "the Lamb of God."

The emphasis in Isaiah 53, moreover, is on the significance of the servant as the one who "bore the sin(s) of many" (53:12). While "sin" is singular, as in John 1:29, in the Hebrew text of 53:12, it is plural in the Septuagint (cf. 53:11–12 LXX: καὶ τὰς ἁμαρτίας αὐτῶν αὐτὸς ἀνοίσει . . . καὶ αὐτὸς ἁμαρτίας πολλῶν ἀνήνεγκεν; cf. 53:4–5: οὗτος τὰς ἁμαρτίας ἡμῶν φέρει). Indeed, in comparison with the Hebrew text, the Septuagint version intensifies the description of how the servant deals with sins (all plural): he carries the sins of others (53:4 LXX: οὗτος τὰς ἁμαρτίας ἡμῶν φέρει), he has been weakened because of their sins (53:5 LXX: διὰ τὰς ἁμαρτίας ἡμῶν), and "the Lord delivered him for our sins" (53:6 LXX: καὶ κύριος παρέδωκεν αὐτὸν ταῖς ἁμαρτίαις ἡμῶν). The servant's death is clearly understood in its Isaianic context to be of vicarious significance; his voluntary suffering and dying on behalf of others is described as the Lord's way of dealing with their sin(s) (cf. 53:4–6). While none of these statements is articulated with the aid of overtly cultic language, one possible exception is the reference to the servant's life being offered as a guilt—or reparation—offering (53:10 HT: אשׁם);[25] in the LXX it becomes a reference to "sin offering" (ἐὰν δῶτε περὶ ἁμαρτίας), though without clear specification as to what will be given as an offering.[26]

Where the truly Johannine innovation lies, in comparison with the depiction of the servant in Isa 53, is in the expansion of scope from the "sin (or 'sins' [LXX]) of many" (53:12) to "the sin of the world." The Johannine focus on the singular "sin" may also go some way toward explaining why John selects the

---

24. Isa 53:7 LXX: "And he, because he has been ill-treated, does not open his mouth; like a sheep he was led to the slaughter, and as a lamb is silent before the one shearing it, so he does not open his mouth" (NETS translation).

25. See further Joseph Blenkinsopp, "The Sacrificial Life and Death of the Servant (Isaiah 52:13–53:12)," *VT* 66 (2016): 1–14. For the view that Isa 53:7 compares the Servant to a lamb unfit for ritual sacrifice, see Jeremy Schipper, "Interpreting the Lamb Imagery in Isaiah 53," *JBL* 132 (2013): 315–25, esp. 323–25.

26. See Eugene Robert Ekblad, *Isaiah's Servant Poems According to the Septuagint: An Exegetical and Theological Study*, Biblical Exegesis and Theology 23 (Leuven: Peeters, 1999), 245–46; cf. Martin Hengel, "The Effective History of Isaiah 53 in the Pre-Christian Period," in *The Suffering Servant: Isaiah 53 in Jewish and Christian Sources*, ed. Bernd Janowski and Peter Stuhlmacher, trans. Daniel P. Bailey (Grand Rapids: William B. Eerdmans, 2004), 125–26; Wolfgang Kraus, "Jesaja 53 LXX im frühen Christentum – eine Überprüfung, " in *Beiträge zur urchristlichen Theologiegeschichte*, ed. Wolfgang Kraus, BZNW 163 (Berlin: de Gruyter, 2009), 158–59.

verb αἴρω rather than [ἀνα]φέρω ("to carry/bear"), as in the Septuagint version of Isa 53 (vv. 4, 11–12),[27] to describe how Jesus deals with sin (1:29). Extensive use of αἴρω is made within the Gospel, ranging from the idea of taking something upon oneself in the sense of carrying/bearing (cf. John 5:10) to taking something away from one position/state to another (e.g., 2:16; 11:39, 41; 15:2; 19:38; 20:2), including Jesus's life (10:18),[28] and often with the connotation of a dynamically upward movement (5:8–9, 11–12; 8:59; 11:41). In other words, the purpose of the act of taking up, for John, is often in order to take away (that is, remove), which suggests that αἴρω, already in John 1:29, lends itself to be interpreted on more than one level.[29] Jesus takes up or raises up "the sin of the world" and, at the same time, takes it away. This may prove significant if, as will be argued later in this essay, there are links between the description of Jesus as "the Lamb of God" and subsequent Johannine references to his "lifting up" on the cross.

The composite elements in John 1:29 are, in all likelihood, intended to be multilayered with regard to their scriptural evocations, while their fusion in the Baptist's statement about Jesus affords some helpful clues as to how salvation *works* according to John. Focusing on the *removal* of sin (singular) rather than the *forgiveness* of sins (plural) dovetails with the Gospel's understanding of sin as a power and condition that, within the Johannine "cosmic drama,"[30] affects the whole of humankind, that is, as part of the conflict between God and Satan,

27. Isa 53:4, 12 (HT): נָשָׂא. See further J. Terence Forestell, *The Word of the Cross: Salvation as Revelation in the Fourth Gospel*, An Bib 57 (Rome: Biblical Institute Press, 1974), 160, who notes that αἴρω is never used in the LXX to denote the bearing of sin(s) and its consequences.

28. Cf. the reference to the Servant's life being *taken* from the earth in Isa. 53:8 LXX: ὅτι αἴρεται ἀπὸ τῆς γῆς ἡ ζωὴ αὐτοῦ. For a brief examination of the use of the verb αἴρω in John's Gospel, see Knöppler, *Die theologia crucis des Johannesevangeliums*, 69–70.

29. Cf. also Bauckham, *Gospel of Glory*, 156–57, although he makes the case for the polyvalent potential of αἴρω in John 1:29 on the basis of intertextual (predominantly Hebrew) links rather than intratextual connections from within John's Gospel. Of particular interest, from an intertextual perspective, is the possible play on the various levels of meaning attached to αἴρω in Isa 53:8, with the first clause (v. 8a) highlighting the notion of "taking away" (ἐν τῇ ταπεινώσει ἡ κρίσις αὐτοῦ ἤρθη: "in his humiliation his judgment was taken away" [NETS]) and the third (v. 8c) lending itself to the connotation of "taking up" (ὅτι αἴρεται ἀπὸ τῆς γῆς ἡ ζωὴ αὐτοῦ: "because his life is being taken from the earth" [NETS]).

30. Schneiders, "Lamb of God," 4; cf. Metzner, *Das Verständnis der Sünde im Johannesevangelium*, 140–43. On examining John's interpretation of Jesus's sacrificial death through the lens of "reconciliatory engagement," see Edward W. Klink III, "The Gospel of John," in *T&T Clark Companion to Atonement*, ed. Adam J. Johnson (London: Bloomsbury T&T Clark, 2017), 515–21.

light and darkness. As becomes increasingly clear from the development of the narrative: to be under the power of Satan, for John, is to be enslaved to sin and death (8:21, 34, 44; 9:41; cf. 10:28; 17:12), that is, to be isolated from God's gift of life in and through Jesus (cf. 15:22, 24; 16:8–9). How Jesus actually deals with sin, as a barrier to the gift of life, may not be spelled out in the Gospel's opening narrative scene, but the composite image of Jesus as "the Lamb of God" strongly suggests that the evangelist already looks ahead to, and certainly includes, the effects of Jesus's death as his way of eliminating sin, particularly in view of the significance attached to the sacrificial death of a lamb (or lambs) in such a wide range of scriptural texts—in fact in all of the most likely scriptural sources. Notwithstanding the absence of explicitly cultic associations in John 1:29, the scripturally informed soteriological qualities of the lamb must be linked in some way to suffering and death; this includes the Isaianic servant's way of dealing with sin by giving his life for the sake of others, and also the blood of the Passover lamb as a way of removing the threat of death.

There is one element in John 1:29, however, that is invariably overlooked, and that is the Baptist's call for others to "see" (ἴδε) the Lamb of God, often translated as "Behold" or "Look." When the Baptist sees Jesus approaching him, he is prompted to identify Jesus with the Lamb of God, but his words are, at the same time, an invitation for the disciples to *see* Jesus as "the Lamb."[31] Indeed the scene as a whole possesses a strongly visual dimension;[32] Jesus is observed through the Baptist's eyes, who, by means of ἴδε, encourages others to look at the one who has until now remained hidden. When Jesus appears the second time (1:36, again with the Baptist's acclamation prefaced by ἴδε), two of the Baptist's disciples follow Jesus (1:35–37; cf. 1:40) and initiate a chain of witnesses that are drawn to Jesus by seeing and believing in him: "Come and see" (1:39, 41–42, 45–46). In this respect John the Baptist acts as a "model of what his followers should do,"[33] in that his own testimony stems from what he himself *saw* when the Spirit descended on Jesus (1:32: τεθέαμαι; 1:33: ἐφ᾽ ὃν ἂν ἴδῃς; 1:34: κἀγὼ ἑώρακα).

John's presentation of the Baptist as a visionary witness who *sees* is again indelibly shaped by the Jewish Scriptures, particularly the prophecies of Isaiah, thus adding even more depth to the Baptist's highly composite testimony about

---

31. See further Zimmermann, "Jesus – the Lamb of God," 94.

32. See Catrin H. Williams, "John (the Baptist): The Witness on the Threshold," in *Character Studies in the Fourth Gospel: Native Approaches to Seventy Figures in John*, ed. Steven A. Hunt et al., WUNT 314 (Tübingen: Mohr Siebeck, 2013), 53–55.

33. R. Alan Culpepper, *Anatomy of the Fourth Gospel: A Study in Literary Design* (Philadelphia: Fortress Press, 1983), 133.

Jesus's soteriological significance: "Behold the Lamb of God who takes away the sin of the world." From the outset, the Baptist draws out the importance of Isaiah as his co-witness, "as the prophet Isaiah said" (1:23), to highlight his identity as the voice in the wilderness proclaiming the way of the Lord (Isa 40:3). This *way* is actualized when Jesus—repeatedly described in these opening scenes as the Coming One—appears and is then acclaimed as "the Lamb of God." Even the visual focus (ἴδε) is reminiscent of the language used by Isaiah to signal the way of the Lord: "See (ἰδού), your God" (40:9 LXX), and then again: "See (ἰδού), the Lord comes with strength" (40:10 LXX).[34] Isaiah's announcement is none other than a call for others to see the Lord as he comes along his way to Zion,[35] just as the Baptist calls upon others to see Jesus, the Lamb of God, as he goes along his way.

Both Isaiah and the Baptist testify, moreover, to what they have seen (12:41: "Isaiah saw his [Jesus's] glory and spoke about him"), with the Baptist even using the words of his prophetic predecessor to furnish his testimony with content and authority. For this purpose he draws specifically on Isaianic traditions about the servant, not only through the acclamation of Jesus as "the Lamb of God who takes away sin" (1:29), but also in John 1:34, if one accepts not "Son of God" but the early reading "the chosen one of God" (ὁ ἐκλεκτὸς τοῦ θεοῦ; cf. Isa. 42:1 LXX: ὁ ἐκλεκτός μου), which echoes the opening lines of the first Servant Song, "My servant whom I uphold; my chosen one, in whom my soul delights." Isaiah 42:1 continues with a reference to God putting his Spirit on the servant, whereas in John's narrative the Baptist acknowledges Jesus's identity as the Lamb and Chosen One of God as a direct result of seeing the Spirit remain on him (1:32–33). The Baptist thus allusively takes up Isaianic prophecies to inform the content of his testimony to the Spirit-endowed figure who, like Isaiah's servant (53:7 LXX), is seen but remains silent.

Thus, already in the opening scene of Jesus's public ministry, various ways of understanding the Johannine theme of *seeing* are introduced: seeing on the basis of divine revelation; seeing on the basis of testimony that is to be passed on to others; seeing as the basis of faith; and a form of *visionary* seeing that already looks ahead to the soteriological effects of Jesus's life, and

---

34. Ἴδε and ἰδού can function in a synonymous manner for John, as indicated by the use of ἰδού in John 19:5 ("Behold the man!") and ἴδε in John 19:14 ("Behold your king!").

35. See also Catrin H. Williams, "The Voice in the Wilderness and the Way of the Lord: A Scriptural Frame for John's Witness to Jesus," in *The Opening of John's Narrative (John 1:19–2:22): Historical, Literary, and Theological Readings from the Colloquium Ioanneum 2015 in Ephesus*, ed. R. Alan Culpepper and Jörg Frey, WUNT 385 (Tübingen: Mohr Siebeck, 2017), 51–52.

especially his death. All of these interrelated motifs are scripturally informed and, on the basis of John the Baptist's invitation for others to see Jesus as "the Lamb of God," they establish a Johannine network of interpretative associations that will be developed—through a variety of configurations—later in the Gospel narrative, as well as providing a scriptural-soteriological frame for that narrative.[36]

## John's "Lifting Up" Sayings—Seeing the Exalted One

Composite allusions drawing from the Jewish Scriptures, and especially from the prophecies of Isaiah about the servant, also occur elsewhere in John's Gospel to unveil other dimensions of its soteriological understanding of Jesus's mission. Among the most striking cases are the three sayings in which the verb ὑψόω is used to describe Jesus being lifted up on the cross and, at the same time, to convey his death as an act of exaltation (3:14; 8:28; 12:32, 34).

The first occasion, in John 3:14, is a comparison of the lifting up (ὑψωθῆναι) of the Son of Man with Moses's act of lifting up (ὕψωσεν) the bronze serpent in the wilderness (3:14)—an act intended to heal the Israelites from the bites of the fiery snakes after they acknowledge their sin (Num 21:4–9). The elevation of the serpent serves, for John, as a kind of type or foreshadowing of Jesus's *lifting up*, with the result that the scriptural incident is compressed to include only the most essential components for the comparison and its vocabulary harmonized with that of the present event through the use of ὑψόω (not ἱστάναι as in Num 21:9 LXX). Interestingly, and significantly, whereas the apotropaic function of the blood of the Passover lamb is described as a "sign" in Exod 12 (cf. also Jub. 49:3: σημεῖον), the pole that holds the serpent is, in the Septuagint translation, also transformed into a visible "sign" for the Israelites (Num 21:8, 9 LXX: ἐπὶ σημείου).[37] These parallels offer significant points of contact between the Johannine understanding of Jesus's identity as "the Lamb of God" (1:29, 36) and his lifting up on the cross (3:14), even offering scripturally evocative hints that

---

36. On Jesus's identification as "the Lamb of God" fulfilling the function of a christological and narratological inclusio, see esp. Jean Zumstein, *Kreative Erinnerung: Relecture und Auslegung im Johannesevangelium*, 2nd ed., ATANT 84 (Zürich: Theologischer Verlag, 2004), 220–21. See further below.

37. Although it is not only the sight of the serpent, but obedience to God's command that brings about salvation (cf. Nielsen, "Lamb of God," 244). This apotropaic function is played down in later Jewish interpretation; cf. Wis 16:6 where the serpent becomes a "symbol of salvation" (σύμβολον σωτηρίας) in that it is a catalyst for a proper attitude to God.

Jesus's death on a cross is, for John, the ultimate σημεῖον.[38] The visibility of a/the sign further aligns with the fact that the intended correspondence in John 3:14 is not between Moses and Jesus but between the effects of the two acts of lifting up. Thus, although the second part of the comparison refers to *believing* rather than *seeing* the one who is lifted up, there is close alignment between seeing and believing on the basis of the parallel structure and content of John 3:15 (πᾶς ὁ <u>πιστεύων</u> ἐν αὐτῷ ἔχῃ ζωὴν αἰώνιον) and Num 21:8 LXX (πᾶς ὁ δεδηγμένος <u>ἰδὼν</u> αὐτὸν ζήσεται).[39] But it is a connection that also involves some degree of contrast: gazing at the serpent led to physical healing (ζήσεται), while seeing Jesus with faith will lead to eternal life (3:15).

If the lifting up of Jesus here alludes to the manner of his death, the widespread figurative use of ὑψόω to denote exaltation is also being activated, since the life-giving purpose (ἵνα) of Jesus's death is also brought into view in John 3:14-15. The comparison is certainly phrased in a way that heightens rather than settles possible ambiguities. The analogy between two literal/physical acts of lifting up (of the serpent, on the one hand, and Jesus, on the other) could have worked with the aid of other Greek verbs, such as αἴρω—the verb used in John 1:29—and this would certainly highlight striking layers of consonance between αἴρω and ὑψόω as far as their Johannine application is concerned.[40] The interpretative possibility that the Lamb of God is said to take away sin by *taking it up* thus dovetails with, and finds further support in, the distinctively Johannine references to Jesus being lifted up on the cross.[41] Having said that, only ὑψόω has the capacity for semantic associations linked to exaltation as well as elevation. The use of the passive form (ὑψωθῆναι) and the element of necessity (δεῖ)—"must be lifted up"—also suggest God as subject (cf. 10:16;

---

38. See, e.g., Gilbert Van Belle, "The Death of Jesus and the Literary Unity of the Fourth Gospel," in *The Death of Jesus in the Fourth Gospel*, ed. Gilbert Van Belle, BETL 200 (Leuven: Peeters, 2006), 11-37, esp. 23-26; cf. Deolito V. Vistar, Jr., *The Cross-and-Resurrection: The Supreme Sign in John's Gospel*, WUNT 2/508 (Tübingen: Mohr Siebeck, 2020).

39. As argued in particular by Jörg Frey, "'Wie Mose die Schlange in der Wüste erhöht hat . . .': Zur frühjüdischen Deutung der 'ehernen Schlange' und ihrer christologischen Rezeption in Johannes 3,14f.," in *Schriftauslegung im antiken Judentum und im Urchristentum*, ed. Martin Hengel and Hermut Löhr, WUNT 73 (Tübingen: Mohr Siebeck, 1994), 183-84.

40. Interestingly, αἴρω (not ὑψόω) is frequently used in the Septuagint to describe the lifting up of a sign/signal (σημεῖον); cf. Isa 5:26; 11:12; 13:2; 18:3; 33:23; Jer 28:12, 27 LXX (noted by Frey, "'Wie Mose,'" 160 n. 34); see also Isa 5:26; 49:22 LXX. In all of these cases, with the exception of Isa 33:23 and 49:22 LXX, αἴρω is used to render the Hebrew verb נשׂא.

41. Cf. Craig S. Keener, *The Gospel of John: A Commentary* (Peabody: Hendrickson, 2003), 1: 456. Bauckham, *Gospel of Glory*, 157.

11:51; 12:34) and acts as a marker that other scriptural elements, in addition to Numbers 21, are being evoked in John 3:14.

This possibility is strengthened by the use of the verb ὑψόω in Isa 52:13 LXX to describe God's promise to exalt his servant: "See, my servant shall understand, and he shall be exalted and glorified greatly" (ἰδοὺ συνήσει ὁ παῖς μου καὶ ὑψωθήσεται καὶ δόξασθήσεται σφόδρα).[42] The juxtaposition of ὑψόω and δοξάζω is a distinctive characteristic of the Septuagint of Isaiah,[43] and their use to denote the exaltation and glorification of the servant can provide a theological-scriptural impetus for the Johannine presentation of Jesus's own exaltation and glorification, including his lifting up on the cross as an event of revelation and salvation. There are several peculiar features in the Septuagint translation of the opening divine oracle (Isa 52:13–15 LXX) that lend support to this proposal.

First, and in contrast to the Hebrew text, all of God's introductory speech in the Septuagint translation is oriented toward the future. The future tense is used to express God's announcement about the exaltation and glorification of his servant (52:13), to describe the servant's dishonoring among people who oppress and afflict him (52:14),[44] and to convey the amazement of nations and kings when they finally see (ὄψονται) and understand him.[45] Second, the casting of all these different facets of God's speech as future *events* means that they lend themselves to mutual interpretation. The most widespread estimation of the introduction to the oracle (52:13 MT and LXX) among commentators is that it offers an anticipatory outline of the exaltation that will *follow* the servant's suffering and death, which is described in the main part of the song (53:1–11). It has nevertheless been proposed, in this connection, that John was prompted to read Isa 52:13 not so much as an anticipatory outline pointing forward to the consequences of the servant's suffering and death but rather as a summary assessment of the message of the song in its entirety: the exaltation of the servant is "the whole sequence of humiliation, suffering, death, and vindication beyond death which chapter 53 describes."[46] However, given the consistently future-oriented focus of Isa 52:13 LXX and of what follows

42. Significantly, as for Isa 52:13, the Septuagint of Isaiah translates the Hebrew verb נשׂא as ὑψόω (cf. also Isa 2:2; 33:10; 52:8; 63:9 LXX), but elsewhere uses αἴρω (in addition to the examples noted in fn. 40 above, see Isa 37:23; 45:20; 46:1, 7; 49:18; 51:6; 60:4; 66:12 LXX).

43. The same correlation, but with the remnant of Israel as referent, occurs in Isa 4:2; 10:15.

44. This involves interpreting the oracle as shifting from a statement *about* the servant (52:13) to one addressing him directly (52:14: σέ and σοῦ).

45. See Nielsen, "Lamb of God," 229–31, 231–33.

46. See esp. Richard Bauckham, *God Crucified: Monotheism and Christology in the New*

in 52:14–15 LXX, I propose that the "death-*as*-exaltation" pattern can already be established on the basis of the Septuagint version of the oracle in 52:13–15, and certainly has the potential to be read in this way: although the servant's appearance and "glory" (δόξα) will be de-glorified (ἀδοξήσει) in the eyes of other people (cf. 52:14; 53:2–3), he will, *at the same time*, be exalted and greatly glorified by God (52:13).

This would mean that the Septuagint version of Isa 52:13–15 points to a twofold vision of the servant—one that characterizes those who see him in a physical sense (52:14) but the other centered on the divine perspective on *seeing* (52:13). This is already highlighted in the opening divine call of the song (ἰδού; cf. Isa 40:9–10 LXX; ἴδε in John 1:29, 36) and is then fulfilled when they—to whom the message about the servant had not previously been announced—will finally see (52:15: ὄψονται) and understand. A much stronger connection is thus forged in LXX Isaiah between the divine challenge to *see* the exaltation and glorification of the servant and the eventual *coming to see* that is attributed to the nations.

Consequently, and returning to John 3:14: the account about the bronze serpent in Numbers 21 and the figurative force of ὑψόω ("lifting up") in Isa 52:13 have a shared emphasis on the act of *seeing* the one elevated/lifted up high,[47] thus supporting the function of John 3:14 as yet another Johannine example of a *composite scriptural allusion* in which motifs associated with the Isaianic servant play a prominent role. In the same way as the Israelites must look at the image of the serpent to be healed (Num 21:8–9), it is necessary to see with faith the one who is lifted high on the cross and exalted in order to receive eternal life (John 3:14b). Soteriological correspondence between these two acts can be ascribed additional interpretative dimensions if the comparison also suggests that the elevated serpent and the crucified Son of Man visibly exhibit the results of human sin and opposition to God. Through their *lifting up*, which connects to the notion of the Lamb of God *taking away* sin by taking it up[wards] and visibly dealing with sin,[48] both the serpent on the pole and

---

*Testament* (Carlisle: Paternoster, 1998), 64. Cf. also C. H. Dodd, *The Interpretation of the Fourth Gospel* (Cambridge: Cambridge University Press, 1953), 247.

47. The visual aspect implicit in this interpretation of the correspondence is highlighted by Knöppler, *Die theologia crucis des Johannesevangeliums*, 155–60. Cf. Francis J. Moloney, *The Johannine Son of Man*, 2nd ed., Biblioteca di Scienze Religiose 14 (Rome: Libreria Ateneo Salesiano, 1975). 59–61; Jörg Frey, "Die '*theologia crucifixi*' des Johannesevangeliums," in *Kreuzestheologie im Neuen Testament*, ed. Andreas Dettwiler and Jean Zumstein, WUNT 151 (Tübingen: Mohr Siebeck, 2002), 228.

48. John Painter, "Sacrifice and Atonement in the Gospel of John," in *Israel und seine*

Jesus as Son of Man demonstrate God's ability to transform the results of sin (Num 21:4–7; cf. John 8:28) into the means of giving life.[49]

At this stage of the Johannine narrative at least, the elusive character of the *exaltation* of Jesus persists. John 3:14 maintains the open-endedness of the image by referring to belief in (πᾶς ὁ πιστεύων), rather than seeing, the elevated Son of Man (3:15). Although verbs of sight are frequently used to denote belief in John's Gospel (e.g., 6:40; 12:21, 45; 14:9), I propose that they may have been deliberately avoided here to ensure that *seeing* is not limited to the visually concrete lifting up of the crucified Jesus.

Further illumination is offered by the second *lifting up* saying in John's Gospel, where Jesus's Jewish opponents are ascribed the role of agents in his elevation: "When you have lifted up (ὑψώσητε) the Son of Man, then you will know that I am he (ἐγώ εἰμι)" (8:28). The primary reference is to the physical raising of Jesus on the cross, but that it points to other levels of meaning is suggested by the way in which it overtly attributes revelatory significance to the crucifixion: the lifting up of Jesus will bring about recognition of his identity as the visible manifestation of God (ἐγώ εἰμι). Once again, as in 3:14, the concrete/visible sign of Jesus being lifted up becomes the catalyst for insight, but it also becomes the locus of judgment (κρίσις) for salvation or condemnation. In other words, whoever accepts this offer of salvation will come to life but its rejection will lead to death; this is why Jesus informs his Jewish interlocutors a few verses earlier (8:24) that they will "die in their sins" (though singular in 8:21), and will consequently be cut off from life, unless they believe that he is ἐγώ εἰμι. Insight and proper recognition are necessary to secure deliverance from sin and death.

The third, and final, "lifting up" saying of the Johannine Jesus occurs in a section dominated by declarations about his imminent death and departure (12:20–36). The arrival of the "hour" amounts to judgment of this world and its ruler (12:31), to the cross as "the place of eschatological triumph, the defeat of sin and death,"[50] which therefore leads Jesus to pronounce that when he is "lifted up from the earth" (ἐὰν ὑψωθῶ ἐκ τῆς γῆς) he will draw "all"

---

*Heilstraditionen im Johannesevangelium*, ed. Michael Labahn, Klaus Scholtissek and Angelika Strotmann (Paderborn: Ferdinand Schöningh, 2004), 292, tentatively proposes that αἴρω in John 1:29 could be translated as "expose."

49. Craig R. Koester, "Why Was the Messiah Crucified? A Study of God, Jesus, Satan, and Human Agency in Johannine Theology Messiah," in *The Death of Jesus in the Fourth Gospel*, ed. Gilbert Van Belle, BETL 200 (Leuven: Peeters, 2006), 178.

50. Lee, "Paschal Imagery," 18.

(πάντας) to himself.[51] With regard to the immediate context of this declaration in John 12—but also the cumulative effect of the three "lifting up" sayings—the primary connotation of ὑψόω here is the physical elevation of Jesus on the cross. That it refers to the manner of his death is confirmed by John's explanatory aside: "he said this to *signify* [σημαίνων] what kind of death he was to die" (12:33; cf. 18:32; 21:19). Once again, the context provides some clarification about the intended meaning of ὑψόω (12:32a), particularly its anticipated consequences (12:32b). The drawing of people to Jesus as a result of his elevation is to be linked to his earlier statement about the necessity for a grain of wheat to die (12:24): by means of his death Jesus brings fruit and draws "all" to himself, as proleptically implied by the request of the Greeks (that is, in all likelihood, a group of gentiles) to *see* him (12:20–22). Again, the description of Jesus being lifted up "from the earth" deliberately plays on the visual aspect of him being set up high for all to see (cf. 3:14), in that it is the exalted Jesus on the cross who can offer salvation for those who *see* him.

What is striking, but rarely noted, is that John's gradual elucidation of the "lifting up" theme coincides with a progressively more explicit outworking of links between Jesus and the Isaianic servant. On the first occasion (3:14) the possible influence of Isaiah's portrayal of the servant is restricted to the verb ὑψόω itself. The connection between them becomes more apparent in the second saying (8:28), particularly due to the linking together of two key Isaianic motifs (ὑψόω and ἐγώ εἰμι). The fullest explication of Jesus's mission through an Isaianic lens (52:12–53:1) occurs in relation to the third, and final, "lifting up" saying: declarations about his future glorification (12:23) and exaltation (12:32, 34) come about as a result of the approach of the Greeks wishing to "see" (ἰδεῖν) him, thus enacting Isaiah's prophecy that nations who had not previously been told about the servant will eventually see (52:15 LXX: ὄψονται).[52] Significantly, the desire of the Greeks to see Jesus (12:21) is not reported, which implies that it is not fulfilled at this point; the *seeing* is deliberately delayed until after Jesus's *lifting up*. Their wish to see Jesus stands, moreover, in stark

---

51. For the view that the phrase "when I am lifted up from the earth" (ἐὰν ὑψωθῶ ἐκ τῆς γῆς) in John 12:32 evokes Isa 53:8 LXX (ὅτι αἴρεται ἀπὸ τῆς γῆς ἡ ζωὴ αὐτοῦ), see Knöppler, *Die theologia crucis des Johannesevangeliums*, 162–63.

52. The influence of Isa 52–53 on John 12:20–43 has been investigated in a number of studies, including Craig A. Evans, "Obduracy and the Lord's Servant: Some Observations on the Use of the Old Testament in the Fourth Gospel," in *Early Jewish and Christian Exegesis: Studies in Memory of William Hugh Brownlee*, ed. Craig A. Evans and William F. Stinespring (Atlanta: Scholars Press, 1987), 221–36; Johannes Beutler, "Greeks Come to See Jesus (John 12,20f)," *Bib* 71 (1990): 341–46.

contrast to the inability of "the Jews" to believe in him because, as John reflects a few verses later, their eyes—"as the prophet Isaiah said"—have been blinded (12:37–40, quoting Isa 53:1 and 6:9–10). The Isaianic witness bubbling under the surface since the early stages of John's narrative—and already in the testimony of the Baptist—now comes to clear expression in John's reflections on the origins and implications of seeing, as well as not seeing, Jesus.

## Seeing the Pierced One

The configuration of certain important Johannine motifs—and their scriptural resources—so far examined in this essay reappear in the passion narrative in John's two final explicit quotations, both of which are clustered together as a double citation to explain specific aspects of the manner of Jesus's death and the state of his crucified body (19:36–37): the piercing of his side—from which blood and water issue forth—enables a Roman soldier to verify that Jesus is already dead (19:34), thus preventing his legs from being broken (19:32–33). If the first of these two quotations, as I suggested earlier, projects the composite image of Jesus as the Passover lamb and righteous sufferer, the primary scriptural source for the second quotation (ἑτέρα γραφή) is Zech 12:10 about the mourning for a (shepherd) figure: "They shall look upon the one whom they have pierced" (ὄψονται εἰς ὃν ἐξεκέντησαν). The textual form of John 19:37 is highly obscure and has generated much scholarly debate. It has some affinities with the Hebrew text ("And they shall look on me, on one who is pierced"), which appears to suggest that the "me" and the "one who is pierced" is none other than God. The Septuagint version of Zech 12:10 evidently seeks to clear up such textual obscurities, but its reading, "And they shall look upon me because they have mocked [me]" (καὶ ἐπιβλέψονται πρός με ἀνθ᾽ ὧν κατωρχήσαντο), bears no resemblance to the citation in John 19:37. They do not have a single word in common.

What, therefore, is the source of the scriptural quotation in John 19:37,[53] and what should be made of the fact that the extant Greek versions (LXX, Theodotion, Aquila) of Zech 12:10 read ἐπιβλέψονται where John has ὄψονται? The use of ὁράω is a less natural translation than ἐπιβλέπω (which means "to look

---

53. For discussion of this issue, see, e.g., William Randolph Bynum, "Quotations of Zechariah in the Fourth Gospel," in *Abiding Words: The Use of Scripture in the Gospel of John*, ed. Alicia D. Myers and Bruce G. Schuchard, RBS 81 (Atlanta: Society of Biblical Literature Press, 2015), 66–69.

upon attentively") of the Hebrew verb in question (נבט) and indicates that John 19:37 has gone its own way and is probably dependent on another source for ὄψονται. Several attempts have been made to trace this source to an early *testimonia* collection,[54] and this is because of the close similarity between John 19:37 and other NT quotations/allusions to Zech 12:10, especially Rev 1:7 with reference to Christ's parousia: "and every eye shall see him (ὄψεται αὐτόν), also those who pierced (ἐξεκέντησαν) him." The difference, then, would be that ὄψονται takes on realized eschatological significance in John 19:37 to denote the "seeing" of Jesus as a result of his crucifixion.

Even so, if we take John's other composite citations as an interpretative guide, it is important to note that *substantive* substitutions or additions to a primary scriptural source text can invariably be traced to, and are exegetically legitimated by, a secondary scriptural source text. This prompts the search for a different solution to the quotation in John 19:37 and the possibility that ὄψονται is to be derived from a scriptural passage other than Zech 12:10—one that exhibits lexical and thematic links with the Zechariah text and also coheres with the reception of the Scriptures attested elsewhere in John's Gospel. The prophecies of Isaiah, including the description of the Isaianic servant, can once again shed light on the textual form of the scriptural citation in John 19:37. Attention has been paid earlier in this essay to the likely contribution of Isaianic prophecies to John's understanding of *seeing*,[55] particularly in relation to faith (John 3:14; cf. 12:38–41, with reference to Isa 6:9–10; 42:18–20; 44:18; 53:1). Two Isaianic declarations are particularly instructive in terms of identifying a composite element in John 19:37, namely Isa 52:10 and 52:15, both in terms of their analogous features with Zech 12:10 and its wider context as well as their resemblance to key Johannine elements.

The similarities between Isaiah 52–53 and Zech 12:9–13 are well documented, not least their descriptions of the death of a figure who is mourned by the people.[56] In Isaiah 52 the suffering of the servant figure is set within the context of God's return and self-manifestation in Jerusalem (cf. Zech 9:9, quoted in John 12:15), which leads to a proclamation of his universal kingship. Particularly striking is Isa 52:10 which, in the Septuagint, reads: "The Lord shall reveal (ἀποκαλύψει; MT: 'has revealed') his holy arm in the sight of all the nations, and all the ends of the earth shall see (ὄψονται) the salvation that

---

54. E.g., Dodd, *The Interpretation of the Fourth Gospel*, 428; Menken, *Old Testament Quotations*, 168–70, 177.

55. See discussion in the previous section, "John's 'Lifting Up' Sayings."

56. Hengel ("Effective History of Isaiah 53," 85–90) proposes that Zech 12:9–13:1 and 13:7–9 offer an eschatological interpretation of Isaiah's suffering servant.

comes from God."[57] Zechariah's depiction of the vision of the pierced one also bears affinities with Isa 52:15, whose announcement about the suffering and future exaltation of the servant is again linked directly to the *seeing* response of many nations (cf. Zech 12:9–13:1): those to whom it was not previously announced about the servant will finally see (Isa 52:15 LXX: ὄψονται), which is the same verbal form as the one used in John 19:37 to describe the *seeing* of Jesus as the pierced one.

To determine the relevance of these possible intertextual and composite connections for the interpretation of the quotation in John 19:37, the function of *seeing* (ὄψονται) within its new Johannine setting needs to be clarified. The immediately preceding section of the crucifixion account could suggest that the subject of both *seeing* and *piercing* is one and the same: that is, the Roman soldier(s) who are responsible for piercing Jesus's side and, by extension, the Ἰουδαῖοι (19:31), although neither is said to see Jesus. The immediate context and John's narrative explanations suggest, nonetheless, that ὄψονται in the scriptural quotation should not be interpreted in this overly limited (and literal) sense, because a different act of seeing—linked specifically to testimony and belief—is also highlighted in connection with the description of blood and water flowing from Jesus's side: "the one who saw (ὁ ἑωρακώς) this has testified so that you may also believe" (19:35). The positive seeing ascribed to the eyewitness means that he sees "the pierced one" with faith,[58] which also makes him a representative figure for future believers (19:35: ἵνα καὶ ὑμεις πιστεύ[σ]ητε), called upon to "participate in an extended and continued fulfillment by gazing upon the crucified Christ."[59] This connotation is further suggested by the indeterminate character of ὄψονται (pl.) in the quotation and also because its verbal form points to the *future* ("they shall see") rather than to a past event.

This interpretation of John 19:37 resonates with the message of the three "lifting up" sayings in the first half of the narrative (3:14–15; 8:28; 12:32–33), together with their own evocations of the connection between "lifting up" and "seeing" in the fourth Servant Song: these declarations, like John 19:37, encapsu-

---

57. For the view that John identifies Jesus as "the arm of the Lord" described by Isaiah (esp. in the LXX), see Catrin H. Williams, "Johannine Christology and Prophetic Traditions: The Case of Isaiah," in *Reading the Gospel of John's Christology as Jewish Messianism: Royal, Prophetic and Divine Messiahs*, ed. Benjamin E. Reynolds and Gabriele Boccaccini, AJEC 106 (Leiden: Brill, 2018), 105–10.

58. See, e.g., Christopher M. Tuckett, "Zechariah 12:10 and the New Testament," in *The Book of Zechariah and Its Influence*, ed. Christopher M. Tuckett (Aldershot: Ashgate, 2003), 111–22, here 116.

59. Bynum, "Quotations of Zechariah in the Fourth Gospel," 71.

late the paradoxical notion that salvation is available to all those who see Jesus as the crucified/pierced one who is lifted up and exalted on the cross. Thus the increasingly more explicit outworking of links between Jesus and the Isaianic servant reaches its culmination in the Johannine presentation of Jesus's death as the means of revelation and salvation for those who see and believe.

Yet this does not exhaust the layers of scriptural signification in John's description of the immediate consequences of Jesus's death. The final quotation in John's Gospel, particularly when its function as the second part of a double citation (19:36–37) is taken into account, also picks up on the invitation issued by John the Baptist, at the beginning of the Gospel narrative, for people to "see" Jesus as "the Lamb of God who takes away the sin of the world" (1:29). This invitation finds its completion or realization when Jesus is seen on the cross.[60] Given the connection between John 1:29 and the interest in Passover imagery elsewhere in the Johannine crucifixion account, it is somewhat surprising that so few attempts have been made to identify an allusion to the Passover lamb, not only in the signaling that the lamb's bones are to remain unbroken (19:36) but also regarding the salvific *significance* of the lamb's death in the description of the flow of blood and water issuing forth from Jesus's side (19:34).[61] The reference to blood and water certainly highlights the importance of belief in the reality of Jesus's death, and possible eucharistic overtones will have been activated primarily through connections with αἷμα language in John 6:53–56. Nevertheless, identifying scriptural resonances in the reference to blood and water draws out, and in fact gathers together, key facets of John's understanding of the effectiveness of Jesus's death as the means for the taking away of sin/death and the gift of life. Blood can be understood to evoke symbolically the substance affording protection and deliverance from death in the context of Passover (hence the description of the blood as a "sign" in Exod 12:13; Jub. 49:3).[62] The water issuing from Jesus's side also points to the life-giving power

---

60. The inclusio framing John 1:29, 36 and 19:36 is frequently noted (e.g., Lee, "Paschal Imagery," 19; Zimmermann, "Jesus – the Lamb of God," 92; Klink, "The Gospel of John," 517, 520), but not the connection with 19:37.

61. Among the few exceptions are Barnabas Lindars, *The Gospel of John*, New Century Bible Commentary (London: Marshall, Morgan & Scott, 1972), 587; Weidemann, *Der Tod Jesu im Johannesevangelium*, 447, 450; Jo-Ann A. Brant, *John*, Paideia Commentaries on the New Testament (Grand Rapids: Baker Academic, 2011), 258: "the accent in John is on Jesus's triumph [as the Passover lamb] over the powers that bring death." Cf. Nielsen, "Lamb of God," 251.

62. Weidemann (*Der Tod Jesu im Johannesevangelium*, 426, 447–48) expands this connection along "satanological" lines (cf. John 12:31; 14:30; 16:11), particularly in view of the

of his death. From an intratextual perspective, it harks back to the numerous references earlier in the Gospel to water as the means of new birth, symbolic of the Spirit that gives life (4:14: 7:38). And from an intertextual perspective, it evokes the scriptural promise, after the passage about seeing "the pierced one," which speaks of the fountain of water opened up for the house of David and the inhabitants of Jerusalem in order for the flowing water to cleanse them from sin and impurity (Zech 13:1 MT). As a result, the composite character of Scripture is attested not only in each of the two quotations individually (19:36–37) but also through their juxtaposition as the Johannine passion narrative draws to its conclusion: together they confirm and clarify the importance of *seeing* the blood and water in relation to the sin-removing and life-giving significance of Jesus's death.

## Conclusion

Any attempt at exploring how multilayered resonances work within John's Gospel must acknowledge that this self-referential text draws on a wide range of discrete images and traditions, with the result that they can interact with each other through various configurations to produce a composite picture of the Johannine understanding(s) of Jesus's death. This essay has focused on one particular network of associations, one held together by a scripturally informed focus on the relationship between seeing and salvation. Scriptural resources, and especially—I have argued—those brought into conversation with Isaiah's prophecies about the servant, play a decisive role in articulating the importance of sight and insight in relation to the soteriological effects of Jesus's death. Diverse intertextual elements also work in close tandem with intratextual features within the Johannine narrative, so that progressive development is identifiable in the outworking of its network of associations as well as a gradual unfolding of the meaning of its embedded, often composite, scriptural references.

This sequential unfolding does, nonetheless, extend beyond John's passion narrative. The elements drawn together at the end of the crucifixion account— the seeing and believing of Jesus's death as the means to life, all of which are said to occur in fulfillment of Scripture—also highlight the inextricable link established within the Gospel between the death and resurrection of Jesus.

---

identification of Mastema as the agent of death in Jub. 49:2, 7. This kind of connection is, nevertheless, not made explicit in the Johannine passion narrative.

Whether one focuses on the relationship between Jesus as "the Lamb of God" (1:29) and the one who baptizes with the Spirit (1:33), or on the heightened ambiguity of John's language of exaltation and glorification, or even on the connection between Jesus's death-removing blood and life-giving water in the crucifixion account, the narrative undeniably accentuates the inseparability of Jesus's death and resurrection insofar as the salvation of believers is concerned. For John the crucified Jesus is indispensable as a focus for faith, so that, in the resurrection narratives, the risen Jesus is seen and identified by the marks of his crucifixion (20:20, 25, 27–28). And so, while the life-giving power of Jesus is *seen* and believed when he dies and yields the spirit (19:30), John's Gospel also makes clear that it is the risen Lord who confers the life-giving Spirit on others by breathing new life (20:22) into those with eyes to see.

# CHAPTER EIGHT

# Sealed for Redemption

*The Economics of Atonement in Ephesians*

T. J. LANG

The language of ransom, gift-exchange, and wealth that coalesces in the early portions of Ephesians resurfaces across the rest of the letter. At the outset Paul's readers learn of their redemption through the currency of Christ's blood (τὴν ἀπολύτρωσιν διὰ τοῦ αἵματος αὐτοῦ, 1:7), which accords with the riches of divine beneficence (κατὰ τὸ πλοῦτος τῆς χάριτος αὐτοῦ).[1] This "economy" (οἰκονομία), as it is termed in verse 10, is again described in verse 14, where it is additionally related to the "pledge of inheritance" (ἀρραβὼν τῆς κληρονομίας) and "redemption" (ἀπολύτρωσις). Redeemed humanity is also defined as God's "acquisition" (περιποίησις).[2] In verse 18, Paul refers to "the wealth of God's glorious inheritance" (ὁ πλοῦτος τῆς δόξης τῆς κληρονομίας αὐτου). According to 2:4, God is "rich" (πλούσιος) in his mercy and, according to 2:7, this is demonstrated in "the extravagant wealth of his charity in generosity to us in Christ Jesus" (τὸ ὑπερβάλλον πλοῦτος τῆς χάριτος αὐτοῦ ἐν χρηστότητι ἐφ᾽ ἡμᾶς ἐν Χριστῷ Ἰησοῦ). In 2:8, Paul clarifies just what this extravagant "charity" (χάρις) is: an "endowment from God" (θεοῦ τὸ δῶρον). In the next chapter, Paul turns to the "economy" (οἰκονομία) given to him (3:2, 9), which is again associated with the language of gift: χάρις in verses 2, 7, 8 and δωρεά in verse 7. Such language is, yet again, coordinated with the

---

1. I refer throughout to the author of Ephesians as Paul, despite modern anxieties about authenticity. Even if not by Paul, the letter is still an important (and, in some sense, authoritative) appropriation of Pauline language, and should be treated as such.

2. Cf. Mal 3:17: "And they shall be mine, says the Lord Almighty, in the day when I make them my acquisition (περιποίησιν), and I will choose them as a person chooses his son who is subject to him" (NETS).

promise of "Christ's inexhaustible wealth (τὸ ἀνεξιχνίαστον πλοῦτος)" (3:8) and the "wealth (τὸ πλοῦτος) of glory" (3:16). The same recurs in chapter 4, with references to "the beneficence (ἡ χάρις) that accords with the measure of Christ's gift (τῆς δωρεᾶς) given to us" (4:7) and to the impending "day of redemption" (εἰς ἡμέραν ἀπολυτρώσεως, 4:30), for which the saints have been "sealed" (ἐσφραγίσθητε) by the Holy Spirit.

The primary interest of this essay is this collocation of sealing and redemption, which appears first in 1:13–14 and then finally in 4:30. Despite the recurrence of this collocation, interpreters have neglected how the nomenclature of sealing may belong to the same sociolinguistic register as that of redemption, thus giving the expression contextual coherence. Sealing, it is usually assumed, refers to some ritual activity, be it baptism, chrismation, or an apotropaic rite.[3] Redemption, it is assumed, refers to something else. To be "sealed for redemption" thus ostensibly amalgamates two discourses, the one involving ritual, the other involving ransom. Irrespective of a specific ritual behind the language of sealing, this terminology also belongs to the discourse of commerce and correlates appropriately with the discussion of humanity's ransom. To be "sealed for redemption" is to be marked as ransomed property, earmarked capital, as in the funds Paul "seals" for delivery to Jerusalem in Rom 15:28. The question is how this whole constellation of commercial terminology in Ephesians—redemption, wealth, gift-giving, pledge of security, inheritance, and so forth—might be synthesized into a coherent account, with sealing included. I focus on the first instance of the sealing/redemption collocation in Eph 1:13–14 and argue for a financial reading in four lexical demonstrations.

After surveying some of the usual readings of sealing in 1:13, the first demonstration lays out the data for the commercial use of sealing language. This is widespread and receives intriguing but oft-overlooked support in Paul himself. The second examines important connections between the descriptions of the Spirit in 1:13 as "of the promise" and then, in the subsequent relative clause in 1:14, as an "ἀρραβών of inheritance." Promise and inheritance are frequently coupled in Paul and elsewhere, and in ways that lay emphasis on the monetary dimension of the inheritance. The third examines the phrase "pledge of inheritance," attending especially to the nature of the ἀρραβών, which is a technical term in commerce, and one with some nuance. The fourth turns to the phrase "for the redemption of the acquisition" and its grammatical relation to what precedes it. The conclusion brings this cluster of transactional phrases and images together and reflects more broadly on the so-called "ransom theory" of atonement.

3. For an efficient summary of previous interpretations, see Tucker S. Ferda, "'Sealed with the Holy Spirit (Eph 1,13–14) and Circumcision," *Bib* 93 (2012): 557–79.

## Sealed by the Spirit in Ephesians 1:13

Because of the subsequent history of liturgical practice and language, interpretations of Paul's description of believers as having been "sealed by the Holy Spirit" in Eph 1:13 (and in 4:30) are inevitably drawn away from the meaning of this image in its immediate context and toward speculation on a ritual *Sitz im Leben* behind it. Andrew Lincoln, for instance, after a brief paragraph introducing this language, quickly pivots to the question of liturgical practice: "But to what precise aspect of the readers' experience does the imagery of 'sealing' correspond?"[4] There is no mischief in this. But such consideration of a liturgical practice of sealing does perhaps too quickly untether that language from the terminology immediately attached to it, namely, the transactional images in verse 14 of an ἀρραβών of inheritance and the redemption of property. How these images hold together, and how the language of sealing might relate to them, is thus left unexamined.

The most common reading of the sealing in Eph 1:13 is with reference to baptism.[5] The explicit association of sealing with baptism is, however, only first extant in the second century.[6] So Hermas can say, "Therefore, the seal is the water (ἡ σφραγὶς οὖν τὸ ὕδωρ ἐστίν). Into the water, therefore, the dead ones descend, and they arise living. To these, then, this seal (ἡ σφραγίς) was proclaimed" (*Sim.* 9.16.4). From the perspective of the second century, language of sealing in a text like Eph 1:13 is indeed likely to evoke baptism. But it is important to bear in mind that there is nothing from the first century that unambiguously connects the two. Even if one is persuaded baptism or some other rite is in view, it is still exegetically sensible to consider why being sealed by the Holy Spirit in verse 13 is linked immediately with the financial images in verse 14.

Others have detected in verse 13 an allusion to circumcision.[7] Thus John

---

4. Andrew T. Lincoln, *Ephesians*, WBC 42 (Grand Rapids: Zondervan, 1990), 39.

5. On the history of this correlation, see Karl Olav Sandnes, "Seal and Baptism in Early Christianity," in *Ablution, Initiation, and Baptism: Late Antiquity, Early Judaism, and Early Christianity*, ed. David Hellholm et al., BZNW 176.II (Berlin: de Gruyter, 2001), 1441–81.

6. Especially informative for much that follows is Joseph Ysebaert, *Greek Baptismal Terminology: Its Origins and Early Development* (Nijmegen: Dekker & Van de Vegt N. V., 1962).

7. See esp. Ferda, "'Sealed with the Holy Spirit (Eph 1,13–14).'" Ferda argues that "regardless of which rite or experience 'sealed' refers to, the author of Ephesians invests that rite or experience with theological significance commonly attached to circumcision" (558). I don't intend to controvert this, but I do contend that, when read in context, the author of Ephesians invests the language of sealing with *economic* significance appropriate to the subjects of inheritance and redemption.

Chrysostom comments on this passage: "The Israelites were also sealed, but with circumcision, just like cattle and other beasts (καθάπερ καὶ τὰ βοσκήματα καὶ τὰ ἄλογα). So also, we were sealed, but as sons, by the Spirit."[8] Chrysostom here compares the sealing of the Christian by the Spirit with the sealing that is Israel's circumcision, but then he polemically distinguishes them, likening circumcision (apparently) to the branding of livestock and sealing by the Spirit to that which is fitting for a son. Chrysostom's association of *seal* with circumcision in this passage is unsurprising. This linkage is common in early Christian literature, such as Barn. 9.6: "And you will say, 'the people were circumcised as a seal' (εἰς σφραγῖδα)." It is sometimes assumed that the first extant author to describe circumcision as a seal is Paul himself in Rom 4:11, referring to Abraham as having received "the sign (σημεῖον) of circumcision as a seal (σφραγῖδα)." There is, however, a noteworthy collocation of sealing and circumcision in Aramaic Levi, which is dated between the fourth and second centuries BCE.[9] The text reads: "Circumcise the foreskin of your flesh and you will appear like us and you will be sealed like us (ותהם חתימין כואתן) with circumcision of [righteo]usness."[10] There is then no reason to presume Paul's alignment of sealing and circumcision is in any way innovative or idiosyncratic. It remains the case, however, that in other extant literature prior to Paul, the predominant term for circumcision is the first one in Rom 4:11: σημεῖον. This is the word God used in his covenant with Abraham: "And you will be circumcised in the flesh of your foreskin, and this will be a sign of the covenant (καὶ ἔσται ἐν σημείῳ διαθήκης) between me and you" (Gen 17:11).

The Pauline correlation of both sign and seal with circumcision is also known in rabbinic texts, and this despite the prevalence of "seal" imagery in early Christian literature and liturgy. So the Babylonian Talmud: "He set a covenant in his flesh and his offspring he sealed with the sign of the holy covenant" (b. Šabb. 137b).[11] "Signs" (σημεῖα), like seals and circumcision, are

8. John Chrystostom, *Hom. Eph.* 2.1.11–14.

9. The earliest manuscript is 4QLevif ar, which dates to the Hasmonean period, but the text under consideration is extant only in fragments from the Cairo Geniza, which dates to the late 9th or early 10th century CE. There is no reason to presume it is not original. For all introductory matters related to this text, see James R. Davila, "Aramaic Levi: A new translation and introduction," in *Old Testament Pseudepigrapha: More Noncanonical Scriptures*, ed. Richard Bauckham, James R. Davila, and Alexander Panayotov (Grand Rapids: Eerdmans, 2013), 121–32.

10. This is the translation of Davila. The Aramaic text from this Cambridge fragment (T-S 16.94) is printed in R. H. Charles, *The Greek Versions of the Testament of the Twelve Patriarchs* (Oxford: Clarendon, 1908), 245.

11. For discussion of other Jewish texts, see Ysebaert, *Greek Baptismal Terminology*, 245–53.

also frequently physical markings, as in the case of the σημεῖον given to Cain in Gen 4:15; or the σημεῖον placed on the hands of Israelites in memory of Passover in Exodus 13:9, 16; or the σημεῖον placed on the foreheads of those who mourn over lawless deeds, thereby sparing them death in Ezek 9:4, 6. Signs and seals in the ancient world are thus cognate phenomena.[12]

It is worth pointing out that an allusion to circumcision in the language of sealing does not exclude the possibility that an alternative rite is actually behind the terminology. Paul, for instance, correlates circumcision with baptism in Col 2:11–12 as he describes believers "in Christ" as "circumcised with a circumcision not done with hands," and then identifies this circumcision as taking place in baptism.[13] Paul (or his earliest tradents) may, therefore, have merged these two ritual acts when referring to believers as "sealed." Whatever the case, there is more to this language than a purported ritual behind it. The preoccupation with the *Sitz im Leben* behind the seal imagery in Ephesians only draws attention away from what is in fact on the foreground of the text: the explicit correlation of sealing with vocabulary related to financial exchange and acquisition. When Paul defines the Holy Spirit who seals believers as a "pledge of inheritance" and then relates that sealing to "redemption of the acquisition," he is not mixing metaphors or mingling terminology from disparate sociolinguistic spheres. To be sealed by the Holy Spirit is to be endorsed as God's ransomed property.

## Sealing Terminology in the Realm of Commerce

Whether or not Chrysostom is correct in interpreting the sealing in Eph 1:13 as an allusion to circumcision, he is correct in viewing it as marking ownership.[14] Seals, like other forms of branding and tattooing, were common in the realm of commerce for identifying property.[15] This use of the word group is ubiquitous in the ancient world. Chrysostom seems to view the seal of circumcision

---

12. The verb σημαίνω, in fact, is even sometimes used for the activity of sealing, and so synonymously with σφραγίζω. See Ysebaert, *Greek Baptismal Terminology*, 208–9.

13. Reading the participle συνταφέντες in v. 12 as modifying the verb περιετμήθητε in v. 11.

14. Commentators on 1:13 routinely note the relation of sealing and marking property, but they do not attempt to connect this idea to what immediately follows.

15. For detailed study of the seal, see Jakob Diehl, "Sphragis: Eine semasiologische Nachlese" (PhD Diss., Giessen, 1938). Also Ysebaert, *Greek Baptismal Terminology*. For tattooing and branding, see C. P. Jones, "Stigmata: Tattooing and Branding in Graeco-Roman Antiquity," *JRS* 77 (1987): 139–55.

specifically as akin to the branding of livestock. This is likewise a common use of the term.[16] We see Christian evidence of this in Rev 7:3–8 and 9:4, with both the noun and the verb used in reference to individuals with the "seal of God" on their foreheads.[17] These individuals are thereby spared the torture of mutant locusts (9:1–12). So also Acts Thom. 26: "God knows his own sheep by his seal."

Besides labeling property, seals were also used to guarantee authenticity and prevent tampering with contents. This is frequent in the documentary papyri. Moulton and Milligan cite P.Oxy. 6.932 (175–199 CE): "if you come, take out six artabae of vegetable-seed, sealing it in the sacks (τοὺς σάκκους σφραγίσας) in order that they may be ready."[18] Deissmann cites BGU 1.249 (second century CE): "seal (σφράγεισον) the wheat and the barley," which he takes to mean "seal (the sacks containing) the wheat and the barley."[19] In Tob 9:5, Raphael provides Gabael with an account of money owed (τὸ χειρόγραφον), and then counts the bags (τὰ θυλάκια) he intends to collect "with their seals intact" (ἐν ταῖς σφραγῖσιν).[20] The seals certify the integrity of the contents. For a papyrological account of the sealing of θυλάκια, see the references to "having sealed the bag" (θυλάκιον ἐσφραγισμένον) in P.Cair.Zen. 1.59069 (257 BCE). The sealing of differently named sacks occurs again in a papyrus dated to 251 BCE: ". . . after sealing the sacks, send . . ." (τοὺς σ[ά]κκους σφραγισάμενος ἀπόστειλον) (P.Petr. 1.25). We perhaps see this same usage in Paul, with the exact same verbal form as the quotation above, when in Rom 15:28 he refers to the "sealing" of the Jerusalem collection for transport, perhaps even in sacks similar to the above quotations:[21] "Therefore, when I finish this and seal for them this income (σφραγισάμενος αὐτοῖς τὸν καρπὸν τοῦτον), I will set out via you to Spain."[22] Like a merchant sealing sacks of grain for sale or transport, so Paul will seal and certify the revenue (καρπός) raised for Jerusalem.[23] Given

16. See Ysebaert, *Greek Baptismal Terminology*, 210–14.

17. Cf. Ezek 9:4–6.

18. James H. Moulton and George Milligan, *The Vocabulary of the Greek Testament* (London: Hodder and Stoughton, 1930), 617 s.v. σφραγίζω.

19. Adolf Deissmann, *Bible Studies: Contributions Chiefly from the Papyri and Inscriptions to the History of the Language, the Literature, and the Religion of Hellenistic Judaism and Primitive Christianity*, 2nd ed., trans. Alexander Grieve (Edinburgh: T&T Clark, 1903), 238–39.

20. For full description of the scenario here, see Tob 4:20–5:3.

21. For further consideration of interpretive options, see Ludwig Radermacher, "Σφραγίζεσθαι: Rm 15:28," *ZNW* 32 (1933): 87–89.

22. Cf. again the parallels to this expression in the papyri noted by Deissmann, *Bible Studies*, 238–39.

23. For καρπός as income or profit in Paul, see also Phil 4:17.

this usage in Rom 15, it is noteworthy that on the three other occasions Paul uses the verb, it is connected with financial terminology, particularly that of earnest, inheritance, and ransom:

**2 Cor 1:22**
the one who seals us, giving the pledge (τὸν ἀρραβῶνα) of the Spirit on our hearts.

**Eph 1:13–14**
you were sealed with the Holy Spirit of the promise, which is a pledge of our inheritance (ἀρραβὼν τῆς κληρονομίας ἡμῶν), for the redemption of the acquisition (εἰς ἀπολύτρωσιν τῆς περιποιήσεως) . . .

**Eph 4:30**
And do not grieve the Holy Spirit of God, with whom you were sealed for the day of redemption (ἐν ᾧ ἐσφραγίσθητε εἰς ἡμέραν ἀπολυτρώσεως).

One context in which the practice of sealing coincides with similar legal and financial subjects is in Roman *tabulae*, the wooden tablets upon which wills (*testamenta*) and mancipation documents (*mancipatio*) were required by law to be composed and then ratified by sealing. Elizabeth Meyer has traced the history of these *tabulae* and their seals in the first century CE.[24] An important development in this time period is the move from the diptych to the triptych, that is, three bounded wooden tablets instead of just two. As Meyer notes, the increased use of the triptych corresponds with "the enhanced importance of sealing."[25] The third *tabula* seems to have been added specifically to protect the seals from exposure because, if not properly sealed, the document would be invalid.[26] Meyer also examines the close relationship between the process of sealing and the growing importance of the expression of *fides* (good faith) on the *tabulae*, which is especially interesting given the correlation of faith and sealing in Eph 1:13.[27] Meyer writes, "sealing and then the adoption of a triptych to protect the seals . . . is also a sign that the tablet itself has come to be seen as grasping and embodying not just a legal act but also *fides*."[28] The relationship between one's expression of faith and one's seal was integral: "If a seal was 'your very self,' in Cicero's words, your *fides*, then wielding it was a powerful pleasure

24. Elizabeth A. Meyer, *Legitimacy and Law in the Roman World: Tabulae in Roman Belief and Practice* (Cambridge: Cambridge University Press, 2004), esp. 125–68.
25. Meyer, *Legitimacy and Law in the Roman World*, 125.
26. For an accessible description, see Suetonius, *Nero* 17.
27. See esp. Meyer, *Legitimacy and Law in the Roman World*, 156–58.
28. Meyer, *Legitimacy and Law in the Roman World*, 156.

and using a triptych to protect the seals ... was to protect yourself."[29] Much more could be said about these documents, the legal significance of sealing, and the intriguing correspondence of personal identity and document in the prior quotation, but it is worth pointing out that Paul himself depicts believers as living *tabulae* with the Spirit's writing on them: "You are our letter, written on our hearts, to be known and read by all, exhibiting that you are a letter of Christ, prepared by us, written not with ink but with the Spirit of the living God, not on tablets (*tabulis*) of stone but on tablets (*tabulis*) of human hearts" (2 Cor 3:2–3 Vulg.).[30]

It is no accident that the terminology of sealing attracts the terminology of commerce. It is consistently the case that when Paul talks about sealing, he is speaking in commercial terms. Whatever ritual technique may have conferred that sealing on individuals (if there was one), it is figured by Paul as a form of commercial certification. The sealed believer is ransomed property, a newly acquired "slave of Christ." As Paul puts it in 1 Cor 7: "For whoever was called by the Lord as a slave is a manumitted person belonging to the Lord, just as the freeperson who was called is a slave of Christ. You were bought with a price" (7:22–23). As Deissmann noted some time ago, Paul's use of these metaphors is in no way novel.[31] It is rather in agreement with the widely known and attested "customs and technical formulae of sacred manumissions in antiquity."[32] To these customs, sealing believers for redemption also belongs.[33]

## Promise and Pledge of Inheritance

Next to consider is the nexus of promise and inheritance. The Holy Spirit who seals believers is first described as "of the promise" and then further defined, via the relative clause in Eph 1:14, as a "pledge of inheritance." The association

29. She goes on: "Authors of a *bona fides* act in a chirograph-style document on a triptych protected their texts with their seals, their seals with the third *tabula*. A person's *fides* was wrapped up and sealed in a bundle tied with string, all of which had to be preserved and defended" (Meyer, *Legitimacy and Law in the Roman World*, 156).

30. Importantly, in 2 Cor 1:22, the Spirit's activity on the hearts of believers is connected with sealing.

31. Adolf Deissmann, *Light from the Ancient East: The New Testament; Illustrated by Recently Discovered Texts of the Graeco-Roman World*, trans. Lionel R. M. Strachan (New York: Harper & Brothers, 1922), 319–31.

32. Deissmann, *Light from the Ancient East*, 320.

33. For the use of seals to mark humans as property, see Ysebaert, *Greek Baptismal Terminology*, 211–12.

of promise and inheritance is standard in Paul. The word *promise* (ἐπαγγελία) appears four times in Rom 4 and in direct relation to Abraham's status as *heir* (τὸ κληρονόμον): "For the promise that he would inherit the world (ἡ ἐπαγγελία . . . τὸ κληρονόμον αὐτὸν εἶναι κόσμου) did not come to Abraham or to his descendants through the law but through the righteousness of faith" (4:13). This is in keeping with Gal 3, where ἐπαγγελία appears eight times and again in direct relation to Abraham's inheritance: "For if the inheritance (ἡ κληρονομία) comes from the law, it no longer comes from the promise (ἐξ ἐπαγγελίας); but God granted it to Abraham through the promise (δι' ἐπαγγελίας)" (3:18). The same connection is maintained in Eph 3:6 as Paul states that gentiles are "co-inheritors" (συγκληρονόμα) with Israel, and so "co-sharers of the promise" (συμμέτοχα τῆς ἐπαγγελίας). Language of promise and inheritance also occurs in other Jewish literature: "It is God who has saved his people and returned the inheritance to all (ἀποδοὺς τὴν κληρονομίαν πᾶσιν) . . . as he promised (ἐπηγγείλατο) through the law" (2 Macc 2:17–18); "May the pious of the Lord inherit the promises of the Lord (ὅσιοι κυρίου κληρονομήσαισαν ἐπαγγελίας κυρίου)" (Pss. Sol. 12:6).[34] The combination of promise and inheritance is thus conventional.[35]

The word ἐπαγγελία is often translated "announcement," "profession," or, of course, "promise," but it can also indicate a financial pledge and perhaps even have the sense of a promissory note—a nuance worth noting given the relation with inheritance and ransom in Eph 1:14. The word is extremely rare in the Greek Scriptures but has this sense of monetary pledge in Esther: "So Mordechai told him what happened, and the promise that Haman had promised (τὴν ἐπαγγελίαν ἣν ἐπηγγείλατο Αμαν) to the king of ten thousand talents into the treasury so that he could destroy the Judeans" (4:7). The verb ἐπαγγέλλομαι is also routinely related to monetary promises or the like: "he pledged (ἐπηγγείλατο) to him three hundred talents" (1 Macc 11:28); "pledging (ἐπαγγειλάμενος) three hundred and sixty talents of silver" (2 Macc 4:8); "he did not pay regularly any of the money pledged (ἐπηγγελμένων) to the king" (2 Macc 4:27); "Menelaus promised (ἐπηγγείλατο) a substantial bribe" (2 Macc 4:45); "boldly pledging (ἐπαγγελλομένη) to give each of them two minas of gold" (3 Macc 1:4); "pledged (ἐπηγγείλαντο) to give him money" (Mark 14:11); "pledged (ἐπηγγείλατο) to give it to him as his possession" (Acts 7:5). Given this widespread pattern of usage, it would not be unreasonable to read ἐπαγγελία in verse 13 with this sense of monetary pledge—a note payable sealed on believers for the inheritance and ransom described in verse 14.

34. Cf. James 2:5.
35. Cf. Gal 3:14.

## The Spirit as "Ἀρραβών of Our Inheritance"

An economic reading of the "promise" in verse 13 is corroborated by the following relative clause, which further defines the promissory Spirit as an ἀρραβών of inheritance. This word is variously translated as "pledge," "earnest," "deposit," "guarantee," or "down payment," all of which convey aspects of its economic nuance. It is a technical term for a provision (usually monetary) that ratifies a contractual relationship, either as a first installment or as security in place of some other provision. In the Greek scriptural traditions, the word only appears in Gen 38, where it describes the ring, necklace, and staff Judah gives Tamar as immediate security for the young goat he tenders in exchange for sex (38:17–20).[36] In the New Testament, the term occurs two other times in Paul and also in relation to the provision of the Spirit. In 2 Cor 1:21–22 Paul writes: "And the God who secured the possession of us along with you for Christ, and anointed us, also sealed us, giving the pledge of the Spirit in our hearts." The commercial imagery in this verse begins at the outset with the use of ὁ βεβαιῶν, which I have adventurously translated "secured the possession of" in agreement with the suggestions of LSJ: "*secure* one *the possession of* a thing"; "*guarantee the validity of* a purchase"; "*warrant* the purchaser's title."[37] Moulton and Milligan also see the association of ὁ βεβαιῶν and ἀρραβών in verses 21–22 as "guaranteeing the delivery of something of which the earnest has already been paid."[38] The key observation in this passage, however, is the connection of sealing, an ἀρραβών, and the donation of the Spirit, all of which perfectly complement Eph 1:13–14. This correlation is confirmed again in 2 Cor 5:5. There the Spirit is again an ἀρραβών given by God. In this case, the ἀρραβών is surety on the eternal house in the heavens that believers have but do not occupy while on earth (5:1–5).

To return to Eph 1:13–14, it is important to consider more precisely what is being described in the depiction of the Spirit as an ἀρραβών of inheritance.[39] There are two possibilities. The first is that the Spirit is an ἀρραβών in the sense of "first installment": an initial offering of something of which more is to come, the total sum of which is the full inheritance. The sense of "first installment" is perhaps supported by Rom 8:23, which associates redemption with the "first offering of the spirit" (τὴν ἀπαρχὴν τοῦ πνεύματος). But, as

36. Cf. here the Hebrew עֵרָבוֹן, from which the Greek ἀρραβών derives.
37. I am not fully committed to this translation, but I do find it instructive.
38. Moulton and Milligan, *Greek Testament*, 108 s.v.
39. For more detailed analysis of nuances in the use of ἀρραβών, see Yon-Gyong Kwon, "Ἀρραβών as Pledge in Second Corinthians," *NTS* 54 (2008): 525–41.

commentators and lexica note, the use of ἀπαρχή here could also have the sense of documentation, as in a "certificate of freedom" or "entrance fee" provided by the Spirit.[40] The second possibility is that the Spirit is an ἀρραβών in the sense of security or deposit: an initial endowment that guarantees the later provision of something else, namely, the inheritance. This latter sense corresponds to the situation in Gen 38 and makes best sense of Paul's usage.[41] The Spirit is a guarantee which, by sealing believers as God's property, also marks them as beneficiaries of a future inheritance—"the wealth of the glory of the inheritance," as it is defined in 1:18. As for the nature of this inheritance, it is elsewhere identified with the kingdom of God (1 Cor 6:9-10; Gal 5:21), the promises to Abraham (Gal 3-4), recompense (Col 3:24), and that which is imperishable (1 Cor 15:50). In 2 Cor 5, the language of inheritance is not used, but the ἀρραβών of the Spirit is linked with a building from God, eternal in the heavens and made without hands (5:1). For all of this, the Spirit is God's deposited guarantee that believers are heirs.

## The Redemption of the Acquisition

After the relative clause defining the promissory Spirit as a pledge of inheritance in verse 14a, Paul returns to the purpose for which the Spirit seals believers in verse 14b: "for/until the redemption of the acquisition" (εἰς ἀπολύτρωσιν τῆς περιποιήσεως). This phrase requires some grammatical deliberation. There are two interpretive options, both of which hinge on how one reads the initial εἰς. The first option is to read the εἰς temporally: "until the redemption of the acquisition." This reading coordinates the phrase with the preceding relative clause: "who is a pledge of inheritance until the redemption of the acquisition."[42] The second option is to read the εἰς in parallel with the immediately following εἰς phrase (εἰς ἔπαινον τῆς δόξης αὐτοῦ), and so as stating the purpose of the sealing in verse 13 (or perhaps reference/respect): "for the redemption of the acquisition." The decision is a difficult one, but parallelism with εἰς ἔπαινον τῆς δόξης αὐτοῦ, which is unquestionably an expression of purpose, inclines me to read εἰς ἀπολύτρωσιν τῆς περιποιήσεως as also expressing purpose, as does the εἰς clause of 4:30 ("you were sealed for the day of redemption [εἰς ἡμέραν ἀπολυτρώσεως]"). Read this way, the explicit purpose

---

40. See LSJ, s.v., where Rom 8:23 is cited under "*birth certificate* of a free person."
41. Cf. also the arguments of Kwon vis-à-vis 2 Corinthians ("Ἀρραβών as Pledge").
42. This reading deviates from the punctuation of NA28.

of the sealing is for the redemption of God's property. The agent of that sealing is the Holy Spirit, who is also a pledge of the believer's coming inheritance, but the specific objective of the sealing is the ransom of God's property.

It is important to distinguish the information about the Spirit as a pledge of inheritance and the purpose of the sealing, which is ransom. In 2 Cor 1:22 the sealing of the believer and the granting of the ἀρραβών are again unmistakably related, but they are not equated. God's act of sealing (ὁ σφραγισάμενος) is co-ordinated with the giving of the pledge (δοὺς τὸν ἀρραβῶνα τοῦ πνεύματος). Also, in 2 Cor 5:5, God's act of acquiring (ὁ κατεργασάμενος) is coordinated with the giving of the pledge (ὁ δοὺς ἡμῖν τὸν ἀρραβῶνα τοῦ πνεύματος). So in Eph 1:13–14, the Spirit who seals believers for redemption is also an ἀρραβών of inheritance. Inheritance and redemption are thus related but distinguishable subjects. Although in 1:7 the redemption is something "we have" (ἔχομεν), in 4:30b the "day of redemption" (ἡμέραν ἀπολυτρώσεως) almost certainly lies ahead, which is why the Spirit who seals believers should not be grieved (4:30a).[43] The Spirit, therefore, is current security along the way to the final completion of the *ransom*, and it is also current security on the way to the future *inheritance*. Ransom and inheritance are intertwined but distinguishable.

Now, to the word ἀπολύτρωσις. "Ransom" is perhaps a better English translation for capturing the financial exchange envisioned by the metaphor here, but "redemption" is the more common English translation.[44] The word ἀπολύτρωσις occurs ten times in the New Testament, seven of which are in Paul. Of those seven, three are in Ephesians (1:7, 14; 4:30). Although ἀπολύτρωσις can be used in an abstract sense for any sort of emancipation, in its concrete sense, an ἀπολύτρωσις occurs when one party offers payment (or ransom money, λύτρον)[45] for the manumission of an enslaved party. The word can also be used for the currency itself, as in this passage from Josephus: "And when they said their ransom money would exceed four hundred talents (τετρακοσίων ταλάντων τῆς ἀπολυτρώσεως), he granted it."[46] Origen provides a succinct description of the total scenario, were one to extend various inferences: "If

43. For consideration of the possibility that even in 4:30 "the day of redemption" is a present reality, see Ernest Best, *A Critical and Exegetical Commentary on Ephesians*, ICC (London: T&T Clark, 1998), 458–59.

44. Presumably following the Latin *redemptio*.

45. A λύτρον is a ransom-price or payment for exchange. Attempts to read it otherwise are often specious. See Nathan Eubank, *Wages of Cross-Bearing and Debt of Sin: The Economy of Heaven in Matthew's Gospel*, BZNW 196 (Berlin: de Gruyter, 2013), 148–51.

46. Josephus, *Ant.* 12.27. This is the only time in Josephus the noun occurs with the ἀπο- prefix. He otherwise refers to ransom money on a number of occasions as λύτρον, which is indeed more common.

therefore we were 'bought with a price' [1 Cor 6:20; 7:23], as Paul agrees, then without a doubt we were bought from someone whose slaves we were, and who demanded whatever price he wished in order to release from his power those whom he held. Now it was the devil, to whom we had been sold by our sins, who held us. He demanded therefore as our price the blood of Christ."[47]

When Paul evokes the metaphor of ransom, a notion of exchange and release is certainly embedded in it. A sense of gift-exchange, for instance, is suggested in Rom 3:24, which connects ἀπολύτρωσις with both χάρις and δωρεά. The capital offered in this χάρις must be, as Origen maintained, Christ's own blood, which is identified as the means of redemption in Eph 1:7 (τὴν ἀπολύτρωσιν διὰ τοῦ αἵματος αὐτοῦ).[48] This is why Christ's blood is further described in that verse in terms of wealth and gift (κατὰ τὸ πλοῦτος τῆς χάριτος αὐτοῦ). The depiction of vicarious death as a type of financial transaction is not unprecedented. A first-century CE inscription from Sardinia attests to one Pomptilla, who "died as a ransom (λύτρον) for her sweet husband."[49] In the first century BCE, Diodorus Siculus describes the Pythagorean commitment to dying for one another and, specifically, to the case of one Damon, whose death was offered as "surety" (ἐγγυητής) for that of his Pythagorean comrade, Phintias: "He said that he would give one of his friends as surety for his death (ἐγγυητὴν τοῦ θανάτου). And when the ruler expressed his wonder whether such a friend was to be found as would take his place in prison, Phintias called upon one of his acquaintances, a Pythagorean philosopher named Damon, who without hesitation came forward at once as surety for his death (ἔγγυος . . . θανάτου)."[50]

The depiction of Christ's blood as a form of currency is also not unusual. According to Acts 20:28, the church of God has been "acquired through his own blood" (περιεποιήσατο διὰ τοῦ αἵματος τοῦ ἰδίου).[51] Similarly, in Rev 5:9, the Lamb is said to have purchased people for God with his blood (ἠγόρασας τῷ θεῷ ἐν τῷ αἵματί σου).[52] Again, in Heb 9:12, Christ's "own blood procures an eternal ransom" (τοῦ ἰδίου αἵματος . . . αἰωνίαν λύτρωσιν εὑράμενος). And again, in 1 Pet 1:18–19, there is the reminder that "you were ransomed with the precious blood of Christ" (ἐλυτρώθητε . . . τιμίῳ αἵματι . . . Χριστοῦ). The

---

47. Origen, *Comm. Rom.* 2.13 (PG 14.911). Paul does not describe the devil as setting a ransom-price. This is something Origen infers but Paul never states.

48. Cf. 2:13.

49. IG XIV 607.

50. Diodorus Siculus, 10.4 (Oldfather, LCL). For further discussion of this passage and the prior inscription, see Simon Gathercole, *Defending Substitution: An Essay on Atonement in Paul* (Grand Rapids: Baker Academic, 2015), 95–98.

51. Cf. the verb περιποιέομαι in this verse with the noun περιποίησις in Eph 1:14.

52. Cf. Rev 12:11.

idea that believers are bought also belongs to Paul: "you were bought (ἠγοράσθητε) with a price" (1 Cor 6:20; cf. 7:23 and also Gal 3:13; 4:5). The notion of purchase-money is implicit in Eph 1:14 with the addition of περιποίησις, the "redemption *of the acquisition.*" That which is redeemed is now God's property, purchased with the currency of Christ's blood (1:7). This is precisely how ransom works: a ransomed person acquires ties of belonging to the person (or god) who ransoms them.[53] Paul does not stop short of describing this as an absolute change in ownership.

The presentation of Christ's blood as legal tender, and believers as having been ransomed by it, is clear enough across the New Testament. But what these passages consistently avoid is any reference to a transaction taking place. The enslaving power is certainly identified. According to Col 1:13–14 the ἀπολύτρωσις of humanity is deliverance "from the powers of darkness" (ὃς ἐρρύσατο ἡμᾶς ἐκ τῆς ἐξουσίας τοῦ σκότους). These same powers are identified across Ephesians (1:21; 2:2; 3:10; 6:12), and even in the singular: "the ruler of the power of the air, the spirit that is now at work among the disobedient" (2:2). But Paul (or any other New Testament author, for that matter) never indicates how the enslaving force has set a price for manumission, or that payment is ever made to them. This seems to me to be the point where expressions of the ransom scheme begin to stammer. Although implications surrounding the transaction will preoccupy later theologians, New Testament authors are uniform in their reluctance to protract the metaphor. The structural elements of the metaphor are, to be sure, present or inferable in Ephesians: believers have been sealed by the Holy Spirit for redemption; Christ's blood is the ransom-capital; "the ruler of the power of the air" (Eph 2:2) enslaves humanity. But there is never a hint of when, where, or how ransom money is exchanged or terms negotiated.

## Conclusion

The economics of atonement in Eph 1:13–14 are as follows: to be sealed by the Spirit is to be marked as God's property, a possession that has been manumitted from slavery to hostile powers and designated an heir. As a ransomed acquisition, the believer is a slave to God, but the Spirit which so marks believers is also security on something else: inheritance. The ransomed believer has thus also become an heir to "immeasurable riches" (2:7). The promissory Spirit that

---

53. Deissmann develops this at length (*Light from the Ancient East*, 319–30).

seals believers is the endorsement guaranteeing that inheritance. It is in the sealing of Rom 15:28 that "sealed by the Spirit" receives its interpretation: as Paul vowed, in concrete terms, to seal the funds earmarked for the Jerusalem saints, thereby certifying those assets, so believers sealed by the promissory Spirit, in more metaphorical terms, are certified as God's acquisition and so earmarked for ransom and heavenly inheritance.

Adolf Deissmann celebrated Paul's use of the ransom metaphor for atonement as "one of the most original and at the same time most popular appraisals of the work of Christ."[54] He hailed it as "one of his profoundest contemplations about the Christ,"[55] and one "admirably meeting the requirements and the intellectual capacity of the lower classes."[56] But Deissmann also identified it as "only vaguely understood among us,"[57] a "frequently misunderstood conception."[58] Modern commentators indeed often sit uneasily with Paul's economic construals of atonement. In his commentary on Ephesians, Stephen Fowl rightly observes that the discussion of redemption in Eph 1:14 occurs "in a context where financial images of exchange abound."[59] Fowl also admits that "the vast majority of patristic authors are all relatively comfortable in recognizing the notion of payment entailed in speaking of redemption here."[60] And yet he concludes: "We should be wary . . . of simply transferring images from the realm of commercial exchange directly into the life of God as if Christ's blood was a form of currency."[61] We may be wary of such conceptions, but Paul was not. There is, to be sure, theological wisdom in never "simply transferring" metaphorical images "directly into the life of God." Metaphors have their hazards. Any metaphor can be developed in unhelpful, risible, or harmful ways. But well-conceived metaphors also have great power.

From Paul, through to the patristic era and beyond, the metaphor of ransom provided the overarching framework within which Christ's death and the human predicament were conceived.[62] Its pervasiveness has since diminished,

---

54. Deissmann, *Light from the Ancient East*, 319.

55. Deissmann, *Light from the Ancient East*, 322.

56. Deissmann, *Light from the Ancient East*, 328.

57. Deissmann, *Light from the Ancient East*, 319.

58. Deissmann, *Light from the Ancient East*, 327.

59. Stephen E. Fowl, *Ephesians: A Commentary* (Louisville: Westminster John Knox Press, 2012), 44.

60. Fowl, *Ephesians*, 44.

61. Fowl, *Ephesians*, 44.

62. For a detailed account and analysis of this history, see the chapter titled "The Devil's Ransom Revisited" in Nicholas E. Lombardo's *The Father's Will: Christ's Crucifixion and the*

and this is perhaps to be attributed to very different social facts concerning the visibility and plausibility of slavery in contemporary Western culture.[63] Ransom from enslavement is not something most of us in Western culture worry about, even while human trafficking remains widespread. The ransom metaphor is thus less viscerally felt and, as Deissmann observed, even frequently misapprehended. For exegetical and historical reasons, it is still vital to appreciate the communicative power of the ransom theory of atonement in its ancient setting. For doctrinal reasons, it is equally vital to be clear about what Paul *does not* say within the logic of the metaphor. According to Paul, God's ransoming of humanity is about liberation from captivity to hostile powers. Ransomed humanity is God's acquisition. There is, therefore, a genuine change in ownership. The currency for humanity's liberation is Christ's blood. The certification of that liberation is the sealing of the Spirit. All of this is affirmed without reference to an actual transaction or any of its terms, much less to something like a theory of the "devil's rights." Paul thus uses the metaphor to say everything he wants to say without elaborating in any detail how the deal was done. Subsequent interpreters would speculate on such details, draw plausible inferences, and press the explanatory reach of the metaphor in a number of contrary and controversial ways. Inevitable as this may be (and sometimes illuminating as this may be), it is important to take seriously the possibility that the inferences and elaborations of later interpreters are ones Paul purposefully or even instinctively avoided.

---

*Goodness of God* (Oxford: Oxford University Press, 2013), 181–239. Also: Eugene Teselle, "The Cross as Ransom," *JECS* 4 (1996): 147–70.

63. Stephen R. Holmes, in his recent analysis of the rise and decline of penal substitution, helpfully demonstrates how "theories of atonement prosper in part because they have a certain cultural plausibility" ("Penal Substitution," in *T&T Clark Companion to Atonement*, ed. Adam J. Johnson [London: Bloomsbury T&T Clark, 2017], 295–314, here 308).

# CHAPTER NINE

# WHAT GOES ON IN THE HEAVENLY TEMPLE?

*Celestial Praise and Sacrifice*
*in Ancient Judaism and Christianity*

MARTHA HIMMELFARB

Ancient Jewish and Christian texts typically imagine God's heavenly dwelling place as either a palace or a temple. These alternatives are in fact two sides of the same coin. As the greatest of kings, God must surely dwell in the greatest of palaces. On the other hand, God's dwelling place is almost by definition a temple, as the term "house of the Lord" for the Jerusalem Temple in the Tanakh suggests. The biblical היכל, which usually means "temple," can sometimes mean the palace of a human king.[1] But despite their close connection, palace and temple imply significantly different pictures. Thus, for example, *palace* suggests that the members of God's angelic entourage are best understood as courtiers, while *temple* implies that they are in some sense priests.

Texts that picture heaven as a palace can easily project the activities of the earthly palace onto the heavenly. God can be described as sitting in judgment (e.g., Dan 7:9–10), for example, just as human kings sit in judgment in their palaces. But the central activity of the earthly temple is sacrifice, and it was clearly a challenge to imagine sacrifice taking place in heaven. Some authors, as we shall see, preferred to avoid the challenge by describing a different kind of cult, a verbal liturgy of praise, while others met the challenge by reimagining sacrifice in terms appropriate to heaven.

This paper considers six Jewish and Christian texts from the Second Temple period and the early centuries of the Christian era—the Book of the Watchers (1 En. 1–36), 2 Enoch, the Songs of the Sabbath Sacrifice, Revelation, the Epistle

---

1. See the entry for היכל in BDB for references, §1964.

to the Hebrews, and the Testament of Levi—that depict heaven as a temple and provide information about its activities. Such a broad approach seems to me the best way to illumine the place of atonement in the heavenly temple. I regret that constraints of space prevent me from considering other texts that depict heaven as a temple or include cultic elements in heaven, such as the Apocalypse of Abraham, the Ascension of Isaiah, and 3 Baruch.[2] They would add to the picture I sketch here in significant ways, but I do not believe that they would change the larger contours. I have also chosen to leave Philo out of the discussion. While his interpretation of the cult's cosmological significance is of great interest, it represents a very different mode of thinking about the temple and provides little by way of direct answer to the question posed by my title.

## The Book of the Watchers and the Heavenly Temple

The first instance in Jewish literature of a depiction of God's heavenly abode as a temple appears in chapter 14 of the Book of the Watchers, which likely reached its final form around the turn of the third to the second century BCE.[3] The work describes Enoch's ascent to heaven in a dream or vision to present to God the petition he has drawn up on behalf of the fallen watchers. But his mission ends in failure. God rejects the petition and rebukes the watchers. The rebuke is the only place in the work that God's heavenly abode is explicitly

2. For discussion of aspects of these works relevant to the heavenly temple, see Martha Himmelfarb, *Ascent to Heaven in Jewish and Christian Apocalypses* (New York: Oxford University Press, 1993), 56–58, 61–66, 89–91; Andrei A. Orlov, *Heavenly Priesthood in the Apocalypse of Abraham* (Cambridge: Cambridge University Press, 2013).

3. Philip F. Esler, *God's Court and Courtiers in the Book of the Watchers* (Eugene, OR: Cascade Books, 2017), offers a book-length argument that the Book of the Watchers pictures heaven not as a temple but as a royal court and that its angels should be understood not as priests but as courtiers. This picture, Esler claims, is better suited to the understanding of the Jews (or as he would put it, Judeans) of the Second Temple period he favors, as an ethnic rather than a religious group. Limits of space prevent me from commenting on his arguments here, but I plan to do so elsewhere. As the discussion in this paper indicates, I am not persuaded.

I should also note recent scholarship that argues that Ezek 40–42 constitutes the first ascent to a heavenly temple in Jewish literature. For this position, Steven S. Tuell, "Ezekiel 40–42 as Verbal Icon," *CBQ* 58 (1996): 649–64, and Paul M. Joyce, "Ezekiel 40–42: The Earliest 'Heavenly Ascent' Narrative?," in *The Book of Ezekiel and Its Influence*, ed. Henk Jan de Jonge and Johannes Tromp (Ashgate: Aldershot, 2007). Joyce's article takes Tuell's as a point of departure. I plan to discuss their arguments, too, at a future date. Again, I am not persuaded.

identified as a temple: "Why have you forsaken the high heaven, the eternal sanctuary . . . ?" (1 En. 15:3).[4] But this identification comes as no surprise in light of what preceded it, for the architecture of the heavenly structures through which Enoch passes is clearly intended to recall the earthly temple.[5] The outer wall and two houses (1 En. 14:9, 10, 15) echo the tripartite structure of the three temples described in the Tanakh (the wilderness sanctuary, Solomon's Temple, and Ezekiel's future temple).[6] Enoch sees cherubim in the ceiling of the first house (1 En. 14:11); figures of cherubim decorate the wilderness sanctuary and Jerusalem Temple. In the innermost house, the throne of the Great Glory (1 En. 14:18–20) recalls Ezekiel's chariot throne, including the wheels, which have no function on a fixed throne.[7] But Ezekiel has prepared readers of the Book of the Watchers for such a throne in the heavenly temple with his identification of the creatures of the chariot as the heavenly originals of the golden cherubim of the Jerusalem Temple (Ezek 10:20).

It is not easy to reach God's throne in the heavenly temple of the Book of the Watchers:

> The Great Glory sat upon [the throne]; his apparel was like the appearance of the sun and whiter than much snow. No angel could enter into this house and look at his face because of the splendor and glory, and no human could look at him. Flaming fire encircled him and a great fire stood by him, and none of those about him approached him. Ten thousand times ten thousand stood before him, but he needed no counselor; his every word was deed. And the holy ones of the watchers who approached him did not depart by night, nor <by day> did they leave him. (1 En. 14:20–23)

The passage is clearly a poem, as indicated by the repeated use of parallelism, and its similarity to the poem describing God seated on his throne before a crowd of angels in Dan 7:9–10 has long been noted. More recently, the publication of the fragments of the Book of Giants from the Scrolls has brought to light a third passage (4Q530 2 ii 16–18) with a picture of the divine throne

---

4. All translations of the Book of the Watchers are taken from George W. E. Nickelsburg and James C. VanderKam, *1 Enoch: A New Translation* (Minneapolis: Fortress, 2004).

5. Himmelfarb, *Ascent to Heaven*, 14–16.

6. In the Greek of Codex Panopolitanus, the wall is a third structure; see the apparatus of George W. E. Nickelsburg and James C. VanderKam, *1 Enoch 1: A Commentary on the Book of 1 Enoch, Chapters 1–36; 81–108* (Minneapolis: Fortress, 2001), 258, 9a.

7. Himmelfarb, *Ascent to Heaven*, 10–11.

room as the scene of judgment and a description of the crowd of angels in terms very close to those of 1 En. 14 and Dan 7, although it should be noted that the passage from the Book of the Giants explicitly places the scene of divine judgment on earth (4Q530 2:16).

There can be no doubt that the three passages are related to each other, but they are probably best understood as independent adaptations of a common tradition for the particular goals of each work.[8] For our purposes what is most significant is the way the vision of the Book of the Watchers differs from the other two visions. While Dan 7 and the Book of the Giants depict God sitting in judgment in the midst of his angelic servants, with books open before him, there is no book in the scene in the Book of the Watchers nor any mention of judgment, and the activities of the angels who stand before the throne are characterized as approaching (or not approaching); verbs that can be translated as "approach" are used of priests engaging in sacrifice in the Torah and the book of Ezekiel.[9] Even the negative formulation, "none of those about him approached him" (1 En. 14:22), has a cultic resonance. The tension between the negative and the subsequent mention of "the holy ones of the watchers who approached him" (1 En. 14:23) is diminished if not resolved if the "holy ones of the watchers" are understood as a distinct and particularly elevated class of angels, although there is some variation in the terms used to refer to these angels in the manuscripts.[10]

Both the act of approaching and the fear that would lead to not approaching fit well with a picture of God's abode as temple. The vision's very brief notice, however, gives no indication of what the angels do if and when they approach. The description of the divine throne room does not include the equipment that makes the earthly cult possible, such as the altars, bowls, and pans that appear in some later works, as we shall see. George Nickelsburg suggests that presence by night and by day (1 En. 14:23) is elsewhere associated with liturgical activ-

---

8. For a recent case for this view, Amanda M. Davis Bledsoe, "Throne Theophanies, Dream Visions, and Righteous (?) Seers: Daniel, the *Book of the Giants*, and *1 Enoch* Reconsidered," in *Ancient Tales of Giants from Qumran and Turfan: Contexts, Traditions, and Influences*, ed. Matthew Goff, Loren T. Stuckenbruck, and Enrico Morano, WUNT 360 (Tübingen: Mohr Siebeck, 2016), 81–96; for previous scholarship on the subject, see 81n2 and 82n3.

9. Nickelsburg, *1 Enoch 1*, 265–66. "Approach" is most often the *qal* of קרב (Exod 12:48, 40:32; Lev 9:7–8; 16:1; 21:17–18; 22:3; Num 1:51; 3:10, 38; 17:28; 18:7; Ezek 40:46; 44:15–16; 45:4), but it can also be נגש (Exod 19:22; 28:43; 30:20; Lev 21:21–23; Num 4:19; Ezek 44:13). Ἐγγίζω, the verb used in the Greek of 1 En.14:23, is used to translate both of these verbs in the LXX.

10. See Nickelsburg, *1 Enoch 1*, 258–59na to 1 Enoch 14:23.

ity and that the angels who approach God's throne are thus best understood as engaging in praise.[11] Although certainty on this point is impossible, the absence of any mention of equipment for the sacrificial cult supports Nickelsburg's suggestion. But whatever they do when they approach, the language of approaching itself, even in the negative and certainly in the positive, serves to identify the angels of the heavenly temple as priests.

It is also worth remembering that the Book of the Watchers is not the first text to suggest a connection between angels and priests. In Ezekiel's vision, the angel who oversees the destruction of Jerusalem is described as "the man clothed in linen" (Ezek 9:2, 3, 11; 10:2, 6, 7); the garments the high priest wears for the Yom Kippur ritual are made of linen (Lev 16:4), as are the breeches worn by ordinary priests (Exod 28:42).[12] From the other angle of approach, Mal 2:7 depicts the ideal priest as an angel: "For the lips of the priest should guard knowledge . . . for he is the מלאך of the LORD of hosts"; מלאך is "messenger" or "angel."[13] Furthermore, Enoch's successful traversal of the halls of the heavenly temple, which suggests that he enjoys a kind of priestly status, is followed by his journey to the ends of the earth in the company of the archangels, with whom he converses freely (1 En. 17–36). That is, although he does not undergo a physical transformation as do the heroes of several later ascent apocalypses, he appears to have achieved angelic as well as priestly status.

The Book of the Watchers is the first work in which the picture of heaven as temple is preserved, but the view of angels and priests in Ezekiel and Malachi indicates that the idea was already in circulation by the time the Book of the Watchers was written. The poorly preserved Aramaic Levi Document is probably roughly contemporary with the Book of the Watchers, and the surviving text makes it virtually certain that it contained an account of an ascent by Levi.[14] Its description of heaven is lost, but it seems likely that a work devoted to Levi as ancestor of the priestly line would have depicted heaven as a temple. The picture of the heavens in the Testament of Levi, which clearly drew on Aramaic Levi, is discussed toward the end of this paper, and it too points in this

11. Nickelsburg, *1 Enoch 1*, 265–66.

12. Translations of texts from the Tanakh and New Testament are taken from RSV unless otherwise noted.

13. RSV: "messenger."

14. For text and translation with introduction and commentary, Jonas C. Greenfield, Michael E. Stone, and Esther Eshel, *The Aramaic Levi Document: Edition, Translation, Commentary*, SVTP 19 (Leiden: Brill, 2004); and Henryk Drawnel, *An Aramaic Wisdom Text from Qumran: A New Interpretation of the Levi Document*, JSJSup 86 (Leiden: Brill, 2004). For the date, Greenfield, Stone, Eshel, *Aramaic Levi Document*, 19–20.

direction. I should emphasize that there is no reason to believe that Aramaic Levi is indebted to the Book of the Watchers. Rather, if I am correct about its content, it provides further evidence for the availability of the idea of heaven as temple in the period before the Maccabean Revolt.

## 2 Enoch

In the course of the second century BCE several admirers of the Book of the Watchers composed works attributed to Enoch or concerned with the story of the watchers—the Apocalypse of Weeks (1 En. 91, 93), the Book of Dreams (1 En. 83–90), the Book of Giants —but it is not until the turn of the era that other works take up Enoch's ascent to the heavenly temple. I shall not discuss the Parables of Enoch (1 En. 37–71) here. While it is deeply indebted to the Book of the Watchers for its picture of Enoch's ascent, it seems to me that its heaven should probably be understood as a palace rather than a temple. I would also note that the consensus that dates the Parables to the turn of the era does not rest on very firm ground.[15]

I focus instead on 2 Enoch. Its dating to the turn of the era is also far from certain, although in the end I am inclined to accept such a date. Second Enoch is preserved in Slavonic, with the earliest manuscripts dated to the fourteenth century, and perhaps in Coptic in fragments dated to the eighth to tenth century.[16] But the evident impact of 2 Enoch's ascent on 3 Baruch means that 2 Enoch, or at least the ascent since the work is composed of several units, must predate 3 Baruch. The manuscript evidence for 3 Baruch, both Greek and Slavonic, is also late. The standard view understands 3 Baruch to have been written shortly after the destruction of the Second Temple on the basis of its setting in the wake of the destruction of the First Temple. This dating of 3 Baruch would make a date for 2 Enoch around the turn of the era plausible.

---

15. On the date, George W. E. Nickelsburg in Nickelsburg and James C. VanderKam, *1 Enoch 2: A Commentary on the Book of 1 Enoch, Chapters 37–82* (Minneapolis: Fortress, 2012), 58–64. The Parables is the only unit of 1 Enoch of which no fragments have been found among the Scrolls, and it is also the only unit for which no Greek evidence survives.

16. On the supposed Coptic fragments, Joost L. Hagen, "No Longer 'Slavonic' Only: 2 Enoch Attested in Coptic from Nubia," in *New Perspectives on 2 Enoch*, ed. Joost L. Hagen, SJ 4 (Leiden: Brill, 2012), 7–34. Hagen dates the fragments on paleographic grounds (15). For criticism of Hagen's arguments for the identification of the fragments with 2 Enoch, Christfried Böttrich, "The Angel of Tartarus and the Supposed Coptic Fragments of 2 Enoch," *Early Christianity* 4 (2013): 509–21.

I believe, however, that this early dating of 3 Baruch is mistaken. I prefer to date 3 Baruch to the fourth century on the basis of its points of contact with the Apocalypse of Paul, which can be dated with some confidence to the second half of that century.[17] If I am correct, 3 Baruch's knowledge of 2 Enoch requires a date for 2 Enoch no later than the fourth century but not necessarily as early as the turn of the era. On the other hand, 2 Enoch's extensive use of the Book of the Watchers almost certainly reflects not the Aramaic original but the Greek translation, and it seems possible that the arrival of the translation in Egypt provided the impetus for the composition of 2 Enoch. The translation can be no later than the first century CE and is likely somewhat earlier, which would make a date for 2 Enoch around the turn of the era plausible.[18]

The Book of the Watchers, like other works of its time, imagines only a single heaven. By the turn of the era, a cosmology that pictured seven heavens was beginning to become popular, and 2 Enoch takes advantage of the opportunities afforded by this new picture to find places for the various angels and cosmological phenomena.[19] Apart from the seventh heaven, where God's throne is situated (2 En. 20–22), there is nothing in the structure or architecture of its heavens that suggests a temple. But in each heaven from the third up, angels offer praise (2 En. 8:8 [third heaven]; 15:1–2 [fourth heaven]; 19:6 [sixth heaven]; 20:4–21:1 [seventh heaven])—or at least they should. When Enoch arrives in the fifth heaven, he finds the watchers who remained in heaven

17. Martha Himmelfarb, "*3 Baruch* Revisited: Jewish or Christian Composition, and Why It Matters," *ZAC* 20 (2016): 41–62, esp. 57–59.

18. Quotations of and allusions to the Book of the Watchers appear in Greek and Latin texts from as early as the late first or early second century. For the texts, Nickelsburg, *1 Enoch 1*, 87–95. Scholars have also noted similarities between the Greek of the Book of the Watchers and the Greek versions of Daniel, particularly LXX Daniel, which is usually dated around the turn of the second to the first century BCE. See James Barr, "Aramaic-Greek Notes on the Book of Enoch (II)," *JJS* 24 (1979): 179–92, at 191; and Erik W. Larson, "The Translation of Enoch: From Aramaic into Greek" (Ph.D. diss. New York University, 1995), 203, 345.

19. On this cosmology and its sources, Adela Yarbro Collins, "The Seven Heavens in Jewish and Christian Apocalypses," in *Death, Ecstasy, and Other Worldly Journeys*, ed. John J. Collins and Michael Fishbane (Albany: State University of New York Press, 1995). It should also be noted that the long manuscripts of 2 Enoch contain not seven but ten heavens; the three additional heavens are described only very briefly (2 En. 21:6). They are widely understood as a later addition to the work; see, e.g., F. I. Andersen, "2 (Slavonic Apocalypse of) Enoch," in *OTP* 1:134, chap. 20 n. a. All references to and quotations from 2 Enoch are taken from Andersen's translation, "2 (Slavonic Apocalypse of) Enoch," *OTP* 1. The chapter divisions there differ from those of A. Pennington, "2 Enoch," *AOT*. Andersen translates two MSS; MS J represents the long form of 2 Enoch, while MS A represents the short form. The ascent is not a clearly demarcated unit; its end is not entirely clear.

silent in their mourning for the punishment of their brothers who descended to earth (2 En. 18:1–6). Enoch assures the watchers of the fifth heaven that he prayed on behalf of their brethren when he encountered them in the second heaven (2 En. 7), though to no avail, and at his urging the watchers of the fifth heaven resume their praise (2 En. 18:7–9).

But while praise is clearly central to 2 Enoch's picture of the heavens, it is not until the seventh heaven that it is described in terms that mark it as a ritual. There groups of angels arranged by rank come forward to worship and then return to their places. In language familiar from the Book of the Watchers, "they do not leave by night, nor depart by day . . . ," and they recite the *trishagion* before the divine throne (2 En. 20:3–21:1).[20] This picture of ritual praise leaves no doubt that 2 Enoch understands the seventh heaven as a temple, and it may suggest that the activity of praise in the lower heavens from the third up means that these heavens too should be understood as part of the heavenly temple. It seems likely that 2 Enoch's picture of angelic praise in the heavenly temple reflects its understanding of the nature of the service in the heavenly temple of the Book of the Watchers, lending ancient support to Nickelsburg's reading noted above.

Finally, another element of 2 Enoch's ascent that contributes to its picture of the heavenly temple is its description of Enoch's physical transformation into a glorious angel in the seventh heaven, a striking development of the Book of the Watchers' picture of Enoch's achievement of equality with the angels. The transformation is accomplished by anointing with oil and clothing in glorious garments (2 En. 22:6–10), both elements of the Torah's account of Aaron's consecration (Lev 8:6–12). In other words, Enoch becomes an angel by becoming a priest.

## The Songs of the Sabbath Sacrifice

But while the Book of the Watchers and 2 Enoch see heaven or the heavens as a temple, neither work imagines a detailed correspondence to the earthly cult, as do the Songs of the Sabbath Sacrifice—an unfortunately fragmentary work from Qumran—and the book of Revelation, the works to be considered next. The Songs consists of thirteen poems for the first thirteen Sabbaths of the year

---

20. The language quoted is taken from MS J, a long form of 2 Enoch; the language of MS A, the short form, differs slightly. The *trishagion* appears in MS J.

according to the 364-day calendar.[21] It survives in ten manuscripts, but they are quite fragmentary, and some of the poems are very poorly preserved, which means that any claims about their content are necessarily tentative. Although it exhibits many points of contact, linguistic and conceptual, with the sectarian corpus, including the calendar, the Songs does not contain any unambiguously sectarian language that would establish definitively its sectarian provenance.[22] The manuscript evidence shows that the work was in existence by the beginning of the first century BCE. Sectarian provenance would mean that the work could not be much earlier.[23]

Let me begin with a brief account of the work, its structure and its language, which is deeply indebted to Carol Newsom.[24] The subject of the Songs is the heavenly liturgy, and the association of each song with a particular Sabbath marks it as a liturgical work, although the setting in which it was recited and its function in that setting are by no means clear. The first five songs describe the establishment of the angelic priesthood, its duties, and the praise offered by the angelic priests. Songs 6–8 constitute a second group. The sixth song describes the praise offered by the seven chief princes, while the eighth song describes the praise offered by the seven deputy princes. The seventh song, the central song of the entire work, begins by calling on the seven angelic councils to offer praise but then turns to describe the praise offered by the heavenly temple itself. The five final songs go on to describe the praise offered in the heavenly temple in more detail, moving from the outer chamber toward the inner sanctum. The architecture of the heavenly temple corresponds closely

21. For a convenient presentation of the individual manuscripts and translations, a composite text and translations, introduction and notes, see James H. Charlesworth and Carol A. Newsom, with H. W. L. Rietz, B. A. Strawn, and R. E. Whitaker, eds., *The Dead Sea Scrolls: Hebrew Aramaic, and Greek Texts with English Translations*, vol. 4B, *Angelic Liturgy: Songs of the Sabbath Sacrifice* (Tübingen: Mohr Siebeck, and Louisville: Westminster John Knox, 1999). For bibliography to 2006, Philip Alexander, *The Mystical Texts: Songs of the Sabbath Sacrifice and Related Manuscripts* (London: T&T Clark International, 2006), 145–63.

22. Sectarian provenance is Newsom's "working hypothesis" in her first publication of the Songs, *Songs of the Sabbath Sacrifice: A Critical Edition* (Atlanta: Scholars Press, 1985), 1–4; quotation, 4. In Charlesworth and Newsom, *Dead Sea Scrolls*, vol. 4B, Newsom suggests that the Songs is a presectarian work, from the same circles as Jubilees and Aramaic Levi ("Introduction," 4–5). After delivering the paper on which this article is based, I learned from Newsom that she is again inclined to view the Songs as a sectarian composition (oral communication, June 6, 2018). Alexander, *Mystical Texts*, treats the Songs as a sectarian work; see esp. 63.

23. Newsom, "Introduction," in Charlesworth and Newsom, *Dead Sea Scrolls*, vol. 4B, 4–5.

24. I follow Newsom, *Songs*, 5–21; more briefly, Newsom, "Introduction," in Charlesworth and Newsom, *Dead Sea Scrolls*, vol. 4B, 3.

to that of the earthly temple, though the structures of the heavenly temple are animate and sometimes multiple rather than singular as on earth. The twelfth song includes a description of the chariot throne of God, while the thirteenth and last song, which is unfortunately extremely fragmentary, mentions the sacrifices offered by the angelic priests and describes the garments they wear. Newsom notes that the language of the last group of songs is less discursive and more evocative or "numinous" than that of the first group.[25]

The Songs is the first of the texts considered here to make explicit reference to atonement. The root כפר appears only once in the surviving text of the Songs, but it appears at a significant spot, near the beginning, in a passage introducing the duties of the angelic priests: "they propitiate his goodwill for all who repent of transgression," וכפרו רצונו בעד שבי פשע (4Q400 frag. 1, col. 1, line 16).[26] The passage in question is quite abstract, with no information about how any of the activities it describes are accomplished, but its placement could be read to suggest that all that follows in the Songs, both the elaborate verbal liturgy and the hints of sacrifice, is part of the process.

The syntax of the clause about atonement deserves some attention. In the Torah כפר is followed occasionally by בעד (Lev 9:7; 16:11, 17, 24) but more often by על (Exod 30:10; Lev 4:20, 26, 31; passim); in both cases those atoned for appear as the object of the preposition. Without "his goodwill," רצונו, the sentence from the Songs would fit this pattern: "they make atonement for all who repent." In the Torah and elsewhere in Scripture, the phrase לרצון means "acceptable," "pleasing," sometimes of sacrifices (Lev 22:20, 21; Isa 56:7; Jer 6:20), but it does not seem possible to construe רצונו in the passage from the Songs in a similar fashion.[27] Newsom notes the parallel in CD 2:5, which lacks the difficulties of the passage in the Songs: לכפר בעד שבי פשע, "to atone for those who repent of transgression."[28]

The closest scriptural parallel to the Songs' usage comes from a non-sacrificial context, the Torah's report of Jacob's thoughts as he prepares gifts to send to Esau: "I will propitiate him (אכפרה פניו) with the gift (במנחה) that goes before me" (Gen 32:21).[29] The translation of וכפרו רצונו as "propitiate his goodwill" understands the phrase on the model of Jacob's words, with the addition of the more standard בעד phrase for the beneficiaries of the propiti-

---

25. Newsom, *Songs*, 14–16; "Introduction," in Charlesworth and Newsom, *Dead Sea Scrolls*, vol. 4B, 3. "Numinous": *Songs*, 16; "Introduction," 3.

26. Trans. Newsom, in *Dead Sea Scrolls*, vol. 4B, 16.

27. Newsom, *Songs*, 104–5.

28. Newsom, *Songs*, 105.

29. Newsom, *Songs*, 105; the translation of Gen 32:21 is mine.

ation. Jacob's words are particularly suggestive for the passage from the Songs because the term appropriately translated "gift" in Genesis is מנחה, a word that appears twice in its meaning of grain offering in the Songs' picture of heavenly sacrifice, as we shall see shortly.

Despite the Songs' fragmentary character, it is clear that the dominant activity in its heavenly temple is praise, offered by both angels and the architectural features of the temple. But, as just noted, the heavenly cult also includes sacrifice, and the placement of sacrifice in the thirteenth and final song surely serves to emphasize its significance. The mentions of sacrifice appear in the space of three lines early in the song: "acceptable [offerings] (מנחו[ת רצון]) . . . all their works . . . for the sacrifices of the Holy Ones (לזבחי קדושים) . . . the aroma of their offerings (ריח מנחותם) . . . and the aroma of their libations (וריח נסכיהם)" (11Q17 frags. 21–22, ll. 3–5).[30] The context is not well preserved; the ellipses in the translation contain only a few letters and otherwise reflect lacunae. The poor state of preservation of this portion of the song means that there may have been more mentions of sacrifice.

All of the phrases for which I have provided the Hebrew consist of words that appear in the Torah's laws of sacrifice; the only exception is "Holy Ones," קדושים.[31] Yet the Songs of the Sabbath Sacrifice combines the words in ways that do not appear in the Torah. In the Torah's laws of sacrifices, the term רצון means "acceptable" in the phrase לרצון (Lev 22:21–22); it never appears preceded by a type of sacrifice in the construct state. "Sacrifices of," זבחי, appears several times in the Torah as part of the phrase זבחי שלמים, "well-being sacrifices" (Exod 29:28; Lev 7:32, 34; 10:14; Num 10:10), but it is never paired with those offering the sacrifices as in the Songs. Finally, in the sacrificial laws of the Torah ריח, "aroma," is always paired with the noun ניחוח, "soothing," thus in English, a pleasant aroma (Lev 1:9, 13, 17; 2:2, 9; 3:5, etc.); the Songs places ריח in the construct state with the offerings that produce the aroma.[32]

The emphasis on aroma, with two mentions in a very brief passage, is significant. P's ריח ניחוח, "soothing aroma," implies that God's enjoyment of sacrifice comes by way of smell, thus reducing somewhat the anthropomorphic

---

30. The translation here is mine. For the word restored by the editors as "offerings" in the first phrase, only the final *t* survives.

31. Noam Mizrahi, "The *Songs of the Sabbath Sacrifice* and Biblical Priestly Literature: A Reconsideration," *HTR* 104 (2011): 35–41, shows that the Songs makes use of terminology from elsewhere in the Tanakh alongside that of P and Ezekiel for the architecture and equipment of the heavenly temple.

32. For a detailed and illuminating discussion of the term ריח, which reaches a somewhat different conclusion, Mizrahi, "*Songs*," 42–48.

assumptions of the idea of sacrifice as food for the gods.[33] It is also noteworthy that of all the terminology preserved in the thirteenth song, only זבח points toward animal sacrifice. It is necessary to be cautious in drawing conclusions since the text is so poorly preserved, but the aromas the Songs mentions are not of animal offerings but of מנחות, grain offerings, and נסכים, libations. It is also noteworthy that the term מנחות appears twice in the passage under discussion (if the restoration of Newsom et al. above is correct). As we shall see shortly, the book of Revelation, too, has difficulty visualizing blood in heaven, and perhaps the fact that those offering the זבחים in the Songs are angels, קדושים, suggests that even those sacrifices are bloodless.

In her commentary to the passage from the thirteenth song, Newsom writes, "The Shirot seems intentionally to vary biblical terminology relating to the technical matters of the cult, perhaps as a means of suggesting the difference as well as the correspondence between the heavenly and the earthly service."[34] With this observation in mind, I would like to consider briefly the similarities and difference between the Songs' use of the sacrificial terminology and the Community Rule's use of purity terminology, as exemplified in the following passage:

> Then God will cleanse by his truth all the deeds of man and will refine for himself the frame of man, removing all spirit of injustice from within his flesh and purifying him (ולטהרו) by the spirit of holiness from every wicked action. And he will sprinkle (ויז) upon him the spirit of truth like waters for purification (כמי נדה) (to remove) all the abominations (תועבות) of falsehood (in which) he has defiled himself through the spirit of impurity (נדה). (1QS 4:20–22)[35]

The terms for which I have provided Hebrew equivalents above are drawn from the Priestly and Holiness sources of the Torah. But in the Community Rule they are supplemented by words drawn from other spheres, such as "cleanse" (יברר), "refine" (יזקק), and "defile" (והתגולל). Furthermore, the Community Rule uses the terms drawn from P and H in ways that go well beyond their use in the Torah. They no longer refer to ritual impurity and to rituals performed by priests in order to remove that impurity. Sprinkling a spirit of truth can-

---

33. On this point, Mizrahi, "Songs," 43–44.

34. Newsom, Songs, 372–73.

35. Trans. Michael A. Knibb, The Qumran Community (Cambridge: Cambridge University Press, 1987), 101, with my substitution of "cleanse" for "purify" for the first verb (יברר) in order to save "purify" for טהר.

not be a physical ritual, especially since the sprinkler is God, not the priests who would sprinkle waters for purification. In other words, the language of the Torah is pushed beyond its boundaries so that purity and sprinkling no longer refer to ritual states but to spiritual ones.[36] In contrast, while the Songs of the Sabbath Sacrifice uses the Torah's terminology of sacrifice in new ways that reflect an understanding of heavenly sacrifice as different from earthly sacrifice, nothing suggests that it understands heavenly sacrifice as spiritual rather than physical.

## The Book of Revelation

The book of Revelation, as noted above, is another rich source for the heavenly temple.[37] Its author, John of Patmos, was a fervent follower of Christ, but he was also a Jew whose writing was deeply informed by the Hebrew Bible and Jewish traditions and who continued to view membership in the people of Israel as a desirable state and to care deeply about the observance of the Torah's ritual laws.[38] The current scholarly consensus places Revelation toward the end of the reign of Domitian, which lasted from 81 to 96 CE, but John Marshall argues for a date between 68 and 70, very close to the traditional date, and such an early date fits well with John's attitude toward observance of the ritual laws of the Torah.[39] On the other hand, the end of the reign of Domitian is certainly not too late for a devoted follower of Christ to be a ritually observant

36. For further discussion of the use of purity language in the Community Rule, including the passage treated below, Martha Himmelfarb, "Impurity and Sin in 4QD, 1QS, and 4Q512," in *Between Temple and Torah: Essays on Priests, Scribes, and Visionaries in the Second Temple Period and Beyond,* TSAJ 151 (Tübingen: Mohr Siebeck, 2013), esp. 152–57.

37. In addition to the many commentaries, there is a significant body of secondary literature on the heavenly temple in Revelation as on almost every other aspect of the book. Here I cite only the most relevant material. For a recent discussion of the heavenly temple in Revelation with some reference to earlier literature, Eyal Regev, *The Temple in Early Christianity: Experiencing the Sacred* (New Haven: Yale University Press, 2019), 222–51.

38. My understanding of John of Patmos as a Jewish writer and my avoidance of the label "Christian" is deeply indebted to David Frankfurter, "Jews or Not? Reconstructing the Other in Rev 2:9 and 3:9," *HTR* 94 (2001): 403–25; John W. Marshall, *Parables of War: Reading John's Jewish Apocalypse* (Waterloo, Ontario: Wilfrid Laurier University Press, 2001); and Alexander Kocar, "A Hierarchy of Salvation in the Book of Revelation: Different Peoples, Dwellings, and Tasks in the End Times," in *Placing Ancient Texts: The Ritual and Rhetorical Use of Space,* ed. Mika Ahuvia and Alexander Kocar, TSAJ 174 (Tübingen: Mohr Siebeck, 2018).

39. For the early date with a discussion of the arguments for the time of Domitian, Marshall, *Parables,* 88–97.

Jew. I avoid using the term "Christian" in my discussion of Revelation on the grounds that it is anachronistic for the first century.

The heavenly temple plays a very important role in Revelation. It makes its appearance at the beginning of John's visions and while it provides a recurring backdrop for the unleashing of the terrors that precede the eschaton, the primary activity in Revelation's heavenly temple is praise: the *trishagion* of the living creatures and the acclamation of the twenty-four elders (Rev 4); the acclamation of the Lamb by the living creatures and the elders (Rev 5); the praise of the multitude from every nation, joined by the angels, the elders, and the living creatures (Rev 7); the praise of the twenty-four elders after the seventh angel blows his trumpet (Rev 11); the new song sung by the hundred forty-four thousand who have the name of the Father on their foreheads (Rev 14); the song of those who had conquered the beast (Rev 15); and the praise of the great multitude, the twenty-four elders, and four living creatures after the fall of Babylon (Rev 19). Even the heavenly altar cries out in praise of God (Rev 16:7), recalling the praise offered by the architectural features of the heavenly temple in the Songs of the Sabbath Sacrifice.[40]

In the opening vision of Revelation, God sits in heaven on a throne from which come forth thunder and lightning and before which lies a sea of glass (Rev 4:5–6); the sea is surely the heavenly counterpart of the "molten sea," the great vessel of Solomon's Temple (1 Kgs 7:23, 24, 39). Four living creatures inspired by Ezekiel's living creatures sing praise before the throne (Rev 4:6–8); their praise plays on the *trisagion* of Isaiah 6. Around the throne John sees twenty-four elders seated on their own thrones (Rev 4:4). They are dressed in white with golden crowns on their heads, and as the creatures offer their praise, the elders toss their crowns before the throne and sing their own words of praise (Rev 4:9–11). The praise and white robes of the elders suggest that the elders should be understood as angelic priests, despite the fact that the title "elder" (πρεσβύτερος) for beings in heaven is, to the best of my knowledge, without precedent and is not a term associated with priests on earth.[41] The tossing of crowns, on the other hand, does not reflect any ritual that took place in the Jerusalem temple, and some scholars have connected it to the ceremonies of Hellenistic and Roman emperor worship.[42]

---

40. As Dale C. Allison ("4Q403 Fragm. 1, Col. I, 38–46 and the Revelation to John," *RevQ* 12 [1986]: 409–14, at 410) notes for the altar's first speech, which does not involve praise (Rev 9:13–14).

41. For the elders, to whom he refers as "Ancient Ones," as angelic priests, Peter J. Leithart, *Revelation 1–11* (London: Bloomsbury T&T Clark, 2018), 229–32.

42. David E. Aune, "The Influence of Roman Imperial Court Ceremonial on the Apoc-

In the scene immediately following, the elders again join the creatures in praise, this time of the Lamb (Rev 5:6–10). In this scene each elder holds a harp (κιθάρα) and "golden bowls full of incense, which are the prayers of the holy ones (τῶν ἁγίων)" (Rev 5:8); it is clear in the Greek that the bowls rather than the incense are the prayers of the holy ones.[43] The harps of the elders are perhaps an echo of the instruments used by the Levites in the Second Temple, although κιθάρα appears most frequently in the Greek Bible in Psalms (Pss 32:2; 42:4; 56:8; 70:22; 80:2; 91:3; 97:5; 107:2; 146:7; 150:3) and Isaiah (Isa 5:12; 16:11; 23:16; 24:8; 30:32), where in all but one instance it translates כנור. The golden bowls of incense recall the account of the dedication of the altar in Num 7, where a golden כף (RSV: "dish"; NJPS: "ladle") filled with incense (Num 7:14, 20, etc.) is among the offerings brought by each of the tribal chiefs in turn. Revelation's word for the bowls, φιάλη, appears in Num 7, but there it translates מזרק, the basin, silver in Numbers, presented by each of the chiefs in turn (Num 7:13, 19, etc.).

The combination of harps and bowls is unprecedented in Jewish Scripture, and here too some have suggested that Revelation's picture is best illumined by reference to its Greco-Roman context, in this case an understanding of the combination of harp and bowl as typifying cultic activity attested in depictions on coins and vases of Apollo holding both a harp and a φιάλη.[44] Such a background may well have contributed to John's association of harp and φιάλη, but it might also be worth remembering here that the Songs of the Sabbath Sacrifice combines elements of the temple cult in ways unknown in the Torah. There is no reason to believe that Revelation knew the Songs; more likely, the two works arrived independently at similar approaches to depicting the heavenly temple as both like and unlike the earthly temple.[45]

---

alypse of John," *BR* 28 (1983): 5–26, at 12–13. See Leithart, *Revelation*, 223, for references to other scholars on related points.

43. I substitute "holy ones" for "saints" in passages quoted from the RSV and NRSV translations of Revelation.

44. Gregory Stevenson, *Power and Place: Temple and Identity in the Book of Revelation* (Berlin: de Gruyter, 2001), 234. David E. Aune (*Revelation 1–5*, WBC 52A [Grand Rapids: Zondervan, 1997], 355–57) notes the Greco-Roman parallels but insists that Revelation intends the bowls to be understood in the context of Jewish ideas about the heavenly cult.

45. On the parallels between the Songs of the Sabbath Sacrifice and Revelation, Allison, "4Q403," 409–14; Håkan Ulfgard, "The *Songs of the Sabbath Sacrifice* and the Heavenly Scene of the Book of Revelation," in *Northern Lights on the Dead Sea Scrolls*, ed. Anders Klostergaard Petersen et al., STDJ 80 (Leiden: Brill, 2009); and Noam Mizrahi, "The Poetics of Angelic Discourse: Revelation 2–3 and the Songs of the Sabbath Sacrifice," *JSNT* 41 (2018): 107–23.

Revelation is the first work discussed in which an altar appears, although the absence of an altar in the Songs of the Sabbath Sacrifice may reflect the poor state of its preservation. Its absence elsewhere and presence in Revelation are notable because the altar is so central to the cult of the Jerusalem temple. The first appearance of an altar in Revelation comes at the opening of the fifth seal, when the souls of martyrs cry out to God from their place under the altar (Rev 6:9–10). Two of the other mentions of an altar in Revelation identify it as the golden altar (Rev 8:3; 9:13), the altar on which incense was offered (Exod 30:1–10; 1 Kgs 7:48); the absence of such an indication for the martyrs' altar may suggest that it corresponds to the bronze altar, the altar on which animal sacrifices were offered (Exod 27:1–2; 30:28; 1 Kgs 8:64).[46]

The bronze altar might seem an appropriate location for the souls of martyrs, but the mention of blood in their cry—"How long will it be before you judge and avenge our blood on those who dwell upon earth?" (Rev 6:10, trans. NRSV)—evokes not a cultic context but passages such as Deut 32:43 ("He avenges the blood of his servants," a passage echoed in Rev 19:2) and Ps 79:10 ("Let the avenging of the outpoured blood of your servants be known among the nations").[47] In response to their plea, the martyrs are given white robes and told to wait until their number is complete (Rev 6:11). The next chapter depicts white-robed martyrs in heaven singing praise to God and the Lamb (Rev 7:9–10). The relationship between these martyrs and those under the altar is not clear.

At the opening of the seventh seal, there is another appearance of an altar or altars, this time with more cultic imagery:

> And another angel came and stood at the altar with a golden censer; and he was given much incense to mingle with the prayers of all the holy ones upon the golden altar before the throne; and the smoke of the incense rose with the prayers of the holy ones from the hand of the angel before God. Then the angel took the censer and filled it with fire from the altar and threw it on the earth; and there were peals of thunder, voices, flashes of lightning, and an earthquake. (Rev 8:3–5)

46. Leithart, *Revelation 1–11*, 302, identifies the altar in question as the bronze altar and insists that, unlike the golden altar that appears in Rev 8, it is not in heaven but on earth. He suggests that the blood of the martyrs is poured out at the base of the altar just as the blood of the *ḥaṭṭāt* offering was poured there. I find this suggestion appealing, but as I note below, the martyrs' reference to their blood does not use cultic language.

47. I substitute "your" for RSV's "thy" in the translation of Ps 79:10.

It is not clear whether this passage intends to distinguish between "the altar" and "the golden altar," but either way, the use of cultic equipment is notable.[48] Revelation's term for the golden censer, λιβανωτός, does not appear in the Greek Bible (LXX), but it should probably identified with the מחתה, fire pan, most often πυρίον or πυρεῖον in the Greek. The firepans for the tabernacle are bronze (Exod 27:3; 38:3), but those of the temple are gold (1 Kgs 7:50). The incense of the passage from Rev 8 recalls the earlier mention of "golden bowls full of incense, which are the prayers of the holy ones" (Rev 5:8); as already noted, the Greek makes it clear that the prayers are the bowls rather than the incense. While the passage from Rev 8 maintains a connection between incense and the prayers of the holy ones, the imagery is quite different.

The integration of the cult of the heavenly temple into the eschatological scenario is a distinctive feature of the book of Revelation. In the passage from Rev 8 the fire from the golden altar causes tremors on earth (Rev 8:5). Later one of the four living creatures gives each of the seven angels a golden bowl (φιάλη again) full of the wrath of God (Rev 15:7). By pouring out their bowls the angels bring further evils on the world (Rev 16).

Finally, it is important to note that blood plays no part in the heavenly cult according to Revelation.[49] This point is particularly noteworthy because the blood of the Lamb is central for Revelation's view of salvation. At the beginning of his words to the seven churches of Asia, John calls Christ the one "who has freed us from our sins by his blood" (Rev 1:5), and when John first sees the Lamb in the heavenly temple, the twenty-four elders offer the following acclamation: "You are worthy . . . for you were slaughtered and by your blood you ransomed for God holy ones from every tribe and language and people and nation" (Rev 5:9, NRSV).[50] It should be noted that "ransomed" translates the Greek verb ἀγοράζω, "buy," which does not appear in cultic contexts in the Greek Bible.

Yet although John sees the Lamb standing "as though it had been slain"

---

48. Leithart, *Revelation 1–11*, 350–51, understands the first altar to be the altar of Rev 6:9–11, which in his view is on earth (302). His suggestion that the angel ascends from the bronze altar on earth to the golden altar in heaven is appealing, but it again assumes a more systematic understanding of the relationship between earthly cult and heavenly in Revelation than is evident from the text itself.

49. For the nineteen (by his count) references to blood in Revelation and discussion, K. C. Hanson, "Blood and Purity in Leviticus and Revelation," *Listening: Journal of Religion and Culture* 28 (1993) 215–30.

50. There is no Greek noun for "holy ones" in this passage, which reads, literally, "by your blood you ransomed for God from every tribe and language and people and nation."

(Rev 5:6), blood plays no part in the description. The multitude singing praise to God and the Lamb have made their robes white by washing them in the blood of the Lamb (Rev 7:14), but presumably the blood is no longer visible. Toward the end of the work, Christ, called there the Word of God, leads the armies of heaven, riding on a white horse and dressed in a robe dipped in blood (Rev 19:13); the armies are dressed in white linen (Rev 19:14), the fabric of priestly garments (Exod 28:42; Lev 6:10, etc.). I am not sure that we are meant to picture the blood of the Word's garment as visible. After all, the robes of the multitude were made white precisely by washing in blood (Rev 7:14). On the other hand, it is possible that visible blood is appropriate to the eschatological battle, which, after all, takes place outside the heavenly temple. But however we picture the garment of the Word, it is clear that for Revelation the heavenly cult does not involve blood. Nor does it involve intercession or atonement. The heavenly cult consists of incense offerings and words of praise. The great atoning sacrifice, the sacrifice of Christ, has already taken place on earth.

Both the Songs of the Sabbath Sacrifice and Revelation, then, see the heavenly cult as primarily a liturgy of praise, but both works also picture elements drawn from the sacrificial cult playing a role. Revelation, as we have just seen, describes incense offerings in heaven, and the Songs mentions specific types of sacrifices and the aroma of offerings. But for Revelation the sacrifice that effects atonement does not take place in heaven, while the placement of the Songs' claim that the angelic priests effect atonement for the penitent suggests that it is not, or at least not only, sacrifice but the entire heavenly cult of praise that does so.

## Epistle to the Hebrews and Testament of Levi

The Epistle to the Hebrews is a homiletical work devoted to demonstrating the superiority of Christ's dispensation to that of the old covenant, likely written at about the same time as Revelation. Its distinctive picture of the workings of the heavenly temple differs in important ways from those of the texts considered so far. Unlike John of Patmos, the author of Hebrews does not claim to have seen the heavenly temple; his account of the atonement effected there by Christ's blood derives its authority from his mode of interpreting Jewish Scripture.

Hebrews invokes God's command to Moses to make the sanctuary according to the pattern he is shown (Exod 25:9) to demonstrate that the earthly temple is "a copy and shadow" (Heb 8:5) of the heavenly temple. Just as the first covenant is inferior to the new covenant that has replaced it, so the earthly temple is inferior to the heavenly. Indeed the earthly temple failed to accomplish its purpose, for had the sacrifices offered by the Levitical priests succeeded in cleansing the people from sin and making them perfect, they would not have had to be offered year after year (Heb 10:1–4). But lasting atonement has finally been achieved, through the one-time sacrifice of Christ, who as high priest "entered once for all into the Holy Place, taking not the blood of goats and calves but his own blood, thus securing an eternal redemption" (Heb 9:12).

Some scholars suggest that the blood Christ bears into the heavenly temple should be understood as metaphorical blood.[51] I see no reason to do so. None of the other descriptions of the heavenly temple considered here—or indeed any other description of the heavenly temple in Jewish and Christian literature that I know—is willing to place blood in heaven, and the author of Hebrews surely intended his readers to be struck and even shocked by his claim. For Hebrews, if the first covenant was inaugurated with blood, so too must the second covenant be, and just as purification according to the Torah required blood, so the blood of Christ constitutes the heavenly counterpart to the blood of those earthly sacrifices—far superior to it, of course, as heaven is to earth (Heb 9:15–28).

Hebrews does not discuss what goes on in the heavenly temple apart from the moment of Christ's entrance with his blood, but its focus on the singularity of Christ's sacrifice implies that there is no ongoing cult in the heavenly temple. This picture accounts for Hebrews' insistence that followers of Christ who abandon him have no hope of atonement (Heb 6:4–8; 10:26–31). Christ's sacrifice was a one-time event, and "there no longer remains a sacrifice for sins" (Heb 10:26).

The distinctive character of Hebrews' picture of the heavenly temple becomes even clearer when it is juxtaposed to that of the Testament of Levi. The Testament of Levi forms part of the Testaments of the Twelve Patriarchs, a Christian work of the mid-second century, thus likely some decades later than Hebrews and Revelation, though it is deeply indebted to Aramaic Levi,

---

51. See, e.g., Harry Attridge in his excellent commentary, *The Epistle to the Hebrews: A Commentary on the Epistle to the Hebrews*, Hermeneia (Philadelphia: Fortress, 1989), 248: "The image should not be pressed . . . to mean that Christ actually brought his blood into heaven. That 'blood' is being used in a metaphorical way is clear, but the precise metaphorical significance is not immediately apparent. . . ." Attridge's notes there refer to others who read the blood as Christ's life (n. 55) or death (n. 56).

the work contemporary with the Book of the Watchers mentioned briefly above. [52] As a first-person account of the career of Levi, the ancestor of the Jewish priesthood, Aramaic Levi is concerned with proper priestly behavior and sacrificial practice. In addition, as noted above, it contained an ascent to heaven, though the ascent has not survived. The relationship between the Testament of Levi and the better-preserved portions of Aramaic Levi makes it likely that the Testament took the earlier ascent as a point of departure for its own, transforming Aramaic Levi's single heaven into seven heavens just as 2 Enoch did for the Book of the Watchers.

The Testament of Levi designates the four highest heavens as holy in contrast to the three lower ones (T. Levi 3:3) and describes the four highest heavens in descending order (T. Levi 3:4–8). I will proceed in ascending order. In the fourth heaven angels offer praise "continually" (T. Levi 3:8). In the fifth heaven angels "bear answers" to the angels of the presence in the sixth heaven (T. Levi 3:7); the nature of these answers is not specified, but perhaps they involve the prayers or deeds of humanity.[53] It is the sixth heaven that is of most interest for us. There the angels of the presence "minister and make propitiation (ἐξιλασκόμενοι) to the Lord for all the sins of ignorance of the righteous, and they offer to the Lord a pleasant odor, a reasonable and bloodless offering (λογικὴν καὶ ἀναίμακτον προσφοράν)" (T. Levi 3:5–6); the pairing "reasonable and bloodless" appears in early Christian texts in relation to both prayer and the Eucharist.[54] Finally, God himself, "the Great Glory," resides in the seventh heaven (T. Levi 3:4).

The Testament of Levi's picture of the heavenly temple shows many points of contact with the pictures already discussed. One heaven is devoted to perpetual praise, and the sacrificial cult centers on aroma. The Testament emphasizes the absence of blood in the heavenly cult by labeling the angels' offering "bloodless." It also makes propitiation or atonement an ongoing aspect of the heavenly cult. In contrast to Hebrews, which tells us that falling away from Christ after the one-time event of Christ's atonement is fatal, the Testament of Levi claims that propitiation for sins of ignorance is ongoing. These two views

---

52. The case for the Testaments as a Christian composition rather than a Jewish composition that underwent Christian editing goes back to Marinus de Jonge's work starting in the mid-twentieth century. For a summary statement, see H. W. Hollander and M. de Jonge, *The Testaments of the Twelve Patriarchs: A Commentary*, SVTP 8 (Leiden: Brill, 1985), 82–85. The translation of passages from the Testament of Levi is drawn from this work.

53. Angels bear the prayers or deeds of humanity to God in 3 Baruch 11–14 (Slavonic: prayers; Greek: deeds).

54. Hollander and de Jonge, *Testaments*, 138, and references there.

are not logically contradictory since the sins they consider belong to different categories, but the emphases are very different. This difference is underscored by another point at which the works differ. For Hebrews, it is Christ's blood in the heavenly temple that effects atonement. For the Testament of Levi, it is the bloodless offering.

## Conclusions

The understanding of angels and priests as counterparts goes back to the end of the period of the First Temple, and it surely implies the existence of a temple and cult in heaven. The earliest description of a heavenly temple appears in the Book of the Watchers' account of Enoch's ascent, likely dating from the late third century BCE; it hints at cultic activity consisting of angelic praise. Sadly, the vision of heaven in the roughly contemporary Aramaic Levi Document has not survived. Perhaps it would have given us a different picture.

The Book of the Watchers was an extremely influential work, and the impact of many aspects of the work is evident in the second century BCE. But it is not until the turn of the era that its picture of a heavenly temple is taken up by other apocalypses. For 2 Enoch and several apocalypses not considered here, the primary activity in the heavenly temple is a liturgy of praise, usually without any mention of the equipment of the sacrificial cult. In some of these works, heaven is identifiable as a temple in part because the visionary's successful ascent is described in terms drawn from priestly consecration.[55] None of these works describes the heavenly cult as effecting atonement.

The Songs of the Sabbath Sacrifice, Revelation, and the Testament of Levi imagine the heavenly temple as the scene of praise but also of some aspects of the sacrificial cult familiar from the earthly temple. The ratio of cultic elements to praise is different in each of these works, and each work takes a distinctive approach to the significance of the heavenly temple reflecting its individual concerns. The Songs represents the whole of the heavenly liturgy and cult as effecting atonement, while the Testament of Levi depicts the sacrifices offered in the sixth heaven as atoning. For Revelation, on the other hand, atonement comes from Christ's sacrifice on earth. Revelation and the Testament of Levi

---

55. Himmelfarb, *Ascent to Heaven*, 51–59 (Apocalypse of Zephaniah and Ascension of Isaiah), 61–66 (Apocalypse of Abraham), 87–91 (3 Baruch). I now understand the Apocalypse of Zephaniah as a Christian work with affinities to the Apocalypse of Paul that suggest a date in the fourth century or not much earlier, as for 3 Baruch.

emphasize incense and aroma, respectively, in their picture of the heavenly cult. The Songs of the Sabbath Sacrifice, too, makes aroma central to the heavenly cult along with grain offerings and unspecified angelic sacrifices. Of all the texts that describe a heavenly temple, only Hebrews dares to imagine blood in heaven in a one-time ritual of atonement.

# Bibliography

Adams, Sean A., and Seth M. Ehorn. "What Is a Composite Citation? An Introduction." Pages 1–16 in *Composite Citations in Antiquity: Volume One: Jewish, Graeco-Roman, and Early Christian Uses*. Edited by Sean A. Adams and Seth M. Ehorn. LNTS 525. London: Bloomsbury T&T Clark, 2016.

Alexander, Philip. *The Mystical Texts: Songs of the Sabbath Sacrifice and Related Manuscripts*. STS 61. London: T&T Clark International, 2006.

Allison, Dale C., Jr. "*4Q403* Fragm. 1, Col. I, 38–46 and the Revelation to John." *RevQ* 12 (1986): 409–14.

———. "Cross: I. New Testament." Page 1042 in vol. 5 of *The Encyclopedia of the Bible and Its Reception*. Edited by Hans-Josef Klauck et al. Berlin: de Gruyter, 2012.

Alster, B. "Tiamat." Pages 867–69 in the *Dictionary of Deities and Demons*. Edited by K. van der Toorn. 2nd ed. Leiden: Brill, 1999.

Andersen, F. I. "2 (Slavonic Apocalypse of) Enoch." Pages 91–221 in *Apocalyptic Literature and Testaments*. Vol. 1 of *The Old Testament Pseudepigrapha*. Edited by James H. Charlesworth. Garden City, NY: Doubleday, 1983.

Anderson, Gary A. *Sacrifices and Offerings in Ancient Israel: Studies in Their Social and Political Importance*. HSM 41 Atlanta: Scholars Press, 1988.

———. *Sin: A History*. New Haven: Yale University Press, 2009.

Ashley, Timothy R. *The Book of Numbers*. NICOT. Grand Rapids: Eerdmans, 1993.

Attridge, Harold. *The Epistle to the Hebrews: A Commentary on the Epistle to the Hebrews*. Hermeneia. Philadelphia: Fortress Press, 1989.

Auffarth, Christoph, and Marvin Döbler. "Cross: II. Christianity. C. Modern Europe and America." Pages 1050–53 in vol. 5 of *The Encyclopedia of the Bible and Its Reception*. Edited by Hans-Josef Klauck et al. Berlin: de Gruyter, 2012.

Aulén, Gustav. *Christus Victor: An Historical Study of the Three Main Types of the Idea of the Atonement*. London: SPCK, 1931.

Aune, David E. "The Influence of Roman Imperial Court Ceremonial on the Apocalypse of John." *BR* 28 (1983): 5–26.

———. *Revelation 1–5*. WBC 52A. Grand Rapids: Zondervan, 1997.

Baden, Joel. *The Composition of the Pentateuch*. AYBRL. New Haven: Yale University, 2012.

———. *J, E, and the Redaction of the Pentateuch*. FAT 68. Tübingen: Mohr Siebeck, 2009.

———. "The Original Place of the Priestly Manna Story in Exodus 16." *ZAW* 122 (2010): 491–504.

Bähr, Karl C. W. F. *Symbolik des Mosaischen Cultus*. 2 vols. Heidelberg: Mohr, 1839.

Balberg, Mira. *Blood for Thought: The Reinvention of Sacrifice in Early Rabbinic Literature*. Oakland, CA: University of California Press, 2017.

Baltzer, Klaus, and Jürgen Kabiersch. "Esaias / Isaias / das Buch Jesaja." Pages 2484–2690 in *Psalmen bis Daniel*, vol. 2 of *Septuaginta Deutsch: Erklärungen und Kommentare zum griechischen Alten Testament*. Edited by Martin Karrer and Wolfgang Kraus. Stuttgart: Deutsche Bibelgesellschaft, 2011.

Barr, James. "Aramaic-Greek Notes on the Book of Enoch (II)." *JJS* 24 (1979): 179–92.

Barth, Gerhard. *Der Tod Jesu Chrisi im Verständnis des Neuen Testaments*. Neukirchen-Vluyn: Neukirchener, 1992.

Bauckham, Richard. *God Crucified: Monotheism and Christology in the New Testament*. Carlisle: Paternoster, 1998.

———. *Gospel of Glory: Major Themes in Johannine Theology*. Grand Rapids: Baker Academic, 2015.

Beale, G. K. *The Book of Revelation: A Commentary on the Greek Text*. NIGTC. Grand Rapids: Eerdmans, 1999.

———. *We Become What We Worship: A Biblical Theology of Idolatry*. Downers Grove: IVP Academic, 2008.

Beavis, Mary Ann, and HyeRan Kim-Cragg. *Hebrews*. Wisdom Commentary 54. Collegeville, MN: Liturgical Press, 2015.

Beentjes, Pancratius Cornelis. "The Book of Ben Sira: Some New Perspectives at the Dawn of the 21st Century." Pages 1–19 in *Goochem in Mokum, Wisdom in Amsterdam*. Edited by Pancratius Cornelis Beentjes. OtSt 68. Leiden: Brill, 2016.

———. *The Book of Ben Sira in Hebrew*. VTSup 68. Leiden: Brill, 1997.

———. "'The Countries Marveled at You': King Solomon in Ben Sira 47:12–22." Pages 135–144 in *"Happy the One who Meditates on Wisdom" (Sir. 14.20): Collected Essays on the Book of Ben Sira*. CEBT 43. Leuven: Peeters, 2006.

Belle, Gilbert Van. "The Death of Jesus and the Literary Unity of the Fourth Gospel." Pages 11–37 in *The Death of Jesus in the Fourth Gospel*. Edited by Gilbert Van Belle. BETL 200. Leuven: Peeters, 2006.

Berg, Shane. "Ben Sira, the Genesis Creation Accounts, and the Knowledge of God's Will." *JBL* 132 (2013): 139–57.

Berger, Peter. *The Sacred Canopy: Elements of a Sociological Theory of Religion*. Garden City, NY: Doubleday, 1967.

Best, Ernest. *A Critical and Exegetical Commentary on Ephesians*. ICC. London: T&T Clark, 1998.

Beutler, Johannes. "Greeks Come to See Jesus (John 12,20f)." *Bib* 71 (1990): 341–46.

Bickerman, Elias J. *Jews in the Greek Age*. Cambridge: Harvard University Press, 1988.

Bieringer, Reimund. "Das Lamm Gottes, das die Sünde der Welt hinwegnimmt (Joh 1,29): Eine kontextorientierte und redaktionsgeschichtliche Untersuchung auf dem Hintergrund der Passatradition als Deutung des Todes Jesu im Johannesevangelium." Pages 207–13 in *The Death of Jesus in the Fourth Gospel*. Edited by Gilbert Van Belle. BETL 200. Leuven: Peeters, 2006.

Blenkinsopp, Joseph. "The Sacrificial Life and Death of the Servant (Isaiah 52:13–53:12)." *VT* 66 (2016): 1–14.

Böttrich, Christfried. "The Angel of Tartarus and the Supposed Coptic Fragments of 2 Enoch." *Early Christianity* 4 (2013): 509–21.

Brand, Miryam T. *Evil Within and Without: The Source of Sin and Its Nature as Portrayed in Second Temple Literature*, JAJSup 9. Göttingen: Vandenhoeck & Ruprecht, 2013.

Brant, Jo-Ann A. *John*. Paideia Commentaries on the New Testament. Grand Rapids: Baker Academic, 2011.

Brettler, Marc Zvi. "Predestination in Deuteronomy 30:1–10." Pages 171–88 in *Those Elusive Deuteronomists: The Phenomenon of Pan-Deuteronomism*. Edited by Linda S. Schearing and Steven L. McKenzie. JSOTSup 268. Sheffield: Sheffield Academic Press, 1999.

Büchner, Dirk. "Ἐξιλάσασθαι: Appeasing God in the Septuagint Pentateuch." *JBL* 129 (2010): 237–60.

Budd, Philip J. *Leviticus*. NCB. London: Marshall Pickering, 1996.

———. *Numbers*. WBC 5. Grand Rapids: Zondervan, 1984.

Burkert, Walter. *Homo Necans: The Anthropology of Ancient Greek Sacrificial Ritual and Myth*. Translated by Peter Bing. Berkeley, CA: University of California Press, 1983.

———. *Kulte des Altertums: Biologische Grundlagen der Religion*. Munich: Beck, 1998.

Bushnell, Horace. "Our Obligation to the Dead." Pages 325–28 in *Building Eras in Religion*. New York: Charles Scribner's Sons, 1881.

Bynum, William Randolph. "Quotations of Zechariah in the Fourth Gospel." Pages 47–74 in *Abiding Words: The Use of Scripture in the Gospel of John*. Edited by Alicia D. Myers and Bruce G. Schuchard. RBS 81. Atlanta: Society of Biblical Literature Press, 2015.

Calabro, David. "A Reexamination of the Ancient Israelite Gesture of Hand Placement." Pages 99–124 in *Sacrifice, Cult, and Atonement in Early Judaism and Christianity: Constituents and Critique*. Edited by Henrietta L. Wiley and Christian A. Eberhart. RBS 85. Atlanta: Society of Biblical Literature Press, 2017.

Capponi, Livia. *Il tempio di Leontopoli in Egitto: Identità politica e religiosa dei Giudei di Onia (c. 150 a.C – 73 d.C.)*. Pubblicazioni della Facoltà di Lettere e Filosofia dell'Università di Pavia 118. Pisa: Edizione ETS, 2007.

Carasik, Michael. *Leviticus* ויקרא. Vol. 3 of *The Commentator's Bible: The Rubin JPS Miqra'ot Gedolot*. Philadelphia: Jewish Publication Society, 2009.

Carlton, Clark. *The Faith: Understanding Orthodox Christianity – An Orthodox Catechism*. Regina: Orthodox Press, 1997.

Carr, David M. *The Formation of the Hebrew Bible: A New Reconstruction*. Oxford: Oxford University Press, 2011.

Charles, R. H. *The Greek Versions of the Testament of the Twelve Patriarchs*. Oxford: Clarendon, 1908.

Charlesworth, James H., and Carol A. Newsom, with H. W. L. Rietz, B. A. Strawn, and R. E. Whitaker, eds. *Angelic Liturgy: Songs of the Sabbath Sacrifice*. Vol. 4B of *The Dead Sea Scrolls: Hebrew Aramaic, and Greek Texts with English Translations*. Tübingen: Mohr Siebeck, and Louisville: Westminster John Knox, 1999.

Chazon, Esther. "Lowly to Lofty: The Hodayot's Use of Liturgical Traditions to Shape Sectarian Identity and Religious Experience." *RevQ* 26 (2013): 3–19.

Collins, John J. *Between Athens and Jerusalem: Jewish Identity in the Hellenistic Diaspora*. 2nd ed. Grand Rapids: Eerdmans, 2000.

Corley, Jeremy. "A Numerical Structure in Sirach 44:1–50:24." *CBQ* 69 (2007): 43–63.

———. "Sirach 44:1–15 as Introduction to the Praise of the Ancestors." Pages 151–81 in *Studies in the Book of Ben Sira: Papers of the Third International Conference on the Deuterocanonical Books, Shime'on Centre, Pápa, Hungary, 18–20 May 2006*. Edited by Géza G. Xeravits and Józsee Zsengellér. JSJSup 127. Leiden: Brill, 2008.

Cottrill, Amy C. *Language, Power, and Identity in the Lament Psalms of the Individual*. LHBOTS 493. New York: T&T Clark, 2008.

Culpepper, R. Alan. *Anatomy of the Fourth Gospel: A Study in Literary Design.* Philadelphia: Fortress Press, 1983.

Davies, Eryl W. *Numbers*. NCB. London: Marshall Pickering, 1995.

Davila, James R. "Aramaic Levi: A new translation and introduction." Pages 121–32 in *Old Testament Pseudepigrapha: More Noncanonical Scriptures*. Edited by Richard Bauckham, James R. Davila, and Alexander Panayotov. Grand Rapids: Eerdmans, 2013.

Davis Bledsoe, Amanda M. "Throne Theophanies, Dream Visions, and Righteous (?) Seers: Daniel, the *Book of Giants*, and *1 Enoch* Reconsidered." Pages 81–96 in *Ancient Tales of Giants from Qumran and Turfan: Contexts, Traditions, and Influences*. Edited by Matthew Goff, Loren T. Stuckenbruck, and Enrico Morano. WUNT 360. Tübingen: Mohr Siebeck, 2016.

Deissmann, Adolf. *Bible Studies: Contributions Chiefly from the Papyri and Inscriptions to the History of the Language, the Literature, and the Religion of Hellenistic Judaism and Primitive Christianity*. 2nd ed. Translated by Alexander Grieve. Edinburgh: T&T Clark, 1903.

———. *Light from the Ancient East: The New Testament; Illustrated by Recently Discovered Texts of the Graeco-Roman World*. Translated by Lionel R. M. Strachan. New York: Harper & Brothers, 1922.

Detienne, Marcel, and Jean-Pierre Vernant, eds. *The Cuisine of Sacrifice among the Greeks*. Translated by Paula Wissing. Chicago: University of Chicago Press, 1989.

Diehl, Jakob. "Sphragis: Eine semasiologische Nachlese." PhD diss., Giessen, 1938.

DiFransico, Lesley R. *Washing Away Sin: An Analysis of the Metaphor in the Hebrew Bible and Its Influence*. BTS 23. Leuven: Peeters, 2016.

Diodorus Siculus. *Diodorus Siculus: Library of History, Volume IV, Books 9–12.40.* Translated by C. H. Oldfather. LCL. Cambridge: Harvard University Press, 1946.

Dodd, C. H. "Ἱλάσκεσθαι: Its Cognates, Derivates and Synonyms in the Septuagint." *JTS* 32 (1930): 352–60.

———. *The Interpretation of the Fourth Gospel*. Cambridge: Cambridge University Press, 1953.

Drawnel, Henryk. *An Aramaic Wisdom Text from Qumran: A New Interpretation of the Levi Document*. JSJSup 86. Leiden: Brill, 2004.

Dunn, James D. G. *Romans 1–8*. WBC 38A. Grand Rapids: Zondervan, 1988.

Eberhart, Christian A. "Atonement. II. New Testament." Pages 32–42 in vol. 3 of *The Encyclopedia of the Bible and Its Reception*. Edited by Hans-Joseph Klauck et al. Berlin: de Gruyter, 2011.

———. "Introduction: Constituents and Critique of Sacrifice, Cult, and Atonement in Early Judaism and Christianity." Pages 1–29 in *Sacrifice, Cult, and Atonement in Early Judaism and Christianity: Constituents and Critique*. Edited by Henrietta L. Wiley and Christian A. Eberhart. RBS 85. Atlanta: Society of Biblical Literature Press, 2017.

———. *Kultmetaphorik und Christologie: Opfer-und Sühneterminologie im Neuen Testament*. WUNT 306. Tübingen: Mohr Siebeck, 2013.

———. *The Sacrifice of Jesus: Understanding Atonement Biblically*. 2nd ed. Eugene, OR: Wipf & Stock, 2018.

———. *Studien zur Bedeutung der Opfer im Alten Testament: Die Signifikanz von Blut- und Verbrennungsriten im kultischen Rahmen*. WMANT 94. Neukirchen: Neukirchener, 2002.

Eberhart, Christian A., and Don Schweitzer. "The Unique Sacrifice of Christ According to Hebrews 9: A Study in Theological Creativity." *Religions* 10/1 (2019). https://www.mdpi.com/2077-1444/10/1/47.

Ederer, Matthias. *Identitätsstiftende Begegnung: Die theologische Deutung des regelmäßigen Kultes Israels in der Tora*. FAT 121. Tübingen: Mohr Siebeck, 2018.

Eilberg-Schwartz, Howard. *The Savage in Judaism: An Anthropology of Israelite Religion and Ancient Judaism*. Bloomington: Indiana University Press, 1990.

Ekblad, Eugene Robert. *Isaiah's Servant Poems According to the Septuagint: An Exegetical and Theological Study*. Biblical Exegesis and Theology 23. Leuven: Peeters, 1999.

Elliger, Karl. "Das Gesetz Leviticus 18." *ZAW* 67 (1955): 1–25.

———. *Leviticus*. HAT 4. Tübingen: Mohr Siebeck, 1966.

Esler, Philip F. *God's Court and Courtiers in the Book of the Watchers*. Eugene, OR: Cascade Books, 2017.

Eubank, Nathan. *Wages of Cross-Bearing and Debt of Sin: The Economy of Heaven in Matthew's Gospel*. BZNW 196. Berlin: de Gruyter, 2013.

Evans, Craig A. "Obduracy and the Lord's Servant: Some Observations on the Use of the Old Testament in the Fourth Gospel." Pages 221–36 in *Early Jewish and Christian Exegesis: Studies in Memory of William Hugh Brownlee*. Edited by Craig A. Evans and William F. Stinespring. Atlanta: Scholars Press, 1987.

Ferda, Tucker S. "Sealed with the Holy Spirit (Eph 1,13–14) and Circumcision." *Bib* 93 (2012): 557–79.

Fine, Steven. *This Holy Place: On the Sanctity of the Synagogue during the Greco-Roman Period*. Christianity and Judaism in Antiquity 11. Notre Dame, IN: University of Notre Dame Press, 1997.

Finlan, Stephen. *Problems with Atonement: The Origins of, and Controversy about, the Atonement Doctrine*. Collegeville, MN: Liturgical Press, 2005.

Fitzmyer, Joseph A. *Romans: A New Translation with Introduction and Commentary*. AYB 33. New York: Doubleday, 1993.

Fletcher-Louis, Crispin H. T. *Christological Origins: The Emerging Consensus and Beyond*. Vol. 1 *Jesus Monotheism*. Eugene, OR: Wipf & Stock, 2015.

———. *The Image-Idol of God, the Priesthood, Apocalyptic and Jewish Mysticism*. Vol. 1 in *Collected Works*. Eugene OR: Wipf & Stock, forthcoming.

———. "King Solomon, a New Adam and Incorporative Representative of God's People (1 Kings 3–4): A Text That Supports N. T. Wright on Paul and the Messiah." Pages 126–47 in *One God, One People, One Future: Essays in Honour of N. T. Wright*. Edited by John Anthony Dunne and Eric Lewellen. London: SPCK, 2018.

———. "The Temple Cosmology of P and Theological Anthropology in the Wisdom of Jesus ben Sira." Pages 69–113 in *Of Scribes and Sages: Early Jewish Interpretation and Transmission of Scripture*. Edited by C. A. Evans. LSTS 50/SSEJC 9. Sheffield: Sheffield Academic Press, 2004.

Foraone, Christopher A., and F. S. Naiden, eds. *Greek and Roman Animal Sacrifice: Ancient Victims, Modern Observers*. Cambridge: Cambridge University Press, 2012.

Forestell, J. Terence. *The Word of the Cross: Salvation as Revelation in the Fourth Gospel*. AnBib 57. Rome: Biblical Institute Press, 1974.

Fowl, Stephen E. *Ephesians: A Commentary*. Louisville: Westminster John Knox, 2012.

Frankfurter, David. "Jews or Not? Reconstructing the Other in Rev 2:9 and 3:9." *HTR* 94 (2001): 403–25.

Frey, Jörg. "Die Deutung des Todes Jesu als Stellvertretung: Neutestamentliche Perspektiven." Pages 87–121 in *Stellvertretung: Theologische, philosophische und kulturelle Aspekte*. Edited by J. Christine Janowski, Bernd Janowski, and Hans P. Lichtenberger. Neukirchen-Vluyn: Neukirchener, 2006.

———. "Edler Tod – wirksamer Tod – stellvertretender Tod – heilschaffender Tod: Zur narrativen und theologischen Deutung des Todes Jesu im Johannesevangelium." Pages 65–94 in *The Death of Jesus in the Fourth Gospel*. Edited by Gilbert Van Belle. BETL 200. Leuven: Peeters, 2006.

———. "Flesh and Spirit in the Palestinian Jewish Sapiential Tradition and in the Qumran Texts: An Inquiry into the Background of Pauline Usage." Pages 367–404 in *The Wisdom Texts from Qumran and the Development of Sapiential Thought*. Edited by Charlotte Hempel, Armin Lange, and Hermann Lichtenberger. BETL 159. Leuven: Leuven University Press, 2002.

———. "Probleme der Deutung des Todes Jesu in der neutestamentlichen Wissenschaft: Streiflichter zur exegetischen Diskussion." Pages 3–50 in *Deutungen des Todes Jesu im Neuen Testament*. Edited by Jörg Frey and Jens Schröter. WUNT 181. Tübingen: Mohr Siebeck, 2005; repr., rev. 2nd ed. UTB 2953. Tübingen: Mohr Siebeck, 2012.

———. "Die '*theologia crucifixi*' des Johannesevangeliums." Pages 169–238 in *Kreuzestheologie im Neuen Testament*. Edited by Andreas Dettwiler and Jean Zumstein. WUNT 151. Tübingen: Mohr Siebeck, 2002.

———. "'Wie Mose die Schlange in der Wüste erhöht hat . . .': Zur frühjüdischen Deutung der 'ehernen Schlange' und ihrer christologischen Rezeption in Johannes 3,14f." Pages 153–205 in *Schriftauslegung im antiken Judentum und im Urchristentum*. Edited by Martin Hengel and Hermut Löhr. WUNT 73. Tübingen: Mohr Siebeck, 1994.

Gane, Roy. *Cult and Character: Purification Offerings, Day of Atonement, and Theodicy*. Winona Lake, IN: Eisenbrauns, 2005.

Gathercole, Simon. *Defending Substitution: An Essay on Atonement in Paul*. Grand Rapids: Baker Academic, 2015.

Gese, Hartmut. "Die Sühne." Pages 85–106 in *Zur biblischen Theologie: Alttestamentliche Vorträge*. 2nd ed. Tübingen: Mohr Siebeck, 1983.

Gilders, William. *Blood Ritual in the Hebrew Bible: Meaning and Power*. Baltimore: Johns Hopkins Press, 2004.

Girard, René. *Violence and the Sacred*. Translated by Patrick Gregory. Baltimore: Johns Hopkins University Press, 1977.

Goshen-Gottstein, Alon. "Ben Sira's Praise of the Fathers." Pages 235–67 in *Ben Sira's God: Proceedings of the International Ben Sira Conference*. Edited by Renate Egger-Wenzel. BZAW 321. Berlin: de Gruyter, 2002.

Greenfield, Jonas C., Michael E. Stone, and Esther Eshel. *The Aramaic Levi Document: Edition, Translation, Commentary*. SVTP 19. Leiden: Brill, 2004.

Gubler, Marie-Louise. *Die frühesten Deutungen des Todes Jesu: Eine motivgeschichtliche Darstellung aufgrund der neueren exegetischen Forschung*. Göttingen: Vandenhoeck & Ruprecht, 1977.

Hachlili, Rachel. *Ancient Synagogue—Archaeology and Art: New Discoveries and Current Research*. HdO 105. Leiden: Brill, 2013.

Hafemann, Scott J., ed. *Biblical Theology: Retrospect and Prospect*. Downers Grove: InterVarsity Press, 2002.

Hagen, Joost L. "No Longer 'Slavonic' Only: 2 Enoch Attested in Coptic from Nubia." Pages 7–34 in *New Perspectives on 2 Enoch*. Edited by Joost L. Hagen. SJ 4. Leiden: Brill, 2012.

Hampel, Volker. *Menschensohn und historischer Jesus: Ein Rätselwort als Schlüssel zum messianischen Selbstverständnis Jesu.* Neukirchen-Vluyn: Neukirchener, 1990.

Hanson, K. C. "Blood and Purity in Leviticus and Revelation." *Listening: Journal of Religion and Culture* 28 (1993): 215–30.

Hartenstein, Friedhelm. "Zur symbolischen Bedeutung des Blutes im Alten Testament." Pages 119–37 in *Deutungen des Todes Jesu im Neuen Testament.* Edited by Jörg Frey and Jens Schröter. WUNT 181. Tübingen: Mohr Siebeck, 2005; repr., rev. 2nd ed. UTB 2953. Tübingen: Mohr Siebeck, 2012.

Hartley, John E. *Leviticus.* WBC 4. Grand Rapids: Zondervan, 1992.

Hays, Richard B. *Echoes of Scripture in the Gospels.* Waco, TX: Baylor University Press, 2016.

Hayward, C. T. R. *The Jewish Temple: A non-biblical sourcebook.* London: Routledge, 1996.

Hengel, Martin. *Crucifixion in the Ancient World and the Folly of the Message of the Cross.* London: SCM Press, 1977.

———. "The Effective History of Isaiah 53 in the Pre-Christian Period." Pages 75–146 in *The Suffering Servant: Isaiah 53 in Jewish and Christian Sources.* Edited by Bernd Janowski and Peter Stuhlmacher. Translated by Daniel P. Bailey. Grand Rapids: Eerdmans, 2004.

Hermisson, Hans-Jürgen. "Das vierte Gottesknechtslied im deuterojesajanischen Kontext." Pages 1–26 in *Der leidende Gottesknecht: Jesaja 53 und seine Wirkungsgeschichte.* Edited by Bernd Janowski and Peter Stuhlmacher. FAT 14. Tübingen: Mohr Siebeck, 1996. English Translation: "The Fourth Servant Song in the Context of Second Isaiah." Pages 16–47 in *The Suffering Servant: Isaiah 53 in Jewish and Christian Sources.* Translated by Daniel P. Bailey. Grand Rapids: Eerdmans, 2004.

Himmelfarb, Martha. *Ascent to Heaven in Jewish and Christian Apocalypses.* New York: Oxford University Press, 1993.

———. *Between Temple and Torah: Essays on Priests, Scribes, and Visionaries in the Second Temple Period and Beyond.* TSAJ 151. Tübingen: Mohr Siebeck, 2013.

———. "*3 Baruch* Revisited: Jewish or Christian Composition, and Why It Matters." *ZAC* 20 (2016): 41–62.

Hobson, Thomas. "Punitive Expulsion in the Ancient Near East." *ZABR* 17 (2011): 15–32.

Holl, Adolf. "Ein liebender Gott will keine Opfer! Sühne, Schuld und Scheitern sind nicht das Zentrum des Christentums, und Gott ist kein Sadist: Warum Jesus mit einem Opferlamm rein gar nichts zu tun hat." *Publik-Forum* 8 (2000): 24–26.

Hollander, H. W., and M. de Jonge. *The Testaments of the Twelve Patriarchs: A Commentary.* SVTP 8. Leiden: Brill, 1985.

Holmes, Stephen R. "Penal Substitution." Pages 295–314 in *T&T Clark Companion to Atonement.* Edited by Adam J. Johnson. London: Bloomsbury T&T Clark, 2017.

Hossfeld, Frank-Lothar, and Erich Zenger. *Psalms 2: A Commentary on Psalms 51–100.* Translated by Linda M. Maloney. Hermeneia. Minneapolis: Fortress, 2005.

Houtman, Cornelis. *Exodus Volume 1,* HCOT. Kampen: Kok, 1993.

———. *Exodus Volume 2,* HCOT. Kampen: Kok, 1996.

———. *Exodus. Volume 3,* HCOT. Leuven: Peeters, 2000.

Hubert, Henri, and Marcel Mauss. "Essai sur la nature et la fonction du sacrifice." *Année Sociologique* 2 (1899): 29–138.

Hughes, Julie A. *Scriptural Allusions and Exegesis in the Hodayot.* STDJ 59. Leiden: Brill, 2006.

Hultgren, Stephen J. *From the Damascus Covenant to the Covenant of the Community: Literary, Historical, and Theological Studies in the Dead Sea Scrolls.* STDJ 66. Leiden: Brill, 2007.

Jacob, Haley G. *Conformed to the Image of His Son: Reconsidering Paul's Theology of Glory in Romans.* Downers Grove: InterVarsity, 2018.

Janowski, Bernd. *Sühne als Heilsgeschehen: Studien zur Sühnetheologie der Priesterschrift und der Wurzel KPR im Alten Orient und im Alten Testament.* WMANT 55. Neukirchen: Neukirchener Verlag, 1982.

Janssen, Enno. *Das Gottesvolk und seine Geschichte: Geschichtsbild und Selbstverständnis im palästinensischen Schrifttum von Jesus Sirach bis Jehuda ha-Nasi.* Neukirchen-Vluyn: Neukirchener, 1971.

Jensen, Robert W. "On the Doctrine of the Atonement." *PSB* 27 (2006): 100–8.

Jewett, Robert. *Romans: A Commentary.* Hermeneia. Minneapolis: Fortress, 2007.

Jones, C. P. "Stigmata: Tattooing and Branding in Graeco-Roman Antiquity." *JRS* 77 (1987): 139–55.

Joosten, Jan. "The Impact of the Septuagint Pentateuch on the Greek Psalms." Pages 147–56 in *Collected Studies on the Septuagint: From Language to Interpretation and Beyond.* FAT 83. Tübingen: Mohr Siebeck, 2012.

Joyce, Paul M. "Ezekiel 40–42: The Earliest 'Heavenly Ascent' Narrative?" Pages 17–41 in *The Book of Ezekiel and Its Influence.* Edited by Henk Jan de Jonge and Johannes Tromp. Ashgate: Aldershot, 2007.

Karrer, Martin. "Hebrews, Epistle to the." Pages 680–89 in Volume 11 of *The Encyclopedia of the Bible and Its Reception.* Edited by Hans-Joseph Klauck. Berlin: de Gruyter, 2015.

Keener, Craig S. *The Gospel of John: A Commentary.* 2 vols. Peabody: Hendrickson, 2003.

Kermani, Navid. *Gott ist schön: Das ästhetische Erleben des Koran.* Munich: C. H. Beck, 1999.

Kessler, Herbert L. "The Codex Barbarus Scaligeri, the *Christian Topography*, and the Question of Jewish Models of Early Christian Art." Pages 139–54 in *Between Judaism and Christianity: Art Historical Essays in Honor of Elisheva (Elisabeth) Revel-Nehere.* Edited by Katrin Kogman-Appel and Mati Meyer. The Medieval Mediterranean 81. Leiden: Brill, 2009.

Kister, Menahem. "'Inclination of the Heart of Man,' the Body and Purification from Evil." Pages 243–84 in *Meghillot: Studies in the Dead Sea Scrolls VIII.* Edited by Moshe Bar-Asher and Devorah Dimant. Jerusalem: Bialik Institute and Haifa University Press, 2010.

Kiuchi, Nobuyoshi. *Leviticus.* AOTC 3. Nottingham: Apollos, 2007.

———. *The Purification Offering in the Priestly Literature: Its Meaning and Function.* JSOTSup 56. Sheffield: Sheffield Academic Press, 1987.

———. *A Study of Ḥāṭā' and Ḥaṭṭā't in Leviticus 4–5.* Tübingen: Mohr Siebeck, 2003.

Klawans, Jonathan. *Impurity and Sin in Ancient Judaism.* New York: Oxford University Press, 2000.

———. *Purity, Sacrifice, and the Temple: Symbolism and Supersessionism in the Study of Ancient Judaism.* New York: Oxford University Press, 2006.

Klink, Edward W., III. "The Gospel of John." Pages 515–21 in *T&T Clark Companion to Atonement.* Edited by Adam J. Johnson. London: Bloomsbury T&T Clark, 2017.

Knibb, Michael A. *The Qumran Community.* Cambridge: Cambridge University Press, 1987.

Knohl, Israel. *The Sanctuary of Silence: The Priestly Torah and the Holiness School.* Minneapolis: Fortress, 1995.

———. "The Sin Offering Law in the 'Holiness School.'" Pages 192–203 in *Priesthood and Cult in Ancient Israel.* Edited by Saul M. Olyan and Gary A. Anderson. JSOTSup 125. Sheffield: Sheffield Academic, 1991.

Knöppler, Thomas. *Die theologia crucis des Johannesevangeliums: Das Verständnis des Todes Jesu im Rahmen der johanneischen Inkarnations- und Erhöhungschristologie.* WMANT 69. Neukirchen-Vluyn: Neukirchener, 1994.

Knust, Jennifer Wright, and Zsuzsanna Várhelyi, eds. *Ancient Mediterranean Sacrifice.* New York: Oxford University Press, 2011.

Kocar, Alexander. "A Hierarchy of Salvation in the Book of Revelation: Different Peoples, Dwellings, and Tasks in the End Times." Pages 101–30 in *Placing Ancient Texts: The Ritual and Rhetorical Use of Space*. Edited by Mika Ahuvia and Alexander Kocar. Tübingen: Mohr Siebeck, 2018.

Koester, Craig R. *Hebrews: A New Translation with Introduction and Commentary.* AB 36. New York: Doubleday, 2001.

———. "Why Was the Messiah Crucified? A Study of God, Jesus, Satan, and Human Agency in Johannine Theology Messiah." Pages 163–80 in *The Death of Jesus in the Fourth Gospel*. Edited by Gilbert Van Belle. BETL 200. Leuven: Peeters, 2006.

Kooij, Arie van der. "6.2 Esaias / Isaias / Jesaja." Pages 559–576 in *Einleitung in die Septuaginta* (LXX.H 1). Edited by Siegfried Kreuzer. Gütersloh: Gütersloher, 2016.

Kooij, Arie van der, and Florian Wilk. "Esaias / Isaias / das Buch Jesaja." Pages 2484–2505 in *Psalmen bis Daniel*, vol. 2 of *Septuaginta Deutsch: Erklärungen und Kommentare zum griechischen Alten Testament*. Edited by Martin Karrer and Wolfgang Kraus. Stuttgart: Deutsche Bibelgesellschaft, 2011.

Kooten, George van. *Paul's Anthropology in Context: The Image of God, Assimilation to God, and Tripartite Man in Ancient Judaism*. WUNT 232. Tübingen: Mohr Siebeck, 2008.

Kraus, Wolfgang. "Jesaja 53 LXX im frühen Christentum – eine Überprüfung." Pages 149–82 in *Beiträge zur urchristlichen Theologiegeschichte*. Edited by Wolfgang Kraus. BZNW 163. Berlin: de Gruyter, 2009.

Kreuzer, Siegfried. "Die Septuaginta im Kontext alexandrinischer Kultur und Bildung." Pages 28–56 in *Im Brennpunkt: Die Septuaginta*, Vol. 3: *Studien zur Theologie, Anthropologie, Ekklesiologie, Eschatologie und Liturgie der Griechischen Bibel*. Edited by Heinz-Josef Fabry and Dieter Böhler. BWA(N)T 14. Stuttgart: Kohlhammer, 2007.

Kuhn, Heinz-Wolfgang. *Enderwartung und gegenwärtiges Heil: Untersuchungen zu den Gemeindeliedern von Qumran*. SUNT 3. Göttingen: Vandenhoeck & Ruprecht, 1966.

———. "Die Kreuzesstrafe während der frühen Kaiserzeit: Ihre Wirklichkeit und Wertung in der Umwelt des Urchristentums." Pages 648–793 in *Aufstieg und Niedergang der Römischen Welt* 2/25/1. Berlin: de Gruyter, 1982.

Kwon, Yon-Gyong. "Ἀρραβών as Pledge in Second Corinthians." *NTS* 54 (2008): 525–41.

Lam, Joseph. *Patterns of Sin in the Hebrew Bible: Metaphor, Culture, and the Making of a Religious Concept*. Oxford: Oxford University Press, 2016.

Lambert, David. *How Repentance Became Biblical: Judaism, Christianity, and the Interpretation of Scripture.* New York: Oxford University Press, 2016.

Lapsley, Jacqueline E. *Can These Bones Live? The Problem of the Moral Self in the Book of Ezekiel.* BZAW 301. Berlin: de Gruyter, 2000.

Larson, Erik W. "The Translation of Enoch: From Aramaic into Greek." Ph.D. diss. New York University, 1995.

Lawson, E. Thomas, and Robert N. McCauley. *Rethinking Religion: Connecting Cognition and Culture.* Cambridge: Cambridge University Press, 1990.

Lee, Dorothy. "Paschal Imagery in the Gospel of John: A Narrative and Symbolic Reading." *Pacifica* 24 (2011): 13–28.

Lee, T. R. *Studies in the Form of Sirach 44–50.* SBLDS 75. Atlanta: Scholars Press, 1986.

Lemke, Werner. "Circumcision of the Heart: The Journey of a Biblical Metaphor." Pages 299–319 in *A God So Near: Essays on Old Testament Theology in Honor of Patrick D. Miller.* Edited by Brent A. Strawn and Nancy R. Bowen. Winona Lake, IN: Eisenbrauns, 2003.

Leppin, Volker. "Cross: B. Medieval Times and Reformation Era." Pages 1047 in vol. 5 of *The Encyclopedia of the Bible and Its Reception.* Berlin: de Gruyter, 2012.

Levenson, Jon D. *Creation and the Persistence of Evil. The Jewish Drama of Divine Omnipotence.* San Francisco: Harper & Row, 1988.

Levine, Baruch A. *Leviticus.* JPS Torah Commentary Series. Philadelphia: Jewish Publication Society, 1989.

Levison, John R. *Filled with the Spirit.* Grand Rapids: Eerdmans, 2009.

Lichtenberger, Hermann. "'Bund' in der Abendmahlsüberlieferung." Pages 217–28 in *Bund und Tora: Zur theologischen Begriffsgeschichte in alttestamentlicher, frühjüdischer und urchristlicher Tradition.* Edited by Hermann Lichtenberger and Friedrich Avemarie. WUNT 92. Tübingen: Mohr Siebeck, 1996.

Lincoln, Andrew T. *Ephesians.* WBC 42. Grand Rapids: Zondervan, 1990.

Lindars, Barnabas. *The Gospel of John.* New Century Bible Commentary. London: Marshall, Morgan & Scott, 1972.

Loader, William. *Jesus in John's Gospel: Structure and Issues in Johannine Christology.* Grand Rapids: Eerdmans, 2017.

Lombardo, Nicholas E. *The Father's Will: Christ's Crucifixion and the Goodness of God.* Oxford: Oxford University Press, 2013.

Lyons, Michael A. *From Law to Prophecy: Ezekiel's Use of the Holiness Code.* LHBOTS 507. New York: T & T Clark, 2009.

Manning, Gary T., Jr. *Echoes of a Prophet: The Use of Ezekiel in the Gospel of John and the Literature of the Second Temple Period.* LNTS 270. London: T&T Clark International, 2004.

Marböck, Johannes. "Der Hohepriester Simon in Sir 50: Ein Beitrag zur Bedeutung von Priestertum und Kult im Sirachbuch." Pages 215–29 in *Treasures of Wisdom: Studies in Ben Sira and the Book of Wisdom, FS M. Gilbert.* Edited by N. Calduch-Benages and J. Vermeylen. BETL 143. Leuven: Leuven University Press, 1999.

———. *Weisheit im Wandel: Untersuchungen zur Weisheitstheologie bei Ben Sira.* BBB 37. Bonn: Peter Hanstein, 1971.

Marshall, John W. *Parables of War: Reading John's Jewish Apocalypse.* Waterloo, Ontario: Wilfrid Laurier University Press, 2001.

Marx, Alfred. *Lévitique 17–27.* CAT 3b. Geneva: Labor et Fides, 2011.

McCauley, Robert N., and E. Thomas Lawson. *Bringing Ritual to Mind.* Cambridge: Cambridge University Press, 2002.

McClymond, Kathryn. *Beyond Sacred Violence: A Comparative Study of Sacrifice.* Baltimore: Johns Hopkins University Press, 2008.

McEwan, Ian. *Atonement: A Novel.* New York: Doubleday, 2002.

Menken, Maarten J. J. *Old Testament Quotations in the Fourth Gospel: Studies in Textual Form.* CBET 15. Kampen: Kok Pharos, 1996.

Metzner, Rainer. *Das Verständnis der Sünde im Johannesevangelium.* WUNT 122. Tübingen: Mohr Siebeck, 2000.

Meyer, Elizabeth A. *Legitimacy and Law in the Roman World:* Tabulae *in Roman Belief and Practice.* Cambridge: Cambridge University Press, 2004.

Meyer, Nicholas A. *Adam's Dust and Adam's Glory in the Hodayot and the Letters of Paul: Rethinking Anthropology and Theology.* NovTSup 168. Leiden: Brill, 2016.

Middleton, J. R. *The Liberating Image: The* Imago Dei *in Genesis 1.* Grand Rapids: Brazos Press, 2005.

Milgrom, Jacob. "Israel's Sanctuary: The Priestly 'Picture of Dorian Gray.'" *RB* 83 (1976): 390–99.

———. *Leviticus 1–16: A New Translation with Introduction and Commentary.* AYB 3. New York: Doubleday, 2000.

———. *Leviticus 17–22: A New Translation with Introduction and Commentary.* AYB 3A. New York: Doubleday, 2000.

———. *Leviticus 23–27: A New Translation with Introduction and Commentary.* AYB 3B. New York: Doubleday, 2001.

———. *Numbers.* JPS Torah Commentary. Philadelphia: Jewish Publication Society, 1990.

———. "Religious Conversion and the Revolt Model for the Formation of Israel." *JBL* 101 (1982): 169–76.

———. "Sacrifices and Offerings." *IDBSup* (1976): 763–70.

———. "Sin-offering or Purification-offering?" *VT* 21 (1971): 237–39.

Milgrom, Jacob, and Daniel I. Block. *Ezekiel's Hope: A Commentary on Ezekiel 38–48*. Eugene, OR: Cascade, 2012.

Mizrahi, Noam. "The Poetics of Angelic Discourse: Revelation 2–3 and the *Songs of the Sabbath Sacrifice*." *JSNT* 41 (2018): 107–23.

———. "The *Songs of the Sabbath Sacrifice* and Biblical Priestly Literature: A Reconsideration." *HTR* 104 (2011): 35–41.

Moffitt, David M. *Atonement and the Logic of the Resurrection in the Epistle to the Hebrews*. NovTSup 141. Leiden: Brill, 2011.

———. "Blood, Life, and Atonement: Reassessing Hebrews' Christological Appropriation of Yom Kippur." Pages 211–24 in *The Day of Atonement: Its Interpretations in Early Jewish and Christian Traditions*. Edited by Thomas Hieke and Tobias Nicklas. TBN 15. Leiden: Brill, 2012.

Moloney, Francis J. *The Johannine Son of Man*. 2nd ed. Biblioteca di Scienze Religiose 14. Rome: Libreria Ateneo Salesiano, 1975.

Morgenstern, Julian. "The Book of the Covenant. Part III – The Ḥuqqim." *HUCA* 8–9 (1931–1932): 1–151.

Moulton, James H., and George Milligan. *The Vocabulary of the Greek Testament*. London: Hodder and Stoughton, 1930.

Mulder, Otto. *Simon the High Priest in Sirach 50: An Exegetical Study of the Significance of Simon the High Priest as Climax to the Praise of the Fathers in Ben Sira's Concept of the History of Israel*. JSJSup 49. Leiden: Brill, 2003.

Muraoka, Takamitsu. *A Greek-English Lexicon of the Septuagint*. Leuven: Peeters, 2009.

Nachmanides. *Commentary on the Torah: Leviticus*. New York: Shilo Publishing House, 1974.

Naiden, F. S. *Smoke Signals for the Gods: Ancient Greek Sacrifice from the Archaic through the Roman Periods*. New York: Oxford University Press, 2013.

Nasrallah, Laura. "The Embarrassment of Blood: Early Christians and Others on Sacrifice, War, and Rational Worship." Pages 142–66 in *Ancient Mediterranean Sacrifice*. Edited by Jennifer Wright Knust and Zsuzsanna Várhelyi. New York: Oxford University Press, 2011.

Newsom, Carol A. *The Book of Job: A Contest of Moral Imaginations*. New York: Oxford University Press, 2003.

——. "Deriving Negative Anthropology through Exegetical Activity: The Ho-dayot as Case Study." Pages 258–74 in *Is There a Text in This Cave? Studies in the Textuality of the Dead Sea Scrolls in Honour of George J. Brooke*. Edited by Ariel Feldman, Maria Cioată, and Charlotte Hempel. STDJ 119. Leiden: Brill, 2017.

——. *The Self as Symbolic Space: Constructing Identity and Community at Qumran*. STDJ 52. Leiden: Brill, 2004.

——. *Songs of the Sabbath Sacrifice: A Critical Edition*. Atlanta: Scholars Press, 1985.

Nibley, Hugh W. "Christian Envy of the Temple." *JQR* 50 (1959/60): 97–123, 229–240.

Nickelsburg, George W. E., and James C. VanderKam. *1 Enoch 1: A Commentary on the Book of 1 Enoch, Chapters 1–36; 81–108*. Minneapolis: Fortress, 2001.

——. *1 Enoch: A New Translation*. Minneapolis: Fortress, 2004.

——. *1 Enoch 2: A Commentary on the Book of 1 Enoch, Chapters 37–82*. Minneapolis: Fortress, 2012.

Nielsen, Jesper Tang. *Die kognitive Dimension des Kreuzes: Zur Deutung des Todes Jesu im Johannesevangelium*. WUNT 2.263. Tübingen: Mohr Siebeck, 2009.

——. "The Lamb of God: The Cognitive Structure of a Johannine Metaphor." Pages 217–56 in *Imagery in the Gospel of John*. Edited by Jörg Frey, Jan G. van der Watt, and Ruben Zimmermann. WUNT 200. Tübingen: Mohr Siebeck, 2006.

Nihan, Christophe. *From Priestly Torah to Pentateuch: A Study in the Composition of the Book of Leviticus*. FAT 25. Tübingen: Mohr Siebeck, 2007.

——. "Resident Aliens and Natives in the Holiness Legislation." Pages 111–34 in *The Foreigner and the Law: Perspectives from the Hebrew Bible and the Ancient Near East*. Edited by Reinhard Achenbach, et al. BZABR 16. Wiesbaden: Harrassowitz, 2011.

Oermann, N. O. *Albert Schweitzer: A Biography*. Oxford: Oxford University Press, 2016.

Orlov, Andrei A. *Heavenly Priesthood in the Apocalypse of Abraham*. Cambridge: Cambridge University Press, 2013.

Painter, John. "Sacrifice and Atonement in the Gospel of John." Pages 287–313 in *Israel und seine Heilstraditionen im Johannesevangelium*. Edited by Michael Labahn, Klaus Scholtissek, and Angelika Strotmann. Paderborn: Ferdinand Schöningh, 2004.

Parrinder, Geoffrey. *Avatar and Incarnation: The Divine in Human Form in the World's Religions*. Oxford: Oneworld, 1997.

Pennington, A. "2 Enoch." Pages 321–62 in *Apocryphal Old Testament*. Edited by H. F. D. Sparks. Oxford: Clarendon, 1984.

Powers, Daniel G. *Salvation through Participation: An Examination of the Notion of the Believers' Corporate Unity with Christ in Early Christian Soteriology*. CBET 29. Leuven: Peeters, 2001.

Preuschaft, Signe, Zin Wang, Filippo Aureli, and Frans B. M. de Waal. "Reconciliation in Captive Chimpanzees: A Reevaluation with Controlled Methods." *International Journal of Primatology* 23 (2002): 29–50.

Propp, William. *Exodus 1–18: A New Translation with Introduction and Commentary*. AYB 2. New York: Doubleday, 1999.

Radermacher, Ludwig "Σφραγίζεσθαι: Rm 15:28." *ZNW* 32 (1933): 87–89.

Regev, Eyal. *The Temple in Early Christianity: Experiencing the Sacred*. New Haven: Yale University Press, 2019.

Rooke, Deborah W. "The Bare Facts: Gender and Nakedness in Leviticus 18." Pages 20–38 in *A Question of Sex? Gender and Difference in the Hebrew Bible and Beyond*. Edited by Deborah W. Rooke. Sheffield: Sheffield Phoenix Press, 2007.

——— "The Blasphemer (Leviticus 24): Gender, Identity and Boundary Construction." Pages 153–69 in *Text, Time and Temple: Literary, Historical and Ritual Studies in Leviticus*. Edited by Francis Landy, Leigh M. Trevash, and Brian D. Bibb. Hebrew Bible Monographs 64. Sheffield: Sheffield Phoenix Press, 2015.

Rosen-Zvi, Ishay. *Demonic Desires: Yetzer Hara and the Problem of Evil in Late Antiquity*. Philadelphia: University of Pennsylvania Press, 2011.

Ryba, Thomas. "Bloody Logic: The Biblical Economy of Sacrificial Substitution and Some of Its Eucharistic Implications." Pages 70–113 in *Sacrifice, Scripture, and Substitution: Readings in Ancient Judaism and Christianity*. Edited by Ann W. Astell and Sandor Goodhart. Notre Dame, IN: University of Notre Dame Press, 2011.

Sacks, Jonathan. "The Most Personal of Festivals." http://rabbisacks.org/the-most-personal-of-festivals/.

Sandnes, Karl Olav. "Seal and Baptism in Early Christianity." Pages 1441–81 in *Ablution, Initiation, and Baptism: Late Antiquity, Early Judaism, and Early Christianity*. Edited by David Hellholm et al. BZNW 176.II. Berlin: de Gruyter, 2001.

Sarna, Nahum M. *Exodus*. JPS Torah Commentary. Philadelphia: Jewish Publication Society, 1991.

Sauer, Georg. *Jesus Sirach/Ben Sira*. ATD – Apokryphen 1. Göttingen: Vandenhoeck & Ruprecht, 2000.

Schenker, Adrian. "What Connects the Incest Prohibitions with the Other Prohibitions Listed in Leviticus 18 and 20?" Pages 162–85 in *The Book of Leviticus: Composition and Reception*. Edited by Rolf Rendtorff and Robert Kugler. VTSup 93. Leiden: Brill, 2003.

Schipper, Jeremy. "Interpreting the Lamb Imagery in Isaiah 53." *JBL* 132 (2013): 315–25.

Schlund, Christine. *"Kein Knochen soll gebrochen werden": Studien zu Bedeutung und Funktion des Pesachfests in Texten des frühen Judentums und im Johannesevangelium*. WMANT 107. Neukirchen-Vluyn: Neukirchener, 2005.

Schneiders, Sandra M. "The Lamb of God and the Forgiveness of Sin(s) in the Fourth Gospel." *CBQ* 73 (2011): 16–29.

Schwager, Raymond. "Christ's Death and the Prophetic Critique of Sacrifice." Pages 109–23 in *René Girard and Biblical Studies*. Edited by Andrew J. McKenna. Semeia 33. Baltimore: SBL, 1985.

Schwagmeier, Peter. "1.2 Exodos / Exodos / Das zweite Buch Mose." Pages 120–36 in *Einleitung in die Septuaginta* (LXX.H 1). Edited by Siegfried Kreuzer. Gütersloh: Gütersloher, 2016.

Schwartz, Baruch. "The Bearing of Sin in the Priestly Literature." Pages 3–21 in *Pomegranates and Golden Bells: Studies in Biblical, Jewish, and Near Eastern Ritual, Law, and Literature in Honor of Jacob Milgrom*. Edited by David P. Wright et al. Winona Lake, IN: Eisenbrauns, 1995.

Schwartz, Baruch J., et al., eds. *Perspectives on Purity and Purification in the Bible*. LHBOTS 474. New York: T&T Clark International, 2008.

Schweitzer, Albert. *J. S. Bach*. Translated by Ernest Newman. 2 vols. London: A & C Black, 1923.

Scott, James M., ed. *Exile: A Conversation with N. T. Wright*. Downers Grove: IVP Academic, 2017.

Seow, Choon Leong. *Job 1–21: Interpretation and Commentary*. Grand Rapids: Eerdmans, 2013.

Ska, Jean-Louis. "Genesis 2–3: Some Fundamental Questions." Pages 1–27 in *Beyond Eden: The Biblical Story of Paradise (Genesis 2–3) and Its Reception History*. Edited by Konrad Schmid and Christoph Riedweg. FAT 2/34. Tübingen: Mohr Siebeck, 2008.

Skehan, Patrick W., and Alexander A. DiLella. *The Wisdom of Ben Sira*. AYB 39. New York: Doubleday, 1987.

Sklar, Jay. *Sin, Impurity, Sacrifice, Atonement: The Priestly Conceptions*. Hebrew Bible Monographs 2. Sheffield: Sheffield Phoenix Press, 2005.

Smith, Jonathan Z. "The Domestication of Sacrifice." Pages 191–205 in *Violent Origins: Walter Burkert, René Girard and Jonathan Z. Smith on Ritual Killing and Cultural Formation*. Edited by R. G. Hamerton-Kelly. Stanford: Stanford University Press, 1987.

Smith, Mark S. *The Genesis of Good and Evil: The Fall(out) and Original Sin in the Bible*. Louisville: Westminster John Knox, 2019.

Snaith, N. H. "The Cult of Molech." *VT* 16 (1966): 123–24.

Sparks, Kenton. "Enūma Elish and Priestly Mimesis: Elite Emulation in Nascent Judaism." *JBL* 126 (2007): 625–48.

Stackert, Jeffrey. "The Composition of Exodus 31:12–17 and 35:1–3 and the Question of Method in Identifying Priestly Strata in the Torah." Pages 175–96 in *Current Issues in Priestly and Related Literature: The Legacy of Jacob Milgrom and Beyond*. Edited by Roy E. Gane and Ada Taggar-Cohen. RBS 82. Atlanta: SBL, 2015.

———. *Rewriting the Torah: Literary Revision in Deuteronomy and the Holiness Legislation*. FAT 52. Tübingen: Mohr Siebeck, 2007.

Stanley, Christopher D. "Composite Citations: Retrospect and Prospect." Pages 203–9 in *Composite Citations in Antiquity*. Volume One: *Jewish, Graeco-Roman, and Early Christian Uses*. Edited by Sean A. Adams and Seth M. Ehorn. LNTS 525. London: Bloomsbury T&T Clark, 2016.

Staubli, Thomas, and Sylvia Schroer. *Body Symbolism in the Bible*. Translated by Linda M. Maloney. Collegeville, MN: Liturgical Press, 2001.

Stevenson, Gregory. *Power and Place: Temple and Identity in the Book of Revelation*. BZNW 10. Berlin: de Gruyter, 2001.

Stökl Ben-Ezra, Daniel. "Atonement III: Judaism." Pages 43–50 in vol. 3 of *The Encyclopedia of the Bible and Its Reception*. Edited by Hans-Josef Klauck et al. Berlin: de Gruyter, 2011.

———. *The Impact of Yom Kippur on Early Christianity*. WUNT 163. Tübingen: Mohr Siebeck, 2003.

Stordalen, Terje. *Echoes of Eden: Genesis 2–3 and Symbolism of the Eden Garden in Biblical Hebrew Literature*. CBET 25. Leuven: Peeters, 2000.

Stowers, Stanley K. "On the Comparison of Blood in Greek and Israelite Ritual." Pages 179–96 in *Hesed Ve-emet: Studies in Honor of Ernest S. Frerichs*. Edited by Jodi Magness and Seymour Gitin. Atlanta: Scholars Press, 1998.

Strauss, Claudia. "Analyzing Discourse for Cultural Complexity." Pages 203–42 in *Finding Culture in Talk: A Collection of Methods*. Edited by Naomi Quinn. New York: Palgrave Macmillan, 2005.

Stuhlmacher, Peter. "Jes 53 in den Evangelien und in der Apostelgeschichte." Pages 93–106 in *Der leidende Gottesknecht: Jesaja 53 und seine Wirkungsgeschichte*. Edited by Peter Stuhlmacher and Bernd Janowski. FAT 14. Tübingen: Mohr Siebeck, 1996. English Translation: "Isaiah 53 in the Gospels and Acts." Pages 147–62 in *The Suffering Servant: Isaiah 53 in Jewish and Christian Sources*. Translated by Daniel P. Bailey. Grand Rapids: Eerdmans, 2004.

Talgam, Rina. "The Representation of the Temple and Jerusalem in Jewish and Christian Houses of Prayer in the Holy Land in Late Antiquity." Pages 222–49 in *Jews, Christians, and the Roman Empire*. Edited by Natalie B. Bohrmann and Annette Yoshiko Reed. Philadelphia: University of Pennsylvania Press, 2013.

Taylor, Joan. "Alexandria." Pages 760–62 in vol. 1 of *The Encyclopedia of the Bible and Its Reception*. Berlin: de Gruyter, 2009.

Teselle, Eugene. "The Cross as Ransom." *JECS* 4 (1996): 147–70.

Theocharous, Myrto. *Lexical Dependence and Intertextual Allusion in the Septuagint of the Twelve Prophets: Studies in Hosea, Amos and Micah*. LHBOTS 570. London: Bloomsbury, 2012.

Tigchelaar, Eibert J. C. "The Evil Inclination in the Dead Sea Scrolls, with a Re-Edition of 4Q468i [4QSectarian Text?]." Pages 347–57 in *Empsychoi Logoi: Religious Innovations in Antiquity; Studies in Honour of Pieter Willem van der Horst*. Edited by A. Houtman, A. de Jong, and M. Misset-van de Weg. AJEC 73. Leiden: Brill, 2009.

Toeg, Aryeh, "מדרש הלכה—לא-במדבר טו כב" ("A Halakhic Midrash in Num. xv: 22–31"). *Tarbiz* 43 (1973–74): 1–20.

Tov, Emmanuel. "The Septuagint Between Judaism and Christianity." Pages 3–25 in *Die Septuaginta und das frühe Christentum – The Septuagint and Christian Origins*. Edited by Thomas Scott Caulley and Hermann Lichtenberger. WUNT 277. Tübingen: Mohr Siebeck, 2011.

Trevaskis, Lee. "Dangerous Liaisons: Sex and the Menstruating Woman in Leviticus." Pages 131–52 in *Text, Time and Temple: Literary, Historical and Ritual Studies in Leviticus*. Edited by Francis Landy et al. Hebrew Bible Monographs 64. Sheffield: Sheffield Phoenix Press, 2015.

Trouillot, Michel-Rolph. *Silencing the Past: Power and the Production of History*. Boston: Beacon Press, 1995.

Tuckett, Christopher M. "Zechariah 12:10 and the New Testament." Pages 111–22 in *The Book of Zechariah and Its Influence*. Edited by Christopher M. Tuckett. Aldershot: Ashgate, 2003.

Tuell, Steven S. "Ezekiel 40–42 as Verbal Icon." *CBQ* 58 (1996): 649–64.

Ulfgard, Håkan. "The *Songs of the Sabbath Sacrifice* and the Heavenly Scene of the Book of Revelation." Pages 251–66 in *Northern Lights on the Dead Sea Scrolls*. Edited by Anders Klostergaard Petersen et al. STDJ 80. Leiden: Brill, 2009.

Ullucci, Daniel C. *The Christian Rejection of Animal Sacrifice*. New York: Oxford University Press, 2012.

———. "Sacrifice in the Ancient Mediterranean: Recent and Current Research." *CBR* 13 (2015): 388–439.

Vahrenhorst, Martin. "1.3 Levitikon / Levitikus / Das dritte Buch Mose." Pages 137–46 in *Einleitung in die Septuaginta* (LXX.H 1). Edited by Siegfried Kreuzer. Gütersloh: Gütersloher, 2016.

VanderKam, James. "The Demons in the 'Book of Jubilees.'" Pages 339–64 in *Die Dämonem: Die Dämonologie der israelitisch-jüdischen und frühchristlichen Literatur im Kontext ihrer Umwelt*. Edited by Armin Lange, Hermann Lichtenberger, and Diethard Römheld. Tübingen: Mohr Siebeck, 2003.

Venit, Marjorie S. "Alexandria." Pages 102–21 in *The Oxford Handbook of Roman Egypt*. Edited by Christina Riggs. Oxford: Oxford University Press, 2012.

Vermes, Geza. "Leviticus 18:21 in Ancient Jewish Bible Exegesis." Pages 108–24 in *Studies in Aggadah, Targum and Jewish Liturgy in Memory of Joseph Heinemann*. Edited by Jakob J. Petuchowski and Ezra Fleischer. Jerusalem: Magnes Press, 1981.

Vistar, Deolito V., Jr. *The Cross-and-Resurrection: The Supreme Sign in John's Gospel*. WUNT 2/508. Tübingen: Mohr Siebeck, 2020.

Waal, Frans B. M. de, and Angeline van Roosmalen. "Reconciliation and Consolation among Chimpanzees." *Behavioral Ecology and Sociobiology* 5 (1979): 55–66.

Watts, James W. *Leviticus 1–10*. HCOT. Leuven: Peeters, 2013.

———. *Ritual and Rhetoric in Leviticus: From Sacrifice to Scripture*. Cambridge: Cambridge University Press, 2007.

Weidemann, Hans-Ulrich. *Der Tod Jesu im Johannesevangelium. Die erste Abschiedsrede als Schlüsseltext für den Passions- und Osterbericht*. BZNW 122. Berlin: de Gruyter, 2004.

Weinfeld, Moshe. "Job and Its Mesopotamian Parallels—A Typological Analysis." Pages 217–26 in *Text and Context: Old Testament and Semitic Studies for F. C. Fensham*. Edited by W. Classen. JSOTSup 48. Sheffield: JSOT, 1988.

Wenham, Gordon. *The Book of Leviticus*. NICOT. Grand Rapids: Eerdmans, 1979.

Westermann, Claus. *Praise and Lament in the Psalms*. Translated by Keith R. Crim and Richard Soulen. Atlanta: John Knox Press, 1981.

Wiesenberg, E. J. "Exogamy or Moloch Worship?" Pages 193–95 in *Jewish Law Association Studies II: The Jerusalem Conference Volume*. Edited by B. S. Jackson. Atlanta: Scholars Press, 1986.

Wilckens, Ulrich. *Jesu Tod und Auferstehung und die Entstehung der Kirche aus Juden und Heiden*. Vol. 1 in *Theologie des Neuen Testaments*. Neukirchen-Vluyn: Neukirchener, 2003.

Williams, Catrin H. "Composite Citations in the Gospel of John." Pages 94–127 in *Composite Citations in Antiquity*. Volume Two: *New Testament Uses*. Edited by Sean A. Adams and Seth M. Ehorn. LNTS 593. London: Bloomsbury T&T Clark, 2018.

———. "Johannine Christology and Prophetic Traditions: The Case of Isaiah." Pages 92–123 in *Reading the Gospel of John's Christology as Jewish Messianism: Royal, Prophetic and Divine Messiahs*. Edited by Benjamin E. Reynolds and Gabriele Boccaccini. AJEC 106. Leiden: Brill, 2018.

———. "John, Judaism, and 'Searching the Scriptures.'" Pages 77–100 in *John and Judaism: A Contested Relationship in Context*. Edited by R. Alan Culpepper and Paul N. Anderson. RBS 87. Atlanta: Society of Biblical Literature, 2017.

———. "John (the Baptist): The Witness on the Threshold." Pages 46–60 in *Character Studies in the Fourth Gospel: Native Approaches to Seventy Figures in John*. Edited by Steven A. Hunt et al. WUNT 314. Tübingen: Mohr Siebeck, 2013.

———. "Persuasion through Allusion: Evocations of Shepherd(s) and Their Rhetorical Impact in John 10." Pages 111–24 in *Come and Read: Interpretive Approaches to the Gospel of John*. Edited by Alicia Myers and Lindsey Trozzo. Lanham: Fortress Academic, 2020.

———. "The Voice in the Wilderness and the Way of the Lord: A Scriptural Frame for John's Witness to Jesus." Pages 39–58 in *The Opening of John's Narrative (John 1:19–2:22): Historical, Literary, and Theological Readings from the Colloquium Ioanneum 2015 in Ephesus*. Edited by R. Alan Culpepper and Jörg Frey. WUNT 385. Tübingen: Mohr Siebeck, 2017.

Wold, Donald J. "The *Kareth* Penalty in P: Rationale and Cases." Pages 1–45 in *SBL Seminar Papers 1979*. vol. 1. Edited by Paul J. Achtemeier. Missoula, MT: Scholars Press, 1979.

Wolff, Hans Walter. *Anthropology of the Old Testament*. Translated by Margaret Kohl. Philadelphia: Fortress, 1974.

Wolter, Michael. *Der Brief an die Römer*. 2 vols. EKKNT 6. Neukirchen-Vluyn: Neukirchener, 2014.

Wright, David P. *Disposal of Impurity*. SBLDS 101. Atlanta: SBL, 1987.

———. "Law and Creation in the Priestly-Holiness Writings of the Pentateuch." Pages 71–101 in *Laws of Heaven—Laws of Nature: Legal Interpretations of Cosmic Phenomena in the Ancient World*. Edited by Konrad Schmid and Christoph Uehlinger. OBO 276. Fribourg: Academic Press; Göttingen: Vandenhoeck & Ruprecht, 2016.

———. "Ritual Theory, Ritual Texts, and the Priestly-Holiness Writings of the Pentateuch." Pages 195–216 in *Social Theory and the Study of Israelite Religion*. Edited by Saul M. Olyan. RBS 71. Atlanta: SBL, 2012.

———. "'She Shall Not Go Free as Male Slaves Do': Developing Views About Slavery and Gender in the Laws of the Hebrew Bible." Pages 125–42 in *Beyond Slavery: Overcoming Its Religious and Sexual Legacy*. Edited by Bernadette Brooten et al. New York: Palgrave Macmillan, 2010.

———. "Source Dependence and the Development of the Pentateuch: The Case of Leviticus 24." Pages 651–82 in *The Formation of the Pentateuch: Bridging the Academic Cultures of Europe, Israel, and North America*. Edited by Jan Gertz, et al. FAT 111. Tübingen: Mohr Siebeck, 2016.

———. "The Study of Ritual in the Hebrew Bible." Pages 120–38 in *Jewish Studies in the 21st Century*. Edited by Frederick E. Greenspahn. New York: New York University Press, 2008.

Wright, N. T. *The Climax of the Covenant: Christ and the Law in Pauline Theology*. Edinburgh: T&T Clark, 1991.

———. *The Day the Revolution Began: Reconsidering the Meaning of Jesus's Crucifixion*. New York: HarperOne, 2016.

———. "God Put Jesus Forth: Reflections on Romans 3:24–26." Pages 135–61 in *In the Fullness of Time: Essays in Honor of Richard Bauckham*. Edited by Daniel Gurtner, Grant Macaskill, and Jonathan T. Pennington. Grand Rapids: Eerdmans, 2016.

———. *History and Eschatology: Jesus and the Promise of Natural Theology*. London: SPCK; Waco, TX: Baylor University Press, 2019.

———. *The New Testament and the People of God*. London: SPCK; Minneapolis: Fortress Press, 1992.

———. *Paul and His Recent Interpreters: Some Contemporary Debates*. London: SPCK; Minneapolis: Fortress Press, 2015.

———. *Paul and the Faithfulness of God*. London: SPCK; Minneapolis: Fortress Press, 2013.

———. *Pauline Perspectives: Essays on Paul, 1978–2013*. London: SPCK; Minneapolis: Fortress Press, 2013.

———. "Pictures, Stories, and the Cross: Where Do the Echoes Lead?" *JTI* 11 (2017): 53–73.

———. "Romans." Pages 393–770 in Volume 10 of *The New Interpreters Bible*, vol. 10. Nashville: Abingdon, 2003.

Yarbro Collins, Adela. "The Seven Heavens in Jewish and Christian Apocalypses." Pages 59–93 in *Death, Ecstasy, and Other Worldly Journeys*. Edited by John J. Collins and Michael Fishbane. Albany: State University of New York Press, 1995.

Ysebaert, Joseph. *Greek Baptismal Terminology: Its Origins and Early Development*. Nijmegen: Dekker & Van de Vegt N. V., 1962.

Zimmerli, Walter. *Ezekiel 1: A Commentary on the Book of the Prophet, Chapters 1–24*. Translated by Ruth Clements. Hermeneia. Philadelphia: Fortress, 1979.

Zimmermann, Ruben. "Jesus – the Lamb of God (John 1:29 and 1:36): Metaphorical Christology in the Fourth Gospel." Pages 83–90 in *The Opening of John's Narrative (John 1:19–2:22): Historical, Literary, and Theological Readings from the Colloquium Ioanneum 2015 in Ephesus*. Edited by R. Alan Culpepper and Jörg Frey. WUNT 385. Tübingen: Mohr Siebeck, 2017.

Zumstein, Jean. *Kreative Erinnerung: Relecture und Auslegung im Johannesevangelium*. 2nd ed. ATANT 84. Zürich: Theologischer Verlag, 2004.

# Contributors

**Max Botner** is Assistant Professor of New Testament at Grand Rapids Theological Seminary

**Justin Harrison Duff** is a Postdoctoral Research Fellow in the School of Divinity, the University of Saint Andrews

**Simon Dürr** is a Research Associate in the Departement of Biblical Studies at the University of Fribourg

**Christian A. Eberhart** is Professor of Religious Studies in the Department of Comparative Cultural Studies at the University of Houston

**Crispin Fletcher-Louis** is Director of Whymanity Research and Training

**Martha Himmelfarb** is Professor of Religion in the Department of Religion at Princeton University

**T. J. Lang** is Senior Lecturer in New Testament in the School of Divinity at the University of Saint Andrews

**Carol A. Newsom** is the Charles Howard Candler Professor Emeritus of Old Testament at Candler School of Theology at Emory University

**Deborah W. Rooke** is Associate Lecturer in Old Testament Hermeneutics at Regent's Park College at the University of Oxford

**Catrin Williams** is Reader in New Testament Studies at University of Wales Trinity Saint David

**David P. Wright** is Professor of Bible and the Ancient Near East at Brandeis University

**N. T. Wright** is Professor of New Testament and Early Christianity in the School of Divinity at the University of Saint Andrews

# Index of Modern Authors

Adams, Seth A., 132n1
Alexander, Philip, 83–84n36, 87n51, 179n21
Allison, Dale C., Jr., 6n10, 184n40, 185n45
Alster, B., 116n13
Andersen, F. I., 177n19
Anderson, Gary A., xviin11, xviin14
Ashley, Timothy R., 31n27
Attridge, Harold W., 189n51
Auffarth, Christoph, 6n8
Aulén, Gustav, 123, 123n28
Aune, David E., 184n42
Aureli, Filippo, 67n1

Baden, Joel, 45n12, 46n13, 62n35
Bähr, Karl C. W. F., 9n20
Balberg, Mira, xvn6
Barr, James, 177n18
Barth, Gerhard, 14n30, 17n39
Bauckham, Richard, 138, 138n23, 140n29, 144n41, 145n46
Beale, G. K., 118n20, 126n40
Beentjes, Pancratius, 91, 91n7, 91n8, 92n10
Belle, Gilbert Van, 144n38
Berg, Shane, 77n22
Berger, Peter, 83, 83n35
Best, Ernest, 166n43
Beutler, Johannes, 148n52
Biale, David, xivn3
Bickerman, Elias J., xivn3
Bieringer, Reimund, 137n17
Bledsoe, Amanda M. Davis, 174n8
Blenkinsopp, Joseph, 139n25
Block, Daniel I., 98n18
Böttrich, Christfried, 176n16

Brand, Miryam T., 70n9, 78n24, 79–80, 79n27, 82n32
Brant, Jo-Ann A., 152n61
Brettler, Marc Zvi, 72, 72n11
Büchner, Dirk, xvin13
Budd, Philip J., 36, 38n37
Burkert, Walter, 8n15
Bushnell, Horace, xiv–xv, xvn5, xvn8, xvn9
Bynum, William Randolph, 149n53, 151n59

Calabro, David, 11, 13
Capponi, Livia, 12n25
Carasik, Michael, 9n17, 9n18, 10n22
Carlton, Clark, 4n1
Carr, David M., 41n4, 76n20
Carter, A. P., 21n1
Charles, R. H., 158n10
Charlesworth, James H., 179n21, 179n22, 179n24, 180n25
Chazon, Esther, 83n36, 87n51
Collins, John J., 12n25
Corley, Jeremy, 99n20, 106n32
Cottrill, Amy C., 79n26
Culpepper, R. Alan, 141n33

Davies, Eryl, 33n31, 38n38
Davila, James R., 158n9, 158n10
Deissmann, Adolf, 160, 160n19, 160n22, 162, 162n31, 162n32, 169, 169n54, 169n55, 169n56, 169n57, 169n58, 170
Detienne, Marcel, xvin10
Diehl, Jakob, 159n15
DiFransico, Lesley R., 78n23
Di Lella, Alexander A., 91n6, 94n12, 98n16, 99n19

Döbler, Marvin, 6n8
Dodd, C. H., xvin13, 146n46
Dunn, James D. G., 17n39

Eberhart, Christian A., xvn6, xvin10, xvii,
    4n2, 5n4, 8n14, 9n19, 10n21, 10n22, 14n29,
    139n9
Ederer, Matthias, 10n22
Ehorn, Seth M., 132n1
Eilberg-Schwartz, Howard, 34n33, 34n34
Ekbald, Eugene Robert, 139n26
Elliger, Karl, 28n17
Eshel, Esther, 175n14
Esler, Philip, F., 172n3
Eubank, Nathan, 166n45
Evans, Craig A., 148n52

Ferda, Tucker S., 156n3, 157n7
Fine, Steven, xivn3
Finlan, Stephen, 4n1, 5n6
Fitzmyer, Joseph A., 17n39
Fletcher-Louis, Crispin, xviii, 89n1, 89n2,
    89n3, 90n4, 90n5, 91n7, 96n13, 107n35
Foraone, Christopher A., xviin14
Forestell, J. Terence, 140n27
Fowl, Stephen E., 159n61, 169, 169n59,
    169n60
Frankfurter, David, 183n38
Frey, Jörg, 84n37, 135n9, 135n10, 136n12,
    144n39, 146n47

Gane, Roy, 42n5
Gathercole, Simon, 167n50
Gese, Hartmut, 10n20
Gilders, William, xvn6
Girard, René, 8n15
Goshen-Gottstein, Alon, 99n21
Greenfield, Jonas C., 175n14
Gubler, Marie-Louise, 14n30

Habershon, Ada R., 21n1
Hachlili, Rachel, xivn3
Hafemann, Scott J., 115n9
Hagen, Joost L., 176n16
Hampel, Volker, 17n39

Hanson, K. C., 187n49
Hartenstein, Friedhelm, 10n21
Hartley, John E., 28n17, 30n20
Hays, Richard B., 127n41
Hayward, C. T. R., 97n15, 100n23, 100n24,
    103n28, 105n31, 106n33, 107n35
Hengel, Martin, 6n9, 139n26, 150n56
Hermisson, Hans-Jürgen, 15n35
Himmelfarb, Martha, xix, 172n2, 173n7,
    177n17, 183n36, 191n55
Hobson, Thomas, 22, 22n7
Holl, Adolf, 5n6
Hollander, H. W., 190n52, 190n54
Holmes, Stephen R., 170n63
Hossfeld, Frank-Lothar, 78n23
Houtman, Cornelis, 32n28, 35n35
Hubert, Henri, 10n20, 13n27
Hughes, Julie A., 86n48, 134n8
Hultgren, Stephen J., 70n7

Jacob, Haley G., 128n44
Janowski, Bernd, 42n5, 68n3
Janssen, Enno, 100n23, 102n25, 107n34
Jensen, Robert, xvin12
Jewett, Robert, 17n39
Jones, C. P., 159n15
Jonge, Marinus de, 190n52, 190n54
Joosten, Jan, 132n4
Joyce, Paul M., 172n3

Kabiersch, Jürgen, 16n37
Karrer, Martin, 20n44
Keener, Craig S., 144n41
Kermani, Navid, 6n8
Kessler, Herbert L., xivn3
Kister, Menahem, 82n33
Kiuchi, Nobuyoshi, 27n14, 27n16, 42n5,
    68n3
Klawans, Jonathan, xivn3, xviin14, 68n3,
    68n4, 75n17, 75n18, 85n46
Klink, Edward W., III, 140n40, 152n60
Knohl, Israel, 22n3, 41n4, 45n10, 47n15,
    59n28, 60n32
Knöppler, Thomas, 135n22, 138n19, 146n47,
    148n51

Knust, Jennifer Wright, xviin14
Kocar, Alexander, 183n38
Koester, Craig R., 20n44, 147n49
Kooij, Arie van der, 15, 15n31, 16n37
Kooten, George van, 116n11
Kraus, Wolfgang, 14–16, 15n31, 15n32, 15n35, 16n36, 16n37, 17, 17n39, 17n40, 139n26
Kreuzer, Siegfried, 12n25
Kuhn, Heinz-Wolfgang, 6n9, 86n67
Kwon, Yon-Gyong, 164n39, 165n41

Lam, Joseph, xviin14
Lambert, David, 69, 69n5
Lapsley, Jacqueline, 72–73, 73n12, 73n13, 78n25, 83n34
Larson, Erik W., 177n18
Lawson, E. Thomas, 62n34
Lee, Dorothy, 136n11, 137n15, 147n50, 152n60
Lee, T. R., 99n19
Leithart, Peter J., 184n41, 185n42, 186n46, 187n48
Lemke, Werner, 71n10
Leppin, Volker, 6n7
Levenson, Jon D., 98n18
Levine, Baruch A., 28n17, 38n39, 38n41
Levison, John R., 87, 87n50
Lichtenberger, Hermann, 14n30
Lincoln, Andrew T., 157, 157n4
Lindars, Barnabas, 152n61
Loader, William, 137n14
Lombardo, Nicholas E., 169n62
Lyons, Michael A., 76n19

Manning, Gary T., Jr., 134n8
Marböck, Johannes, 100n23, 107n34, 107n35, 107n36
Marshall, John W., 183, 183n38, 183n39
Martyn, J. Louis, 123
Marx, Alfred, 30n21, 38n40
Mauss, Marcel, 10n20, 13n27
McCauley, Robert N., 62n34
McClymond, Kathryn, xvin10, 8
McEwan, Ian, xiii

Menken, Maarten J. J., 132n5, 138n21, 150n54
Metzner, Rainer, 137n17, 140n30
Meyer, Elizabeth, 161, 161n24, 161n25, 161n27, 161n28
Meyer, Nicholas A., 70n7
Middleton, J. R., 116n11
Milgrom, Jacob, xvin13, 22, 22n4, 22n6, 23, 23n8, 27n15, 28n17, 29n19, 31n23, 31n25, 37n37, 40n1, 41n2, 41n4, 42n5, 54n16, 55n22, 59n29, 68n3, 98n18
Milligan, George, 160, 160n18, 164, 164n38
Mizrahi, Noam, 181n31, 181n32, 182n33, 185n45
Moffitt, David M., xvn7, 20, 20n45, 122
Moloney, Francis J., 146n47
Morgenstern, Julian, 29n18
Moulton, James H., 160, 160n18, 164, 164n38
Mulder, Otto, 99n19, 103n28, 109n38
Muraoka, Takamitsu, xvin13

Nahman, Moses ben, 9n17
Naiden, F. S., xvin10, xviin14, 11n23
Nasrallah, Laura, xvn8
Newsom, Carol A., xviii, 74n15, 83n35, 84n40, 84n41, 179, 179n21, 179n22, 179n23, 179n24, 180, 180n25, 180n27, 180n28, 180n29, 182, 182n34
Nibley, Hugh W., xivn3
Nickelsburg, George W. E., 173n6, 174–75, 174n9, 174n10, 175n11, 176n15, 177n18, 178
Nielsen, Jesper Tang, 136n13, 138n20, 143n37, 145n45, 152n61
Nihan, Christophe, 41n4, 43n6, 54n16, 54n17, 55n22, 55n23, 56n26, 61n33, 63n36

Oermann, N. O., 113n3
Orlov, Andrei A., 172n2

Painter, John, 146–47n48
Powers, Daniel G., 17n39
Preuschaft, Signe, 67n1
Propp, William, 62n35

Radermacher, Ludwig, 160n21
Regev, Eyal, 183n37
Rietz, H. W. L., 179n21
Rooke, Deborah W., xviii, 25n11, 30n22, 59n28
Roosmalen, Angeline van, 67n1
Rosen-Zvi, Ishay, 81n30
Ryba, Thomas, 10n20

Sacks, Jonathan, xiii
Sandnes, Karl Olav, 157n5
Sarna, Nahum M., 33n30
Sauer, Georg, 100n23, 110n40
Schenker, Adrian, 28n17
Schipper, Jeremy, 139n25
Schlund, Christine, 133n6
Schneiders, Sandra M., 137n15, 140n30
Schroer, Sylvia, 81n31
Schwager, Raymond, 8n15
Schwagmeier, Peter, 12n25
Schwartz, Baruch J., 42n5, 59n29
Schweitzer, Don, 9n19
Scott, James M., 120n24
Seow, Choon Leong, 74n14
Ska, Jean-Louis, 76n20
Skehan, Patrick W., 91n6, 94n12, 98n16, 99n19
Sklar, Jay, xvin13, 42n5
Smith, Jonathan Z., xvin10
Smith, Mark S., 76n20, 76n21
Snaith, N. H., 28n187
Sparks, Kenton, 44n8
Stackert, Jeffrey, 41n4, 55n22
Stanley, Christopher D., 132n3
Staubli, Thomas, 81n31
Stevenson, Gregory, 185n44
Stökl Ben-Ezra, Daniel, xivn3, 68n3
Stone, Michael E., 175n14
Stordalen, Terje, 76n20
Stowers, Stanley K., xviin14
Strauss, Claudia, 75n16
Strawn, B. A., 179n21
Stuhlmacher, Peter, 14n30

Talgam, Rina, xivn3
Taylor, Joan, 12n25
Teselle, Eugene, 170n62
Theocharous, Myrto, 132n4
Tigchelaar, Eibert J. C., 82n32
Tov, Emanuel, 15n33
Trevaskis, Lee, 31, 31n24, 31n25, 31n26
Trouillot, Michel-Rolph, 18–19, 19n42
Tuckett, Christopher M., 151n58
Tuell, Steven S., 172n3
Tyndale, William, 4

Ulfgard, Håkan, 185n45
Ullucci, Daniel C., xviin14

Vahrenhorst, Martin, 12n25
VanderKam, James C., 80n29, 173n6, 176n15
Várhelyi, Zsuzsanna, xviin14
Venit, Marjorie, 12n25
Vermes, Geza, 28n17
Vernant, Jean-Pierre, xvin10
Vistar, Deolito V., Jr., 144n38

Waal, Frans B. M. de, 67n1
Wang, Zin, 67n1
Watts, James W., 10n22, 25, 25n10, 26n13
Weidemann, Hans-Ulrich, 138n20, 152n61, 152n62
Weinfeld, Moshe, 74n15
Wenham, Gordon, 24n9
Westermann, Claus, 79n26
Whitaker, R. E., 179n21
Wiesenberg, E. J., 28n17
Wilckens, Ulrich, 14n30
Wilk, Florian, 15n31
Williams, Catrin H., 132n2, 132n5, 134n7, 141n32, 142n35, 151n57
Wold, Donald, 22, 23
Wolff, Hans Walter, 81n31
Wolter, Michael, 17n39
Wright, David P., xvin13, xviii, 41n2, 41n3, 43n8, 44n8, 46n14, 54n16, 55n22, 56n24, 59n29

Wright, N. T., xviii–xix, 6–7, 113n1, 113n2, 114n4, 114n5, 114n7, 115n8, 117n15, 118n19, 120n25, 123n29, 125n35, 125n36, 125n38, 127n41, 129n47

Yarbro Collins, Adela, 177n19
Yitzchaki, Shlomo, 9n17

Ysebaert, Joseph, 157n6, 158n11, 159n12, 160n16, 162n33

Zenger, Erich, 78n23
Zimmerli, Walter, 28n17
Zimmermann, Ruben, 137n14, 137n16, 141n31, 152n60
Zumstein, Jean, 143n36

# Index of Subjects

Aaron, 90, 91, 101, 102, 105–6, 107, 118, 136, 178
Abihu, 59
Abraham, 80, 115, 124, 137, 163, 165
Abrahamic covenant, 121, 125, 127, 158
Adam, 89, 91, 94, 99, 105–7
adoption, 63
adultery, 30
afterlife, 22
Alamo, 18–19
Alexandria, 12
alien sinful will, 80
altar, 44, 98, 104, 108, 109, 110, 186–87; bronze, 95, 186, 187n48
analogical exegesis, 132
angels, 174–75, 177, 178, 179, 181, 182, 190
Anselm of Canterbury, 6, 19
anthropology, xviii, 70, 71, 74, 114; body-based, 81n31; negative, 83, 84, 85, 86, 87
Apocalypse of Abraham, 172
Apocalypse of Paul, 191n55
Apocalypse of Weeks, 176
Apocalypse of Zephaniah, 191n55
Apostles' Creed, 6
appeasement, 43
Aqedah tradition, 137, 138n23
Aramaic Levi Document, 80, 175–76, 179n22, 190, 191
arboreal symbolism, 103–5
aroma, 181–82, 188, 192
Ascension of Isaiah, 172
"at-one-ment," 4, 91, 92, 95
atonement: defining, 3–7, 130; economics of, 168; in heaven, 188, 190; terminology of, 135; in worship, 111
attribution, 13n28

Augustine, 19
authenticity, 160
avatars, 19–20

baptism, 157, 159
Barabbas, 123
Barkhi Nafshi, 81, 82
Battle of the Alamo, 18–19
beauty, 103, 106, 110
believing, 144, 147, 151
bestiality, 30
biblical theology, 115–16
Bildad, 74, 83, 85
blasphemy, 60
blood: as currency, xv, 155, 167–68; in heaven, 182, 187–88, 189, 190, 192; ingestion of, 27, 35–36; in Passover, 137–38, 152; as purifying, 10; rites, 40n2, 43, 57
bones, 133–34, 149
Book of Dreams, 176
Book of Giants, 176
Book of the Watchers, 172–76, 177, 178, 190, 191
"born of a woman," 85
bowls, 185, 187
branding, 159–60
broken, 149
bronze serpent, 143, 146
burnt offering, 8, 61–62

capital punishment, 28, 32, 60n30
catchword associations, 132, 134
cereal offering, 8
certificate of freedom, 165
chaos, 116–17, 119, 129
chariot throne, 180

cherubim, 173
Christology, 14, 120
*Christus Victor*, xix, 123
circumcision, 34–35, 157–59; of the heart, 71–72
citizen, 55–58
commerce, 159–62
community, 24, 26, 50
Community Rule, 182
compartmentalization, 75n16
compensation, 69
composite allusions, 134–43; scriptural, 146
composite citations, 131–34, 150
conceptual blending theory, 136n13
condemnation, 147
confession, 77
consecration, 10
conversion, 63
cosmology, xviii, 113, 177
cosmos, 97, 110
covenant, 16, 112, 120–21, 125, 127; new, 189; old, 188–89
Covenant Code (CC), 49, 54–56
creation, 94–98, 105, 110, 111, 112, 116; new, 121–22, 126, 129
cross, 5–6n7, 18
crucifixion, 6, 18
culture, 170n63
"cut off," 27–38, 59, 68

David, 68, 91, 119, 120
Day of Atonement, xiii, 7–8, 9, 11, 27, 29, 37, 44, 45, 56, 57, 58, 59, 60, 61, 122, 135
death, 59, 80n29, 147
death penalty, 28, 32, 60n30
debt redemption, 14
demons, 80–82
deposit, 164
descendants, 38
designation, 13n28
Deuteronomy, 49, 54–56
disobedience, 71
divine glory, 109
Domitian, 183
down payment, 164
dust, 84

earnest, 164
Eastern Orthodoxy, 4
eating, 35
economy, 155, 168
elevation, 147
Elijah, 102
Eliphaz, 74, 75, 83, 85, 86
Enoch, 172–73, 175, 177–78
Enosh, 99, 106
entrance fee, 165
*Entstörung*, 5n5
Esau, 67, 180
eschatological joy, 87
eschatology, 114, 120, 121
Eucharist, 14, 16, 152, 190
Eve, 106
evil, 117, 126, 129
exaltation, 143, 144–45, 151, 154
exchange, 166–67
excision, 60n30
excommunication, 22, 25, 26, 33n31, 38n37
exogamy, 28n17
expiation, 4. *See also* atonement
extirpation, of family line, 68
Ezekiel, 108, 119, 173

faith, 150, 151, 154, 161
family line, 59, 60, 68
fasting, 69
fat, eating of, 35
Feast of Booths, 55
Feast of Unleavened Bread, 32–33, 56, 57
fertility, 34
festivals, 56, 57
fire offering, 10–11
flesh, 84n37
flood, 77
forgiveness, xv, 78, 140
free moral agency, 69, 73

genealogical extinction, 60
gentiles, 124, 148, 163
*gēr*, 55–58, 61, 62, 63
Gibeonites, 68
gift, 167

glorification, 145, 146, 154
glory, 103, 109, 119
good works, 102
Gospels, 122–23, 127
grain offerings, 182
Greco-Roman culture, 185
guarantee, 164
guilt, xiii, 48, 123; offering, 8, 139

hand-leaning gesture, 11–13
harps, 185
Hasmoneans, 120
ḥaṭṭā't, 40–63. See also sin offering
heart of stone, 73
heaven, 98, 108, 172–76
Hebrews (epistle), 20, 188–89, 190–91, 192
helplessness, 79
Herodians, 120
Hezekiah, 102
high priest, 105–10
holiness, 35, 37, 39
Holiness Code, 41, 45, 76, 77
holy of holies, 98, 126, 130
holy people, 24
Holy Spirit: gift of, 127; gives life, 153; indwelling of, 125, 142; as inheritance, 156, 162, 164–65, 166; power of, 122; presence of, 126; as purifying, 83, 87; sealing of, 157–59, 168–69, 170
honor, 103
hope, 118–20, 127–28
human existence, 87
humanity, 105–7
human nature, 69, 84
human origins, 97
humiliation, 69, 73, 145
humility, 75

Ibn Ezra, Abraham ben Meir, 9n17, 13
identification, 13n28
identity, 24
idolatry, 30, 117–18, 119, 123–24, 125, 128
illness, 80n29
image of God, 114–15, 117, 128
immigrant, 55–58, 61

immorality, 84
impurity, 10, 33, 43, 49, 70, 75, 84, 182; of corpses, 33; of females, 85–86
imputed legalism, 125
incarnation, 4, 19
incense offerings, 188, 192
incest, 30
inheritance, 156, 157, 159, 161, 162–63, 165, 166, 168
intertextuality, 137, 140n29, 153
intratextuality, 96, 97, 137, 153; heptadic, 96
Isaac, 137
Isaianic servant, 138–39, 148–49, 150, 152

Jacob, 67, 180
Jesus Christ: blood of, 155, 167–68, 170, 189; death of, 115, 116, 121–26, 131; exaltation of, 147; as Lamb of God, 135–43; as Messiah, 123; resurrection of, 17–19, 154
Job, 74–75
Johannine scholarship, 131
John the Baptist, 18, 135, 136, 141–43, 152
Joshua, 102
Joshua son of Jozadak, 99
Josiah, 102
Judah, 164
Judaism, 4, 7
judgment, 147, 171, 174
justice, 129
justification, 129

karet penalty, 21, 22–26, 32n28
kingdom of God, 122–24, 126, 165
kingship, 89

Lamb of God, 126, 135–43
lambs, 133, 135
lament psalms, 79
land, 63
Last Supper, 14
law code, 25
Leontopolis, 12, 15, 16n37
Leviticus, 7n13
libations, 182
"lifting up" sayings, 140, 143–49, 151

Maccabees, 119–20
Malachi, 119
Manasseh, 73
marriage, 34
martyrs, 186
materiality, 84
mediums, 28
menstruating women, 30–31
messianic substitution, 124–26
metaphors, 114, 162, 168, 169
misfortune, 80n29
models, 112, 114
Molek, 27–28, 32, 57
monetary pledge, 163
Moses, xviin13, 16, 109–10, 119, 143–44
most holy place, 44
motifs, 114, 134, 146

Nachmanides, 9n17, 10n20, 10n22
Nadab, 59
national holiness, xv, 46, 49, 56
Nebuchadnezzar, 73
Nehemiah, 99, 102–3
New Testament, 14–15
Nicene Creed, 6
*niphal* form, 24–26, 29, 59
Noah, 99

obedience, 71, 77n22
offenses, 22–24, 30
oneness, 111
Onias IV, 16n37
orphan, 55, 56

pagans, 124
palace, 171
Parables of Enoch, 176
parallelism, 173
Passover, 37–38, 56, 57, 122–24, 126, 127, 133, 137–38
Passover lamb, 143, 152
Paul, 14, 17, 18, 124–26
penal substitution, 115, 125, 170n63
Philo, 13, 172
Phinehas, 91

"pierced one," 149–53
piety, 82
Plato, 121, 125
Plea for Deliverance, 81
pledge, of inheritance, 162–63, 164
praise, 181, 184, 188, 191
Priestly and Holiness traditions, 40, 75
priests, 100, 175, 178, 184
Primeval History, 76
prohibitions, 47, 56
promise, 156, 162–63
property, 159–60, 162
propitiation, 4, 180–81, 190. *See also* atonement
prostration, 109
Protestants, 115, 121, 124
punitive expulsion, 25
purgation, 40. *See also* atonement
purification, 10, 43
purity, 57

Qumran Hodayot, 69, 70, 83–87, 134

ransom, 61n33, 155, 156, 159, 161, 166, 167, 169, 170, 187
rationalism, 121
rebellion, 125
reconciliation, 67, 77, 114
redemption, 114, 156, 157, 165–68
Red Sea, 119
release, 166–67
repentance, 69, 73, 77
representation, 91, 92, 100
resident aliens, 33, 36, 55–58
resurrection, 18, 122, 128–29, 154
Revelation, 145, 182, 183–88, 191
ritual, 156
ritual slaughter, 8–9
Roman Catholicism, 6n7, 115
romanticism, 121–22
royal priesthood, 117, 126, 128–29
rule keeping, 114–15

Sabbath, 32, 46, 54, 59, 60
sackcloth, 69

sacral offenses, 23
sacrifice, xiv, xvi, xvii, 5, 7–11, 39, 57, 114, 180, 181, 183, 189; animal, 45, 128, 182; child, 28n17; communion, 8; *tamid*, 137
sacrificial compensation, 69
Sadducees, 120
salvation, xvii, 5, 18, 145, 147, 148, 152, 153
Satan, 140–41
satisfaction, 6
Saul, 68
scapegoat, 7, 11, 44, 136
sea, 116–17, 119, 126, 129, 184
sealing, 156, 157–62, 168–69, 170
Second Temple Judaism, 70, 73, 79, 81, 82, 85, 88, 90, 116, 132, 138, 171, 172n3
sectarian provenance, 179
seeing, 142, 144, 146, 147, 148, 150, 151, 153
self-humiliation, 69, 83
Septuagint, 12, 17, 132, 133–34
serpent in the wilderness, 143–44, 146
servant song, 145
Seth, 99, 106
seventh heaven, 177
sex, 28n17
shame, xiii
Shem, 99, 106
*Sifra*, 7n13
signs, 158–59
Simeon, 91, 94, 95, 96, 99, 102, 108
sin, xvii; deliberate, 31; as disease, 79; elimination of, 138, 140; and idolatry, 117, 124, 125; and impurity, 10, 70; inadvertent, 46–47, 48, 51, 58, 68; intentional, 44, 47, 58–62, 68; sexual, 30, 57; unforgivable, 24
sin offering, 5, 8, 9, 48, 139. *See also ḥaṭṭāʾt*
slavery, 168, 170
societal values, 25
Solomon, 89, 91, 105, 111, 119, 184
Songs of the Maśkil, 86
Songs of the Sabbath Sacrifice, 178–83, 188, 191, 192
Son of Man, 146
soteriology, 14, 114
stones of delight, 101, 104
story, 112
substitution, xix, 16, 115, 123–26

suffering, 150–51
Suffering Servant Song, 14
*Sühne*, 5
symbolism, 103–5

tabernacle, 36, 45, 95, 96, 105, 118, 119, 121, 127
table, 104
*tabulae*, 161
Tamar, 164
tattooing, 159–60
temple: altar of, 104, 185, 186; building of, 118; as Eden, 105; in heaven, 172–76, 184; in Jerusalem, 4; as microcosm, 97, 98, 110; vs. palace, 171
terminology, 162
Testament of Levi, 189–91
testimony, 150, 151
Texas Revolution, 18–19
thanksgiving psalms, 81, 87
theodicy, 74
theophany, 108–10
*theosis*, 4
throne, 173–74, 180
transformation, 78, 81, 82–84, 87, 178
transliterations, 40n1, 44
trees, 103–5
twelve tribes, 101, 104

uncircumcised heart, 71–72
uncleanness, 31, 38
unquiet sea, 116–17

*Vayikra Rabbah*, 7n13
vicarious substitution, 16, 19
victory, 120–21, 123–24, 126
visionary seeing, 142

water, 87, 152–53, 154, 157
wealth, 167
Western culture, 170
Western theology, 113–14, 122
widow, 54–55, 56
wisdom, 107
witnesses, 141

wizards, 28
words of praise, 188
worldview, 24
worship, 36, 92, 94–95, 99, 104–5, 118–19, 128

Yahweh, holiness of, 35
Yom Kippur, xiii, 37, 122, 175. *See also* Day of Atonement
Zechariah, 119
Zerubbabel, 99

# INDEX OF SCRIPTURE AND ANCIENT SOURCES

**OLD TESTAMENT**

**Genesis**

| | |
|---|---|
| 1 | 95, 96, 118, 130 |
| 1:2 | 116 |
| 1:9–10 | 96, 108 |
| 1:14–19 | 96 |
| 1:26 | 98, 106 |
| 1:26–28 | 89, 96, 106, 116n11 |
| 1:26–29 | 96 |
| 1:28 | 98 |
| 2–3 | 76, 76n21, 77n22, 85, 86 |
| 2:1–2 | 97 |
| 2:4b–3:23 | 76n20 |
| 2:7 | 77, 84, 86 |
| 2:8 | 137 |
| 2:9b | 76n20 |
| 2:17 | 76–77 |
| 3 | 76n21, 84 |
| 3:5 | 77 |
| 3:19 | 86 |
| 3:22 | 76n20, 77 |
| 4:1–24 | 76n20 |
| 4:15 | 159 |
| 6:5 | 77 |
| 6:5–8 | 76n20 |
| 6:6abβ | 76n20 |
| 7:1–2 | 76n20 |
| 7:3b–5 | 76n20 |
| 7:7 | 76n20, 117n14 |
| 7:10 | 76n20 |
| 7:12 | 76n20 |
| 7:16b | 76n20 |
| 7:17 | 76n20 |

| | |
|---|---|
| 7:22–23aα | 76n20 |
| 7:23b | 76n20 |
| 8:2b–3a | 76n20 |
| 8:6–13 | 76n20 |
| 8:20–22 | 76n20 |
| 8:22 | 77 |
| 9:3–4 | 27 |
| 9:11 | 110 |
| 9:14 | 108n37 |
| 9:20–27 | 76n20 |
| 10:1b | 76n20 |
| 10:8–15 | 76n20 |
| 10:21 | 76n20 |
| 10:24–30 | 76n20 |
| 17:11 | 158 |
| 17:14 | 23, 24, 34, 34n34, 59n28 |
| 18:27 | 85, 86 |
| 22 | 138n23 |
| 22:7 | 137 |
| 25:8 | 27n15 |
| 32:21 | 67, 180 |
| 38 | 164, 165 |
| 38:17–20 | 164 |

**Exodus**

| | |
|---|---|
| 3:1–10 | 42n6 |
| 3:12 | 119n22 |
| 4:22–23 | 89 |
| 4:23 | 119n22 |
| 7:16 | 119n22 |
| 7:26 | 119n22 |
| 8:16 | 119n22 |
| 9:1 | 119n22 |
| 9:13 | 119n22 |
| 10:3 | 119n22 |

| | |
|---|---|
| 10:7 | 119n22 |
| 10:8 | 119n22 |
| 10:11 | 119n22 |
| 10:24 | 119n22 |
| 10:26 | 119n22 |
| 12 | 143 |
| 12:1–8 | 38 |
| 12:2–7 | 138 |
| 12:3–5 | 137n18, 138 |
| 12:6LXX | 137n18 |
| 12:10LXX | 133 |
| 12:13 | 138, 152 |
| 12:14 | 138 |
| 12:15 | 23, 24, 32, 59n28 |
| 12:17 | 138 |
| 12:19 | 23, 24, 32, 33, 57, 59n28 |
| 12:21 | 137n118 |
| 12:22 | 133, 137 |
| 12:23 | 138 |
| 12:25 | 46 |
| 12:25–27 | 138 |
| 12:27 | 137n118 |
| 12:31 | 119n22 |
| 12:38 | 62n35 |
| 12:43 | 137n118 |
| 12:43–49 | 62n35 |
| 12:45 | 54n17 |
| 12:46 | 133 |
| 12:48 | 174n9 |
| 12:48–49 | 33, 57 |
| 13:9 | 159 |
| 13:16 | 159 |
| 14:21–22 | 119n23 |
| 15:7–8 | 119n23 |
| 16 | 46 |

| | | | | | |
|---|---|---|---|---|---|
| 16:1–3 | 46n13 | 29:38–41 | 137 | 3 | 12 |
| 16:6–20 | 46n13 | 29:43 | 60n31 | 3:2 | 9, 12 |
| 16:10 | 108 | 30:1–10 | 42n6, 186 | 3:5 | 181 |
| 16:21 | 46n13 | 30:6–10 | 42n6 | 4 | 40n2, 42, 44, 46, |
| 16:22 | 46n13 | 30:10 | 43n8, 44n9, 180 | | 47, 58, 61 |
| 16:22b–25 | 46n13 | 30:12 | 44n8 | 4:1–35 | 41n2 |
| 16:31–35a | 46n13 | 30:16 | 44n9 | 4:2 | 47, 48, 58n27 |
| 16:36 | 46n13 | 30:17–21 | 96 | 4:2–12 | 43 |
| 19:6 | 117n18 | 30:20 | 174n9 | 4:3 | 43, 136 |
| 19:22 | 174n9 | 30:28 | 186 | 4:4 | 9 |
| 20:1–17 | 54n18 | 30:33 | 22n3, 24, 35, | 4:5 | 100n22 |
| 20:5 | 119n22 | | 59n28 | 4:5–7 | 42n6, 43 |
| 20:8–10 | 32 | 30:38 | 22n3, 24, 35, | 4:12 | 40n2 |
| 22:20 | 54 | | 59n28 | 4:13 | 47, 48 |
| 22:20–22 | 55 | 31:12–17 | 46, 60n30 | 4:13–21 | 43, 49–51 |
| 22:20–23 | 55 | 31:14 | 23, 24, 59n28 | 4:14 | 43, 61 |
| 22:30 | 55 | 31:14–15 | 32, 32n28 | 4:16–18 | 42n6, 43 |
| 23:1–8 | 55 | 31:18a | 97 | 4:20 | 43n8, 180 |
| 23:9 | 54, 55 | 32 | 119 | 4:21 | 40n2 |
| 23:10–11 | 55, 56n24 | 34 | 109, 110 | 4:22 | 47, 48 |
| 23:12 | 54 | 34:6 | 110 | 4:22–26 | 43 |
| 24:8 | 16 | 34:6–7 | 110n39 | 4:23 | 43, 48 |
| 25 | 43n6 | 34:8 | 109 | 4:25 | 43 |
| 25–27 | 42n6 | 35–40 | 46 | 4:26 | 9, 43n8, 180 |
| 25–31 | 46, 95, 96, 105 | 35:2 | 32 | 4:27 | 47, 48, 58n27 |
| 25–40 | 8 | 35:2–3 | 46 | 4:27–31 | 43, 51–52 |
| 25:9 | 188 | 38:3 | 187 | 4:28 | 40n1, 43 |
| 25:31–36 | 105 | 39:26 | 105 | 4:30 | 43 |
| 27:1–2 | 186 | 39:32a | 97 | 4:31 | 9, 43n8, 180 |
| 27:3 | 187 | 40 | 118, 130 | 4:32 | 43 |
| 28 | 101 | 40:2 | 59 | 4:32–35 | 43 |
| 28–29 | 90 | 40:32 | 174n9 | 4:34 | 43 |
| 28:2 | 101, 109 | 40:33b | 97 | 4:35 | 43n8 |
| 28:9–12 | 90, 101 | 45:9 | 105 | 5:1–13 | 42n6, 45 |
| 28:17–21 | 101 | | | 5:6 | 43n8 |
| 28:21 | 90 | **Leviticus** | | 5:10 | 43n8 |
| 28:28–30 | 101 | 1–7 | 8, 9, 10, 11, 41n2 | 5:13 | 43n8 |
| 28:30 | 90 | 1–16 | 22 | 5:14–26 | 42n6 |
| 28:36 | 105 | 1:4 | xvin13, 9, 11, 12, | 5:16 | 43n8 |
| 28:40 | 101, 109 | | 43n8 | 5:18 | 43n8 |
| 28:41 | 100n22 | 1:5 | 9, 9n17 | 5:26 | 43n8 |
| 28:42 | 175, 188 | 1:9 | 181 | 6:10 | 188 |
| 28:43 | 174n9 | 1:11 | 9 | 6:17–23 | 41n2, 42n6 |
| 29:28 | 181 | 1:13 | 181 | 6:22 | 41n2 |
| 29:33 | 43n8 | 1:17 | 181 | 6:23 | 40n2, 43n8 |
| 29:36 | 43n7, 43n8, 44n9 | 2:2 | 181 | 7:1–10 | 30 |
| 29:36–37 | 43n8 | 2:9 | 181 | 7:7 | 43n8 |

| | | | | | |
|---|---|---|---|---|---|
| 7:20 | 23, 24 | 14:49–53 | 40n2 | 17:5–7 | 30 |
| 7:20–21 | 22n3, 59n28 | 14:53 | 43n8 | 17:6 | 61n33 |
| 7:21 | 23, 24, 36 | 15:13–15 | 44 | 17:7 | 61n33 |
| 7:25 | 24, 35, 59n28 | 15:15 | 43n8 | 17:8 | 57, 61n33 |
| 7:26 | 36 | 15:24 | 31 | 17:8–9 | 36 |
| 7:26–27 | 61n33 | 15:28–30 | 44 | 17:9 | 23, 24, 36 |
| 7:27 | 23, 24, 27n16, 35, 59n28 | 15:30 | 43n8 | 17:10 | 23, 27, 57, 59n28, 61n33 |
| 7:28–36 | 30 | 16 | 7, 8, 40n2, 58, 60, 61, 62, 135 | 17:11 | xv, 7n13, 27, 44n8, 61n33 |
| 7:32 | 181 | 16:1 | 59, 174n9 | 17:11–14 | 61n33 |
| 7:34 | 181 | 16:1–28 | 44, 47 | 17:12 | 57, 61n33 |
| 8–10 | 59 | 16:3 | 44 | 17:13 | 57, 61n33 |
| 8:6–12 | 178 | 16:4 | 175 | 17:14 | 23, 59n28 |
| 8:15 | 10, 43n7, 43n8 | 16:5 | 40n2, 61, 62 | 17:15 | 57 |
| 8:23–24 | 10 | 16:5–11 | 44 | 17:15–16 | 55 |
| 8:30 | 10 | 16:6 | 43n8 | 18 | 28n17, 30n21, 31, 63 |
| 8:34 | 43n8 | 16:8 | 40n2 | | |
| 9:2–3 | 45n11 | 16:9 | 62 | 18:5 | 106 |
| 9:3 | 135 | 16:10 | 43n8 | 18:19 | 31 |
| 9:7 | 43n8, 45n11 | 16:11 | 43n8 | 18:21 | 60n31 |
| 9:7–8 | 174n9 | 16:11–16 | 44 | 18:24–28 | 63 |
| 10:3 | 60n31 | 16:14–15 | 9 | 18:25 | 75 |
| 10:14 | 181 | 16:14–16a | 44 | 18:26 | 57 |
| 10:17 | 43n8 | 16:15 | 44, 62 | 18:28 | 75 |
| 11:44–45 | 60n31 | 16:16 | xviiin13, 10, 42n6, 43n8, 44, 58 | 18:29 | 23, 30, 59n28 |
| 12:6 | 135 | | | 19:2 | 27, 60n31, 76 |
| 12:7 | 43n8 | 16:16–18 | 43n8 | 19:8 | 23, 24, 36, 59n28 |
| 12:7–8 | 43n8 | 16:17 | 43n8 | 19:9–10 | 55, 56 |
| 12:8 | 43n8 | 16:17b–19 | 44 | 19:10 | 57 |
| 14:4–7 | 40n2 | 16:18–19 | 9 | 19:12 | 60n31 |
| 14:7 | 43n7 | 16:19 | 10, 43n7, 44 | 19:22 | 43n8 |
| 14:8–32 | 44 | 16:20 | 10, 43n8 | 19:23 | 46 |
| 14:10 | 44 | 16:20–22 | 40n2, 44, 136, 136n11 | 19:33–34 | 55, 56, 57 |
| 14:12–13 | 135 | | | 20 | 28n17, 30n21, 38 |
| 14:14 | 10 | 16:21 | 12, 13 | 20:2 | 28, 57 |
| 14:18 | 43n8 | 16:22 | 136, 136n11 | 20:2–5 | 60n30 |
| 14:19 | 44 | 16:24 | 43n8 | 20:3 | 59n28, 60n31 |
| 14:19–20 | 43n8 | 16:24–25 | 44, 62 | 20:3–5 | 23, 24, 27 |
| 14:20 | 43n8 | 16:27 | 40n2, 43n8 | 20:4–5 | 28 |
| 14:21 | 43n8, 135 | 16:29 | 57, 61 | 20:5 | 59n28 |
| 14:22 | 44 | 16:29–34 | 61 | 20:6 | 23, 24, 28, 59n28 |
| 14:28–29 | 43n8 | 16:30 | 43n8 | 20:7 | 60n31 |
| 14:30–31 | 44 | 16:32–34 | 43n8 | 20:17 | 23, 38, 59n28 |
| 14:31 | 43n8 | 17–26 | 41 | 20:17–21 | 30n21 |
| 14:34 | 46 | 17:4 | 23, 24, 30, 36 | | |
| 14:44 | 43n7 | 17:5 | 61n33 | | |

| | | | | | | |
|---|---|---|---|---|---|---|
| 20:18 | 23, 30, 59n28, 85, 86 | **Numbers** | | 15:24 | 58, 58n27 | |
| 20:24–26 | 56 | 1:51 | 174n9 | 15:24–26 | 47, 49–53, 61 | |
| 20:26 | 60n31 | 3:10 | 174n9 | 15:25 | 43n8, 58n27 | |
| 21:1–6 | 33 | 3:38 | 174n9 | 15:25–26 | 46 | |
| 21:6 | 60n31 | 4:18 | 59n28 | 15:26 | 46, 53, 57, 58n27, 61 | |
| 21:14 | 34, 56n26 | 4:19 | 174n9 | 15:27 | 40n1, 58n27 | |
| 21:17–18 | 174n9 | 5:8 | 43n8, 44n9 | 15:27–28 | 46 | |
| 21:21–23 | 174n9 | 6:1–21a | 45n10 | 15:27–29 | 47, 49–53 | |
| 22:2 | 60n31 | 6:10–11 | 45 | 15:28 | 43n8, 58n27 | |
| 22:3 | 23, 24, 27n14, 38, 174n9 | 6:11 | 43n8 | 15:29 | 46, 53, 57, 58n27, 61 | |
| 22:9 | 38 | 6:14 | 45 | 15:30 | 46, 57 | |
| 22:10 | 54n17 | 6:16 | 45 | 15:30–31 | 23, 31, 46, 47, 58–62, 59n28, 61 | |
| 22:13 | 56n26 | 7 | 185 | 15:31 | 46 | |
| 22:18 | 57 | 7:13 | 185 | 15:32–36 | 46, 59 | |
| 22:20 | 180 | 7:14 | 185 | 15:35 | 32 | |
| 22:21 | 180 | 7:19 | 185 | 15:41 | 46 | |
| 22:21–22 | 181 | 7:20 | 185 | 16:1a | 45n12 | |
| 22:25 | 54n17 | 8:12 | 43n8 | 16:2aβ–11 | 45n12 | |
| 22:32 | 60n31 | 8:19 | 43n8 | 16:16–24 | 45n12 | |
| 23 | 37 | 8:21 | 43n8 | 16:22 | 109n38 | |
| 23:8 | 43n8 | 9:12 | 133 | 16:26–27a | 45n12 | |
| 23:22 | 56, 57 | 9:13 | 23, 24, 37, 59n28 | 16:35 | 45n12 | |
| 23:26–32 | 8 | 9:14 | 57 | 16:42 | 108 | |
| 23:27 | 44n9 | 10:10 | 181 | 17:11–12 | 43n8 | |
| 23:28 | 44n9 | 11:4 | 62n35 | 17:28 | 174n9 | |
| 23:29 | 23, 24, 37, 59n28 | 13–14 | 45 | 18:7 | 174n9 | |
| 23:30 | 23, 24, 29 | 13:1–17a | 45n12 | 19 | 33, 40n2 | |
| 24 | 60 | 13:21 | 45n12 | 19:1–10 | 33n32 | |
| 24:10–23 | 46, 60n31, 62 | 13:25–26bα | 45n12 | 19:9 | 40n2 | |
| 24:16 | 57 | 13:32 | 45n12 | 19:10 | 57 | |
| 24:22 | 57 | 14:1a | 45n12 | 19:13 | 23, 33, 59n28 | |
| 25 | 55n24 | 14:2–10 | 45n12 | 19:20 | 23, 33, 59n28 | |
| 25:2 | 46 | 14:26–39 | 45n12 | 20:6 | 109n38 | |
| 25:6 | 54n17 | 15 | 46, 62 | 20:10–12 | 60n31 | |
| 25:9 | 44n9 | 15:1–16 | 62 | 21 | 145, 146 | |
| 25:23 | 54n17 | 15:2 | 46 | 21:4–7 | 147 | |
| 25:35 | 54n17 | 15:13–16 | 46, 57 | 21:4–9 | 143 | |
| 25:40 | 54n17 | 15:15 | 46 | 21:8 | 143, 144 | |
| 25:45 | 54n17 | 15:17–18 | 63 | 21:8–9 | 146 | |
| 25:47 | 54n17, 57 | 15:17–21 | 62, 63 | 21:9 | 143 | |
| 25:53 | 57 | 15:18 | 46, 62, 63 | 25:8 | 43n8 | |
| 26:41 | 71 | 15:21 | 46 | 25:13 | 43n8 | |
| | | 15:22–23 | 47–49 | 27:14 | 60n31 | |
| | | 15:22–31 | 42, 45–47, 54n16 | | | |
| | | 15:23 | 46 | | | |
| | | 15:23–24 | 46 | | | |

| | | | | | |
|---|---|---|---|---|---|
| 28–29 | 135 | 28:43–44 | 55n21 | **2 Kings** | |
| 28:3–10 | 137 | 29 | 119 | 17:7–20 | 71 |
| 28:22 | 43n8 | 30:1–2 | 71 | 19:6 | 60n31 |
| 28:30 | 43n8 | 30:1–10 | 71 | 19:22 | 60n31 |
| 29:5 | 43n8 | 30:3–9 | 72 | 21:1–15 | 71 |
| 29:7–11 | 8 | 30:6 | 71, 72 | | |
| 29:11 | 43n8, 44n9 | 30:8 | 72 | **2 Chronicles** | |
| 31:50 | 44n8 | 31:10–13 | 55 | 4:3 | 110n41 |
| 35 | 63 | 32 | 119 | 30:15–20 | xviin13, 138n20 |
| 35:15 | 57 | 32:43 | 186 | 30:27 | 98 |
| 35:31 | 44n8 | | | 33:10–17 | 73 |
| 35:31–33 | 44n8 | **Judges** | | | |
| 35:33–34 | 63 | 13:20 | 109n38 | **Ezra** | |
| | | | | 9:3–15 | 73 |
| **Deuteronomy** | | **2 Samuel** | | | |
| 1:39 | 77 | 7:14 | 79 | **Nehemiah** | |
| 5:12–14 | 32 | 19:36 | 77 | 1:2–3 | 125n37 |
| 5:14 | 54, 54n18 | 21:1 | 68 | 1:4–11 | 73 |
| 7:6 | 56 | 21:3 | 68 | 9:6–37 | 73 |
| 10:15 | 56 | 21:6 | 68 | | |
| 10:16 | 71 | | | **Esther** | |
| 10:18 | 54n19 | **1 Kings** | | 4:7 | 163 |
| 10:18–19 | 55 | 3–4 | 89, 105, 111 | | |
| 12:12 | 54n18 | 3:3–15 | 111 | **Job** | |
| 12:18 | 54n18 | 3:9 | 77, 90, 91 | 4 | 74 |
| 14:2 | 56 | 3:16–25 | 90 | 4:7–8 | 74 |
| 14:21 | 55, 56 | 4:20a | 90 | 4:14–16 | 74 |
| 14:29 | 54n19 | 4:29 | 90, 91n6 | 4:17–19 | 74, 75 |
| 15:1–11 | 55n20, 56n24 | 6–7 | 105 | 4:19 | 86 |
| 15:12–18 | 56n24 | 6:18 | 105 | 8:4–7 | 74 |
| 16:11 | 54n18, 54n19, 55 | 6:29 | 105 | 8:20–22 | 74 |
| 16:14 | 54n18, 54n19, 55 | 6:32 | 105 | 10:9 | 86 |
| 17:14–20 | 90 | 6:35 | 105 | 11:13–16 | 74 |
| 18:13 | 56 | 7:18–19 | 105 | 14:1 | 85 |
| 23:8 | 55n21 | 7:22 | 105 | 15:14 | 85 |
| 23:14–15 | 55 | 7:23 | 184 | 15:14–16 | 75 |
| 24:17 | 54n19, 55 | 7:23–26 | 96 | 19:9 | 86 |
| 24:19–21 | 54n19 | 7:24 | 184 | 22:2–11 | 75 |
| 24:19–22 | 55, 55n20 | 7:26 | 105 | 22:21–27 | 74, 75 |
| 26:11 | 55 | 7:39 | 184 | 25 | 74 |
| 26:12 | 54n19 | 7:48 | 186 | 25:4 | 85 |
| 26:12–13 | 55 | 7:50 | 187 | 25:4–6 | 74, 75 |
| 26:15 | 98 | 8 | 119 | 30:19 | 85, 86 |
| 27:19 | 54n19, 55 | 8:64 | 98, 186 | 33:6 | 85, 86 |
| 28 | 119 | 10–11 | 91 | 34:15 | 86 |
| 28:1 | 71 | 21:27–29 | 69 | 42:6 | 85, 86 |
| 28:15 | 71 | | | | |

**Psalms**

| | |
|---|---|
| 2 | 116n12, 120 |
| 8 | 89, 96, 106, 116n11, 128 |
| 8:2 | 96 |
| 8:5 | 106 |
| 8:6 | 96 |
| 8:6–9 | 107 |
| 8:7 | 96, 107 |
| 8:11 | 96, 107 |
| 8:12c | 96 |
| 8:13a | 107 |
| 13:7 | 125n37 |
| 32 | 73 |
| 32:2 | 185 |
| 33:21LXX | 133 |
| 36:8–9 | 104 |
| 42:4 | 185 |
| 44:17 | 60n31 |
| 47 | 120 |
| 51 | 78, 78n23, 79, 81 |
| 51:7 | 85 |
| 51:12–13 | 78 |
| 52:8 | 103 |
| 52:10 | 103 |
| 56:8 | 185 |
| 63:3 | 104 |
| 63:8 | 104 |
| 68:6 | 98 |
| 70:22 | 185 |
| 72 | 116n12, 120, 130 |
| 77:16 | 119n23 |
| 77:19 | 119n23 |
| 78:38 | 69 |
| 79:10 | 186, 186n47 |
| 80:2 | 185 |
| 87 | 120 |
| 89 | 116n12 |
| 89:33 | 79 |
| 90:3–9 | 75 |
| 90:12 | 75 |
| 90:17 | 75 |
| 91:3 | 185 |
| 92:12–14 | 103 |
| 92:13–15 | 103 |
| 96 | 116n12 |
| 97:5 | 185 |
| 98 | 116n12 |

| | |
|---|---|
| 104 | 109 |
| 104:1c–2a | 109 |
| 106:9 | 119n23 |
| 107:2 | 185 |
| 114:3 | 119n23 |
| 114:5 | 119n23 |
| 119 | 80 |
| 125:1 | 125n37 |
| 128:1 | 104 |
| 128:2 | 104 |
| 128:3 | 103, 104 |
| 128:4 | 104 |
| 128:5 | 104 |
| 128:11–13 | 104 |
| 146:7 | 185 |
| 150:3 | 185 |

**Isaiah**

| | |
|---|---|
| 2:2 | 145n42 |
| 4:2 | 145n43 |
| 5:12 | 185 |
| 5:26 | 144n40 |
| 6 | 184 |
| 6:9–10 | 149, 150 |
| 7:15–16 | 77 |
| 10:15 | 145n43 |
| 11:1–10 | 116n12 |
| 11:12 | 144n40 |
| 13:2 | 144n40 |
| 16:11 | 185 |
| 18:3 | 144n40 |
| 23:16 | 185 |
| 24:8 | 185 |
| 26:21–27:1 | 110 |
| 29:16 | 86 |
| 30:32 | 185 |
| 33:10 | 145n42 |
| 33:23 | 144n40 |
| 35 | 116n12 |
| 37:6 | 60n31 |
| 37:23 | 60n31, 146n42 |
| 40 | 110, 119, 127 |
| 40–55 | 127 |
| 40:3 | 142 |
| 40:3–11 | 120n24 |
| 40:5 | 109 |
| 40:9–10LXX | 146 |

| | |
|---|---|
| 40:10LXX | 142 |
| 42:1 | 142 |
| 42:1LXX | 142 |
| 42:18–20 | 150 |
| 43:16 | 119n23 |
| 43:28 | 60n31 |
| 44:4 | 103 |
| 44:18 | 150 |
| 45:9 | 86 |
| 45:20 | 146n42 |
| 46:1 | 146n42 |
| 46:7 | 146n42 |
| 49:18 | 146n42 |
| 49:22 | 144n40 |
| 51:6 | 146n42 |
| 51:7 | 60n31 |
| 51:9–11 | 119n23 |
| 52 | 119, 127 |
| 52–53 | 148n52, 150 |
| 52:7–12 | 120n24 |
| 52:8 | 145n42 |
| 52:10 | 150 |
| 52:12–53:1 | 148 |
| 52:13 | 145, 145n42, 145n44, 146 |
| 52:13–15 | 145, 146 |
| 52:13–53:12 | xvii, 3, 13–17, 18 |
| 52:14 | 145, 145n44, 146 |
| 52:14–15 | 146 |
| 52:15 | 15, 148, 150, 151 |
| 53 | 139, 140 |
| 53:1 | 15, 149, 150 |
| 53:1–11 | 145 |
| 53:2–3 | 146 |
| 53:4 | 139, 140, 140n27 |
| 53:4–6 | 139 |
| 53:5 | 139 |
| 53:6 | 139 |
| 53:7 | 138, 139n24, 139n25, 142 |
| 53:8 | 79, 140n28, 140n29, 148n51 |
| 53:10 | 14, 139 |
| 53:11 | 16 |
| 53:11–12 | 139, 140 |
| 53:12 | 139, 140n27 |

| | | | | | |
|---|---|---|---|---|---|
| 54 | 127 | 9:6 | 159 | **Habakkuk** | |
| 54:12 | 101 | 9:11 | 175 | 2:20–3:6 | 110 |
| 55 | 127 | 10:2 | 175 | | |
| 55:3 | 89 | 10:6 | 175 | **Zephaniah** | |
| 55:12–13 | 116n12 | 10:7 | 175 | 2:8 | 60n31 |
| 56:7 | 180 | 10:20 | 173 | | |
| 59:17 | 109 | 11:19 | 73, 78 | **Zechariah** | |
| 60:1–3 | 108 | 16 | 73 | 1:16–17 | 120n24 |
| 60:4 | 146n42 | 16:63 | xviiin13 | 2:13 | 98 |
| 63:7 | 138 | 18 | 72 | 8:3 | 120n24 |
| 63:9 | 146n42 | 20 | 73 | 9:9 | 150 |
| 65–66 | 116n12 | 20:43 | 83 | 12:9–13:1 | 150n56, 151 |
| 66:12 | 146n42 | 23 | 73 | 12:10 | 149, 150 |
| | | 36:25 | 87 | 13:1 | 153 |
| **Jeremiah** | | 36:25–27 | 83 | 13:7–9 | 150n56 |
| 1:3 | 125n37 | 36:26b–27a | 73 | 19:9–13 | 150 |
| 4:4 | 71 | 36:27 | 73, 78, 87 | | |
| 5:4–5 | 72 | 36:31 | 78, 83 | **Malachi** | |
| 5:13 | 72 | 40–42 | 172n3 | 2:7 | 175 |
| 5:21 | 72 | 40:46 | 174n9 | 3:1 | 120n24 |
| 6:10 | 72 | 43 | 120n24 | 3:17 | 155n2 |
| 6:20 | 180 | 43:13–17 | 98 | | |
| 8:4–9 | 72 | 44:7–9 | 71 | **NEW TESTAMENT** | |
| 9:3 | 72 | 44:13 | 174n9 | | |
| 9:26 | 71 | 44:15–16 | 174n9 | **Matthew** | |
| 11:1–8 | 71 | 44:22 | 34 | 1:23 | 127n42 |
| 18:3–6 | 86 | 45:4 | 174n9 | 8:17 | 15 |
| 25:30 | 98 | 45:18–20 | 138n20 | 13:28 | 117n17 |
| 28:12 | 144n40 | 45:21–25 | 138n20 | | |
| 28:27 | 144n40 | | | **Mark** | |
| 31:33–34 | 72 | **Daniel** | | 14:11 | 163 |
| 32:39–40 | 72 | 4 | 73 | 14:41 | 123n30 |
| | | 7 | 174 | 15:6–15 | 123n31 |
| **Ezekiel** | | 7:9–10 | 171 | | |
| 1 | 109, 110 | 8:9–10 | 173 | **Luke** | |
| 1:1–2 | 125n37 | 9:4–19 | 69, 73 | 5:30 | 123n30 |
| 1:26–28 | 108 | | | 7:34 | 123n30 |
| 3:11 | 125n37 | **Hosea** | | 10:18 | 117n15 |
| 3:15 | 125n37 | 14:5–7 | 103, 104 | 22:37 | 15 |
| 5:15 | 60n31 | 14:8 | 104 | 22:53 | 117n15 |
| 6:9 | 83 | | | 23:39–43 | 123n32 |
| 7:1–4 | 71 | **Jonah** | | 23:47 | 123n33 |
| 9:2 | 175 | 3:5–10 | 69 | 24:7 | 123n30 |
| 9:3 | 175 | | | | |
| 9:4 | 159 | **Micah** | | | |
| 9:4–6 | 160n17 | 1:2–4 | 110 | | |

## John

| | |
|---|---|
| 1:14 | 121 |
| 1:23 | 132n2, 142 |
| 1:29 | 126, 135, 136, |
| | 136n11, 137, 137n15, 139, |
| | 140, 140n29, 141, 142, 146, |
| | 147n48, 152, 152n60, 154 |
| 1:32 | 141 |
| 1:32–33 | 142 |
| 1:33 | 141 |
| 1:34 | 141 |
| 1:35–37 | 141 |
| 1:36 | 126, 135, 137, 141, |
| | 146, 152n60 |
| 1:39 | 141 |
| 1:40 | 141 |
| 1:41–42 | 141 |
| 1:45–46 | 141 |
| 2:16 | 140 |
| 2:17 | 132n2 |
| 3:14 | 143, 144, 145, 146, |
| | 147, 148, 150 |
| 3:14–15 | 144, 151 |
| 3:15 | 144 |
| 4:14 | 153 |
| 5:8–9 | 140 |
| 5:10 | 140 |
| 5:11–12 | 140 |
| 6:31 | 132 |
| 6:40 | 147 |
| 6:45 | 132n2 |
| 6:53–56 | 152 |
| 7:38 | 132, 153 |
| 8:21 | 141, 147 |
| 8:24 | 147 |
| 8:28 | 143, 147, 148, 151 |
| 8:34 | 141 |
| 8:44 | 141 |
| 8:59 | 140 |
| 9:41 | 141 |
| 10:1 | 120n6 |
| 10:1–18 | 134 |
| 10:8 | 120n26 |
| 10:16 | 144 |
| 10:18 | 140 |
| 10:22 | 120n27 |
| 10:28 | 141 |

| | |
|---|---|
| 10:34 | 132n2 |
| 11:39 | 140 |
| 11:41 | 140 |
| 11:51 | 145 |
| 12 | 148 |
| 12:13 | 132 |
| 12:15 | 132, 150 |
| 12:20–22 | 148 |
| 12:20–36 | 147 |
| 12:20–43 | 148n52 |
| 12:21 | 147, 148 |
| 12:23 | 120 |
| 12:24 | 148 |
| 12:31 | 120, 147, 152n62 |
| 12:32 | 143, 148, 148n51 |
| 12:32–33 | 151 |
| 12:33 | 148 |
| 12:34 | 143, 145, 148 |
| 12:37–40 | 149 |
| 12:38 | 132n2 |
| 12:38–41 | 150 |
| 12:40 | 132 |
| 12:45 | 147 |
| 13:18 | 132 |
| 14:9 | 147 |
| 14:30 | 152n62 |
| 15:1–10 | 134 |
| 15:2 | 140 |
| 15:22 | 141 |
| 15:24 | 141 |
| 15:25 | 132n2 |
| 16:8–9 | 141 |
| 16:11 | 152n62 |
| 17:12 | 141 |
| 18–19 | 133 |
| 18:28 | 133 |
| 18:32 | 148 |
| 19:5 | 142n34 |
| 19:14 | 133, 142n34 |
| 19:24 | 132n2 |
| 19:29 | 133, 137 |
| 19:30 | 154 |
| 19:31 | 133, 151 |
| 19:32–33 | 149 |
| 19:34 | 149, 152 |
| 19:35 | 151 |

| | |
|---|---|
| 19:36 | 132, 133, 138, |
| | 138n21, 152, 152n60 |
| 19:36–37 | 149, 152, 153 |
| 19:37 | 132, 149, 150, 151 |
| 19:38 | 140 |
| 20:2 | 140 |
| 20:19–23 | 129n45 |
| 20:20 | 154 |
| 20:25 | 154 |
| 20:27–28 | 154 |
| 21:19 | 148 |

## Acts

| | |
|---|---|
| 7:5 | 163 |
| 8:32–33 | 15 |
| 20:28 | 167 |

## Romans

| | |
|---|---|
| 3 | 125 |
| 3:24 | 167 |
| 4 | 163 |
| 4:11 | 158 |
| 4:13 | 163 |
| 4:25 | 17–20 |
| 5:20–21 | 125 |
| 5:21 | 117n18 |
| 6:5 | 20 |
| 7 | 125 |
| 7:23 | 125n37 |
| 8 | 128 |
| 8:19–22 | 117n16 |
| 8:23 | 164 |
| 10:16 | 15 |
| 12 | 128 |
| 15 | 161 |
| 15:21 | 15 |
| 15:28 | 156, 160, 169 |

## 1 Corinthians

| | |
|---|---|
| 1:18 | 6 |
| 6:9–10 | 165 |
| 6:20 | 167, 168 |
| 7 | 162 |
| 7:22–23 | 162 |
| 7:23 | 167, 168 |
| 15 | 126 |

15:50 165

**2 Corinthians**
1:21–22 164
1:22 161, 162n30, 166
3:2–3 162
3:18 118n19
5 165
5:1 165
5:1–5 164
5:5 164, 166
5:21 124

**Galatians**
3 124, 163
3–4 165
3:10–14 115
3:13 168
3:14 163n35
4:5 168
5:21 165

**Ephesians**
1:7 155, 166, 167, 168
1:13 157, 159, 159n14, 164
1:13–14 156, 161, 164, 166
1:14 162, 163, 165, 166, 167n51, 169
1:21 168
2:2 168
2:4 155
2:7 168
2:8 155
2:13 167n48
3:2 155
3:6 163
3:7 155
3:8 155, 156
3:9 155
3:10 168
3:16 156
4:7 156
4:30 156, 157, 161, 165, 166, 166n43
6:12 168

**Philippians**
4:17 160n23

**Colossians**
1:13–14 168
2:11–12 159
3:24 165

**Hebrews**
2:14 9n19
6:4–8 189
7:27 9n19
8:5 189
9:12 167, 189
9:15–28 189
9:22 xv, xvn7
10:1–4 189
10:10 9n19
10:12 9n19
10:14 9n19
10:26 189
10:26–31 189
13 128
13:12 127n42

**James**
2:5 163n34

**1 Peter**
2 15
2:9 117n18
2:24–25 15

**1 John**
2:2 135
4:10 135

**Revelation**
1:5 187
1:6 117n18
4 184
4:4 184
4:5–6 184
4:6–8 184
4:9–11 184
5 184

5:6 187–88
5:6–10 185
5:8 185, 187
5:9 167, 187
5:9–10 128n43
5:10 117n18
5:12 126
6:9–10 186
6:10 186
6:11 186
7 184
7:3–8 160
7:9–10 186
7:14 188
8 186n46, 187
8–9 126n39
8:3 186
8:3–5 186
8:5 187
9:1–12 160
9:4 160
9:13 186
9:13–14 184n40
12:11 167n52
13 126n39
14 184
15 184
15:3–4 126n39
15:7 187
16 187
16:7 184
19 184
19:13 188
19:14 188
21 130
21:1 129n46
21:1–5 126n39

**APOCRYPHA**

**Tobit**
4:20–5:3 160n20
9:5 160

**Wisdom of Solomon**
16:6 143n37

| | | | | | |
|---|---|---|---|---|---|
| 18:5–9 | 138n21 | 45:7–8 | 102, 103 | 50:3 | 94, 96, 96n14, |
| | | 45:7–23 | 102 | | 108n37 |
| **Sirach** | | 45:8 | 101, 102 | 50:5–7 | 95, 96, 101, 102, |
| 1–43 | 100 | 45:11 | 101 | | 110 |
| 1:8 | 111 | 45:12 | 91, 102, 103 | 50:5–13 | 94 |
| 1:11–20 | 104 | 45:13 | 105 | 50:6 | 94 |
| 1:27–30 | 104 | 45:15 | 91 | 50:6–7 | 94 |
| 2:7–17 | 104 | 45:20 | 102, 103 | 50:7 | 94, 108, 108n37 |
| 2:11 | 110n39 | 45:23 | 94 | 50:8 | 94, 101, 102, 104, |
| 2:18c–d | 110n39 | 45:23–25 | 91 | | 110 |
| 5:4–6 | 110n39 | 45:25 | 91 | 50:8–10 | 95, 102 |
| 5:5–21 | 111 | 45:26 | 91, 99n21 | 50:9 | 94, 101, 102, 104 |
| 7:11b | 106 | 46:2 | 102 | 50:10 | 94, 101, 103, 104 |
| 7:27–31 | 91, 104 | 47:2–11 | 91 | 50:11 | 102, 103, 110 |
| 13:15–16 | 110 | 47:12–23 | 91 | 50:11–13 | 94, 95, 96, 106 |
| 14:17–18 | 110 | 47:15 | 91n6 | 50:12 | 94, 102, 110 |
| 17 | 106 | 47:19–21 | 91 | 50:12–13 | 99 |
| 17:1–8 | 106 | 47:20–21 | 91 | 50:12–14 | 94 |
| 17:1a | 77n22 | 47:23–25 | 91 | 50:13 | 95, 102, 103 |
| 17:3–4 | 96 | 48:1 | 102 | 50:14 | 94, 95, 97, 108 |
| 17:7 | 77n22 | 48:15–16 | 91 | 50:14–19 | 95, 96, 97 |
| 17:12a | 106 | 48:17 | 102 | 50:14–20 | 95 |
| 17:13 | 106 | 48:20 | 109 | 50:14–21 | 94 |
| 24:1–23 | 96, 107 | 49:1 | 102 | 50:16 | 94, 98, 99 |
| 24:25–29 | 105 | 49:4 | 91 | 50:16–19 | 94 |
| 24:32 | 102 | 49:8 | 108 | 50:17 | 94, 95, 110, 111 |
| 26:1–18 | 101 | 49:11–12 | 103 | 50:17–19 | 99 |
| 26:16 | 101 | 49:11–13 | 99 | 50:17–21 | 94 |
| 26:17 | 101 | 49:13 | 103 | 50:18b | 95 |
| 36:1 | 94 | 49:14–16 | 99 | 50:19 | 94, 95, 108 |
| 36:14–15a | 108 | 49:15 | 99 | 50:20 | 94, 95, 102 |
| 39:12 | 102 | 49:15–16 | 99 | 50:20–21 | 95 |
| 39:13 | 102 | 49:16 | 92n9, 94, 95, 99, | 50:21 | 99, 103 |
| 39:19 | 110 | | 104, 105, 106 | 50:23 | 91 |
| 43:1–12 | 96, 110 | 49:16–50:1 | 97 | 50:29 | 104 |
| 44–49 | 91, 98, 99, 100 | 49:16–50:4 | 95 | | |
| 44–50 | 99, 103 | 49:16–50:21 | xviii, | **Baruch** | |
| 44:1–15 | 106 | | 92–94, 95, 96, 100 | 2:10–3:8 | 73 |
| 44:2 | 103 | 50 | 97, 99, 104, 107, | 2:27–35 | 72 |
| 44:7 | 103 | | 108 | | |
| 44:13 | 103 | 50:1 | 99, 100, 102, 103, | **1 Maccabees** | |
| 44:15 | 107 | | 106 | 11:28 | 163 |
| 44:16–17 | 99 | 50:1–2 | 97 | | |
| 44:18 | 110 | 50:1–4 | 94, 102, 105, 111 | **2 Maccabees** | |
| 44:19 | 103 | 50:1–21 | 91, 99 | 4:8 | 163 |
| 45:6–22 | 91 | 50:1–24 | 99 | 4:27 | 163 |
| | | 50:2 | 94, 97, 102 | | |

| | | | | | | |
|---|---|---|---|---|---|---|
| 4:45 | 163 | **Jubilees** | | 8:29 | 87 | |
| | | 1:20 | 80 | 9:23 | 84 | |
| **3 Maccabees** | | 7:27 | 80 | 9:24 | 84n38, 84n39 | |
| 1:4 | 163 | 10:1–2 | 80 | 11:24–25 | 84 | |
| | | 12:20 | 80 | 15:10 | 87 | |
| **2 Esdras** | | 12:20–21 | 80 | 18:6 | 85n42 | |
| 11:2–3 | 125n37 | 22:16–17 | 124n34 | 18:7 | 85n43 | |
| | | 49 | 138 | 19:13–17 | 87 | |
| **OLD TESTAMENT** | | 49:1 | 138 | 19:14–15 | 84n39 | |
| **PSEUDEPIGRAPHA** | | 49:2 | 138, 153n62 | 19:15 | 85n45 | |
| | | 49:3 | 143, 152 | 19:23 | 84n38 | |
| | | 49:7 | 138, 153n62 | 20:15 | 87 | |
| **1 Enoch** | | 49:12 | 138 | 20:27 | 85n42 | |
| 1–36 | 171 | 49:13 | 138, 138n21 | 20:27–28 | 70 | |
| 14 | 174 | 49:19 | 138 | 20:27–30 | 86 | |
| 14:9 | 173 | 49:20 | 138 | 20:27–31 | 69 | |
| 14:10 | 173 | | | 20:28 | 84n39, 85n45 | |
| 14:11 | 173 | **Psalms of Solomon** | | 20:30 | 85n43 | |
| 14:15 | 173 | 12:6 | 163 | 21:9–10 | 85n44 | |
| 14:18–20 | 173 | | | 21:10–11 | 84 | |
| 14:20–23 | 173 | **Testament of Levi** | | 21:30 | 84n38 | |
| 14:22 | 174 | 3:3 | 190 | 21:34 | 87 | |
| 14:23 | 174, 174n9, | 3:4 | 190 | 21:35 | 84n38 | |
| | 174n10 | 3:4–8 | 190 | 22:8–9 | 84n38 | |
| 15:3 | 173 | 3:5–6 | 190 | 23:13 | 84n38 | |
| 15:11 | 80n29 | 3:7 | 190 | 23:13–14 | 85n44 | |
| 17–36 | 175 | 3:8 | 190 | 23:29 | 87 | |
| 19:1 | 80n29 | | | 23:34 | 87 | |
| 37–71 | 176 | **DEAD SEA SCROLLS** | | | | |
| 83–90 | 176 | | | **1QS** | | |
| 91 | 176 | **Aramaic Levi Document** | | 4:20–22 | 182 | |
| 93 | 176 | 3:9 | 80 | 11:21 | 84 | |
| | | | | 11:22 | 85n42 | |
| **2 Enoch** | | **CD** | | | | |
| 7 | 178 | 2:5 | 180 | **4Q400** | | |
| 8:8 | 177 | 2:16 | 81 | frag. 1, col. 1, line 16 | 180 | |
| 15:1–2 | 177 | | | | | |
| 18:1–6 | 178 | **1QHᵃ** | | **4Q435** | | |
| 18:7–9 | 178 | 4:29 | 87 | 2i 1–5 | 81 | |
| 20–22 | 177 | 4:31 | 85n45 | | | |
| 20:3–21:1 | 178 | 5:31 | 85n44 | | | |
| 20:4–21:1 | 177 | 5:31–33 | 69 | **4Q436** | | |
| 21:6 | 177n19 | 5:32 | 84n38, 84n39 | 1i 5b–6, 10–1ii 4 | 81 | |
| 22:6–10 | 178 | 5:36 | 87 | | | |
| | | 8:20 | 87 | **4Q504** | | |
| **Ezekiel the Tragedian** | | 8:22–23 | 84 | 18:12–19 | 72 | |
| 184–87 | 138n21 | | | | | |

**4Q510–11**
frags. 28–29 l. 4          86

**4Q530**
2 ii 16–18                173
2:16                      174

**11Q17**
frags. 21–22, ll. 3–5     181

**11QPsᵃ 19**
ll. 15–16                 80

**11QPsᵃ 24**
ll. 11–13a                79

**11QT**
16:14–17:2               xviin13
26:9                     xviin13

**ANCIENT JEWISH SOURCES**

**Josephus**

*Jewish Antiquities*
2:312                    138n20
3:172–78                 105n30
3:179–187                110
3:184                    105n30
13:72                    12n25

*Jewish War*
5:212–13                 110
5:217                    110
5:21                     98n17

**Philo**

*On the Life of Moses*
2:71–145                 110
2:119–121                105n30
2:133                    105n30

*On the Special Laws*
1:93–94                  105n30
1:198                    13

**RABBINIC WORKS**

**Babylonian Talmud**

*Šabbat*
137b                     158

*Yoma*
5a                       xv
36                       13

**Mishnah**

*Keritot*
1:1                      21n2

*Menaḥot*
9:8                      13

**Tosefta**

*Menaḥot*
10:12                    13

**Other Works**

*Exodus Rabbah*
15:13                    138n20
17:3                     138n20

*Mekhilta on Exodus*
12:6                     138n20

**APOSTOLIC FATHERS**

*Barnabas*
9.6                      158

*Shepherd of Hermas*

*Similitudes*
9.16.4                   157

**NEW TESTAMENT PSEUDEPIGRAPHA**

*Acts of Thomas*
26                       160

**CLASSICAL AND CHRISTIAN WRITINGS**

**Chrysostom**

*Homilies on Ephesians*
2.1.11–14                158n8

**Cicero**

*Pro Caelio*
61.12                    118n21

**Horace**

*Epistulae*
1.19.41                  118n21

**Terence**

*Andria*
126                      118n21

**PAPYRI**

**BGU**
1.249                    160

**Flinders Petrie Papyri**
1.25                     160

**Oxyrhynchus Papyri**
6.932                    160

**Zenon Papyri Cairo**
1.59069                  160